# LANGUAGE
# PROCESSING
# IN ATYPICAL
# POPULATIONS

D1517541

To my children, Alexander and Eric,

for what they have taught me about love,

life, and individual differences in learning.

# LANGUAGE PROCESSING IN ATYPICAL POPULATIONS

## Vivien C. Tartter

SAGE Publications
*International Educational and Professional Publisher*
Thousand Oaks   London   New Delhi

*For information:*

SAGE Publications, Inc.
2455 Teller Road
Thousand Oaks, California 91320
E-mail: order@sagepub.com

SAGE Publications Ltd.
6 Bonhill Street
London EC2A 4PU
United Kingdom

SAGE Publications India Pvt. Ltd.
M-32 Market
Greater Kailash I
New Delhi 110 048 India

Printed in the United States of America

Library of Congress Cataloging-in-Publication Data

Tartter, Vivien C.
Language processing in atypical populations / by Vivien C. Tartter.
p. cm.
Includes bibliographical references (p. ) and index.
ISBN 0-7619-1468-4 (acid-free paper)
ISBN 0-7619-1469-2 (pbk. : acid-free paper)
1. Language and languages. 2. Psycholinguistics. 3. Communication. 4. Biolinguistics. 5. Sign language. 6. Language disorders. I. Title.
P106 .T285 1998
400—ddc21                                        98-9077

This book is printed on acid-free paper.

98  99  00  01  02  03  04  10  9  8  7  6  5  4  3  2  1

Acquisition Editor:       Catherine Rossbach
Production Editor:        Wendy Westgate
Typesetter/Designer:     Rose Tylak
Cover Designer:          Candice Harman

# Contents

# Preface

In 1986, I published *Language Processes,* a book that I intended would provide a comprehensive overview of primary language—the language we grow up thinking in—and its processing. I was struggling myself with how to define language, and whether it was unique to us, part of our biological heritage. To consider those questions, in addition to reviewing the available data on language structure and its normal processing and acquisition, I turned to research often covered only scantily in psycholinguistic texts, that is, on language and communication in atypical populations. This includes the systems used by animals naturally (and the success or failure of projects aimed at teaching them human language), the language recovery or creation patterns of children isolated from language and/or social contact, the signed languages of the deaf, language and its recovery after brain damage, and communication patterns in psychosis. Unlike most presentations that concentrate on the dominant generative-linguistic and cognitive-psychological views, I thus also entertained data and theory on language and its processing offered by communication scientists and comparative, behavioristic, clinical, and neuro-psychologists.

In revising the book, I wanted to add research on secondary language processing (reading and writing and second language acquisition) and more focused discussion on social processes in language. This meant adding sections to many chapters in addition to updating them, and also adding chapters on sociolinguistics and bilingualism. It seemed best therefore to divide the field into two books, one covering "normal language," both primary and secondary language, and the other, this volume, focusing on the intriguing findings from atypical populations. Language in these populations is presented for its intrinsic interest and to address questions on the essence of language, how it is shaped by normal cognitive, perceptual, and social constraints, and how it can be rehabilitated when these constraints are abnormal.

The chapters in this book have been thoroughly updated. In addition, new sections have been added, examining, in addition to the teaching of human language to common chimpanzees, work with bonobos (pygmy chimpanzees), a parrot, and dolphins (Chapter 2); expanding the learning of language by child isolates to include first language learning by deaf adults (Chapter 3); considering language-learning disabilities and cases of retardation with apparent language preservation (Chapter 3); and discussing ethics in working with atypical populations (Chapters 2 and 3). In keeping with the addition of a chapter on reading and writing in the companion volume, here I have added new sections covering developmental (Chapter 2) and acquired (Chapter 5) dyslexia.

The chapters on language in atypical populations in the original book were singled out for commendation in *Contemporary Psychology,* which described them as

> an unusually comprehensive discussion of the issues relating to language use in alternative populations [with] implications for general language processes. This important and underutilized perspective is well-articulated here, permitting the reader to reconsider in detail fundamental questions about human language (e.g., design features) in light of each language population. (Carroll, 1987, p. 230)

This revision maintains the original's structure as well as comprehensive and open-minded approach to the issues, encouraging readers to think for themselves about difficult, emotional, and, I think, fascinating issues.

As in my previous book, I have tried to do justice to the complexities and controversies inherent in study of any complex phenomenon: I present different sides of the issues, data supporting each side, and techniques for reaching logical and consistent conclusions. Too often, I believe, texts present things as black and white and deny the reader the challenge of thinking an issue through and the fun of analysis, indecision, and controversy. I do share my biases, but I sincerely invite readers into the discussion and to take the other position.

*Language Processing in Atypical Populations* is intended for readers already familiar with basic linguistics and psycholinguistics—advanced undergraduates, graduate students, or professionals with some background in psycholinguistics. Important concepts and methods from "normal" psycholinguistics are reviewed in the first chapter and before applications to a particular atypical population. However, these reviews are expected to be reminders rather than basic presentation.

I see this book ideally serving as a second-semester text in a one-year course. It should be of special interest to individuals pursuing work with clinical populations (e.g., speech and language pathologists). I have found that many undergraduates who do not think they are interested in cognitive psychology and psycholinguistics become "hooked" as they consider the intrinsically interesting clinical populations and possibilities for rehabilitation. Thus this book may be an excellent supplemental text for a basic one-semester course in psycholinguistics. While it may be used with any standard text, it is an ideal companion to *Language and Its Normal Processing,* also published by Sage Publications, which develops the same themes in the context of normal language.

My principal goal in writing *Language Processes* was to share the fun and excitement I have had working in psycholinguistics. This arises in playing with language (in language games and creating language stimuli). It also arises in thinking through complex issues and the "tickle" of vacillating between resolutions. And it comes about in creating a clever design to shed light on some aspect of language processing. "Normal" psycholinguistics is particularly accessible because one's laboratory is everywhere; observations can be done on every conversation. "Atypical" psycholinguistics is often a person's first glimmer that language and its processing cannot be taken for granted, that there are questions to be asked. I have included many examples of dialogues from atypical subjects to stimulate such questions. I have also presented case histories against which the language behaviors can be judged. Finally, I have tried to contextualize information about testing, experimental design techniques, and reasoning to encourage play with these creative, scientific tools.

It is my profound hope that through open discussion of controversy, emphasis on methods of analysis and criticism, presentation of psycholinguistics from the diverse perspectives of its various researchers, and encouragement of active involvement, readers will be stimulated to continue thinking about language and its processing well after they have completed this book (and, I hope, its companion). The first course I had in psycholinguistics added a major dimension to my life and I would like to pass that gift on.

## REFERENCE

Carroll, J. J. (1987). Psycholinguistics in the round: Complementary perspectives on the experimental investigation of language. *Contemporary Psychology, 32,* 229-231.

# Acknowledgments

I am grateful to my family for the patience and support they offered during my labors on this book.

This book owes much to both my teachers and my students. Professor Sheila Blumstein, to whom the first edition was dedicated, shaped my love for and thought on psychology of language more than 20 years ago. Integral to her psycholinguistics course were units on brain damage and language and the chimpanzee language projects, and through such exposure I learned what consideration of atypical populations could tell us about language and its processing. Professor Richard Millward encouraged my study of computer science, linguistics, and biology along with cognitive psychology, before such a thing was done; the interdisciplinary focus of this book had its seed in his open vision. Professor Peter Eimas honed my knowledge and appreciation of experimental methods. Former graduate students Alexandra Economou, Hilary Gomes, and Malca Resnick broadened my thinking in aphasia, right-hemisphere discourse processes, dyslexia, child language acquisition, and metaphor. Whole classes at City College used and critiqued the text in manuscript form, and their comments improved its accessibility.

I am grateful to Dane Harwood and Arty Samuel, who read and critiqued the first edition in its entirety, which significantly affected this edition as well. The original of Chapter 4 benefited from a review by Richard Meier.

I thank also colleagues with whom I have collaborated and whose ideas have significantly affected my outlook on our field: Arty Samuel and Donna Kat, Ursula Bellugi, Susan Fisher and Richard Meier, Oliver Patterson and Pamela Laskin.

# 1

# PERSPECTIVES ON LANGUAGE IN ATYPICAL POPULATIONS

Possibly from the beginnings of our consciousness of ourselves as human, we have reflected on our language, seeing it as one reason we are special, apart from, and, at least from our perspective as humans, superior to animals. The symbolism inherent in linguistic meaning allows us to consider the abstract, the nonimmediate, the unreal. Through language—oral traditions and writing systems—we communicate across generations and over long distances. Thus we build on the knowledge of others, constructing civilizations that seem vastly different from (and superior to) those of any other animal group. In fact, most features that have ever been considered profoundly and essentially human—religion, culture, tool use, the ability to imagine death—depend in some way on language.

We may ask, What gives language these unique powers? Is language intrinsic to us, arising uniquely and automatically from *innate* specifications (ones inborn, not known through learning), and then affecting learning and conceptualization of both language and nonlinguistic thought *recursively* (feeding back to act similarly on itself)? Or is language only a special tool that some ancestors were clever enough to develop and pass on to descendants, and that we could likewise pass on to other species?

During the last several decades, research in learning principles, artificial intelligence, and animal communication systems has attempted to place human lan-

F: I think you could say it's a hoarse voice,

L: [In a low voice] You could say it's more of a horse.

F: Now, does that mean it's a horse talking?

L: No! [Amused] It's me talking. [Chuckles] You know what your voice sound like when you('re) um, when you're sort of sick? Your voice can go hoarse. [Makes voice sound hoarse]

**Figure 1.1.** Severe Retardation in a 14-Year-Old (L.) With Language Preserved Relative to Drawing Ability

SOURCE: J. E. Yamada (1990), *Laura: A Case for the Modularity of Language,* pp. 85, 139. MIT Press. © Massachusetts Institute of Technology. Used by permission.

guage in broad evolutionary and cognitive contexts. In this regard, could this paragraph, expressing new ideas in a never-before-used, structured sequence, be only a result of reflex associations? Is production or comprehension of such a paragraph within the capability of a computer? Consider the complex communities in beehives or anthills, the sophisticated intelligences of monkeys, apes, whales, and dolphins. Could we be the only social animals to share abstract ideas through a natural communication system? Have the attempts to teach parrots, chimpanzees, gorillas, and dolphins human languages been successful, or do they only crudely simulate a small subset of our language skills?

In the last several decades, research in humans' use of human language has also addressed the foundations of language. On the one hand, human intelligence, at least as defined by IQ tests, includes different "verbal aptitude" measures, each with a broad range considered "normal." This suggests that language skills vary across human beings and correlate with some, but not all, other cognitive functions. On the other hand, young children simply seem to soak language up, in what seem to be similar ways, unconsciously, quickly, and effortlessly mastering a grammar so complex that they (we) have difficulty *explicitly* learning it in "grammar school." And there are idiot savants in language—people with severe retardation who, nevertheless, use language creatively and correctly. Contrast the ability of 16-year-old Laura to draw people with her ability to create and sustain a conversation, displayed in Figure 1.1 (Yamada, 1990, pp. 85, 139). Her drawing illustrates her nonverbal IQ of 40. What intelligence gives her language such sophistication?

To what extent is language the unfolding of a genetic program? To what extent are language skills part of our general cognitive functions, like reasoning, remembering, or problem solving? To what extent is linguistic knowledge and ability a separate, hardwired "cognitive *module*," a processor independent of our other cognitive processes? Answers to these questions have been approached this century through study of normal language acquisition and processing, computer models of normal language, and comparison of structures in languages throughout the world, both historically and contemporaneously. These data and their implications for the essence of language may be explored in the companion volume, *Language and Its Normal Processing*.

Evidence has also accrued this century from study of what may be languagelike behaviors in other species as well as in humans for whom the nature-nurture patterns that normally underlie language acquisition and processing have been disrupted. Disruptions can be *genetic* as in Laura, *social* as in the isolation caused by abuse or neglect or personality disorder, *sensory-perceptual* as a result of deafness, or *neurocognitive* as a consequence of brain damage or learning disability. This book explores these data, addressing the issue of whether (and how) normal language is "special." As in the companion volume, the discussion focuses the data to define human language and how it is shaped by human social, perceptual, and cognitive constraints.

## A BRIEF HISTORY OF PSYCHOLINGUISTICS

Three basic lines of inquiry form the historical foundations of modern study of the psychology of language, which underlies today's study of language(-like) behaviors in atypical populations: (a) whether and which language abilities are innate, (b) how words are associated with meanings and with one another, and (c) why there are language disorders and how these might be treated. The very first recorded psycholinguistic experiment, in fact, formally addresses the question of innate language abilities and the foundation of word meaning through study of an atypical population—linguistically isolated infants—a population studied for the same purposes today, as we will see in Chapter 3.

Herodotus (1954/1986) wrote that before 600 B.C., an Egyptian king, Psammetichus, ordered a shepherd to rear two newborn infants without any exposure to language. (Today's isolates are neglected children who are studied while being rehabilitated, not mere "guinea pigs" in a scientific design.) Psammetichus reasoned that the language the children would speak innately would be the human ancestral language, which he expected to be Egyptian. Two years later, the children uttered the sounds *becos*. Investigation established that *becos* was the Phrygian word for bread. "In consideration of this the Egyptians yielded their claims and admitted the superior antiquity of the Phrygians" (p. 130). Today's research on isolates does not presume to discover the first language but the genetically specified language scaffold and the times or *critical periods* when it may most easily be built on by learning from a language model.

The next recorded developments in the study of language in atypical populations, as in most disciplines in Western civilization, were in ancient Greece. The Greeks considered only adult human language to be "typical," distinct from both animal and child communications. They viewed the human vocal tract and its apparent adaptation for language as reflecting a natural (innate) basis for language skill, with experience sharpening our ability to control articulation. The Greeks also analyzed deafness, seeing it, unfortunately, as a disorder of language-thought that *resulted* in hearing loss because thought was inextricably related to language, and language, to hearing.

Beginning with the Renaissance, six new views of language emerged that today still affect its study in atypical populations. Francis Bacon described language as a multilevel process, with speech constituting only one level. The idea that redundant, multileveled, and overlapping processes underlie a single language function has been employed to rehabilitate language after brain damage or in children who have some avenues for language processing impaired.

A second important Renaissance perspective on language was that of Descartes, who attributed more aspects of language to instinct. In particular, he considered not only the urge to communicate and general language capacity instinctive, but also some ideas themselves—such as religion and time. These *innate ideas* give all people, in his view, common frames of reference. The modern linguistic outlook, shaped by Chomsky (1972, 1986), claims inspiration from Descartes, holding that our language arises from the operation of an innate *universal grammar (UG)*, which specifies general structural language features (called *principles and parameters*) that can be set in innately constrained ways by the language the child hears.

This perspective on language contrasts sharply with Locke's, who rejected the notion of the innateness of anything other than the basic language capacity. For Locke, language and thoughts were acquired by experience, and the interesting question was how concepts are formed and linked. His answer was "association"—of events that occur together in time or that appear similar to one another. Associationism inspired *behaviorists,* who teach animals (and people) new associations (as shown in Figure 1.2) by associating a new stimulus with an existing reflex *(classical*

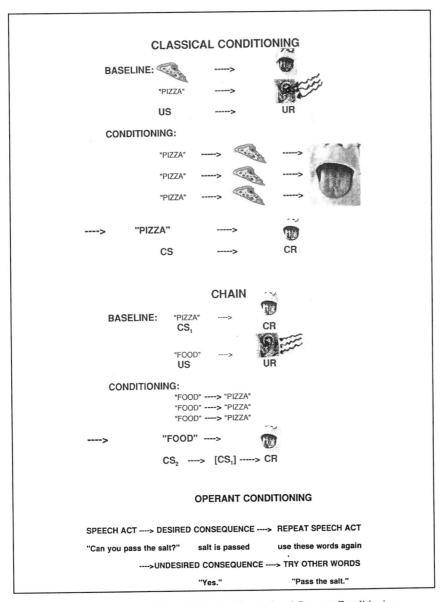

**Figure 1.2.** The Formation of Associations in Classical and Operant Conditioning

NOTE: In classical conditioning, we begin with a reflex, an innate, unlearned (or unconditioned) connection between a stimulus (unconditioned stimulus, US) and a response (unconditioned response, UR), here, a pizza slice and salivation. Repeated pairing of the sounds of the word *pizza* with the food causes the sound to produce salivation, to become a conditioned stimulus (CS). This process can be repeated, pairing a new neutral stimulus (here the word *food*) with the word *pizza* in a "chain," so that this secondary stimulus also produces salivation. In operant conditioning, a behavior is followed by a stimulus that either increases *(reinforcement)* or decreases *(punishment)* the chance that it will be repeated.

*conditioning)* or by associating a behavior with its consequences, following it in time by a "pleasant" *(reinforcement)* or "unpleasant" *(punishment)* stimulus to change the likelihood that that behavior recurs *(operant conditioning)*. Locke's ideas and behaviorist principles have been used in the attempts to teach human language behaviors to animals and in rehabilitating people who fail to acquire language automatically.

A fourth historical influence on the psychology of language is the changing view of people's place in the animal kingdom. In *The Descent of Man,* Darwin (1871/n.d.) acknowledged that the language faculty "has justly been considered as one of the chief distinguishors between man and lower animals" (p. 461) and is necessary for complex thoughts. However, he attempted to show that human beings share with other animals vocal and nonvocal emotional gestures, the capacity and urge to imitate, and the abilities to think and reason. Thus the rudiments of language skills are present elsewhere in the animal kingdom, and our abilities may be accounted for by evolution. This view leads to the modern comparative approach to language and communication.

Newtonian *mechanism* and its offspring, *structuralism,* shaped many fields of scientific inquiry, including linguistics and cognitive psychology. The structuralist seeks to discover indivisible elements and rules for their combinations into complex structures. In language (as a first pass), we might consider words to embody the elements of linguistic meaning, and grammar, the rules for combining them to convey new, more complex meanings. A structuralist perspective on language in atypical populations expects disability or primitive processing (in animals, say) to preserve language primitives over the complex structures they constitute, and to map language components to specific brain structures. Thus it provides an organizational framework for the data we will be examining.

The final important historical development is *physiological mechanism,* the belief in physiological underpinnings of language and cognition, of the brain as the organ of mind. Before the nineteenth century, following Aristotle, it was generally thought that speech was essential to language and that deafness represented a cognitive disorder resulting from language deficiencies. In the nineteenth century, deafness became recognized as a sensory disorder, and teaching methods for the deaf developed. In addition, damage to specific locations of the brain was discovered to affect some language skills apart from others and apart from general cognitive skills. This led to a hypothesis of a language "faculty" separate from other cognitive faculties, and from speech specifically. These views have focused study on the manual languages of the deaf and the relative sparing and disintegration of different language abilities after brain damage or in learning-disabled populations.

## REVIEW OF NORMAL LANGUAGE AND ITS PROCESSING

Readers of this book are expected to be somewhat conversant in psycholinguistics, from the companion volume *Language and Its Normal Processing* or from another source. To ground the methods and data from study of language in atypical populations, here I briefly review the outlooks of the major contributing disciplines and schools of modern thought as well as the salient findings on language structure and processing by normal adults and children. More explicit presentation and references can be found in the companion volume.

---

**Box 1.1. The Historical Roots of Study
of Language in Atypical Populations**

— *The innateness question:* What is natural (genetic, biological, and human-instinctive) about language, and what is learned?
— *Associationism:* How are concepts (word meanings) acquired through experience?
— *Darwinism:* Are there roots of linguistic behaviors in other cognitions or elsewhere in the animal kingdom?
— *Physiological mechanism:* How is language organized in the brain (and in the speech-hearing, gesture-vision systems)?
— *Structuralism:* To the extent that language is a complex composed in a rule-governed way of primitive units, do we see "primitive" language reflecting only the units, selectively impairing the rules and resulting combinations?

---

## Modern Outlooks on Meaning and Its Processing

The essence of language is the *communication,* or active, intentional transfer of meaning from a speaker to a hearer. Meaning occurs most obviously in words but also in parts of words and in word combinations. The smallest unit of language to convey meaning *productively* (regularly through combination with other units) is the *morpheme.* The word *words* consists of two morphemes, the "content word" *word* and the "inflectional" suffix *s,* signifying the plural.

Morpheme combination conveys meaning beyond simply summing the meanings of the constituent morphemes. The sentence "The lion chased the elephant" renders the lion more threatening than the elephant by virtue of its being the chaser; the phrase "his marriage was an icebox" is *literal*ly a lie, but implies *figurative*ly or *metaphor*ically a distant relationship. The more threatening role of the lion and the distance in the marriage, and the "figurativeness" of "icebox," are conveyed in no morpheme in particular but, somehow, through their combination.

### Linguistic Approaches to Meaning

Linguists have attempted to analyze meaning structurally by defining the morpheme and categories of morphemes and by analyzing the meaning conveyed in language into primitive general features. A *content* or *open-class* morpheme refers to a specifiable idea, as opposed to a *function* or *closed-class* morpheme, which is a language's tool for combining content morphemes into *phrase* units. "Open" indicates that the class can grow to reflect any new idea; function words and inflections like the plural or tense have limited, "closed" membership. Roughly, nouns, verbs, adjectives, and adverbs constitute content words, while articles *(determiners),* conjunctions, and prepositions are function words.

Content morphemes may be analyzed further into component features, shared by several morphemes of the language. For example, *people, wife, butterfly,* but not *rock, computer,* or *book,* are *animate; mother, angel, peace,* but not *shock, death, homework,* are *pleasant;* and *adult, horse, tree,* but not *infant, colt, sapling,* are *mature.* A semantic *system* consists of the organized representation of such general meaning features and their map to the morphemes of the language.

General meaning features underlie patterns of thought peculiar to a language and culture: Relationships being cold/hot or containing features in common with trips or journeys enables metaphors like the marriage-icebox one or marriage as a roller coaster (Lakoff & Johnson, 1980). A *dead* metaphor, one we have frequently experienced and no longer see as metaphoric, certainly would be represented with such features. But intrinsic to many concepts may be such metaphoric features that enable a quick understanding of a new metaphor consistent with the prevailing thought patterns of the culture.

Linguists use feature systems to account for logical relations in the language, such as meaning similarity *(synonymy* or *paraphrase),* in which different words, but the same feature values, are used, or meaning opposition *(antonymy, contradiction, anomaly)* in which features with antagonistic values are paired. Features may be further analyzed with respect to degree of generality (the most general are semantic *markers;* the least, *distinguishers*) and with respect to whether they are *defining* (necessary for a concept—like *feathered* for "bird") or *characteristic* (typically occurring with the concept—like *flies* for "bird").

### Philosophical Approaches to Meaning

How a word or morpheme signifies reality is a thorny philosophical issue. First, note that words and morphemes are *arbitrary;* they do not directly reflect their meaning except in odd cases like *onomatopoeia* (e.g., *bang* or *splash*) in which a word sounds like its referent. Second, note that a word does not merely refer to or *denote* a portion of the experienced world; it focuses attention on particular features of it *and* it arouses associations with previous uses of the word, or *connotation.* Thus a "dirty" or slang word (e.g., *ass*) and its polite euphemism *(buttocks)* denote the same aspect of reality but connote differently, activating, respectively, associations of the gutter or a doctor's office.

Consider the word *thorny* in the first sentence of the last paragraph. *Thorny* concretely denotes a property of some plants—painful, pointed extensions from a main stem. *Concrete* refers to the ability to experience the meaning directly through the senses, to image the thorn. *Issue* is abstract, denoting an idea that we may have generalized from many different concrete experiences but that does not connect directly with any one of them. Issues are "thorny" only in a *symbolic* sense: They do not have thorns but "extensions" on which one can get "snagged" mentally, as one can get physically snagged on a real thorn. Using the word *thorn* brings to bear the physical plant characteristics on the abstract *issue.* That word meaning is far removed from any specific real experience makes it a philosophically intriguing association.

*Psychologists' Models and Methods for Studying Meaning*

Some psychologists have studied meaning as a classical association (see Figure 1.2): Through reflexive learning, we connect the sound of a word and the sensory experience of its *referent* (the thing it refers to). The meaning of the word then is a *mediating response* ($R_m$), the arousal of this connection. (This is far from a symbol!) $R_m$s have been studied as sensory images and as more abstract, emotional reactions that locate the word with respect to other words in *semantic space,* defined by pleasantness *(evaluation), intensity,* and *potency.*

Evidence for images as word meaning has emerged from people's *introspections* (what they think they are experiencing). More objectively, *reaction time* studies have shown that it takes longer to conceptualize words that denote opposite ends of a figure than those that denote adjacent points, suggesting that our thought is arranged spatially (Kosslyn, 1988). *Masking* or *interference* studies have shown too that people are slower or less accurate at deciding whether a sentence describing something visual (like "a rosebush has thorns") is true *(sentence verification)* if they are reading it (a visual task) than if they hear it, suggesting that thinking about something one has seen uses some of the same mental operations (visual imagery) as seeing the print (Eddy & Glass, 1981).

The three-dimensional abstract-emotion type $R_m$s have emerged from the *semantic differential* task (Osgood, Suci, & Tannenbaum, 1957/1978). Here subjects rate words with respect to a number of oppositional or *bipolar* scales, like *beautiful-ugly* or *hot-cold.* The pattern of co-occurrence of ratings across words reveals a similar three-dimensional structure for different languages and cultures.

Moving beyond simple associationism, cognitive psychologists have conceptualized our mental representation of word meaning as a complex interconnection of shared abstract semantic features. At one level are features of the word itself, the sounds or letters and their ordered connection. Thus we easily generate sound associations (rhymes or words beginning with a particular letter); likewise, we may temporarily lose some of this information, misspeaking a word in a *slip of the tongue,* or forgetting part of it as when a word is on the *tip of the tongue (TOT),* and we still know what sound it starts with.

The word-name features connect to meaning features shared by many words because our slips and TOTs are not random but often result in substitution of a word of similar meaning or sound. Meaning is conceptualized separately from the word-name layer, and its representation is a matter of some debate. One model, the *prototype* model (Rosch, Mervis, Gray, Johnson, & Boyes-Braem, 1976), suggests that we understand a general category like *bird* by evoking all its instances, with typical examples of the category ("robin" as opposed to "penguin" or "ostrich" or "hummingbird") most strongly evoked. Indeed, *lexical* (Is *robin* a word?) or *semantic* (Is *robin* a bird?) *decisions* are speeded more (i.e., evoked faster) for typical than atypical instances when subjects are *primed* (prompted) first with the category name.

Another model of meaning represents categories as lists of characteristic and defining features (Smith, Shoben, & Rips, 1974). *Verification* tasks, deciding the truth of a sentence like "A robin is a bird," appear to be accomplished by comparing the overlap of features of both instance and category. If there is considerable overlap (as would be true for the prototype) or almost no overlap (for a nonmember), decisions are made very quickly. With intermediate overlap, decisions are slow, presumably accomplished by a methodical process of examining the instance for each of the category's defining features.

The last models of meaning consider it to be a vast, semihierarchically structured network of associations (Collins & Loftus, 1975; McClelland, Rumelhart, & the PDP Research Group, 1986) with frequently associated points being more strongly interconnected or *weighted* than those less frequently associated. Accessing a concept arouses related ones through *spreading activation* proportionally to their weighting with the concept. Thus a property like "having feathers" is more weighted to the category "bird" than to any instance of it (which makes it faster to verify that birds have feathers than that robins do), and typical examples are weighted more to a category than are atypical ones.

Not only are words tied to their component sounds, articulatory commands, and letters, as well as to abstracted connotative and denotative features, shared by other words, they are also tied (a) to sensory experience allowing us to describe what we perceive and (b) to words with which they can co-occur in phrases. Each word specifies both the roles that it can enter into in phrases and the *arguments* that it takes (the other concepts it needs to flesh out its meaning).

Thus a word may be associated with words that sound like it (*clang* associations), that are similar to it (robin-canary—*paradigmatic* associations), that occur in similar contexts (egg-cereal—both breakfasts: *slot-filler* associations), or that co-occur in phrases (soft-pillow—*syntagmatic* associations). When we hear or see a word or portion of one, connections to it are activated in proportion to their psychological distance from it (the more distant, the less activation), the number of intervening connections (the more intervening, the less activation), and the weight of the connection (the greater the weight, the more activation).

So, a "dirty" word and its euphemism do not mean the same thing because they do not produce the same patterns of activation; they differ in slot-filler, connotative, and syntagmatic associates. And a *homonym,* one word with several meanings (like *pen*—a writing tool and a place to keep animals), briefly activates associations to all its uses, rendering its experience different from a "synonym" with only one meaning (e.g., *sty*).

*Processing Meaning in Conversation*

When words are used in fluent speech, the speech stream progressively activates meanings, with overlap resulting in the most strongly activated representations. A word sense can conflict with other senses in the sentence, which then *inhibit* or decrease its arousal: *Pig pen* reinforces the "sty" sense of *pen* and inhibits the "writing" sense. Figurative, metaphorical associations are aroused simultaneously and similarly to literal meanings, particularly for dead figures of speech (as was *thorny* when applied to issues). Understanding a new figure of speech involves creating or considerably strengthening an association: Usually a highly weighted feature of the predicate or *vehicle* is strengthened with respect to the subject or *topic* of the metaphor, for which it had only weak prior associations. This change in association strength may be accompanied by a feeling of tension release, the appreciation of the metaphor.

To only a limited extent, deriving or expressing meaning in language involves a relatively passive arousal of existing associations. Literal as well as figurative language implicates active, constructive processes as conversation partners elect to be cryptic about information each knows to be known to the other, to explicate information deemed unknown or new to the other (which thus must entail creating new associations or strengthening old weak ones), to build upon common ground established previously in the relationship or in the immediate discourse or currently in the shared context. Because language usually is used to communicate new ideas, what is new must be actively constructed, not merely reactivated.

### Conclusions for Atypical Populations

In studying linguistic meaning processing in atypical populations, therefore, we can ask:

- Is word meaning normally symbolic?
- Are abstract and figurative associations as available as concrete associations?
- Are word names, meanings, and sensory representations normally connected?
- Is meaning normally constructed and expressed given the context and relations between the participants?
- Are irrelevant associations normally inhibited by context?
- Is semantic memory normally organized with prototypical instances more strongly connected to a category than peripheral examples?
- Can the individual construct the new meanings inherent in figurative language and normal informative conversation?

## Modern Outlooks on Syntax and Its Processing

Syntax is the rule-governed way in which morphemes combine to form higher units of meaning. In "The lion chased the elephant," the "chaser" and "chasee" are so indicated by their relation to the verb, through syntax. This is done in several different ways: (a) the *order* in the sentence, (b) the *arguments* a verb specifies that it takes and nouns specify they supply, and (c) the inflections or function words that signal a particular relation.

In English, but not many other languages, order is the most important determinant. The first noun is usually the *subject* or *agent,* and the one following the verb, the *object* or *patient.* (English is a subject-verb-object or *SVO* language.) In a *cue competition* where native English speakers must judge who is doing what to whom, such as in "The pencil sharpen the boys," "pencil" is deemed the agent, despite the facts that "boys" is the likely subject given that "sharpen" without a final -s suggests a plural subject and semantics suggests an animate one, as well as the plausibility of the "pencil" being sharpened.

Order may be changed in English, as in the *passive,* "The elephant was chased by the lion." Then the agent is signaled by the function word "by" and the inflections "was -ed" on the verb. In other languages a specific morpheme may be affixed to the agent and a different one to the patient, as I did with chas*er* and chas*ee.* In such languages, syntactic relations are still clear although order is freer than in English. There, inflection dominates in competition: The most significant cues in any language are those most reliable and frequent (MacWhinney, 1987).

In all languages, in addition to order and inflection, some syntactic relations are cued through lexical knowledge. With a word are coded the relations it can enter into or demand in addition for complete expression: agents are usually animate; *chasing* requires a chaser and chasee; *chasing* may be to or from a particular location.

## Linguistic View of Syntax

Syntax is the most abstract level of language, entailing relations exclusively within the language. It is quite complex because of the variety of ways that the basic sentence relations—the *deep structure* (or now, *D-structure*)—can manifest in the *surface structure (S-structure),* the structure to be articulated. In English the agent usually begins the sentence, and the *topic* or *old information* is also usually first, grounding the sentence. If the agent is the *focus* or *new information,* it should be in the predicate, resulting in the passive.

At some level the passive and the active versions of a sentence express the same sentence relations, differing largely in their order in the surface structure. In early views of syntax (see Chomsky, 1965), passives and actives were therefore considered to have the same deep structure, with the different surface structures resulting from a process of *transformation*—that is, moving, adding, or deleting *constituents*—a word or a set of words that may be grouped because they constitute a *phrase*—of a structural unit combining morphemes.

Currently, D-structures are considered to contain *all* information to be expressed in S-structure (this includes topic and focus, so passive and active sentences are seen as differing in deep structure). Transformations can only *move* constituents to their final positions in the sentence to be articulated. Movement leaves a *trace* of the constituent in the positions it once occupied. The trace is not articulated but its residue in S-structure both binds it to its *filler* (expressed) constituent and influences grouping or *parsing* of elements.

For example, we may articulate *want to* as *wanna* when *want* and *to* are contiguous. One meaning of the sentence "Teddy is the man I want to succeed" is "I want Teddy to succeed." If that is the intended meaning, we cannot and do not use *wanna.* Even though *want* and *to* seem to be adjacent, a trace of Teddy intervenes between them (I want [Teddy] to . . . ) so they are not contiguous in S-structure.

The "Teddy" sentence is a complex sentence, one that is actually composed of two sentences: Teddy is the man, and I want Teddy to succeed. The possibility of a single sentence recursively enfolding or *embedding* other sentences is a powerful feature of language, accounting for much of its productivity and complexity. Conjoining the constituent sentences is accomplished in part by eliminating the redundant *noun phrase (NP),* here the second "Teddy," the trace of which must be connected to its expressed form, here many words away. The dependency relations in a sentence often span distances of many intervening words. Thus they *cannot entail only sequential associations* (a *behavioral chain,* where one thing leads only to the next, modeled by *finite state grammar*) but must use complex context-sensitive "rules."

Chomsky (1965) distinguishes *competence,* the rules speaker-hearers know, from performance, what they actually utter (false starts, mistakes, and so on). Competence emerges through the interaction of UG (which predisposes children to expect traces tacitly, for instance) with a *corpus* or body of utterances despite frequent performance errors and missing critical examples of the language *poverty-of-the-stimulus* problem. According to Chomsky (1986), the primary goal of linguists is elucidating the innate principles of language and their modification—parameter-setting—by language experience. Our syntactic knowledge and operations, perhaps along with other features of language, are considered to be special and unique mental processes, encapsulated from other cognitive operations, their own brain *module* (Fodor, 1983).

### Parsers and Psychological Approaches to Syntax

Chomsky's evolving theories of generative grammar have been tested through implementation on computer and through experiments measuring speed, accuracy, and memory for sentences differing in structure and/or meaning. First, it is important to note that we do do syntactic processing: We can map the relations in a nonsense sentence like "The pencils sharpened the boy" or in a semantically undetermined sentence like "The lion chased the elephant." We are sensitive to basic sentence structure, mentally marking the break between main and subordinate clauses in complex embedded sentences. And studies show that at the position where a trace is hypothesized, the filler is primed relative to other words in the sentence. However, syntactic operations are ephemeral: We quickly forget exactly how a sentence was worded or structured, remembering only the meaning.

With respect to how we parse, studies have shown that simple sentences, those with no embedding and minimal transformation, are generally more quickly verified than complex sentences that involve both more, and more esoteric, syntactic operations. Sentences that contain overt cues to their structure, such as the function word *that,* which introduces a relative clause (as in, "the book [that] I read yesterday . . . ), are faster and more accurately understood than those with such words omitted. But sentences in which semantics alone could determine the relation—*irreversible* sentences (such as "The boy sharpened the pencil," where *boy* is the only NP that could be the agent)—take less time to understand than reversible sentences.

As a sentence is presented, we briefly seem to consider all possible meanings and structures, weeding out those that do not fit as new words rule out ambiguous meanings and alternative structures. The parses and meanings that we first attempt are those most common and consistent in the language, and speakers usually provide overt cues in surface structure to less common ones if they are intended. It is not clear that we precisely follow a rule-governed grammar to parse. Rather, we may use general *heuristics,* informed guesses, as to the likely structure: The first NP is the likely subject and agent of the sentence, the nearest preceding NP is the subject/agent of the embedded clause *(minimum distance principle),* and so on.

### Conclusions for Atypical Populations

When examining sentence production and comprehension in atypical populations, we may ask,

- Do they appropriately use syntax as well as semantics to construct sentence relations?
- Are they sensitive to the phrase structure of sentences?
- Are complex sentence structures as well as simple ones used in conversation?
- Can they keep track of long-distance dependencies?
- Do they appropriately weigh competing and/or redundant cues in processing sentences?
- Do they use inflection and/or order as the language dictates?
- Are they sensitive to the frequency and regularity of usages in their language?
- Do they recognize or produce agrammatical sentences?

## Modern Outlooks on Speech and Its Processing

### Linguistic Approaches to Speech (Phonetics and Phonology)

Linguists parse the speech stream into different layers of structure. The overall intonation and loudness changes constitute *suprasegmental* information, some of which is paralinguistic and some of which is linguistic. *Paralinguistic* information refers to things like emotional overtone and speaker identity; it is not relevant linguistically but carried together with language-relevant information. Suprasegmentals used in language mark clauses or differentiate questions from statements by tone of voice alone.

Speech *segments* include syllables, which consist of *phonemes,* the smallest unit of sound that can distinguish words in a language. In turn, phonemes are composed of *phonetic features,* distinctive articulatory gestures falling in discrete auditory regions. Examples of phonetic features are *voicing* (when the vocal folds start vibrating relative to the release of air) and *place of articulation* (where closure is in the mouth). Each language combines phonetic features into phoneme categories uniquely, using some optimum number of features and phonemes. Languages optimize distinctiveness, the number of separate units that need to be identified in memory, and the complexity of combinations: The fewer features, the fewer that need be recognized, but the more that must be combined to produce unique different words.

Languages also combine sounds using regular rules. For example, in English, the past tense -ed and the plural -s are pronounced differently depending on the sound that ends the word they affix to. If it is voiced, the affix is also voiced (/d/ or /z/); if voiceless, the affix is voiceless (/t/ or /s/); if it matches the affix in place and manner of articulation (-d, -t for the past and -s, -z for the plural), the affix has the neutral, *schwa* vowel and the voiced variant. Thus we have cat/s/, dog/z/, and hors/əz/; walk/t/, close/d/, and end/əd/. These *morphophonemic* variants correspond to rules of *assimilation,* making sounds blend when they are near, and *dissimilation,* making near sounds more distinctively different. The regularity of the change and its easy extension to nonsense words (make *wug* and *niss* plural or past) suggest that it is a productive rule, within native English speakers' competence.

### Psychologists' Approaches to Speech

Discovering the relevant information in the speech stream is a problem in pattern recognition, which has been traditionally studied structurally: The stimulus, here speech, is methodically changed and the changes are mapped to changes in what is perceived or how it was produced. For speech, as for many other signals, there is no direct mapping between individual gestures, acoustic properties, and phonetic feature, phoneme, or syllable distinctions. Segments *seem* to be produced sequentially, analogous to strings of letters, but, in fact, emerge from a complex of overlapping quasi-*simultaneous* gestures, the acoustic consequences of which are *smear*ed across several segments. There is no discrete moment in time when we are articulating or hearing, for example, a /g/ independent of the following vowel; you can feel your tongue tip arching for the "ee" (/i/) or lips pursing for /u/ *as* your tongue back touches the roof of your mouth in /gi/ and /gu/. Thus the vowel and consonant are coarticulated and perceived simultaneously, with their "cues" smeared together. "Smear" extends over several segments (there are long-distance dependencies in speech as well as syntax), and paralinguistic information is smeared with linguistic information.

That speech appears to be perceived and produced sequentially, but is not, and because investigators have not readily found gestures or acoustic properties that *invariably* occur with readily identifiable segments, they have proposed that *speech is special,* processed differently, perhaps by an innate module, from other auditory signals. Speech seems to be better identified by the left cerebral hemisphere (the putative "language" hemisphere) than the right when competing signals are presented to both ears simultaneously *(dichotic listening);* native speakers often discriminate phonemes not much better than they can identify them and quite differently from nonnative speakers *(categorical perception);* speech may be identified by combining auditory information with lipreading and/or the feel of the mouth (the *McGurk* effect), which do not influence nonspeech auditory signal perception; impoverished signals that are barely recognizable as speech are perceived differently when listeners are induced to hear them as speech than when they are not so induced *(duplex* perception). These, among other demonstrations, together with our incredibly rapid, seemingly effortless skill at recognizing and producing speech, have suggested that we have specially evolved to process speech.

However, it has also been noted that the "specialness" of speech may arise from more general perceptual and cognitive constraints. Speech is a skill that is extremely practiced and central to human socialization. From early infancy we spend considerably more time attentively listening to and reproducing the speech patterns we hear than any other auditory signals. It is possible that effects like categorical perception arise from the learning—overlearning—of the speech patterns of our native language. Indeed, some of the speech-is-special effects can be approximated with nonspeech signals if subjects are given intense practice and feedback.

Moreover, some animals have been shown to perceive human speech similarly to us. Because there would be no reason for them to have an innate human speech perceiver, we can hypothesize that our speech sounds have mapped to regions of general *auditory sensitivity.* That is, rather than the human species evolving special language skills, human communication evolved to use what was perceptually most salient. The principal difference between humans and animals with respect to auditory sensitivity lies not in the initial discriminability of the sounds but in our learning to tie them together into phoneme categories (different for different languages) organized around the most typical instance that we hear of each, and then to map these semantically (Kuhl, 1993).

Speech perception is intimately tied to the use of speech to signal language. Tests of *on-line* speech processing, that is, intercepting perception of discourse as it is happening, demonstrate lexical influences: It is easier and faster to recognize a phoneme in a word than in a nonword, for instance. Likewise, degrading a phoneme in a word by masking it with noise or splicing it out is less observable than doing so in a nonsense-word string. We seem to be able to activate the missing information from the common co-occurrence of the surrounding sounds and their connections to our memory representation for all the sounds of the word. Indeed, as semantic memory and syntax appear multileveled and semihierarchical, so it appears are speech perception and production. Some processing units respond to low-level acoustic cues (or motor commands), some to their synthesis into phonemes or syllables (or target smoothly coarticulated gestures), some to their synthesis into morphemes or words, complete with semantic representation, and some to their synthesis into sentences and so on, including the necessary suprasegmental processing.

*Conclusions for Atypical Populations*

With respect to atypical populations, we may ask the following about their language-signal processing:

- Is the signal appropriately redundant, with information about many segments conveyed simultaneously and smeared across the signal through coarticulation?

- Is there a hierarchical organization interconnecting low-level signal features and commands with higher-order ones, ultimately into a lexical representation?

- Are all levels of the hierarchy, from the lowest through suprasegmental contours, normally perceived and produced?

- In nonspeech systems (American Sign Language and animal communication), do we see similar specializations (increased discriminability for relevant distinctions, or categorizations, better processing in the language hemisphere, or *lateralization*)?

- If the signal used is not perceived and produced in the ways deemed critical for speech, does that affect higher-level communication properties like meaning conveyance and syntactic structures? That is, are the abstract properties of speech in some way essential to language?

## Pragmatics: Language in Social Context

In looking at language and its processing, we must never forget the broad social context in which they occur. Language serves to bond humans in communities and to convey information between them, to regulate these communities. As such, language always serves a paralinguistic function as well as the linguistic ones, reflecting the group(s) speakers affiliate with and distance from. We see this as language changes, not to enhance information transmission but to mark group identity (*change from above* in dialect movements) through "accent," word choice (the latest [or not] slang), particular syntactic constructions (like *negative concord*—I ain't got no), and even distinctive word games and word taboos (Labov, 1972a, 1972b).

When people converse, they expect their partners to communicate according to social conventions. Importantly, these include the *cooperative principle* (Grice, 1989, see pp. 22-40, "Logic and Conversation," and pp. 41-57, "Further Notes on Logic and Conversation"), that participants make their contributions to the conversation

1. as informative as, but not more informative than, is necessary;
2. true;
3. relevant;
4. clear, unambiguous, and brief.

To accomplish this, speakers must correctly assess what listeners need for understanding, where they might get confused, and what common ground they share that need not be restated. Speakers may increase the intimacy of an interaction by referring to "private" common ground and by demanding deeper processing from the listener such as in interpreting a private joke or a new figure of speech dependent on shared experience. They may also decrease intimacy by making reference to or using language known to be unknown to a participant.

With respect to atypical populations, we may ask,

- Is language use appropriately informative, redundant, truthful—cooperative?

- Does speech style switch with different participants, reflecting appropriate sensitivity to the needs of the audience?

- Is current context and past shared experience used in an appropriately effortful way to derive common ground?

## Language Acquisition

### The Data

Babies are born prepared to attend socially to people, prepared to attend to the sound of speech, and already discriminating many speech sounds, some of which will be used in their language. Within the first week of life, they learn to recognize their mother's voice and *their* language, distinguishing it from foreign languages. Within their first nine months, they learn enough to begin unitizing speech for language, moving from segmenting by intonation and stress to recognizing the confluence of the frequently experienced segmental and suprasegmental information that characterizes words, clauses, and eventually phrases (Jusczyk, 1997). At the same time, infants develop their sound production, deliberately and systematically practicing syllables in *canonical babbling.*

Toward the end of their first year, infants generally utter their first word, which is distinguished from babbling by the reliability with which the sounds occur for a specific context. The first word is thought to accompany an important cognitive development, a beginning symbolism, the recognition that objects continue to exist even when not directly sensed, that is, *object permanence.* Vocabulary grows slowly for a time, and then for most children suddenly takes off, a *vocabulary spurt,* perhaps indicating that the child understands something about the general concept of naming. Shortly after the vocabulary spurt, children combine words—the beginnings of syntax. At this time they seem to see language as a system, requesting names for concepts or, in bilingually reared children, separating vocabulary from the two languages and requesting translation equivalents.

Children differ in how they acquire language. Two general types of acquisition have been described: *referential/analytic* and *social/expressive.* Referential children focus more on analyzing language into components and ways to combine them; count nouns are heavily represented in their early vocabulary. Expressive children focus on language as a means of bonding, so they tend to imitate holistic, unanalyzed utterances to maintain the flow of speech. Their first words are drawn from many grammatical categories and may include whole phrases. Both types of children, of course, learn to analyze language and to use it socially. The characterizations are of their preferential approach to early language, although Bates, Bretherton, and Snyder (1988/1991) claim that learning-style differences are evident through the first several years.

After the first two years, language develops very rapidly, with semantic growth aiding syntactic understanding (e.g., the understanding that boys sharpen pencils and not conversely aids acquisition of the passive concept for "The pencils were sharpened by the boy") and syntactic understanding aiding semantic development ("a dax" must refer to a noun, so *dax* must be that thing whose name I don't know), known as *semantic* and *syntactic bootstrapping,* respectively. By the age of 4, children have some command of many syntactic complexities, including embedded sentences, connecting traces with their fillers, and a variety of conjunctive relations like time (after I did this, I did that) and causality.

### General Theories of Language Acquisition

The rapid acquisition of language complexities has indicated to some that the child has help from an innate guide or *bioprogram,* sometimes called the *language acquisition device (LAD)* and sometimes UG. It has been hypothesized that this bioprogram is active only during a critical period, estimated at ending sometime before puberty. Arguments for UG include common language acquisition milestones (first word, vocabulary spurt, early syntax) in children learning different languages but also across children of a given culture, each of whom is exposed to a different and nonrepresentative sample (or poverty of the stimulus) of structures in the parents' discourse to them.

However, studies have shown that infants and children do not need to have perfectly consistent examples but, like animals, can exploit statistical regularity (i.e., *usual* but not always occurring constructions). Children seem to acquire structures first that are semantically important *(form follows function),* frequently occurring, and regular. To the extent that this is true, it does not implicate an innate language-learning guide but a general cognitive mechanism, which is sensitive also to properties of the particular language to be learned. Likewise, rather than basic linguistic principles and specific parameters being innate, what may be innate are broad heuristics for language processing, heuristics such as (a) the *taxonomic principle* (words name categories of objects, not individual items) or principle of *contrast* (if there are two words, they will each reference different categories), (b) a *distinctiveness principle* (attend to sounds that are stressed and precede or follow silence), or (c) the minimum distance principle (group words that are near to one another into phrases, so that the nearest noun is likely the subject of an embedded clause). To some extent, these heuristics may be specific to language, dealing with, for example, how language refers, but, by and large, they are general cognitive and perceptual guides applied to language.

There is also the possibility that parents help their children learn by simplifying, regularizing, and exaggerating their language *(motherese),* making the underlying patterns more accessible to the learners. Typically, parents' language to young children or about them in their presence tends to center on the common environment ("yes, there's the kitty") or on an activity that the child is engaged in. Thus the parent "cooperatively" provides language for what the child is likely to be thinking about, facilitating learning. As children get older and more sophisticated, conversation with them becomes more abstract and decontextualized, perhaps because the parents model the child's increasingly abstract conversation, or perhaps because of the parents' natural response to the older-appearing person.

## Conclusions for Atypical Populations

With respect to atypical populations, we may ask,

1. Is language acquisition part of the human bioprogram, or do animals taught human language show similar milestones and heuristics?

2. Is there a critical period for language acquisition, or do people learn it similarly at any age?

3. After brain damage or in language-learning disabilities, what is the pattern of preservation and disruption: For example, can the social process be preserved and the referential not be (or conversely), and what is the effect on language?

4. Do parents model/teach language differently to children learning language atypically or at atypically late ages?

## Literacy and Secondary Language Processes

In the United States, most people grow up speaking only one language, and many are taught a second language in school. Most people learn to read and write, often in school. Literacy and fluency in English are necessary in the United States to advance in school and then in society. In many parts of the world currently, and certainly historically, most people have had no need of literacy but have needed more than one language for intertribal and international communication and trade. Sometimes two (or more) languages are acquired together from birth; then both are "primary." More often, the second language (L2) is acquired after the first (L1), as is literacy. In this case, these become *secondary* language skills, learned in part by applying models of language acquired from experience with primary language. At the same time, acquiring secondary language skills helps to deepen understanding of the primary language, seeing how it does code the world but also how it could do so differently; seeing how the language itself is recoded in print.

*Second Language Acquisition*

L2 acquisition is often not as complete as that of L1, with learners retaining an accent, both phonological and "syntactic," as they fail to learn to use subtle morphology and syntax completely. This "failure" may be due to the later time of learning, perhaps after a critical period for the LAD. It may also come from a *dis*advantage conferred by a more mature mind better able to remember large chunks of language and therefore less likely to fortuitously analyze language into appropriate morphemes (*the less-is-more hypothesis;* Newport, 1990). And it could arise from a lack of incentive and practice by older speakers, who are more likely to have and to retain a community in L1, and so need L2 less. Be that as it may, there are documented cases of adults attaining full fluency in a second language (and forgetting the first), but it is more common to attain greater fluency the younger one starts.

L2 acquisition does not normally proceed as does acquisition of L1, in part because there is L1, so the learner need not begin from the beginning, say, with the taxonomic assumption. At the same time, there is little evidence that learners try L1's constructions for L2, or that they learn by explicitly contrasting the way the two languages work. There appears to be a little of each of these approaches, but, by and large, structures in L2 are acquired in the same order as when that language is L1: form follows function; the more frequent and regular a structure, the earlier it is learned; semantically clear and perceptually salient constructions are attended to earlier.

Knowing more than one language seems to slow low-level language skills (like speeded picture naming) but to advance metalinguistic skills and literacy (e.g., Bialystok, 1988). Even in nonfluent L2 learning, the user does not seem to code L2 through L1 but to map it directly to concepts and to interconnect words and constructions within it. Slow, low-level skills may arise from a weaker association and lesser experience of a word in either language with a concept because some weight is apportioned to the concept's connections in the other language.

Multilinguals often combine their languages, particularly when in the company of other multilinguals. To the monolingual, this gives the appearance of ignorance of one of the languages, but in fact such *code-switching* is rule-governed, reflecting competence in both languages as well as in seamlessly interweaving them. It also is "cooperative," drawing on the common ground and community identity of fellow multilinguals.

The bilingual processes just reviewed assume a community of speakers of L2 into which the learner voluntarily enters. Historically, there have been situations in which there is either limited interaction among adult speakers of different languages (as when traders arrive in a new country for only a short time) or limited common language of adult speakers suddenly living as a community (as slaves or immigrant workers from a number of tribes on a single plantation). In these cases a primitive communication system develops, a *pidgin,* characterized by limited syntax used inconsistently, no function words, and considerable repetition or *reduplication* of morphemes. Children of pidgin speakers reared together develop a more structured, complex communication system, a *creole,* in which some content words take on function, and order is regularized to convey syntax. Bickerton (1984) hypothesizes that creolization happens spontaneously, as the *bioprogram,* UG, works on the primitive pidgin during the child's development.

## Reading and Writing

Across the world and through history, writing has been used for different purposes and therefore reflects and emphasizes different properties of spoken language. In our culture, writing is used to record and relate stories and knowledge as well as to aid memory. In acquiring literacy, we must experience the conventions of narrative storytelling as well as the relationship between speech and print.

There are three significant "routes" to understanding print: (a) connections between concepts and ways of expressing them in language *(contextually driven* or *top-down processing);* (b) connections between *graphemes* (letters or unitary letter combinations like "sh" or "tion") and speech (which thence connect to concepts), the *indirect* or *phonological route;* and (c) connections between the print and concepts *direct*ly on a *visual route.* (The latter two are *bottom-up* or *data-driven* processes.)

Forming all three sets of connections requires substantial language experience. Being able to move efficiently from print to concepts, so that one can "read to learn," requires extensive experience beyond "learning to read" or translating print to speech. Fluent readers going directly from print to concepts at the speed of thought have had much practice with language generally and with reading and writing specifically.

As fluent readers, it may be hard to recognize that our writing does not perfectly reflect our speaking. We do not directly capture in writing intonation, body language, pauses, and so on. Rather, we code them in writing either with punctuation (which you may remember was hard to learn and still may be a struggle) or with words like *sarcastically* or *disbelieving.* Print takes advantage of a "hard" memory and so uses longer sentences with more complex constructions and fewer overt "cues" to structure than speech. Finally, to connect graphemes and sounds requires that we analyze the continuous speech stream into grapheme-sized segments, which, for our roughly phonemic alphabet, does not happen naturally; children recognize syllables, *onset*s (the first sound of a syllable), and *rime*s (the syllable remainder) before they segment phonemically, and those who write without a phonemic alphabet may never code phonemically. So we must learn to think about our language in a new way for print. And, therefore, acquiring literacy teaches us not only to read and write but to understand our spoken language differently and more deeply.

## Conclusions for Atypical Populations

Given that secondary language processes depend on primary language, we might expect them to be more vulnerable than primary language to misdevelopment due

---

**Box 1.2. Levels and Perhaps-Essential Properties
of Language in Typical Populations**

---

Primary Language
Speech
— *Rapid fading:* The speech signal is ephemeral and must be stored in memory.
— *Hierarchically structured:* A continuous speech stream is composed of segments (phonetic features, combined into phonemes, combined into syllables, combined into words, phrases, clauses, and sentences) cemented through suprasegmentals.
— *Simultaneous and smeared:* Each segment is highly context-dependent, incorporating characteristics of neighboring segments and incorporated or smeared into neighboring segments.

Semantics
— *Arbitrary:* A word need not resemble its referent; they connect solely through use and experience.
— *Abstract:* Word meaning is not a simple association to an aspect of reality but a distant and generalized experience dependent on associations to other words.
— *Symbolic:* Words do not simply refer or denote; meaning is a more complex relation, dependent on the semantic system. Thus language can be innovative and figurative, generating new meanings through use.

Syntax
— *Productive:* Morpheme combinations are not fixed, although general "rules" governing them pertain, allowing an interesting infinite variety.
— *Hierarchical:* Languages evidence a constituent structure, with morphemes combining into words, which combine into low-level phrases, which combine into higher-level phrases, and so on through to the sentence.
— *Recursive:* Syntactic units can be created by incorporating units like themselves, as when a sentence is formed by conjoining or embedding other sentences.

Primary and Secondary Language
— Most people learn language "automatically," perhaps aided by a perfect confluence of cognitive development and language input, and perhaps with the assistance of a specially evolved language acquisition device, or bioprogram, operative during the critical period of early childhood.
— Children raised bilingually acquire two languages thus.
— Otherwise, a second language and literacy are acquired through more explicit teaching at a later age, piggybacking on primary language knowledge.
— Secondary language develops metalinguistic skills.

---

to learning disability, brain damage, or deviant language-learning exposure. Anything that could affect primary language should have a ripple effect on processes dependent on it. Moreover, because to some extent secondary language processes require abstracting a model of primary language, a cognitive problem in abstraction not evident in primary language could emerge in secondary language processing. On the other hand, secondary language could sometimes be easier than primary: print, for example, is visual and so could advantage individuals with auditory or speech-specific problems (to the extent that the indirect, phonological route may be bypassed); print provides a permanent "memory" unlike the *rapidly fading* speech signal; a second language less dependent on order might be easier for someone with particular language-learning disabilities affecting sequencing.

## ORGANIZATION OF THIS BOOK

In this chapter, I briefly outlined historical perspectives on language and then reviewed some salient characteristics of normal language and how it is processed, as revealed this century in a variety of disciplines. As we have seen, there has been a tendency for those who study language to ascribe language's normal emergence and symbolic power to unique-to-human processes that come into play naturally during normal childhood. Clearly, there are elements of this reasoning that are circular: People mature and language develops, but that does not mean that language develops through people's maturation. Even our cursory review illustrates the difficulty of parsing genetic factors specific to language acquisition (like the taxonomic principle) from general cognitive factors (like less is more) from environmental factors (like parents initially talk about the concrete context the child is experiencing).

To consider what *causes* our language abilities and language's communicative power, we need to compare normal language systematically and objectively with communication in groups who do not have normal human genetics and/or upbringing. This book presents data on language (-like behaviors) from such comparison groups as well as theories as to the cause of similarities and differences with normal language. We consider the comparison groups (a) to sharpen our concept of what language is and what its defining and characteristic properties are, (b) to evaluate whether and how language is special, and (c) to determine the human social, sensory, and cognitive mechanisms that shape language. We also briefly consider how our knowledge of language processes can help rehabilitate people who do not acquire language normally or who lose it through organic disorder.

The populations we will examine are animals (Chapter 2), language-learning-disabled and retarded children (Chapter 3), socially (neglected) or linguistically (orally reared deaf) deprived children (Chapter 3), deaf signers (Chapter 4), aphasics (brain damaged; Chapter 5), and psychotics or neurotics (personality/socially "damaged"; Chapter 6). Each population reflects a change from the typical language environment in at least one of the following factors: genetic specification, social environment and language models, cognitive constraint (what the human mind can or cannot do), and perceptual constraint (what properties of language derive from the *oral-aural* [speech-hearing]) modality.

We begin at the outset with a noncontroversial but empty definition of language: *Language is the way humans communicate. Communication* is formally defined as the active transfer of information from one to another. The two critical terms are *active* and *information. Active* implies *deliberate* processing on the part of the communicator; communication does not take place between a person and a tape recorder. Following the information-theoretic approach, *information* is defined rigorously as a lessening of uncertainty. In this view, telling a person something she or he already knows does *not* communicate that content but could communicate that the narrator is boring or noncooperative. In this view too, redundant signals (like the smear in speech or the predictability provided by grammar) do not often *add* information; redundancy reduces uncertainty only to the extent that the information failed to get through (it was obscured by outside noise or by the listener's inattention).

To this simplistic definition of language—typical human communication—we may consider adding some characteristic properties that we isolated in our review of typical language, properties such as symbolic nature, hierarchical and recursive structure, a rapid fading and simultaneously and redundantly (smeared) signal. As we proceed, we will develop a much more detailed, concrete, and, probably more controversial, definition.

As we have seen, language provides humans with a powerful means of regulating their complex *soci*eties, and normally it develops socially. Human beings are not alone in having social communities with social order: any sexual animal must communicate with potential mates and rivals; nurtured offspring and their caregivers must communicate; colonies like hives, herds, and flocks must coordinate. We have also seen that language provides and uses powerful cognitions, symbolic representation. However, human beings are not alone in symbolizing: Animals solve complex problems to locate food or defy predators. In Chapter 2, we compare our communication system with animals' to see if, and in what ways, language may be unique. We look for similarities, indicative of common evolutionary pressures, and differences, which will help us specify significant features of full-powered language. Chapter 2 also looks at attempts to teach nonhuman animals language, which, as we will see, have helped to define the critical features of language and how they are normally attained. Finally, we explore philosophers' and comparative psychologists' definitions of language and apply them to the animal systems, and retroactively to typical human language, asking, for example, at what age children "have language" or whether the amalgamation of second languages into pidgins or creoles qualifies as language, given rigorous application of these defining attributes.

---

## REFERENCES

Bates, E., Bretherton, I., & Snyder, L. (1991). *From first words to grammar: Individual differences and dissociable methods.* New York: Cambridge University Press. (Original work published 1988)

Bialystok, E. (1988). Levels of bilingualism and levels of linguistic awareness. *Developmental Psychology, 24,* 560-567.

Bickerton, D. (1984). The language bioprogram hypothesis. *Behavioral and Brain Sciences, 7,* 173-221.

Chomsky, N. (1965). *Aspects of a theory of syntax.* Cambridge: MIT Press.

Chomsky, N. (1972). *Language and mind.* New York: Harcourt Brace Jovanovich.

Chomsky, N. (1986). *Knowledge of language: Its nature, origin, and use.* New York: Praeger.

Collins, A. M., & Loftus, E. F. (1975). A spreading activation theory of semantic processing. *Psychological Review, 82,* 407-428.

Darwin, C. (n.d.). *The descent of man.* In *The origin of species and the descent of man* (pp. 445-495). New York: Modern Library. (Original work published 1871)

Eddy, J. K., & Glass, A. L. (1981). Reading and listening to high and low imagery sentences. *Journal of Verbal Learning and Verbal Behavior, 20,* 333-345.

Fodor, J. A. (1983). *The modularity of mind.* Cambridge: MIT Press.

Grice, H. P. (1989). *Studies in the way of words.* Cambridge, MA: Harvard University Press.

Herodotus. (1986). *The histories* (A. de Selincourt, Trans.). Harmondsworth, Middlesex, England: Penguin. (Original work published 1954)

Jusczyk, P. W. (1997). *The discovery of spoken language.* Cambridge: MIT Press.

Kosslyn, S. M. (1988). Aspects of a cognitive neuroscience of mental imagery. *Science, 240,* 1621-1626.

Kuhl, P. K. (1993). Early linguistic experience and phonetic perception: Implications for theories of development of speech perception. *Journal of Phonetics, 21,* 125-139.

Labov, W. (1972a). *Language in the inner city: Studies in the Black English vernacular.* Philadelphia: University of Pennsylvania Press.

Labov, W. (1972b). *Sociolinguistic patterns.* Philadelphia: University of Pennsylvania Press.

Lakoff, G., & Johnson, M. (1980). *Metaphors we live by.* Chicago: University of Chicago Press.

Lowry, R. (1987). *The evolution of psychological theory* (2nd ed.). New York: Aldine.

MacWhinney, B. (1987). The competition model. In B. MacWhinney (Ed.), *Mechanisms of language acquisition* (pp. 249-308). Hillsdale, NJ: Lawrence Erlbaum.

McClelland, J. C., Rumelhart, D. E., & the PDP Research Group (Eds.). (1986). *Parallel distributed processing* (Vol. 2). Cambridge: MIT Press.

Newport, E. L. (1990). Maturational constraints on language learning. *Cognitive Science, 14,* 11-28.

Osgood, C. E., Suci, G. J., & Tannenbaum, P. H. (1978). *The measurement of meaning.* Urbana: University of Illinois Press. (Original work published 1957)

Rieber, R. W. (Ed.). (1980). *Psychology of language and thought: Essays on the theory and history of psycholinguistics.* New York: Plenum.

Rosch, E., Mervis, C. B., Gray, W. D., Johnson, D. M., & Boyes-Braem, P. (1976). Basic objects in natural categories. *Cognitive Psychology, 8,* 382-439.

Smith, E. E., Shoben, E. J., & Rips, L. J. (1974). Structure and process in semantic memory: A featural model for semantic decisions. *Psychological Review, 81,* 214-241.

Yamada, J. E. (1990). *Laura: A case for the modularity of language.* Cambridge: Bradford Books of MIT Press.

## STUDY QUESTIONS

1. Given what you know about normal language, speculate on which features may be innate, part of a fundamental human predisposition to structure and process our communication linguistically. Do you think animal communication has languagelike features? If so, which features? Which features do you expect to find to be uniquely human?

2. We will be exploring language (-like) behavior in children reared with no or impoverished language until well past infancy, in deaf people who are raised from birth with sign language, in people who suffer brain damage in the language hemisphere (aphasics), and in people who have either childhood or adult-onset psychosis. For each group, consider which aspects of normal language are likely to be preserved and which changed by their atypical condition and experience. Explain your guesses.

# 2

# LANGUAGE: A HUMAN-SPECIFIC ACCOMPLISHMENT?

What, if anything, is it about language that makes it "special"? Do animals have the same or similar modes of communication? Or is there some reasonable set of criteria we can establish to distinguish animal communication from human communication, aside from the obvious one of who is the communicator? Do all humans have language? Does a newborn infant, for instance? Or is there a point in development when the infant passes from another form of communication to language as we know it? How, given only the child's communications, do we recognize this point, do we define the shift from nonlanguage to language? Whatever the criteria used to recognize the shift, do all languages satisfy these standards equally well, or are some languages more primitive than others, meeting fewer of these criteria? Similarly, are some animal communication systems more advanced than others, meeting language standards more precisely?

Obviously, to consider such questions, we must establish what we mean by language, what constitutes language and what does not. As we will see, we also need to establish what constitutes communication, and the definitions of language and communication and the distinctions between them are by no means settled.

This chapter presents some animal communication and human nonlanguage communication systems as alternative systems of social interaction and for consideration of possible biological and evolutionary mechanisms responsible for our language. In the attempt to establish reasonable criteria for language and communication, these other systems are also compared with language as reviewed in the last chapter. In later chapters, we will use the criteria established here to evaluate different human primary communication systems.

## OTHER COMMUNICATION SYSTEMS

There are many reasons to study animal communication, aside from its intrinsic fascinations. First, although it seems "simpler" than human communication (perhaps because we expect that it should be), it still manages to regulate social interaction, as language does for us. If animal communication is easier to understand, we may be able more readily to deduce principles of communication that also apply to human language. Second, by comparing ourselves and other species, we may make hypotheses about our development through evolution and about biological mechanisms underlying our current abilities. Third, we can test the age-old view that humans hold a special place in the cosmos *(anthropocentrism)* by studying other species to yield proof either of human uniqueness or of the interconnectedness of life.

In this section, I present selected descriptions of systems that animals use in interacting to provide comparison points for evaluating human communication.

### Evolutionary Theory: Some Caveats

Our anthropocentric, egotistical slant on reality causes us often to think carelessly about evolution, distorting its principles so that we emerge as its perfected product. Before comparing ourselves with other species, we should be quite clear on the nondistorted principles of evolution.

First and foremost, it is important to recognize that *evolution is neither a goal-directed process nor a force but a random process of change modified by environmental constraints.* The change results from variation in the transmission of genetic information. Many of the fluctuations produced genetically cannot survive beyond infancy and so are not propagated. Some of the fluctuations cause the organism to be at a disadvantage in competing for the necessities of its life, and so, over time, there become fewer of these individuals. Some fluctuations cause the individual to be less attractive to potential mates than others. Lesser access results in less opportunity for reproducing these traits. The last is *sexual selection;* the whole process of winnowing less advantageous characteristics is *natural selection.*

At any particular instant, the existing characteristics of a species may be those in the process of being winnowed; that is, as we are now, we are not the end product of evolution but some point in a long chain, and there is no way of knowing which point. (Indeed, like the dinosaurs, we may be a species that will become extinct.) Moreover, any individual existing at the same time we are is as much the product of eons of selection as we are; we are not necessarily better adapted to this millennium than are our pets, our plants, and our cockroaches.

We must be vigilant in our consciousness of the nonpurposiveness of evolution; not everything we see is either optimal or advantageous, nor is everything now extinct necessarily unfit for the current environment. Horselike creatures abounded in South America before humans and then became extinct for some reason; when their descendants were reintroduced after the discovery of the New World, conditions were again favorable for them and they proliferated (Darwin, 1871/n.d.). We have many ailments resulting from walking upright; our posture derived from a structure suited to quadrupeds and is not optimal for standing erect. Presumably, this disadvantage was compensated for by some advantage to being upright, but we should not think we are perfectly designed, or that "Nature" intended or designed us to walk erect. These considerations are important because, on the basis of assumed evolutionary principles, we tend to call other animals primitive—an arrogant and erroneous tendency!

So, the first consideration is that evolution is nonpurposive and neither we nor any existing species is an end product. A second point to be kept in mind is that in discussing the evolution of language, we are confined to deductions based on existing species, all of which, as already emphasized, have been subject to the selection pressures of evolution. This contrasts with speculations about posture, for instance, because we have, in the (imperfect) fossil record, skeletal remains. We cannot find similarly hard evidence (pun intended) on the early forms of language because language does not fossilize. What the record can disclose to us are properties of the skull and vocal anatomy and aspects of the social life of our precursors. From these we can infer their biological potentials and their communication needs. Some of these inferences will be discussed later in this chapter; however, such inferences are necessarily quite speculative.

We turn now to examine existing communities and their communication systems, to calibrate the effectiveness and specialness of ours, and to derive speculations for its evolution. Along with the other caveats noted in this section, we must always be aware that in studying other organisms' communication systems, we are prejudiced. We are outsiders to their "culture," their sensory capacities, and their communicative needs. Necessarily we are judging them with respect to our view of our abilities, and thus may be missing important data.

As I have stated, the definitions of communication and language are controversial. I enjoy controversy and will try to present all sides of the issue before presenting my own stand. Because there are authoritative opinions that differ from mine, feel free to disagree with my view: You will be in good company, wherever you stand. However, be consistent and thoughtful in evaluating systems of communication; if you change your mind or your definition of communication as you go along, retrace your steps and make sure you accept all the new implications.

## Communication and Signal Systems

In this section, I analyze signal systems of some organisms, which, through contrast to our system, exemplify an influential definition of language and communication—Hockett's (1960). I will present Hockett's view explicitly after debating the arguments.

---

**Box 2.1. Evolutionary Principles and Our Prejudices**

— *Anthropocentrism:* The human tendency to view other organisms as inferior to us, to view humans as the center of creation.
— *Natural selection:* A combination of random genetic variation and environmental constraints that results in organisms optimally suited to compete for necessary resources. The optimal organism for a particular ecological niche may not do well in another, and conversely. Hence natural selection effects a progression only to the extent that environmental conditions are stable.
— *Sexual selection:* The natural selection of genetic variants that increase access to mates.
— Evolution is nonpurposive, not goal-directed.
— Extinction is not a sign of failure but of inability to adjust to perhaps cataclysmic and temporary events at a critical time.
— Social and cognitive behavior does not fossilize, so we only infer its existence by analogy to current organisms and their capacities.

---

A preliminary definition of *communication* could be that it is the means by which one organism influences the behavior of another. By this definition, a fly buzzing around a frog communicates its edibleness to the frog, influencing the frog to catch it with its tongue. (The fly never communicates again.) Most people would not think this is communication; why not? Note that the fly is emitting/transmitting signals—a noise, a movement, perhaps an odor—that the frog is specially tuned to receive and respond to. Note also that the communication is not only one-way: If the frog misses the fly, the attempt will communicate "danger" and the fly will flee. Thus, if we reject this as communication, we conclude that communication involves something more than transmission of a signal, reception of a signal, or an "accidentally coordinated" transmission-reception system.

Perhaps communication entails the transmitter and receiver working together for a common good. This would exclude the fly-frog situation (and competitive human transactions). It still allows some situations that most would agree are also too "primitive." For example, when a tree is plagued by tent caterpillars, it immediately changes its metabolism, removing nutrients from the infested leaves and sending poisons or "medicines" to them. The poisons can kill the caterpillars either directly or indirectly by weakening them through "starvation" or causing them to migrate to other leaves, increasing their chances of being spotted by caterpillar-eating birds.

Now, the communication is not between the leaf and the caterpillar, a fly-frog situation. Schultz (1983) has shown that in addition to their having an immediate effect on the leaves, the poisons become airborne and *are picked up by neighboring trees!* Reception of this chemical message causes the neighbors to change their metabolisms, increasing the poisons in their own leaves, in "anticipation" of future attacks. In effect, the transmitter tree has "announced" the caterpillar invasion.

Obviously, trees able to receive such messages are more likely to survive than those that cannot defend themselves in advance, so the selective pressures should be clear. Obviously also, this system works for the common good, so, to separate it from human communication, we need additional necessary characteristics. One candidate is "feedback"; if a tree falls prey to caterpillars in the forest, it receives no indication from its neighbors that it has been heard.

Reflex communication systems with feedback working for the common good are still distinct from our communication, as we see from the mating ritual of the stickleback fish (Tinbergen, 1952, 1955). At the appropriate time of year, the male stickleback stakes out a territory and builds a tunnel nest. While he is doing this, his body changes color, developing a red mark, and his appetites change; he is suddenly attracted to swollen-looking things and aggressive toward things with red on them. The female also changes; she becomes swollen with eggs and develops an attraction for things red—simply as the result of the time of year. When the nest is completed, the male approaches the female and begins a zigzag dance. The female, attracted to the moving red spot, follows, and the male beelines to, and through, his nest. The pursuing female becomes stuck in the narrow tunnel. The male, prodding at the base of her tail, causes her to drop her eggs and become thin enough to exit through the nest. The male then fertilizes the eggs.

With respect to communication, both male and female transmit signals of courtship readiness (the red mark and the swollen belly). Each responds to the other's signal (by dancing and pursuing). Both give feedback; if the female stops following, the male will renew courtship, suggesting that he is responsive to her response of pursuit. Finally, the participants have a common goal (at least to the outside observer)—procreation. What makes this situation of interest to us is that despite these characteristics, the principle seems the same as in the tree "communication." The behaviors, as laboratory experiments have shown, are reflex responses to particular stimuli (like the tree releasing a chemical in response to a wound). Thus this "communication" is simply a biologically programmed reflex sequence. A female will as readily follow, or a male attack, a piece of red cardboard as a real male. A male is as attracted to another male swollen with food as he is to a real female. The fish respond to *sign stimuli,* characteristics of an object, rather than recognizing the object or situation as a whole. "Communication" appears to take place because the right stimuli appear at the right time. Fortuitous synchrony of signals may also underlie human communication, as in the urgent response to infants' cries or the attraction of their eye contact or laugh, or perhaps even in the parents initially talking about the shared context to which the baby is attending.

The fortuitous development of a red spot in the male and an attraction to red in the female is a product of natural selection; individuals who missed the signals of the opposite sex would not be likely to reproduce themselves. In other species, the fine-tuning of transmitter and receiver characteristics has been demonstrated to be under genetic control—a situation that has an obvious advantage. It has been demonstrated in species capable of crossbreeding that do not normally do so in nature.

For example, different species of crickets (Bentley & Hoy, 1972; Hoy, 1974; Hoy & Paul, 1973) have a characteristic mating song. For instance, two species have songs consisting of a high-amplitude trill followed by a low-amplitude trill.

In one of the species, the low-amplitude portion consists of a train of pulse pairs, while in the other species, it consists of a train of single pulses. Females of each species prefer the songs of their own species, resulting in no natural crossbreeding. If the species are crossbred in the laboratory, however, the offspring produce a song with characteristics between the songs of their two parents, suggesting that song character is under genetic control. And the females of the hybrid group prefer the new songs of their hybrid brothers to the songs of either parent! Thus *reception is under the same genetic control as transmission,* guaranteeing that male and female will find each other.

Our analysis thus far suggests that the bare rudiments of communication include effecting a behavior change in another, toward a common goal, with feedback from the other causing a change in the transmitter. In other words, communication must be two-way. Although the crickets and the frogs seem to be communicating only primitively, that should not stop us from noting the biological mechanism for coordinating "communication." Hybrid vocalizations have been produced by cross-breeding monkeys (Gautier & Gautier-Hion, 1982), so the effect is not limited to "simple" creatures. It may underlie human communication as well, for instance, in yoking speech production and speech perception to produce categorically percep-tible and producible features (see *Language and Its Normal Processing,* Chapter 7; Stevens, 1989).

An important difference between the situations we have just examined and language is that the former are inflexible; the communicators have no choice about what they will transmit or receive and no way to modify it. In the next section, I compare more flexible animal communication systems with ours.

## Flexible Communication: The Birds and the Bees—and Primates

In the signal systems just described, each organism emits behavior and produces a fixed response in the receiver. Allowing some learning, some productivity, some individual differences, or somewhat less predictability may result in more human-like communication but still be obviously biologically determined.

Male and female white-crowned sparrows "sing" in response to various stimuli. Only the male sings the mating song, called the *male song.* Like the stickleback's red spot and the cricket's mating song, the male song attracts a mate and establishes territory. Again, like the stickleback and the cricket, the sparrows seem to be specially tuned to recognize this song and no other. What makes this song interest-ing, though, is that it differs for birds of the same species who grow up in different geographic regions; it has dialects.

Males sing a song specific to their region, which females of the region respond to preferentially. Moreover, when prompted to sing through injection with male hormones, females sing their dialect alone (Baker, Spitler-Nabors, & Bradley, 1981).

The dialect difference indicates that there must be a learning component given that the birds of the species all derive from the same gene pool regardless of where they grow up. The preference for the dialect features of their home territory in both male and female sparrows shows that learning is constrained so that male transmission to regional females is guaranteed.

In an ingenious set of experiments, Marler (see Marler & Mundinger, 1971, for review) has shown how learning can be constrained. He raised baby sparrows under various conditions of isolation, controlling their exposure to male song. If the birds were deafened so that they could not hear adults, their song shared only overall length with normal sparrow song, showing that a minimum of song production is *hardwired* (i.e., genetic, requiring no environmental exposure). If the birds were raised without an adult model but with other baby sparrows so they had social stimulation and could hear themselves sing, their song sounded sparrowlike but contained none of the dialect features. This suggests that the birds may have a hardwired idea of song, a production goal that is achieved through monitoring and correction. It also suggests that the dialect features are not part of this hardwired idea but need to be learned.

Now, the most intriguing aspect of Marler's experiments is the criticalness of the time of introduction of the dialect features. If the baby sparrow was exposed to a tape-recorded male song during a certain time in infancy, very little exposure was necessary to have him sing the song complete with dialect features. Beyond about 50 days of age, no amount of exposure would cause him to sing as other members of his group sang. (A period when there appears to be a learning readiness and beyond which learning is difficult or impossible is called a *critical period.*) And, finally, Marler found that tape-recorded exposure to noises or birdsong other than that of the white-crowned sparrow even during the critical period did not result in the birds' learning these songs.

As Marler did, we may explain these results by assuming that there is a biologically determined limit on learning. At birth, the birds have a crude "blueprint," the hardwired idea (sparrow UG?) of what sparrow song should sound like. This focuses attention on the species' song to the exclusion of songs of other species or irrelevant noises in the environment. During the critical period, this blueprint is finely tuned (parameters are set) depending on surrounding input. At the end, the revised blueprint determines what the bird will sing (or respond to).

Similar models have been proposed for development of other perceptual systems and for the development of speech perception (see Eimas & Tartter, 1979); I pointed out the analogy to UG. A tunable blueprint allows genetic specification as well as guided flexibility for learning. It is interesting to note that Marler's initial claims of a fixed critical period during which song learning could not take place and the failure of the birds to learn any but white-crowned sparrow song may depend on the "poverty" of a tape recorder as teacher. Baptista and Petrinovich (1984) found that birds exposed to a bird "tutor," with whom they could visually and vocally interact, learned song after the critical period—even the song of a different species. Moreover, they observed a bird in the wild learn new dialect features after siring and rearing his first brood. Thus, if the stimulus is adequate socially, the learning period is not so critical. This too may be a significant analogy for human language learning.

With the white-crowned sparrow, we see one mechanism for introducing complexity into a message of sexual readiness—learning. In the western marsh wren, we see productivity in messages of sexuality, probably shaped by sexual selection.

The vocal repertoire of the western marsh wren is elaborate, numbering between 100 and 200 separate songs, far more than the eastern marsh wren. The western wren, moreover, has 1½ times the brain tissue devoted to song than the eastern wren and is capable of learning many more songs, even when reared under similar exposure conditions (Kroodsma, 1983). The extensive repertoire appears critically linked to sexual competition: The males duel each other vocally for territory. A dominant bird will sing; an inferior bird echoes the song, more quietly. If the inferior bird anticipates the next song, the tables are turned, and the previously dominant bird winds up echoing the other and losing his territory. Therefore, it is to the bird's advantage to be hard to anticipate, to have an extensive repertoire. (These claims have been supported by experiments using tape-recorded songs as the "dominant" model and observing the singing and territorial response of other birds to the tape.) Kroodsma has shown in another bird species (canaries) that females respond preferentially to (their) males with more varied song repertoires (Griffin, 1984).

The extensiveness of the repertoire, the ability to mimic new songs, and the suggestion that new songs may be created to extend the repertoire shows a flexibility not seen in the other systems we have looked at. The bird appears to be able to express territory ownership through diverse songs as opposed to having a fixed link between song and signaled state. Perhaps our elaborate repertoires have also been shaped by sexual selection. Labov (1972) describes a verbal dueling by inner-city speakers of the African American English Vernacular, *sounding* (discussed in some detail in *Language and Its Normal Processing*). Leadership in the "gangs" is attained in part by having a good repertoire of sounds, and in part by the verbal flexibility to create them following the correct linguistic formulae: The better sounders are the leaders. Thus dominance in human groups likewise can be established by displaying the most extensive repertoire.

Although the bird systems incorporate many features that we have proposed as critical for a communication system—transmission-reception centered on a common goal, feedback, and flexibility—they are different from language. To capture the difference, we must make a critical leap now from discussion of the communicators and communication situation to discussion of *what* is being communicated. In all the situations described thus far, the "topic" has been *the transmitter's signaling of his or her current state*—"I am ready to mate," "I am being attacked by caterpillars," "I am an eligible male from your social group," and so on. Moreover, in all these situations, *the sign stimulus can be used to indicate only one state,* to produce one response; it cannot enter into new "sentences" to take on additional meanings. (Note that this is true even for the marsh wren; he can express his state in a variety of ways but cannot use them to describe a new state, which would be a new meaning.)

A system that seems to allow expressions of new meanings belongs to an insect—the bee. (You may be surprised to find an advanced communication feature [see Figure 2.1] in a "primitive" insect rather than in an "advanced" mammal. Catch

"THOSE SOCIAL INSECTS ARE EVERYWHERE THESE DAYS."

**Figure 2.1**  (© 1997 by Sydney Harris.)

yourself: Your surprise derives from both anthropocentrism and the erroneous idea that there is some linear progression from primitiveness to complexity in current species!) Bees communicate with one another about the quality, quantity, and location of food sources (von Frisch, 1974). Some aspects of this communication are like sign stimuli; when the bee returns from a flower, she has its pollen on her legs and its quality can be judged immediately by her coworkers. Given that the pollen "represents" itself, it can indicate only one state.

To specify quantity and location of the food source, the bee engages in an elaborate dance, which her coworkers mimic, touching her and dancing with her, until they are satisfied they "understand" and fly off to the food. Locations close to the hive are distinguished from those far from the hive (> 50 meters) by the nature of the dance: A dance in a circle indicates a near source; a dance in a figure eight—*the waggle dance*—a distant one. Quantity and quality are specified for a near source by the intensity (speed; the excitement?) of the circular movement. If several foragers return from different locations, all locations will be transmitted initially, and the hive-dancing will ultimately synchronize to the "best" source.

For a distant source, direction as well as quantity and quality must be specified so the foragers can "beeline" to the source. As Figure 2.2 shows, the bees indicate direction by "translating" the angle they must fly from the hive to the food source with respect to the sun's position into the angle that the figure eight forms with respect to either the sun's position or the vertical axis of the hive. This translation turns out to be complex: The sun's position changes as the day progresses; the

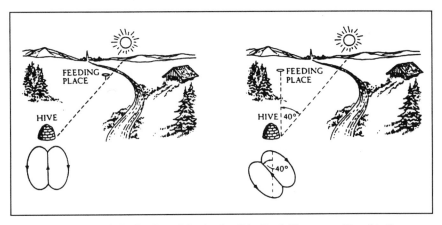

**Figure 2.2.** Schematic Indication of the Angle of the Bee's Dance as a Signal to the Direction of the Food Source With Respect to the Sun

SOURCE: From K. von Frisch's Nobel lecture "Die Entschlussung der Bienensprache." Copyright © by The Nobel Foundation 1974. Used by permission.

amount of change depends on the time of day, time of year, and latitude. And it seems that the bees compensate for the sun's position by using a calibration determined by the current rate of sun movement (Gould, 1980). When it is cloudy, the bees use as reference the point in the sky with some specific amount of polarized light relative to other points in the sky, the amount of which is a "dialect feature" and differs from hive to hive (Brines & Gould, 1979). If the hive is kept in the dark, then the dance is performed by using the vertical axis as determined by gravity— requiring a transfer of visual information, where the sun is (as seen going to the food source), into kinesthetic information, where the pull of gravity is. Thus the dance is quite flexible, not a fixed response.

While von Frisch detailed the waggle dance with respect to food, the bees are not confined to using it to describe food locations. Griffin (1984) points out that bees perform the dance to indicate any resource needed by the hive: building materials for repair, water if the hive is overheated, or food. Moreover, he notes that there must be some communication system as yet undiscovered whereby the foragers learn which supplies are needed by the workers maintaining the hive, caring for the young, and so on.

The dance language of the bees poses problems for those who would find characteristics of human communication that make it distinct from all other communication systems. As with other systems we have examined, here we have a special transmitter-receiver system, working for the common good. And there is flexibility—different hives use different dialects—indicating learning. There is feedback from receiver to transmitter in the touch as she mimics the dance. It is productive; new utterances are generated as different direction-goodness-of-supply-distance combinations are needed. Finally, bee dancing reflects some consideration of the other's "perspective"; updates are made for the new sun position, and a bee will concede her discovery to a better one communicated by another guide.

---

**Box 2.2. Characteristic Features of Communication Systems**

— Coordination of transmission and reception of the signal, seen in any successful predator-prey relationship, as well as in the perhaps genetically coordinated abilities of a male bird to sing and a female to respond to the song, or of a person to produce and perceive phonemes.

— Coordination toward a common goal, seen in sexual displays. While the common goal eliminates a predator-prey relation from the sphere of communication, it may eliminate too some conversations that we would like to consider communication.

— Use of a feedback loop: The transmitter modifies the signal depending on the receiver's response—this therefore includes predator-prey relations.

— Flexibility of communication:
  — Dialect features implying a learning component
  — Ability to change the communication to indicate a new situation, as when the bees modify their dance for different reference points
  — Ability to use a signal to elicit a behavior in unusual circumstances, deliberate deception
  — Ability to vary the signal, to communicate one's communication skill

— Topic and Productivity
  — Signals an external state like the location of food or type of predator as opposed to fear or singing skill
  — Signals used productively to construct new utterances

---

Nevertheless, the dance language can be described easily as a reflex-response sequence. The mapping of external stimulus to bee response is invariant and probably innately specified. Bees probably have no choice but to dance to describe the food source location following the simple rules just mentioned. They probably also have no choice but to mimic the best food source. Is human language a similar reflex expression of rules, but with more rules, giving us more apparent flexibility?

## Communication in Mammals

At this point, I hope to have stimulated you to see perhaps disturbing similarities between the natural communication abilities of "primitive" colonies—plants, birds, and bees—and of advanced cultures—ours. You may be tempted to reject the similarities because you see such a gap between them and us. For that reason, it is worth looking at nonhuman mammal communication, because mammals 'R' us and because the communication features found to date are not so different from "them." Examination of the mammal communication features therefore may help you bridge the gap and see our place in the continuity of life. I will not describe mammal communication in detail but will give an overview with selected examples.

Unfortunately, perhaps because mammal behavior is so complex, it is difficult to describe any one communication system completely. For example, researchers have looked at auditory signaling in whales and determined for the humpbacked whale that a given burst of song lasts as long as 30 minutes and consists of call types (whistles, rumbles, and so on) produced in a set order for each whale but with different examples of each call in different cycles of the order (Payne & McVay, 1971). (This is analogous, perhaps, to an SVO sequence with different examples of call types corresponding to different nouns [S and O] or verbs.) It suggests that these whale signals exhibit syntax unlike the other signals we have discussed. However, discussion of the whale "system" is limited because the "code"—what the songs mean—has not been broken, nor is it known whether other whales recognize or respond to the songs.

Primates (monkeys and apes) and other land mammals are easier to study than oceanic mammals because they may be more easily followed and observed. Study of mammal behavior has fallen into three interacting categories: their social structure, their call systems and body language (both visual and olfactory), and their cognitive abilities. Their call systems and cognitive skills have usually been investigated in relation to a human model to see if they do what we do in similar ways. (This bias may render our view of other mammals' communication overly simplistic but does allow for important analogies to human behavior.) Different investigators have concentrated on different types of mammals with respect to each of these aspects, so my review will not describe any system fully.

### Overview of Social Structure and Signaling

Generally, mammals have a strong social structure: They reproduce sexually, and the females (at least) care for their young, necessitating some forms of signaling between male and female, parent and child. In addition, many mammals exhibit a "tribal" structure, hunting, grazing, grooming, baby-sitting, playing, or fleeing danger as a herd. This means there must be signaling among members to coordinate these group activities. (Of course, social structures also exist in schools of fish, hills of ants, vees of geese, knots of toads, and so on.) The question is whether this signaling is different from other systems we have looked at.

Primate communication displays usually indicate the transmitter "state" that we have seen in other animals—readiness to mate, territory ownership, pain, or presence of a desired food source or undesirable enemy. Groups with social structure usually also indicate dominance relations (perhaps inseparable from territory marking)—what we call the "pecking order" from observing chickens in a barnyard. There is also usually some means of recognition between offspring and parent and some way for the offspring to signal their needs to their parent(s).

Signals occur in many modalities: For example, monkeys may scream (auditory), bare their teeth (visual), emit an odor (olfactory), clutch one another (tactile). The signals are perhaps more complex or variable compared with those of some of the organisms we have looked at. For example, a single emotional state, such as fear, may be expressed by several different calls (Jurgens, 1982). Or the feeling of aggression (produced here by stimulating an "aggression center" in the monkey's brain) may be expressed differently depending on the animal's dominance position within the tribe (Delgado, 1977).

"Messages" can vary to describe a stimulus more specifically than perhaps in some of the other systems we have examined: Vervet monkeys give distinctly different calls when confronted with leopards, eagles, and snakes. Vervets hearing those calls give distinct responses—running into trees, looking up, and looking down, respectively, even when the calls are played by tape recorder in a sterile laboratory setting (Cheney & Seyfarth, 1992). Infant vervets show the same reactions but produce the calls in response to a broader range of stimuli, indicating that there is an innate component that is finely tuned through environmental exposure. Snowdon (1982) has demonstrated similar call variations dependent on environmental stimulation in another type of monkey, cotton-top tamarins.

Despite the additional complexity or specificity of the relationship between signal and stimulus, nonhuman primate communication seems similar to the signal systems already described. Thus far, no syntax has been revealed, nor is there much indication of productivity—creation of new messages. And the "messages" still reflect an invariant relationship between internal motivational state and call, the difference being perhaps that the primate is able to indicate fear of leopards as opposed to eagles, while trees are only able to indicate general attack.

Of course, the systems may seem primitive both because we expect and want them to be (so we win) and because we do not yet fully understand them. We must also be careful to ensure that we communicate something different before declaring that we do: Isn't each of our utterances under the control of a given motivational state and environmental cue? Is the only difference (if it holds up to further study) that vervets distinguish through calls three predators while we distinguish many more?

*Neural Analogies*

Study of the neural mechanisms underlying perception and production of primate vocalizations can provide meaningful analogies for human communication because we are not-too-distant relatives. What has been discovered for the monkey as well as for "lower" animals such as the cricket (Zaretsky, 1971) or songbird (Leppelsack & Vogt, 1976; see Eimas & Tartter, 1979, for review) is that there are specific brain cells that respond in very regular ways to aspects of the communication signal. This has been discovered through "single-cell recording."

Every *neuron* (nerve cell) has an electrical charge. When the neuron is at "rest," it exhibits a baseline level of electrical discharging called *spontaneous activity*. When the neuron is stimulated, its activity level changes, either increasing, called *excitation,* or decreasing, called *inhibition*. When an EEG (electroencephalogram) is taken, the electrical activity of the whole brain—the sum of these individual charges—is measured. It is possible to measure *individual* neuron activity by attaching a microelectrode directly to a cell; this is *single-cell recording*. Whereas an EEG tells us about general alertness, single-cell recording indicates the specific stimuli to which a particular neuron responds. Presumably, if we determine the stimuli to which each neuron reacts (the neuron's *receptive field*), we can derive a general picture of how the brain works. (Neurons may be stimulated directly with a small jolt of electricity, the technique used in stimulating aggression in monkeys of different dominance, described earlier. By seeing how the animal reacts when the cell[s] is stimulated, we can determine what the cell[s] is responsible for.)

The simplest model of the brain's workings is a *detector model;* one cell responds to one stimulus type. If detectors can be found, the matter of perception is straightforward: Each neuron is invariantly tuned to particular features of the stimulus stream, and perception takes place as all the neurons respond to their particular features. We can conceptualize the system as a network of sign stimuli-fixed responses: The sign stimulus is the feature that the neuron reacts to; the response is excitation or inhibition.

There are many difficulties involved in the research and the conceptual framework presented here, which I will briefly describe. The first, as I mentioned for speech in Chapter 1 (see Chapter 7 of the companion volume for a more complete exposé), is that direct or invariant maps between a signal property and response (phonetic feature) have rarely been found in speech because of its inherent simultaneity and smear. A second problem is that searching for detectors is like looking for the proverbial needle in a haystack. There are a vast number of neurons and a vast number of stimuli and stimulus features; matching the perfect stimulus with its neuron requires luck. In fact, we never know that we have discovered a detector: All we know is that that cell responds to the stimulus we tested. Yet it may also respond to a number of others that we have not tried, so our interpretation of its sensitivities may be erroneous. A third problem is that knowledge of a single unit's response, even if accurate, does not tell us what role that neuron plays in the perception or consciousness of the stimuli in the whole organism.

With all these opportunities to overlook the "needle in the haystack," it is noteworthy to find a neuron set that responds to stimuli important to the animal. In production, Apfelbach (1972) has isolated neurons in the gibbon brain that, when stimulated, cause the animal to produce its calls—with different brain regions for different calls. In perception, Wollberg and Newman (1972; Newman & Wollberg, 1973a) isolated neurons in the auditory cortex of the squirrel monkey (the *cortex* is a layer of cells at the surface of the brain that is responsible for higher cognitive and perceptual functions) responsive to the species' vocalizations.

In an extensive study of one call type, Newman and Wollberg (1973b) found detectors for identifying the speaker. The call is the *isolation peep,* a sound the squirrel monkey produces when separated from its troop, which is answered in kind by the troop members. This dialogue continues until the lost monkey makes visual contact with the troop. There are two kinds of cells in the auditory cortex responsive to the isolation peep: One responds to the structure of the peep over wide frequency and intensity ranges, as might be found across individuals, and the other, to specific acoustic variants of the peep, perhaps selective for an individual or a dialect feature of that troop. Thus we see a biological mechanism for group and speaker identification in a species for which such identification is vital.

Some nonhuman primates, macaques, show brain hemisphere differences, a *laterality effect,* in processing the calls of their species, as humans show in dichotic listening (Peterson, Beecher, Zoloth, Moody, & Stebbins, 1978). Specifically, acoustic distinctions that differentiate call types are more discriminable when presented to the monkey's right ear than when presented to its left, but pitch differences for the same call show a left-ear advantage. In addition, surgical removal of a particular region in the left hemisphere only, in which damage in humans produces language problems (see Chapter 5), causes macaques to lose their ability to discriminate the calls (Heffner & Heffner, 1984). (Lateralization of species-specific sounds has also been demonstrated in birds [Nottebohm, 1970; reported in Marx, 1982] both in production and perception. The neural song center, moreover, is larger—has more neurons—in birds with larger repertoires.)

## Higher-Level Cognitive Skills

Apart from looking directly at their communication systems, we may assess communicative capabilities through the cognitive skills of the communicators in other situations. For example, we may ask what symbolic thinking is and whether animals can do it, whether or not they use symbols in their natural communication. If they can, then we may redirect our investigation of the animal's communication system to search for evidence of symbol use, and we may attempt to teach the animal a system that uses symbols directly, like language. In fact, many of the recent advances in understanding complexities in primate communication such as the different call types for different predators were found because the investigators had the expectation that there must be higher-order communications as the animals had been shown elsewhere to be "smart." And, as we will see, there have been extensive attempts to teach some primates human-type language, derived from similarly heightened expectations.

Many mammals have shown that they are capable of responding not just to the stimulus situation but to abstract information deduced from it. For example, chimpanzees recognize themselves in a mirror and use the reflection to clean their fur, perhaps demonstrating self-awareness (Gallup, 1979). (This is an abstraction because to conclude that it is a self-image, the animal must respond to something like the identical nature of the motion of the image and the self, and must overlook differences between the mirror reflection and typical self-view.) They also respond appropriately to pictures: One anecdote tells of a home-reared chimpanzee finding a picture of iced tea in a magazine and showing it to her owner as she dragged the person toward the refrigerator (see Premack, 1976); another tells of a chimpanzee watching a film of the capture of an orangutan in the wild and hooting and throwing things at the image of the captors (Premack, 1976). Experiments have demonstrated that a chimpanzee watching a videotape of a person faced with a problem will appropriately select a photograph of a tool to be used in the solution (Premack, 1986; Premack & Woodruff, 1978). Thus the chimps appear to interpret photographs or movies, "identify" with them, and use them to receive information. (Pigeons also respond to photographs. They discriminate photographs containing human beings from those that do not, regardless of the angle the person was photographed from or his or her position, age, dress, and so on; Herrnstein & Loveland, 1965.)

Nor are mammals confined to perceiving concrete properties of objects. For example, one chimpanzee (after extensive language-type training; see Sarah in the next section) seemed to be able to understand causality. Premack (1976, 1986) trained her to insert between two states of an object an instrument that could have caused the change in state (apple-knife-apple slice, sponge-glass of water-wet sponge). She readily generalized to new pairs (e.g., to place the knife between a sponge and a cut sponge). In another task, chimpanzees were trained to respond differently to the concepts "same" and "different," selecting from among three objects the object that differed from the other two along some *untrained* dimension.

Finally, mammals seem to show an awareness of their signals and are able to use them "symbolically," for the purposes of *deception*. The critical point here is that in using a signal deceptively, an animal must be able to (a) produce the signal when its normal stimulus is absent and (b) produce the signal to elicit a response in another—presumably therefore demonstrating awareness of the likely response of the other (Griffin, 1984). Some deceptions are perhaps uninteresting, because they are hardwired, like a bird's stereotypically feigning a broken wing to lead a predator from the nest. In this case, the crippled behavior is elicited reflexively by two "sign stimuli": a *bona fide* broken wing or a predator. It is clearly symbolic only when the animal modifies the deception in response to feedback from the target. (Griffin, 1984, discusses cases thought to be stereotypical where animals do seem to modify their "reflex" intelligently.)

A clear case of deliberate, nonstereotypical deception was reported by Bruemmer (1983). He observed a weighty male sea lion land on top of a tiny baby, certain to suffocate it. The baby's mother "flirted" with the male, biting his neck, a signal of estrus, but she was not in estrus. A male's reflex reaction to such a signal is to chase the signaler, here a successful ploy. Once the male moved off her baby, she stopped her signal and left him. Therefore, it appears that she was aware of the effect of her signal and had it under nonreflex control.

Woodruff and Premack (1979) experimentally induced similar deceptive behavior in chimpanzees (including Sarah). They allowed chimps to observe a trainer placing food in one of two bins. The chimps could not themselves reach the food but could signal a new trainer, who had not observed the food placement, to indicate its location. The new trainer was by design either cooperative, sharing the food with the chimps, or competitive, hoarding the food. The chimps spontaneously developed means of signaling the trainers—orienting their bodies toward the food bin while watching the trainer, looking back and forth from the food bin to the trainer, and, occasionally, spontaneously pointing to the correct container. Moreover, after becoming acquainted with the personalities of the trainers (and being allowed to fetch the food if the trainer was unsuccessful in finding it), the chimps began to suppress these signals when the competitive trainer was present. This indicates that the signals were not uncontrolled reflexes and that the animals were aware of their effects.

Finally, one chimp lied to the competitive trainer, using the signals to indicate the container that did not have the food!

## Summary

In this section, we examined naturally occurring animal behaviors that seem to exhibit flexibility like that we find in human language. We also considered potential mechanisms for some of these behaviors. Thus we saw in birds and bees the existence of dialects, presumably acquired during a critical period, through modification of an innate blueprint for communication by particular environmental experience. We saw productive use of a simple system of rules by bees to describe the location of a food source with modifications for varying reference points. We found large vocabularies for signaling internal states and environmental causes in birds and primates, what is perhaps a syntax system in whales, and evidence of complex conceptual structures in apes. In the primate, we found evidence of specialized neural centers for communication, perhaps analogous to ours, and we found call detectors, suggesting potentially analogous detectors in people. Thus far, no communication system has been found that demonstrates the extensive flexibility, productivity, and restructuring found in ours, but that may be because, in looking at alien systems, we are unable to recognize what we see. An alternative method for comparing human capabilities with those of other animals is to find out what they "see" when looking at our language. We turn next to attempts to teach human language to animals, in part to determine whether animals can learn language, adding evidence to the view that there is an evolutionary continuity implied in the common cognitive substrates of languagelike behaviors, and in part to examine the criteria for language that the trainers used.

## HUMAN LANGUAGE AND NONHUMANS

Given apes' extraordinary intelligence, a number of investigators have examined whether it is possible for them to learn humanlike language under specific training situations. The earliest attempts used a spoken language, English, with chimpanzees raised like children in upper-middle-class homes (Brown, 1958). The chimps adapted readily to human life, learning to dress, wash dishes, brush their teeth, and so on. However, despite specific training, they learned to produce very few words, perhaps because their vocal tracts differ anatomically from ours, making our sounds impossible for them to produce. Note here the biological constraint on speech acquisition.

Subsequent attempts took this biological constraint into account, and, recognizing the apes' superlative manual dexterity, visual discrimination abilities, spontaneous imitation, and use of gestures, attempted to teach them language skills in visual-manual forms. Either artificial "languages" were constructed using plastic chips (Premack, 1971) or computer-graphic symbols as words (Rumbaugh, Gill, &

---

**Box 2.3. Biological Mechanisms and Analogies in Communication**

— *Sign-stimulus/reflex-response:* The innate, genetically controlled response to a particular feature of a critical stimulus, like the female stickleback's following of a red spot, whether a cardboard one or an attractive male fish.
— *Tunable blueprints and critical periods (a bioprogram):* A model for the genetic control of some types of learning. The organism is born with a crudely specified concept of a critical pattern and with a window of adaptability for learning critical features of that pattern. During that window, the organism soaks up features coordinated with those that match the innate concept, modifying the blueprint for the concept.
— *Genetic control of transmission and reception:* A single biological mechanism ensuring that a female will respond to the call of the male. Demonstrated through creation of hybrids in the laboratory, where hybrid sisters (crickets) prefer the song of their brothers to those of either parent.
— *Detectors and centers:* Areas of the animal's brain that when stimulated produce characteristic calls of the species, or that respond to such calls with a characteristic activation pattern.
— *Laterality:* A neural center on one side of the brain only, which is differentially responsible for species communication—in people, as well as birds and some nonhuman primates.

---

von Glaserfield, 1973), or a natural visual-gestural language, American Sign Language (ASL; Gardner & Gardner, 1969; Patterson, 1978a, 1978b; Terrace, Petitto, Sanders, & Bever, 1979) was employed. (ASL is described in detail in Chapter 4. For now, note that it is not fingerspelling, it is very different from English syntactically and morphologically, and it has the full power of expression of any human language.) Attempts to produce languagelike behavior have also been extended to other animals: to seals and dolphins (see Herman, Kuczaj, & Holder, 1993), which are presumed intelligent like humans, and to a parrot (Pepperberg, 1981, 1983, 1987), which can vocalize and sound like humans.

The attempts varied not only in what kind of language was taught but also in the extent to which production, comprehension, or both were emphasized. They also varied in the extent to which the learning situation mimicked child-rearing conditions, tying communication to *social* interaction in a homelike environment (either human or that natural for the animal's group). The alternative to the social model was an explicit conditioning model in which, like circus performers, the animals accomplish a humanlike task through *shaping*, being rewarded (e.g., given food) for successive approximations to the target behavior.

Evaluation of the success of the projects has at times been enthusiastic: Apes outperform children (e.g., Gardner & Gardner, 1975; Savage-Rumbaugh & Lewin, 1994), and animals understand semantic relations, anomaly, syntactic violations (e.g., Herman et al. 1993). (The evaluation has at times been emotional and nasty too; see Wade, 1980.) The enthusiasm is usually tempered after more careful analysis suggests that much of what the animal seems to be doing is enriched by the very capable language-interpretation skills of human observers, skills that we may apply also in (too) richly interpreting children's behaviors or in feeling we are conversing when interacting with a user-friendly computer. Probably the most significant example of enthusiasm reversal was the public turnaround by Terrace:

> From my own experience while directing Project Nim [. . .] By Nim's third birthday, I was sufficiently impressed with his combinations to conclude that they constituted the best evidence to date of an ape's grammatical competence. When I subsequently discovered, through frame-by-frame analyses of videotapes of Nim signing with his teachers, that Nim's combinations were artifacts of his ability to imitate his teacher's signing, I concluded that apes could not create sentences . . . In a review of Premack's work, I argued that sequences such as *Mary give Sarah apple* were rote sequences consisting of three nonsense syllables whose meanings Sarah [the chimpanzee] did not know *(Mary, give, and Sarah)* and one paired-associate *(apple)* whose meaning Sarah understood in a particular context. (foreword, pp. xv-xvi, to Savage-Rumbaugh, 1986)

For us, the debate is meaningful because it has caused careful (although at times heated) consideration of what our language is, how to test for it, and how it differs from other skills. My purpose in reviewing the literature—indeed, the purpose of the experimenters originally—is twofold. The first is to show evolutionary continuity: Although no other animal discourses the way we do, given the process of evolution, we should look for common cognitive skills that have diverged, producing *human* language (not surprisingly) *only in humans.* (Likewise, no animal has a hand like ours, but we see structural analogues in the hands of the apes and in the wings of birds.)

My second purpose is to test our definitions of languagelike behavior and our concepts of how they are produced. Use the presentation to challenge your *critical* skills: Be cautious in either your acceptance or your rejection of the animals' abilities as we review this literature. A dog who paws his owner's lap leash-in-mouth is communicating his desire to go outside, using an association, the leash, to outside. Is this a symbol? Does it become more symbolic if it is a spoken word or gestured sign? Do we need more than this type of association to conclude that an animal (or person) has languagelike abilities?

## Systems for Simulating Language in Other Animals

As already stated, there have been two general approaches to language in animals: teaching the animal a naturally occurring language like English or ASL or developing an artificial language. The advantages of using a natural language are its unquestionable power: It is not an approximation to human language but is a human language, and is therefore capable, in the hands of skilled users, of expressing metaphor, recursion, and so on. Moreover, it is flexible; it may be produced anywhere and any time with no special materials. Its disadvantages, experimentally, stem from the advantages. It takes years for people to achieve fluency in a language and we would like to quantify results in a shorter time. We would like to be confident that teachers of the language are fluent in it. If experimenters learn sign only before training their animals, they are unlikely to be fluent, effective teachers. And because of the freedom to express language anywhere, it is hard to maintain a complete and accurate record of utterances to establish frequency of errors, insights, and so on. It has been shown that we recall semantically and syntactically correct sentences more easily than anomalous or scrambled sentences (see Chapter 5 of the companion volume). A human-memory record of animal performance is thus naturally biased, that is, more likely to include good sentences than nonsense.

The main sign language projects involved Washoe and Nim (chimpanzees) and Koko (a gorilla). The animals were taught sign in a homelike environment through observation of their trainers communicating with them and through *molding* of signs, the trainer shaping the animals' hands into the sign, usually when referents were present. When the animal reached for or was handed an object, the trainer labeled it and, after a time, required the animal to use the label to obtain the object. This was presumed to simulate the natural language-learning situation. During the course of the Washoe and Nim projects, different trainers (undergraduate or graduate research assistants) participated. This may have retarded the animal's learning because different trainers would have different sign proficiency, and there would be a social disruption as a trusted friend disappeared. (Project Nim especially has been criticized on this ground.)

At this time, the only ongoing sign language project is that of Koko, in part because of the public critique of Project Nim by its scientists, which reduced at least funding, if not enthusiasm, for the project. In most cases, the apes participating in the projects were moved from pampered lives with high social involvement with humans to isolation. In some cases, this was to cages in medical facilities. Some of the apes returned to the wild, involving expensive and human-labor-intensive rehabilitation to life in the wild. Linden (1986) provides a thought-provoking and heart-rending discussion of the politics and ethics of treatment of these subjects, nonhuman but certainly sentient and possibly linguistic.

Intriguingly, in the medical facilities the animal caretakers found it worthwhile to tape pictures of signs and their translations to the cages for, whenever they walked in, the animals frantically tried to communicate with them in sign. Of course, when one enters an animal shelter there is a distressing cacophony of animal sounds as the caged animals beg for attention, release, and perhaps even an imagined home. Whether the signing apes are communicating more than that in a more languagelike manner is moot, but the impact of the more human-appearing behavior is distressing.

The artificial language projects I will review include the chimpanzees, Sarah and Lana (with Sherman, Austin, and Kanzi), and the dolphins, Phoenix and Akeakamai. I also present Alex, the parrot, who learned a subset of spoken English, so restricted that it resembles an artificial language, though using a natural medium.

Sarah was one of the earliest chimpanzee language projects, and her project evolved into some of the cognition assessments described in the previous section

(Premack and Woodruff). The Lana project is ongoing and has evolved markedly over the course of time in response to criticism and increasingly sharper definitions of language, communication, and so on. The dolphin project is recent, ongoing, and, in my opinion, worth presenting as a foil because I see little evidence that the scientists have considered either what language is or the criticisms leveled at their predecessors in the ape projects.

Sarah's artificial language used a board and plastic magnets that could be mounted on it. Lana used a computer with a screen and keyboard, with shapes corresponding to words. In some of the freer-form work emanating from the Lana project, the keyboard setup was replaced with a portable board or photographs of the objects. In the dolphin project, two systems were used: One dolphin learned to respond to high-frequency electronically emitted whistles and the other, to gestures of a trainer. In both cases a particular whistle or gesture was paired with an object, location, or action, that is, constituted a word.

Note that the artificial languages are constructed with explicit, not tacit, knowledge and do not, like natural language, evolve historically through use. In examining these languages, it is important to consider whether they truly show the complexity of a real language or only give the appearance of complexity through the translation into English.

## Sarah

### Teaching Naming

Sarah, Premack's (1971, 1976, 1986) chimpanzee, was taught to associate pieces of plastic with particular objects in the environment, using classical and operant conditioning (reviewed in Figure 1.2). Each plastic piece represented a concept and differed from other plastic pieces in size, shape, or color. Sentences were written vertically on the board. Sarah learned thus names of foods; names of trainers; names of properties like different colors and shapes; names of names of properties like "color of," "shape of"; words describing language like "name of"; prepositions; syntactic markers like plural, interrogative, and negative; and ways of forming compound strings ("Sarah put apple in dish and banana in pail") and complex strings ("if red on green Sarah take apple").

The training and testing methods were the same for simple and complex concepts and constructions, so I will describe only a few. To teach the token symbol for apple, for example, first rapport was established so that Sarah felt comfortable eating in front of the trainer. Then the trainer presented her with a piece of apple together with the plastic piece that was to represent it. Gradually, the apple was made more and more difficult for Sarah to reach while the plastic piece was attainable. (Gradual removal of a cue, such as the object apple, is called *fading*.) When Sarah picked up the plastic piece, she was reinforced with the apple. Reinforcing successive approximations of the desired behavior, *shaping* the behavior, the trainer next taught her to place the plastic on the board before she received the apple.

Other plastic pieces were similarly paired with other fruits. To test if she had learned the associations, she was presented with a piece of fruit and choice of plastic symbols and was reinforced only if she selected the symbol naming the fruit.

Properties were taught in the same way; plastic pieces that were to stand for, for example, red and yellow, were presented respectively, in conjunction with apples and bananas. For an apple, Sarah had to choose red and no other colors. Trainers' names and "verbs" like *give* and *take* were similarly paired with situations in which one was appropriate and the others not.

Testing always required that Sarah select from among a set of (usually two) chips, the correct one for the concept.

### Teaching "Syntax"

Once particular tokens were learned, they were required to be *chained,* strung together for reinforcement. The procedure was the same: If Mary was in the room and Sarah wanted the apple, she was shaped to say "Mary apple," then "Mary give apple," then "Mary give apple Sarah." (Minor difficulties arose when Sarah had to give food to someone else—important for differentiating the meaning difference between "Mary give Sarah" and "Sarah give Mary"; these were overcome by reinforcing Sarah with something else when she correctly designated someone else as receiver. Children show a similar bias, with the self being the first instance of the recipient semantic relation or *case* [Dore, 1975].) Conjunctions were taught by placing two sentences next to each other, then merging them so one was underneath the other and then removing the extra subject and verb. Questions were taught by replacing a symbol in a learned string with a bit of plastic representing "?" and requiring that Sarah substitute the correct symbol, that is, fill in the "blank," for the interrogative marker.

### Teaching More Complex Concepts

Complex concepts like "color of," "name of," and "if-then" were taught in similar fashion, worth describing because it may not be clear how to use this simple procedure for abstract concepts. Once the color names were learned, the symbol for color was introduced in the string "red color-of apple," and the response of "red" to "? color-of apple" was reinforced. Note that at times the actual fruit was in the last position, in which case a color match could be performed, but at other times the symbol for the fruit was there—and apple was represented by a blue plastic chip. So the correct response was in fact "red color-of blue-plastic-chip = apple"— which Sarah had no trouble making. Once the color-of symbol was learned, it could be used to teach new color names. "Name-of" was acquired by substituting its symbol between an object's name symbol and the object, and like "color-of," once learned, it could be used to teach new names.

"If-then" was taught as a label for a particular kind of discrimination, one that many animals have no difficulty performing. An animal can be trained to make one response for reinforcement in the presence of one stimulus (called a *discriminative stimulus*) and a different response in the presence of another one—to pull a lever if there is a green light, and to turn around if there is a red one, for instance. Sarah was taught to take one food if green was present and a different one if red was present, and was then taught a symbol to describe this activity—"if green take apple." Once she learned to respond to this sentence, the "if-then" symbol could be used to teach new conditions for behavior. This was her most challenging task.

Is this language? At this time, I will not formally critique Sarah's performance so that you may have the opportunity to consider it yourself. Be careful in your consideration: I have used standard terms describing syntax and semantics to describe her behavior and I have "translated" her chip strings into English. This is likely to bias you into thinking of this as language because it looks like our language. Is your ATM constructing sentences symbolically or productively? Is Sarah doing what you do when you talk or some more rote process like the machine? Examination of Sarah's sentences without benefit of translation, as in Figure 2.3, may help you decide.

It is important to keep in mind also how Sarah was tested, with simple commands and questions to assess comprehension and with fill-in-the-blank tests given a limited number of alternatives to assess production. Is this a strong test of language capability? Finally, it is important to realize that her performance was a consistent 80%, much better than chance, but do you think people make errors 20% of the time when asked to name a color?

## Lana, Sherman, Austin, and Kanzi

The original star performer in the other artificial language project was also a female chimpanzee, Lana, and she was joined subsequently by two male chimpanzees, Sherman and Austin (Savage-Rumbaugh, Rumbaugh, & Boysen, 1980). The project has been extended to a different species, the pygmy chimpanzee or bonobo, of which a male, Kanzi, is the star performer.

Lana was raised with a computer that ministered to her needs. She was taught to type requests into the computer to get food, drink, music, and so on. Each key was labeled with a symbol, called a *lexigram;* such as ⊗ = M&M, ⊙ = juice, ⬙ = pudding. When Lana pressed a food key within a correct sequence of key presses, she was reinforced by the machine delivering her request, much as we are served by a candy machine. (The sequence was shaped beginning with single key presses and increasing string length, as Sarah's sentences were shaped.)

First, Lana had to hit a key that Rumbaugh et al. translated as "please." This caused the machine to start to process her sentence; without it, the computer would not know to begin a parse. Next, Lana had to press a key naming an agent, initially "machine," and subsequently, trainers' names. Next came a verb key, "give," in the case of objects like food or drink, or "make" for actions like music or window opening. Then came the name of the request, "M&M" or "music," and, finally, a

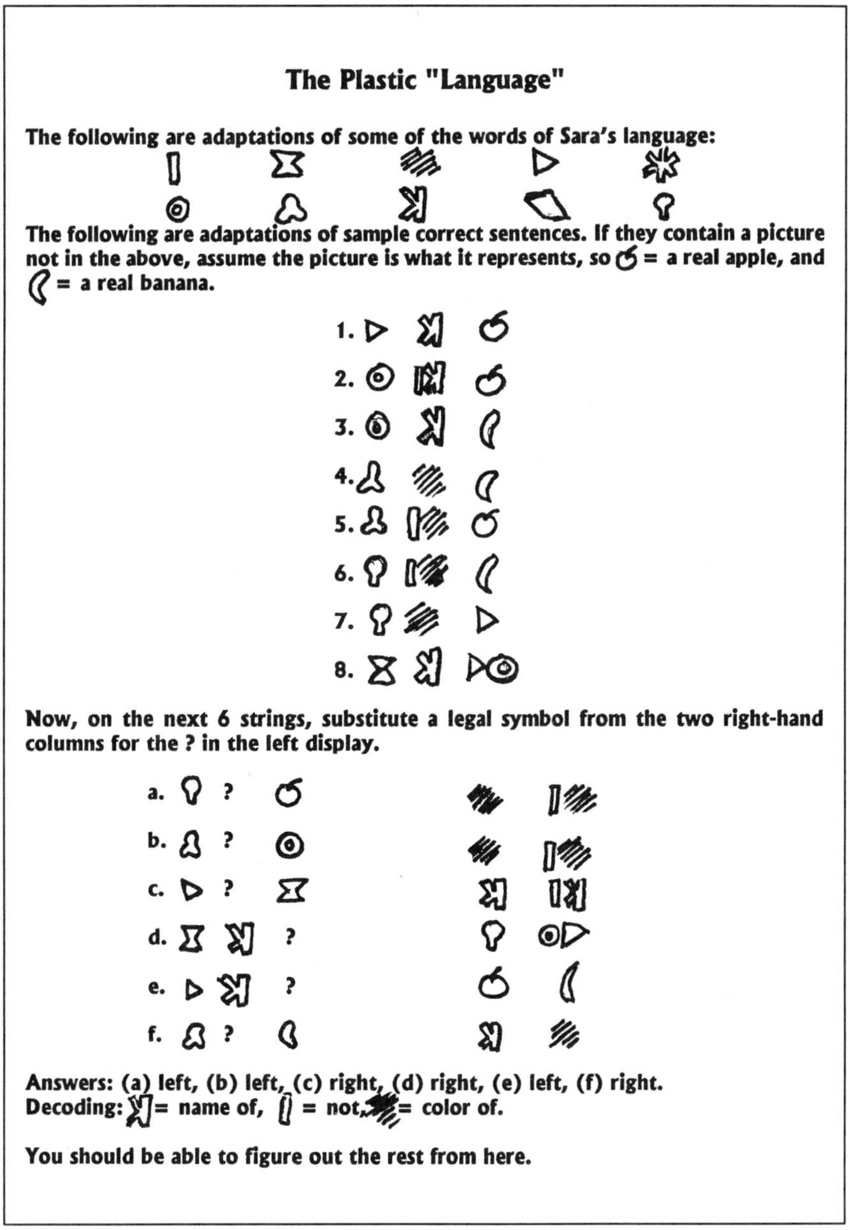

## The Plastic "Language"

The following are adaptations of some of the words of Sara's language:

The following are adaptations of sample correct sentences. If they contain a picture not in the above, assume the picture is what it represents, so = a real apple, and = a real banana.

1.

2.

3.

4.

5.

6.

7.

8.

Now, on the next 6 strings, substitute a legal symbol from the two right-hand columns for the ? in the left display.

a.

b.

c.

d.

e.

f.

**Answers:** (a) left, (b) left, (c) right, (d) right, (e) left, (f) right.
**Decoding:** = name of, = not, = color of.

You should be able to figure out the rest from here.

**Figure 2.3.** The Plastic "Language"

NOTE: This figure contains adaptations of some of the words of Sarah's language followed by adaptations of sample correct sentences. If the sentences contain a picture not displayed among the words, it is intended to depict the actual object, a real apple or a real banana. After the correct sentences, there are six strings containing a question mark, and two choices on the right to substitute for it to create a correct sentence. Try to do so.

The correct answers are at the bottom of the figure. Realize that you know more about this game than Sarah did. You have been told that the symbols stand for words, and you know what a word is. You also have some information on how she was trained and on what concepts she learned, so you could guess the symbol meanings. She, of course, had none of this knowledge. But she had many more trials.

The questions are as follows: (1) Are you able to play the game? (2) Do you know what the sentences mean? (3) If you can figure out the meanings, do so. Was this what you did in playing the game?

**Figure 2.4.** (© 1997 by Sydney Harris.)

terminal lexigram, rendered as "." which instructed the machine that the request was finished and it should begin to parse. Correct performance might yield a sentence translated as "Please machine give M&M." As Sarah was taught more complex sentences, so was Lana—as already mentioned, she could use a trainer's name in place of "machine" and one of several verbs. She also was taught to use prepositional phrases like "Please Tim give [the] milk out [of the] room."

As it turned out, Lana's entire syntax can be accounted for as substitutions in one of several frames and her language easily modeled by computer (Thompson & Church, 1980). Table 2.1 shows her language output in relation to these frames, and the relative frequency of occurrence of each sentence type. However, in addition to making requests in the formats she had been taught, Lana made some spontaneous, "creative" strings, shown in Table 2.2, tabulated for the same period as Table 2.1. Lana's teachers also saw creativity in her generalizing the symbol for "apple" to "orange," which included the possible invention of a syntactic construction (apple-which-is-orange, shown in Table 2.3). Read the dialogue in Table 2.3 critically and

**Table 2.1** Stock Phrases Produced by Lana

| *Format* | *Total Occurrence*[†] |
|---|---|
| question [ pronoun or noun ] give [ object name, food name, or proper name ] to Lana in room | 630 |
| (?you give bread to Lana in room) | |
| please machine give piece of [ food name ] | 310 |
| (please machine give piece of bread) | |
| question you make [ door or window ] [ open or shut ] | 35 |
| (?you make door open) | |
| question [ proper name or pronoun ] move [ in or out ] room | 53 |
| (?Lana move out room) | |
| question [ proper name or pronoun ] [ tickle or groom ] [ proper name or pronoun ] | 116 |
| (?you tickle Lana) | |
| [ common or proper name ] name this [ color ] | 1,181 |
| (shoe name this red) | |
| [ single symbols ] | 465 |

SOURCE: "Do Apes Use Language?" by Sue Savage-Rumbaugh, Duane M. Rumbaugh, and Sara Boysen, *American Scientist, 68*, 1980, pp. 49-61. Reprinted by permission.

NOTE: Variable elements given in boxes; example follows each format.

[†]Total number of times variants of stock format—including complete versions—were produced.

see if you agree that this is a semantic and syntactic creation. In the context of the full dialogue, isn't it more likely a sequence of errors or accidents, resulting in an interpretable one?

While Lana's training emphasized production of long ordered strings, Sherman and Austin were taught the same "language" in a different manner, one emphasizing comprehension, labeling, and question-answering skills (Savage-Rumbaugh & Lewin, 1994; Savage-Rumbaugh, Rumbaugh, & Boysen, 1978). Specifically, they were taught to name foods and then respond to the machine's "what's this?" with the correct food name. If they were correct, they were reinforced by the opportunity to request the machine to deliver some other food. The communication was made more interactive by the machine's naming a food the animal could not see but could request. Savage-Rumbaugh et al. argued that this training allows the formation of a more general notion of a name because the same symbol is used to answer questions, make requests, and indicate the presence of an object. Moreover, because the object itself was invisible, the use of the lexigram was considered symbolic, referring to some mental representation of the object rather than the object itself. (Do you agree that this is what a symbol is? Do you have a better definition, for which you could devise a test for the chimpanzees?)

**Table 2.2** Novel Phrases Produced by Lana

| Phrase | Occurrences | Phrase | Occurrences |
|---|---|---|---|
| question you name this | 9 | open yes | 2 |
| question give drink this | 8 | question you give Lana Columbus | 2 |
| name this shoe | 8 | make window open machine | 2 |
| name this cup | 8 | milk out | 2 |
| question drink this | 6 | please milk out | 2 |
| out please | 6 | please make machine | |
| question you give beancake shut open | 6 | music window open | 2 |
| please milk out room | 5 | question you tickle Lana please | 2 |
| question you tickle Lana go | 5 | go please | 2 |
| this ball | 5 | yes out room | 2 |
| question you tickle Lana behind room | 4 | please out room | 2 |
| want yes | 4 | please you move Columbus | 2 |
| question you tickle Lana into room | 4 | bowl name this pudding | 2 |
| question you tickle Lana in room | 4 | please machine groom | 2 |
| question you give Columbus in Lana to room | 4 | question you give go | 2 |
| you open | 3 | question Lana Columbus | 1 |
| question you tickle Lana to Lana | 3 | tickle question | 1 |
| question you tickle Lana to Lana behind room | 3 | drink yes | 1 |
| out room | 3 | hand eye foot | 1 |
| please milk room | 3 | window keyboard | 1 |
| out room yes | 3 | give Lana chow | 1 |
| to out room | 3 | question you give Lana juice | 1 |
| question you give milk open | 3 | question you give bread to machine | 1 |
| question you give milk shut open | 3 | orange coke | 1 |
| question you give this orange drink | 3 | question Lana in room | 1 |
| question you give this to Lana in room | 3 | eat yes | 1 |
| question you open | 2 | question you give to Lana in | |
| yes money | 2 | machine out room | 1 |
| question Lana you out room | 2 | question you give juice to Lana in | |
| give out room | 2 | cup out room | 1 |
| | | question you give bread Lana | 1 |
| | | question Lana give bread to room | 1 |
| | | give Lana milk | 1 |
| | | question you give Lana | 1 |

SOURCE: "Do Apes Use Language?" by Sue Savage-Rumbaugh, Duane M. Rumbaugh, and Sara Boysen, *American Scientist, 68*, 1980, pp. 49-61. Reprinted by permission.

Having received this general training individually, Sherman and Austin were placed together in the computer room and each given access to information about the existence of foods that the other chimpanzee did not have. Then the machine would query the informed animal with "what's this?" with the other animal able to observe the question and the answer. The observer could then request the named food, using the information obtained from the other chimp. Then both animals received their food reward. Both animals adapted to this procedure without further training. Moreover, both animals could match the lexigram the other animal used to request the food or could point to a picture of it, from which Savage-Rumbaugh

**Table 2.3**  A Dialogue Between Lana and Tim Leading to a Creative Naming Structure

| | | |
|---|---|---|
| Tim: | ?What color of this. | 10:10 a.m. |
| Lana: | Color of this orange. | 10:11 a.m. |
| Tim: | Yes. | |
| Lana: | ?Tim give cup which-is red. [This was probably an attempt to request the orange. However, because a red cup was part of her object/color naming materials, Tim responded with the latter object.] | 10:13 a.m. |
| Tim: | Yes. [Thereupon he gave her the cup, which she discarded.] | 10:14 a.m. |
| Lana: | ?Tim give which-is shut. | 10:16 a.m. |
| | ?Shelley give. | |
| Tim: | No Shelley. | 10:16 a.m. |
| Lana: | Eye. [A frank error, probably.] | 10:16 a.m. |
| | ?Tim which-is orange. | 10:21 a.m. |
| Tim: | What which-is orange. | 10:21 a.m. |
| Lana: | ?Tim give apple which-is green. [At this point, Lana frequently confused keys for the colors orange and green.] | 10:22 a.m. |
| Tim: | No apple which-is green. [In other words, "I have no green apple to give."] | |
| Lana: | ?Tim give apple which-is orange. [Thereupon she bounded with apparent enthusiasm to the door to receive "the orange-colored apple."] | 10:23 a.m. |
| Tim: | Yes. [And he gave it to her.] | 10:23 a.m. |

SOURCE: Quoted from Rumbaugh (1977), pp. 178-179.

et al. inferred that the observer was constructing an "image" of its referent. This interaction has been designated by Savage-Rumbaugh et al. as "conversation."

Finally, the interaction game was made more complex with one chimpanzee witnessing a food being hidden, the recovery of which required a tool he did not have but that the other chimpanzee did. So, he could request the tool to obtain the food to share, removing the communication from the food by one step (Savage-Rumbaugh, 1986; Savage-Rumbaugh & Lewin, 1994). An anecdote suggests that they were indeed communicating. Once, Sherman mistakenly requested a key, appeared dumbfounded when Austin retrieved the key, looked at the keyboard where the key lexigram was still illuminated (indicating that he knew that the symbol was relevant), and with agitation changed the request to "wrench." Austin noted the change in the keyboard display, although it marked a break from routine, and dropped the key and retrieved the wrench. (Of course, this anecdote is sensible to the human observer. How many instances of uninterpretable "corrections" might there have been that no one has bothered to tally or report?)

Savage-Rumbaugh and Lewin attribute the appearance of symbol use and humanlike interaction to a situation pragmatically conducive to discourse: The interactors have a clear intent, full knowledge of each other's knowledge and the utility of sharing it, and the chance to use the system to signal that intent.

Again, I reserve criticism of Lana's, Sherman's, and Austin's skills until after discussing all the projects. However, you should consider the following questions: (a) Are these chimps demonstrating different skills from Sarah's? (b) Are their keypress sequences equivalent to human sentences? (c) *Have* they demonstrated a symbol use like naming, or a simple association? (d) Is Sherman's and Austin's interchange actually a conversation? (e) Is substitution of a new symbol in a highly trained sequence what we mean by creative symbol use of language?

The animal most recently tested using the keyboard system is Kanzi, a bonobo, a different kind of chimpanzee. Savage-Rumbaugh and Lewin (1994) report that bonobos are naturally more similar to humans than other chimpanzees in respects that might suggest their natural communication skills are a better analogue of ours. They look more like humans, walking on two feet, and their facial expressions are more like ours, with smiling for pleasure and outright laughter. This means we feel more at ease when we try to communicate with them, and perhaps they feel more at ease with us. They also spontaneously gesture and vocalize more than common chimpanzees. And they seem more sociable, copulating for pleasure and bonding, not just fertility. This means that they naturally must signal sexual interest; their bodies do not exhibit sign stimuli to signal mating readiness. Thus they must naturally have a system for social interaction and may therefore be more primed to learn a communication system devised by humans.

Kanzi was the first nonhuman primate to be exposed to language training in infancy. This was fortuitous: The researchers were trying to teach his mother the keyboard system while he was an infant-in-arms. The teaching of his mother proceeded like that of the other chimpanzees, with food rewards and the like, and was not particularly successful. When his mother was removed from the project (to conceive again), Kanzi was 14 months old and began formal training with the keyboard. To everyone's surprise, he seemed to comprehend the lexigrams, pressing the symbol for "apple" and then picking an apple up, and similarly spontaneously naming other foods before selecting them from the refrigerator. This learning had been acquired passively, as he watched his mother's training.

To enrich Kanzi's opportunity to communicate through the language, a portable keyboard was made and he was given free access to human companions and a 50+-acre forest-playground. Tests of his production accuracy were conducted by an observer who was unfamiliar with the forest, and so could only follow and record what he said and did but could not model productions and actions for him. He spontaneously produced his own word combinations within one month. Without specific training, he understood the reversibility of agent and patient roles in a "tickle" situation (A tickles B or B tickles A), and sometimes directed games in which he was neither agent nor patient, simply an observer. (Recall the difficulty in getting Sarah to give food to anyone else; we might expect similar difficulty in getting an ape [or child] to designate someone else as "star.")

By 5½ years, Kanzi had 13,691 recorded productions of which at least 10% were combinations of lexigrams, with a fixed order of action-patient, probably copied from the English of his trainers. Savage-Rumbaugh and Lewin (1994) consider Kanzi's utterances to reflect grammar. Their most important criteria for demonstrating grammar are as follows:

1. Each component has independent symbol status, so that each word of a two-word utterance participates in other utterances and provides its own meaning.

2. The *relationship* between the symbols is reliable and meaningful like an agent, patient, or causal relationship is meaningful.

3. A grammatical rule affects *categories* of symbols (like nouns), not individual symbols alone.

4. A grammatical relationship is indicated formally, either through morphological marking or order.

5. Rules are productive and so can apply to new symbols (paraphrase of Savage-Rumbaugh & Lewin, 1994, pp. 158-159).

(Consider whether these are reasonable criteria for grammatical competence, and whether they capture the intricacies of human grammar. Do these distinguish an ordered sequence with no long-distance dependencies—the finite state grammar not considered powerful enough to model human syntax—from one capable of embedding, recursion, and context dependencies, as are all human language? If not, don't we need more criteria to say that an animal is using humanlike syntax?)

Kanzi had satisfactorily established comprehension of the lexigrams as independent symbols (criterion 1) and used them in new combinations (criterion 5). His clear comprehension of agent and patient roles and his consistency in ordering the patient after the action satisfied criteria 2 and 4; his allowing many different symbols to serve as patient, criterion 3. Also of interest, he appeared to create his own syntactic rule, reflecting the ape mind, if not the human one. He combined verbs, like "tickle bite," always in the order of the action requiring more distance between the participants, followed by the action of greater intimacy. This ordering follows the protocol in bonobo play situations, with Kanzi's language mirroring his reality.

In addition to his spontaneous use and apparent comprehension of the keyboard symbols, Kanzi also appeared to understand spoken English and to be able to follow commands, fetch objects, and point to pictures of named objects at least as well as a 2-year-old child tested similarly. These tests employed two experimenters, one to give the subject the instruction, and another, who does not hear the spoken stimulus—that is, is "blind" to the correct response—to provide the alternatives and record the subject's response.

Perhaps most interesting are the anecdotes. Kanzi is told that there is a "surprise" for him in a particular room, which he questions, and then is told that the surprise is his mother, who has been absent for several months. He looks stunned, runs to the room, and gestures for it to be opened, shrieking when he sees his mother. Another time he is told that if he gives Austin a mask, he will be given cereal, and he gives Austin the mask and then points to the cereal. Both instances suggest comprehension, and comprehension of something not indicated by immediate context but only through the language. Of course, we do not know how rare such insights were, or whether there were instances that are incomprehensible and reflect possible errors, like the several utterances preceding the "apple-which-is-orange."

Kanzi's prodigious performance was repeated by another infant bonobo, but not by an infant common chimpanzee, suggesting the biological substrate may be different for the two primates, with the bonobos' more conducive to languagelike behavior. The infants' learning, but not the adults', suggests, moreover, that there may be a critical period for language acquisition in nonhuman primates—and perhaps in humans.

## The Dolphins

Compared with these projects, the dolphin project is much less exciting and much less scientifically controlled with respect to consideration of what language is. The trainers, of course, here were constrained by the difficulty of interacting with animals who live in the water and do not have hands to gesture or manipulate keys or plastic, nor humanlike perceptual systems. They developed two systems for communicating with the dolphins, which the dolphins themselves could not use, separating, perhaps critically, comprehension from production.

Phoenix was taught to respond to electronically produced whistles, and Akeakamai, to gestures. In each case, there was a one-to-one map between a stimulus (gesture or whistle) and a word. The words represented objects in the dolphins' tank (ball, hoop, frisbee), actions the dolphin could perform with these objects (fetch, toss, jump over), and location descriptions (left, right). Sentences consisted of ordered sequences of up to five of these terms: A two-word sentence might be "frisbee over" (jump over the frisbee); a three-word sentence might be "right frisbee over" (jump over the frisbee on the right); a four-word sentence might be "left hoop pipe fetch" (take a pipe to the hoop on the left); and a five-word sentence would modify both objects like "right water left basket fetch" (take the basket on the left to the water stream on the right; Herman et al., 1993).

Each animal learned each system well and, of course, was able to generalize appropriately from specifically trained syntactic constructions to novel ones. Herman et al. define novelty as a word not trained *in that sequence* being understood in the sequence. They also define different semantic relations for the objects depending on the predicate: an object to be moved or transported (e.g., pipe fetch) versus an object as a location (e.g., left pipe). At times, they call these syntactic relations, representing direct and indirect objects. And they seem to consider that the animals understand syntactic and semantic anomaly because, if they are asked to transport the untransportable (water), they do not respond, or they respond to the portion of the command sequence that is possible to execute.

Now, are these simple sentences in your view? Do the whistles or gestures really constitute word names? Is the dolphin's correct remembering of five discrete associates and executing them in order reversed from the one produced a demonstration of parsing and semantic understanding? Is failing to do the impossible—move the pool—understanding of pragmatics? Whether or not these animals exhibit

**Figure 2.5** (© 1997 by Sydney Harris.)

humanlike language, is their performance here as cognitively complex as Sarah's was, let alone Kanzi's?

As Thompson and Church did for Lana's utterances, Premack (1986) collapses the dolphins' "sentence" comprehension skills into a rote formula:

> On the basis of successful transfer performance, Herman et al. attributed to the animals a finite-state grammar; thereafter, they speak freely of "syntactic categories," "semantic propositions," "lexical component," "syntactic rules," and the like. This flurry of linguistic terms is gratuitous, for to account for the dolphins' performance we need . . . two rules . . . : (1) (Property) Object Action and (2) (Property) Object Action$_2$ (Property) Object . . . Object, property, and action do not derive from linguistic theory, . . . [but from] perceptual theory and cognition. An individual knowing nothing of either "word" or "sentence" could walk through the world and point to examples of action, object, and property. (p. 15)

To this we may add, moreover, that we know that animals—rats and pigeons!—can be taught to perform a behavioral chain, an ordered sequence where each action cues the next, and that behavioral chains are describable by a finite state grammar. Human language is more powerful than a finite-state grammar, requiring variably sized units and embedding possibilities. Is executing a behavioral chain the equivalent of parsing?!

*Alex, the Parrot*

---

A good contrast with the exaggerated claims of language skills in the dolphin are the tempered claims and careful performance tests of the African grey parrot, Alex (Pepperberg, 1981, 1983, 1987). Alex, like many parrots, can produce speech-like sounds, originally thought to illustrate a purely imitative capacity. Using precisely specified conditioning procedures (like Premack's with Sarah), Pepperberg has demonstrated that this is more than imitative because it can also be used to answer questions—labeling objects—and to request objects. She has also, again like Premack did with Sarah, tested Alex's nonlanguage cognitive abilities using the languagelike behavior he was taught. In addition to being very clear as to the conditioning procedures, this project is very careful in applying linguistic terms to Alex's behavior, and also intelligent in building on some of the critiques of the historically earlier ape studies discussed above and below. For example, in training labeling, Pepperberg was careful not to have Alex name only the food he would be reinforced by, but other foods and toys, to separate cleanly a request for the food from a "label"-type skill.

Alex was not taught to string words specifically, nor were syntactic functions taught. He seemed to have acquired a working vocabulary of up to (in 1987) 80 different items, which named objects' properties (color, shape, number of sides, material like paper or wood), which he could select on command or identify in response to "What's this?" His performance on controlled tests was about 80% correct, not perfect but far above the 50% chance. On the color, shape, property tests, he performed as well (approximately 80%) on objects he had never seen before.

He also acquired the word *no,* which he applied to refuse an object he did not want or a task he did not like. Other indications that the *no* was functional were the parrot behavior of throwing the undesired object back at the trainer or threatening to bite if the request was repeated.

Alex also appeared to have learned some class concepts and was able to use the descriptors "color," "shape," or "mah-mah" (= material) to respond to questions about what was the same or different between two presented objects—suggesting that he also understood the categories "same" and "different." As of 1987, he had not learned to respond "same" or "different" when queried about two objects, although he could both produce and comprehend color names of objects. Finally, Alex was able to use his trained vocalizations to number groups of up to six objects.

The difference between Pepperberg's discussion of Alex's performance and the claims of Herman et al. with respect to the dolphins is best illustrated by quotation. Note the modest discussion of cognitive skill and the absence of highfalutin linguistic terms:

> Although we stress that there exist distinctions between the forced-choice condi-
> tional discrimination tests often used to investigate nonhuman conceptual abilities

and our test protocol, which includes referential (vocal labeling) . . . , we note that Alex may have learned a form of conditional response: For example, "If I hear 'A' (a categorical label), I must respond with an 'a' (a label for the instance of that category)." But this performance implies, we claim, that our subject had acquired at least a rudimentary concept of the relationship between A and its instances. (Pepperberg, 1983, p. 184)

I do not believe that the more tempered discussion results from Alex's displaying fewer language skills than the dolphins. He demonstrates both comprehension and production (while the dolphins only evidence comprehension) and an ability to understand, as well as the dolphins do, "sentences" like "What's same?" "What's this?" "Do you want this?" and "Tell me what it is again." The dolphins may demonstrate better sequence memory, but is that language?

## Sign Language Projects With Apes

The advantage of using a human language like ASL in teaching language to chimpanzees is that we know that it has the potentials of creativity, spontaneity, grammatical complexity, and so on, of human language, although we do do not know whether the animal will be able to take advantage of these potentials. Basically, the ape-signing projects all used the same procedure as the speaking projects, with the young apes raised in upper-middle-class environments with trainers instructed to sign with each other and with the animal. Unlike the artificial language projects, the animal's signing was not always reinforced, and the animal's understanding as determined by obedience to commands such as "It's bedtime" or "Brush your teeth" was more emphasized than the animal's productions. (As I indicated, the later artificial language projects stressed both comprehension and production.) As most pet owners believe, the animals seemed to be able to learn to respond appropriately to many sentences.

### Washoe

The most studied signing ape, and perhaps the most fluent, is Washoe, a chimpanzee raised from about 8 months old by Gardner and Gardner (1969, 1975; Gardner, Gardner, & van Cantfort, 1989). From the beginning, she seemed adept at imitating complex actions, sometimes after a delay, like bathing her doll in the same manner as she herself was bathed. Imitation of signs also occurred, but generally not as an echo of the trainer's most recent utterance. For example, after being told many times that it was time to brush her teeth or here was her toothbrush, she noticed her toothbrush in the bathroom and spontaneously signed toothbrush. Using this, the trainers shaped her to request her toothbrush after meals, reinforcing her with permission to leave the table. Note that it was Washoe's utterance that started the training, and that it was not specifically prompted when it first occurred.

Washoe's spontaneity in use of signs indicated more creative use of language than did the other chimpanzees, perhaps because use of a name for her was not so tightly confined to specific situations. For example, when being tickled, an activity chimpanzees love, and having it stop, Washoe would try to make her ticklers continue. Using this, they taught her the sign for "more," which she then generalized to "more food" and more other activities. "Open" was also generalized in an interesting manner, initially taught for a specific standard door and later spontaneously extended to refrigerator doors, drawers, and faucets. Washoe used the sign for "flower" to describe flowers as well as to label anything with an odor, for example, tobacco and kitchens—until she was taught the sign for "smell." More important than her meaning generalizations of particular signs was her spontaneous stringing together of signs and creative sign combinations. Without syntactic training, she produced "gimme tickle" and for "open the refrigerator," "open food drink." (Her trainers, of course, signed sentences but never had used these constructions.) Also, upon seeing a swan for the first time, she signed "water bird," having known each component individually and apparently creating a new compound.

After four years of training, Washoe had acquired 132 signs that she used to (a) name objects, classes of objects, and photographs of objects; (b) answer questions; (c) make requests; and (d) create short sentences. Many of these skills were demonstrated in controlled test situations, in which, of course, the anecdotes of spontaneous creativity are not. Gardner and Gardner (1975) compared her sign acquisition favorably with that of children.

The project continued with additional chimpanzees, including an infant, Loulis, who was given to Washoe to adopt when her own infant died (Fouts & Fouts, 1989; Fouts, Fouts, & van Cantfort, 1989). The chimpanzees signed to one another when no humans were around, requesting hugs for comfort, tickling, or "gimme that" for a limb to be groomed. Washoe, the dominant animal, also signed to others to go away as accompaniment to dominance postures. The humans intentionally did not sign to Loulis for more than five years, at which time 73 signs were reliably observed in his vocabulary, signs he could have learned only from his chimpanzee companions.

### Koko

Patterson (1978a, 1978b) also reported development of spontaneous compound creation in her signing gorilla, Koko, who labeled a stale roll "cookie rock," a zebra "white tiger," and a Pinocchio doll "elephant baby." She reported that Koko joked and lied spontaneously; caught chewing a crayon, for example, she pretended to color her lips. She also is said to use "first" and "later" appropriately, indicating a linguistic concept of time; she described previous emotional experiences together with her reaction (given a lot of prompting); and she spontaneously conversed with another gorilla who had learned ASL.

The major difficulty in assessing this project is that Koko's progress is anecdotally reported, not substantiated through scientific processes (see the foreword to Savage-Rumbaugh, 1986). There are no catalogues of utterances to check for general production patterns to see if these novel productions are indeed creative or are errors. There is no independent evaluator to determine comprehension, as in the Kanzi project. There are no unedited videotapes available, nor is access to Koko possible without Patterson mediating (Linden, 1986).

### Nim

Terrace et al. (1979) reported a large vocabulary acquisition in a chimpanzee (Nim Chimsky) and spontaneous stringing of signs together. Unlike the other signing projects, they attempted to catalogue Nim's utterances, their frequencies, and the contexts in which they occurred. Perhaps for this reason, Terrace and his colleagues reached markedly different conclusions about the animal's language skills. Table 2.4a shows Nim's two- and three-sign combinations and Table 2.4b shows four-sign combinations. Take time to study these strings and consider whether they indicate the existence and use of productive syntax. And consider with respect to the observations just mentioned for Koko and Washoe that, given enough time at a typewriter, by chance, a monkey could produce Hamlet—amid a lot of nonsense.

## Critiques of the Ape Language Studies

Ultimately you must decide for yourself what language is and whether it has been demonstrated in nonhumans. In this section, I present the principal criticisms of the studies (and criticisms of the criticisms) to help you reach a reasoned decision.

Generally speaking, there are two errors, easy to make, that have been attributed to all the ape language studies, *perhaps also applicable to studies of human language.* The first is known as a *Clever Hans* error. Clever Hans was a horse who performed in the early 1900s. He displayed what looked like a remarkable ability to solve spoken arithmetic problems by tapping out the correct answer with his hoof. Initial suspicions of trickery by his owner were ruled out because his owner did not need to be in the room when Hans was queried, questions could be whispered to Hans, and so on. However, it did turn out that Hans was not understanding the spoken words or the arithmetic problem: If two people gave Hans the numbers to add, one in each ear, so that no one knew the correct solution, Hans failed.

It turned out Hans was a very clever horse—able to read body language. All questioners would lean forward, tense, as Hans started to tap out his answer. The tension increased as he approached the answer. When he reached it, the questioner visibly relaxed, and when Hans perceived this, he stopped. Because everyone gives similar tension-relaxation signals, Hans's trainer per se did not have to be present, but there had to be at least one person present who knew the right answer (incidentally, his trainer really thought that he could do arithmetic and refused to believe it after Hans's performance was explained; Brown, 1958).

**Table 2.4a**   Nim's Most Frequent Two- and Three-Sign Combinations

| Two-Sign Combinations | | Frequency | Three-Sign Combinations | | | Frequency |
|---|---|---|---|---|---|---|
| play | me | 375 | play | me | Nim | 81 |
| me | Nim | 328 | eat | me | Nim | 48 |
| tickle | me | 316 | eat | Nim | eat | 46 |
| eat | Nim | 302 | tickle | me | Nim | 44 |
| more | eat | 287 | grape | eat | Nim | 37 |
| me | eat | 237 | banana | Nim | eat | 33 |
| Nim | eat | 209 | Nim | me | eat | 27 |
| finish | hug | 187 | banana | eat | Nim | 26 |
| drink | Nim | 143 | eat | me | eat | 22 |
| more | tickle | 136 | me | Nim | eat | 21 |
| sorry | hug | 123 | hug | me | Nim | 20 |
| tickle | Nim | 107 | yogurt | Nim | eat | 20 |
| hug | Nim | 106 | me | more | eat | 19 |
| more | drink | 99 | more | eat | Nim | 19 |
| eat | drink | 98 | finish | hug | Nim | 18 |
| banana | me | 97 | banana | me | eat | 17 |
| Nim | me | 89 | Nim | eat | Nim | 17 |
| sweet | Nim | 85 | tickle | me | tickle | 17 |
| me | play | 81 | apple | me | eat | 15 |
| gun | eat | 79 | eat | Nim | me | 15 |
| tea | drink | 77 | give | me | eat | 15 |
| grape | eat | 74 | nut | Nim | nut | 15 |
| hug | me | 74 | drink | me | Nim | 14 |
| banana | Nim | 73 | hug | me | hug | 14 |
| in | pants | 70 | sweet | Nim | sweet | 14 |

SOURCE: Reprinted with permission from "Can an Ape Create a Sentence?" by H. S. Terrace, L. A. Petitto, R. J. Sanders, and T. G. Bever, 1979, in *Science 206*, pp. 891-902. Copyright 1979 American Association for the Advancement of Science.

Can the apes be responding to their language situations as Clever Hans was? With the exception of the apes communicating with the machine (which could not give unconscious hints), the answer is that it is a possibility for all of them, and, in fact, when tested by people who do not know either the language or the correct answer, all of the apes do worse (see Premack, 1971, for example). However, one could argue that these trainer-blind situations are not a fair test of language given that language is social, and a situation where one person cannot really understand another is not terribly social. While this is the only way to test communication without unconscious cuing, a blind test sets up a pragmatic situation in which communication is impossible—as is evidenced by the silence, monosyllabic responses, or irrelevancies of children unfamiliar with testing situations and strange examiners.

Throughout the presentation of the animal performance, I have sounded the second general note of caution. We all have a tendency to interpret another's utterance as we would if we were making it ourselves. This leads to misunderstand-

**Table 2.4b** Nim's Most Frequent Four-Sign Combinations

| Most Frequent Four-Sign Combinations | | | | Frequency |
|---|---|---|---|---|
| eat | drink | eat | drink | 15 |
| eat | Nim | eat | Nim | 7 |
| banana | Nim | banana | Nim | 5 |
| drink | Nim | drink | Nim | 5 |
| banana | eat | me | Nim | 4 |
| banana | me | eat | banana | 4 |
| banana | me | Nim | me | 4 |
| grape | eat | Nim | eat | 4 |
| Nim | eat | Nim | eat | 4 |
| play | me | Nim | play | 4 |
| drink | eat | drink | eat | 3 |
| drink | eat | me | Nim | 3 |
| eat | grape | eat | Nim | 3 |
| eat | me | Nim | drink | 3 |
| grape | eat | me | Nim | 3 |
| me | eat | drink | more | 3 |
| me | eat | me | eat | 3 |
| me | gum | me | gum | 3 |
| me | Nim | eat | me | 3 |
| Nim | me | Nim | me | 3 |
| tickle | me | Nim | play | 3 |

SOURCE: Reprinted with permission from "Can an Ape Create a Sentence?" by H. S. Terrace, L. A. Petitto, R. J. Sanders, and T. G. Bever, 1979, in *Science 206*, pp. 891-902. Copyright 1979 American Association for the Advancement of Science.

ings in human relationships as we all have experienced, so it can obviously lead to misunderstandings when talking to animals. We assume, for instance, that if Lana types out "Please machine give M&M." she understands about politeness, punctuation, and what an M&M and machine are. What evidence do we have that she understands any of this? That she eats the M&M after asking for it? Certainly that does not count as evidence because, as long as she likes M&Ms, she is likely to eat them (as we would) whether or not that was what she thought she was getting. Even if she asked for water, got an M&M, and did not eat it, that would be no more evidence that she understood the symbolic relation between the lexigram and its referent than is an animal's going to its food bowl for food and its water bowl for water (see Mistler-Lachman & Lachman, 1974, for similar criticisms).

The same caution can be applied to the so-called creative communications of the apes: A human observer understanding "water bird" and seeing a swan assumes that Washoe is naming the bird, creatively. But as Terrace et al. (1979) pointed out, it is possible that Washoe was first naming the lake the swan was sitting on and then naming the animal, bird, both words that she knew. This would indicate perhaps symbol use and good labeling skills, but not a syntactic combination with a whole meaning more than the component meanings. That creative combination may have been in the eye of the beholder, not in the mind of the animal at all. With the anecdotal reports of Patterson on Koko, we have many similar examples; Koko's signing "lips" as she chewed the crayon may not have been an attempt to sign lipstick cleverly and deceptively but merely a description of what the crayon was between. Our assignment of deceptive intent exceeds the data.

A third criticism made of all the production studies was a failure to analyze the produced strings in context, to consider the contingencies that governed them. Terrace et al. kept complete records of their interaction with Nim on videotapes, and review of those tapes suggested that although Nim's utterances got longer, the length did not arise from application of syntactic rules: Two frequent two-sign combinations were "play me" and "me Nim"; a three-sign utterance was "play me Nim"; and a four-sign utterance "Nim me Nim me." That is, the four-sign utterance is a repetition of a two-sign utterance, not a construction of a sentence embedding a sentence, for example. Usually, also, the increased length was just repetition for emphasis—like reduplication in pidgin "language," perhaps?

A second feature of Nim's signing that Terrace et al. found troublesome was that it reflected little spontaneity (although Gardner et al., 1989, contend this is a result of a rigid, unnatural training style). For the most part, Nim responded to trainers' questions or imitated what the trainer had just said but did not initiate conversations himself. And he tended to sign simultaneously with the trainer (interrupt), indicating that he was not actually attending to the conversation (although this is often true for small children). And, unlike children, Nim never asked for names of things. Finally, Terrace et al. reviewed the videotapes and films available from the other signing projects and found little difference between Washoe's or Koko's behavior and Nim's. I note that the Kanzi project followed Terrace's critiques of the spontaneous production projects, and Savage-Rumbaugh was careful to rule out imitation as the trigger for Kanzi's productions. Patterson criticized Terrace's study but did not offer substantial counterevidence ("Ape Language," 1981); the Gardners (Gardner et al., 1989) have responded that their animals spontaneously sign, combine signs, and imitate only as do children, with this documented independently by at least two observers working on their project.

*Animal Language Revisited*

With these things in mind, let's reexamine the language-teaching projects. All the animals have shown the capacity to associate one visual object or gesture with another, to learn many such associations, and, in some cases, to use the associations "correctly," in a prescribed order, generating longer and longer ordered sequences. For all the animals tested, as for common experimental animals like rats and pigeons, these abilities are commonplace: A rat taking one arm of a t-maze in response to one stimulus and the other to another is associating stimulus and action, performing actions (the running of the maze) in a prescribed order, and, during *extinction* (when the usual reward is withheld), exhibiting frustration behaviors indicative of expectation (an image of the anticipated reward?) and disappointment.

Some of the language projects have developed associations between visible objects and abstract properties of objects, like color-of or same-as. The questions are these: Do associations equal names? Does order in association reflect syntax, and do ordered associations equal sentences? Do groups of ordered associations produced by different individuals equal conversations?

If you have difficulty conceptualizing the productions as anything but words, sentences, and conversations, consider the use of a candy machine as a behavioral chain. Suppose we say that a gesture of fiddling for coins "means" please, a gesture of putting one in a slot "means" machine, a gesture of putting another in a slot "means" give, and one of pulling a particular lever "means" M&Ms. Then we could conclude that someone using a candy machine is uttering the sentence "Please machine give M&Ms." Note that the order of performing the gestures must be maintained; putting money in after pulling the lever is "ungrammatical" and will not yield the candy. Is any string of ordered gestures potentially a sentence, or is there something that characterizes language apart from its ability to alter the environment and its sequential order?

Aside from these general problems, common to all the animal language studies, we can criticize some studies specifically. For example, as you may have realized, Sarah could just be performing multiple discriminations. In the presence of the object apple, she learned to place a blue plastic triangle or an orange square on the board to get reinforced. (We called the blue triangle "apple" and the orange square "red.") In the presence of the object banana, she learned to place two other plastic pieces on the board. This does not appear to be a terribly difficult task. It is not clear even that she knows the difference in "meaning" between blue triangle and orange square (between "apple" and "red") or between the superordinate categories "name of" and "color of," given that she never had to choose between "apple" and "red" when answering questions about them; she only had to select from either color names or fruit names. Thus her entire language task could be performed as a large discrimination: If there is an apple present or a blue triangle on the board, then orange square is the right answer, or if there is a blue triangle and a red cross (potential "color-of" symbol) on the board, then orange square is the right answer. (Can human language also be merely a large discrimination?) Written this way, it sounds more like the rules for a board game than like a sentence. Indeed, college students taught to "play" Sarah's game as Sarah was, without being told that these plastic bits were words, were very successful at it and never realized that it was a language (Premack, 1979)! Did *you* read the symbols as language in Figure 2.3, or problem-solve them?

Lana's language can be criticized in the same manner as Sarah's, except that Lana was allowed more freedom of expression and had access to all her words at the same time; they were not selected for her. You can look at her spontaneous productions like "please make machine music window open" (Table 2.2) as the spontaneous creation of a compound sentence. On the other hand, you might observe that "machine" should precede "make" in her syntax and therefore this was an error, that she had no way of knowing that there is such a thing as machine music distinct from live music—in short, that this is a random set of key presses that *we* happen to be able to interpret. You might support this view with the nonsensical nature of some of her other creations, "question you give milk shut open" or "question you tickle Lana to Lana behind room." And isn't the "apple which-is-orange" sequence (Table 2.3) a matter of random keystrokes until the trainer "relaxed," reinforcing her with the orange, when at last she said something he could interpret? (Note the errors: a request for a cup, which is not there, then for a "which-is shut," then a poorly formed "Shelley give" when Shelley is not there, and so on.)

Some of these criticisms of Lana's language the Rumbaughs accepted, particularly after training Sherman and Austin (Savage-Rumbaugh et al., 1980). They concluded that there is a difference between a label's representing an object in symbolic fashion and a label's association with an object. Apart from association, they list the following as criteria for representation:

- the ability to name apart from requesting objects
- the ability to describe an object given the label
- the ability to locate the object given the label
- the ability to refer to the object from the label when the object is absent

Note that these criteria include both production and comprehension skills, and that for Sherman and Austin, both were explicitly taught, as were the additional flexibilities listed here. For the most part, the chimpanzees have failed to show these skills and in fact only demonstrate things that they do in their own natural communication—desire objects or grooming, and indicate drive states and objects in the environment. Note that the dolphins also only locate objects given the label and have not demonstrated any higher-order category skills.

A critical feature of communication in Savage-Rumbaugh's (revised) view is the *interchangeability* of transmitter and receiver, the fact that both production and comprehension of the strings are evidenced. Of interest, Premack (1986) found too that it was necessary to *train* the comprehension skills for chimpanzees like Sarah, who could well produce the plastic chip sequences to describe a situation. After several comprehension trials, they seemed to understand the general relation of comprehension and production, so a new symbol could be introduced in either task and would immediately generalize to the other task. The dolphins, of course, cannot interchange roles.

*Conversational pigeons?* Do you agree that the interchangeability of transmission and reception is critical in demonstrating symbol use? Consider a parody of Sherman's and Austin's conversation, illustrated in Figure 2.6, by two pigeons, Jack and Jill, trained by Epstein, Lanza, and Skinner (1980). Jack and Jill were each explicitly trained to perform a chain involving conditional discriminations. Together, they give the appearance of asking each other for information and then using it to share food.

Jack was taught first to peck one of three different-colored keys (left, middle, or right) depending on which of three vertically arranged keys was lit (top = red,

**Figure 2.6.** Communication Between Jack and Jill

SOURCE: Reprinted with permission from "Symbolic Communication Between Two Pigeons *(Columba livia domestica)*" by R. Epstein, R. P. Lanza, and B. F. Skinner, 1980, in *Science 207,* pp. 543-545. Photos by R. Epstein. Copyright 1979 American Association for the Advancement of Science.

NOTE: (A) Jack (left) asks Jill (right) for a color name by depressing the WHAT COLOR? key. (B) Jill looks through the curtain for the hidden color. (C) Jill selects the color name while Jack watches. (D) Jack rewards Jill with food by depressing the THANK YOU key. (E) Jack selects the correct color as Jill goes to food. (F) Jack is rewarded with food.

middle = green, bottom = yellow); that is, if the top key, labeled "R," was lit, he would peck a red key (on the left); if the G key was lit, he would peck a green key; and if the Y key was lit, a yellow key. After learning this discrimination, he was taught to peck two other keys in sequence: a key labeled "what color" that caused the R, G, and Y keys to light so he could make the above response (these are *secondary reinforcers;* activating those keys signals eventual delivery of the primary reinforcer, the food), and after they lit, a key labeled "thank you" that lit his color keys for his choice (also secondary reinforcers). After his discrimination, of course, he received food.

Meanwhile, Jill was taught to peck R, G, or Y keys depending on whether a red, green, or yellow color key was lit. By gradually moving the color key to behind a curtain, the experimenters taught Jill to look for it behind the curtain, beginning her search when a "what color" key was lit. Then the two pigeons were put together to have an apparent conversation, as illustrated in Figure 2.6: Jack would ask Jill "what color?" Jill would go and look and then tell him by pressing the R, G, or Y key, and he would reinforce her by pressing the "thank you" key and then select his "decoding" of her "symbol" by pressing the appropriate colored key. Epstein et al. (1980) concluded:

> It has not escaped our notice that an alternative account [to sustained natural, symbolic communication] of this exchange may be given in terms of the prevailing contingencies of reinforcement. . . . The performances were established through standard fading, shaping, chaining, and discrimination procedures. A similar account may be given of the Rumbaugh procedure as well as of comparable human language. (p. 545)

Savage-Rumbaugh and Rumbaugh (1980) attacked the pigeon study on the grounds that the pigeons were rigidly trained for each of their sequences, whereas Sherman and Austin appeared to respond spontaneously to each other's typing once they had learned the symbol names. In addition, they considered it critical, as we have discussed, that Sherman and Austin could switch roles and could generate responses other than keystroking, like pointing to photographs. Having examined the pigeon study, do you feel now that this interchangeability and flexibility is critical? Given that the training procedure for each role for Sherman and Austin was also labored, as was their coming together, might the pigeons not also be trained to exchange roles and so on? Would this then constitute human-like communication?

## Conclusions

As you can see, the animal-human-language attempts have raised interesting questions on criteria for linguistic phenomena, and the researchers' debates have developed stronger criteria. In this regard, we should note the following:

At least in animals, comprehension and production of symbols are two separate processes and must be deliberately connected. The interchangeability of the communication roles appears critical both to realize true symbol acquisition and to evidence true communication.

The most compelling projects are pragmatically reasonable, taking into account the animal's need to communicate and awareness of others' ability to understand. Producing a string for food yields automaton "language." Savage-Rumbaugh (1986) attributes the success with Sherman and Austin to her design and specific shaping of a situation in which both attended to each other's behavior; one had information that the other did not and both were aware of that; the transmitter was aware that his information was worth transmitting; the receiver was aware that it was worth getting; both shared context and experiences so that they could appreciate the other's needs and actions; and both had access to symbols with which to exchange the information.

Symbol use entails, at least, the application of the symbol to name, not just request, objects, and recognition of the object given the symbol. Recognition must be evidenced both by indication of the object itself and by provision of descriptors of the object when the object is absent. In this respect, the dolphins fail to do anything but respond to a signal of an object with the object when it is present.

Grammar involves more than correct serial ordering of items. Each item must have an independent contribution, evident in other combinations, but each combination must convey a meaning independent of the individual items, arising only through the combination. The compound "water bird" for "swan," if this was intended, would constitute a combinatorial meaning beyond that of the parts. To instantiate grammar, the meaning given by combination must apply to abstract categories of symbols, categories defined through *function in the language.*

The pool's nonmovability in the dolphin program is not a linguistic property but a real-world one. Likewise, our elementary school definition of *noun* as the name of a person, place, or thing is real world. But *what makes a noun a noun is not those real-world properties,* that is, the things it stands for, but *the kinds of frames it stands in—the category of noun is defined by its use in the language.* Almost all of the projects demonstrated understanding of different serial orders, but none made it clear that abstract grammatical categories were understood or manipulated. Even Kanzi's tickle-bite is not a higher-order grammatical category, a compound where each item loses its individuality, but a coordination—tickle, then bite.

While it is not clear that any of the animals have demonstrated full human language skills, it is clear that they can appear to, and that they have many skills that may underlie true language abilities: associative learning, prodigious memories, prodigious memories for serial order, prodigious memories for serial order of associations and intentional communications, as every pet owner knows. Language may be unique to humans, but the substrates of language were likely present in human-animal ancestors.

## LANGUAGE AND COMMUNICATION: NECESSARY CHARACTERISTICS

In this section, I specify criteria for language and communication that have been proposed in the past and that have guided our previous discussion, and I add some based on our analysis of language. We will then apply these rules to human communication to separate what we do in common with animals from what we do uniquely. Finally, we will look generally at what is known about the biological basis of human language to determine how the unique skills occur.

### Design Features for Communication

In Chapter 1, we defined *communication* as the active transfer of information from one (the transmitter) to another (the receiver). By this definition, all the situations we have described constitute communication.

Theorists have introduced additional refinements that at least grade the levels of communication, if not distinguish communication systems from noncommunication systems. One refinement is further consideration of the concept of *active and deliberate* processing on the part of the receiver; we must distinguish perception from communication. When we touch an outstretched hand or see a tail waving to and fro, we get a tactile or visual sensation, automatically, and also a message of friendliness from person or dog. The first is a mechanical, relatively passive sensation; the second, communication. Distinguishing the second from the first is not always easy; MacKay (1972) defines an event as communicating if it serves an *internal organizing function* for the receiver by providing information that alters the receiver's interpretation of the world. (Of course, changes in internal organization and mental representations are hard to measure.) Note that information in this sense is consistent with our earlier definition of it as a reduction of uncertainty, and allows what is transmitted to be false or imaginary; it will reduce uncertainty, but incorrectly. In this case, the touch of the hand has only a transitory effect, but the handshake changes the receiver's concept of the social situation, of the transmitter, and so forth.

The next characteristic we may consider is *active transmission along with reception.* A person cannot communicate with a tape recorder, nor can a tape recorder communicate with a person. The person who made the tape does, via the recording. This holds true for literature, art, and music; the inanimate does not communicate but the creator does. (Consider the story of a professor who stopped attending classes, delivering lectures by tape recorder. One day he came in to see how things were going and found no students but 30 tape recorders in record mode on the students' desks. Is this communication? Of what? To whom?)

Obviously, an inanimate object cannot communicate, although by being perceived it can affect an observer's behavior. Less obviously, an animate being who is perceived may not be communicating—but is just being seen, heard, and so on. Communication takes place only when the transmitter is deliberately, intentionally emitting the signals to affect the receiver's conception of the world. Passive emissions—light bouncing off an individual, indicating that he or she is there, a stomach gurgling, a flat EEG—however interpretable they are to a skilled observer, are not messages but *symptoms.* Nature may have coordinated transmission and reception of symptoms in sign stimuli, but they are no more deliberate than a radio transmitter's effect on a radio. This kind of interaction is *signaling,* and the "rules" determining the receivers' responses are the *code system.*

A signal, whether it is intentionally communicated or coincidentally appears through nature, must have an arbitrary relation to the state it signals. Chasing someone out of a territory is not a signal but a direct causation; marking the territory so that the intruder "interprets" its ownership and leaves is a signal system. Cherry (1957) made this distinction for human communication versus human interaction— pushing someone is not communicating but telling him to move is, even though the effects may be the same. We can see arbitrariness in the signaling systems involving sign stimuli: Neither readiness to mate nor pursuit have a direct relation to red (the stickleback fish). Readiness to mate, of course, has a direct relation to pursuit, but the relation of each to red is mediated by a shared but arbitrary code. The stickleback fish system is an arbitrary, nonintentional signal, not communication.

The difficulty with *intentionality* as a criterion separating signaling from communicating is that it is very difficult to prove intentionality. One way, as we saw, is to find instances of deception, because deception indicates a flexible relationship between the message and the environment-controlling stimuli. Another way is to look for the transmitter's response to feedback. The existence of feedback and response to it, called *evaluation,* are other requirements for communication.

Feedback is a signal the receiver makes about the symptom or message. Evaluation is the transmitter's interpretation of the feedback and use of it to alter the message. Feedback and evaluation essentially reverse communication direction; the receiver becomes transmitter when giving feedback, and the transmitter becomes receiver when evaluating it. As Sherman and Austin demonstrated, communication must be a closed loop with transmitter and receiver simultaneously playing both roles. A gives a message to B while receiving feedback from B. B receives a message from A while transmitting feedback. And this can spiral continuously—B may be watching for feedback from A about A's reaction to B's feedback.

If A is watching for feedback and changes behavior as a result of it, we can infer that A internally represented the outcome of the communication, evaluating the outcome and determining whether there is a mismatch between what happened and what A *intended* to have happen. Thus we can infer intentionality. Symptoms such as red spots on the stickleback, a flat EEG, or a scream indicating a predator are not altered when the transmitter perceives their effects; they are tied to the stimulus, not the interaction. Note that the criteria of intentionality and evaluation imply that the transmitter can react to his own actions as others will react (Morris, 1964); the transmitter's reaction as receiver to his own communication, *monitoring,* forms the basis of his internal representation for communication.

### Summary

To be communication for our purposes, a signal must be actively, intentionally transmitted; must be actively received, changing the organizational state of the receiver; and must generate feedback from the receiver to the transmitter, potentially changing the transmitter's behavior.

## Evaluation: Communication and Noncommunication Systems

### Plants and Animals

Given the criteria just established, most of the situations described in preceding sections of this chapter do not constitute communication for one reason or another. The fly and the frog fail because there is neither internal representation of the other's internal state nor intentionality of communication. The fly signals no more to the frog than a grain of corn does to a bird. This basic response to another-as-stimulus has been classified (adapted from Hinde, 1972) as the lowest form of interaction, the *vegetable level.*

The tree interaction also fails but may be considered another, higher level of interaction. In this case, the failure is due to failure to monitor for feedback as well as failure of intentionality. (Note, though, that the transmitter and receiver trees could switch roles and at least metabolically have similar "internal representations.") This constitutes a higher level in terms of the nature of the stimulus reacted to—it is not the transmitter as a whole stimulus but a signaled aspect of its state (in this case, being devoured). When the signal is based on a bodily process, such as sending poison to the wound or leaving a scent on a trail, the interaction is at the *tonic level.*

The stickleback interaction must be divided into separate signals. The development of the red spot or swelling with eggs are indications of state. They differ from the tree because they are not a sustained-over-time state but a discontinuous one, and the reception of the information is likewise discontinuous, for the female responds to red only when she is pregnant. This is the *phasic level* of interaction because the signals work only at certain phases of the organism's life. The courtship dance and pursuit behavior are at a higher level, the *signal level,* because transmission is triggered by perception of the other, and the transmitter is responsive to feedback. The courtship rituals of the cricket and birds also fit into the signal level.

The remaining two levels are the *symbolic level* and the *language level,* distinguished from the preceding levels by the variability in signals, the amount that can be communicated, and the referential nature of the symbols (not signals). In this classification scheme, they differ from each other in that language may communicate abstract ideas, whereas the symbolic level is restricted to the concrete.

The classification scheme just described, although useful, is anthropocentric and based heavily on prior notions of hierarchy in the animal kingdom. This scheme places interaction between plants and the animals that feed on them at the vegetable level; "lower" vertebrates, at the phasic level; "lower" vertebrates and birds at one stage and birds and "lower" mammals at another stage of the signal level; nonhuman primates at the symbolic level; and language is restricted to humans. Beginning with a classification of primitive to complex, researchers can find classes of interaction that likewise go from primitive to complex, but this is circular reasoning. I presented the distinctions made by the system because the divisions based on the communications alone, apart from the interactors, are reasonable and provocative about the nature of communication.

I will discuss the distinction between symbolic and linguistic levels of communication in animals as "design features" for language. However, we still must decide whether the "higher" forms of interaction—of the bees, mammals, and pigeons—constitute interaction, communication, or symbolic communication. Despite the elaborateness of the bee system, it seems reasonable to conclude that bees are not communicating but signaling. On the transmitter's side, there is no choice about what to say. That does not mean that a bee does not produce novel utterances, but simply that if she visits one food supply, her behavior when she returns is totally predictable. The receivers also need not concern themselves with the adequacy of her message, her previous finds and descriptions, and so on; they can be confident that it absolutely represents her experience and what theirs would be too if they were there. Their "feedback" in dance does not cause the message to change or cause the transmitter to try other "words" to make it clear. In fact, their feedback, as automatic mimicry, need not be considered feedback at all but more akin to "social" yawning—we yawn once someone else starts, not as a signal to them but as an uncontrollable response.

It is easy to eliminate the pigeon "conversation" from communication given the criteria just established, because the pigeons are not aware of each other, let alone intentionally communicating together. They certainly looked for environmental signals (different lights lighting up), which happen to be under the other bird's control (and the experimenter's), but did not obviously search for a change in the other's world representation. Here, the fact that they cannot change roles suggests that they cannot have a representation of the other's experience and cannot evaluate the effect of the communication in light of such a representation.

What is troublesome about the analysis of the pigeon "conversation" is that it is tempting to conclude that the chimpanzees, Sherman and Austin, are communicating, that they do have such a representation; however, aside from their abilities to switch roles, their behavior can be described in the same way as that of the pigeons. (This implies that ability to switch roles *is* a defining feature of communication.) Moreover, while examination of the untrained interaction patterns and cognitive capacity of the monkeys, apes, and sea lions suggests that they certainly can form mental representations and can put themselves in the place of others ("identifying" with characters in videotapes and the like), it does not suggest definitively that they form such representations in normal interactions.

Under extreme, unusual circumstances, when the bull sea lion is suffocating the infant, or when the "competitive" trainer is not obeying the social code, or when food is withheld until some action is performed, the need arises to represent the other's frame of mind to induce an extraordinary response, but, ordinarily, responses elicited through signal interaction are sufficient to maintain social order. To my knowledge, normally in nonhuman social colonies, little information is transmitted; colony members have little choice in what to signal and no choice in how to interpret the signal; there is much less uncertainty. With behavior between colony members always conforming to the social rules, there is no chance of being misinterpreted, no need to monitor for feedback to see if the signal was correctly received: Perfect understanding is guaranteed. If you could guarantee perfect understanding without using language, would you bother? Perhaps teaching our language to animals is so laborious and those who have learned some so seldom use it with each other *because* the animals naturally have signaling success without it. So why should they bother?

## Human Signal and Communication Systems

Now that we have applied a set of criteria to animal interaction and concluded that, at least to our alien eyes, much of it is not actually communication, the time has come to apply the same set of criteria to humans, to make sure that we pass, at least in some instances. There are many forms of human "communication" of which language is only one; there is also body language and paralanguage as part of our natural interaction, and pantomime, art, music, and literature as studied—perhaps secondary—forms of interaction.

*The arts.* Let us look first, briefly, at these secondary forms of interaction. There can be no question that in the arts there is active, deliberate, intentional transmission—the artist works to create and convey the message. For each of the arts, also, the perceivers try, presumably actively, to decode the message. The problem in this case is the feedback loop. Frequently the artist is not around to receive audience reaction and/or is not monitoring for it. (Is Shakespeare communicating with us?) Frequently, too, the artist does not care what the audience reaction is, deliberately forbidding publication until after death, or ignoring critical reviews, lack of sales, and general unpopularity. So even if there is a reaction the artist could consider, it is often ignored or not used to change the message or its form.

By our criteria, then, artistic expressions are simply expressions, not communications. Of course, the medium—pantomime, art, a map—may be used to convey an idea in normal interaction and is then subject to normal feedback loops. And there are artists or performers who are sensitive to audience response and change their styles around it and so are, in a general way, communicating. But, for the most part, these secondary forms, because they cannot be affected by feedback, must not be considered communication if we consistently apply our criteria. (It is interesting to consider, if you disagree, whether it is the playwright or the actor who is communicating.)

*Nonverbal primary communication.* Now consider the primary forms of human interaction in typical face-to-face conversation between two people, called *dyadic interaction.* In addition to the content of the conversation, there are many other potential messages. Conversation consists of a series of floor switches: First A talks, then B talks, then A talks again. Most conversations consist of *ordered floor switches* (Duncan & Fiske, 1977). In our culture, while A holds the floor (and wishes to keep it), A mostly looks away from B, occasionally looking at B for feedback. A is also talking and gesturing continuously. When A comes to the end of what she or he has to say, speech and gestures cease in a regular away; the sentence is completed, intonation declines, the hands return to a neutral resting position, and so on. A also looks directly at B, further signaling B to take the floor. If B wanted to break in during A's turn, B also would indicate that in a rule-governed way: raising the eyebrows, beginning a hand gesture and mouth gesture and holding it, but not articulating. When A got the message, A would let B in, as before.

In addition to floor regulation, speech comprises signals of phonetic content, speaker identity, emotional overtone (and stress/deception), and syntactic information (as in pauses and intonation changes). These are transmitted, in some cases unintentionally and uncontrollably by the speaker, and possibly perceived/interpreted by the listener.

Finally, as most of us are aware, several kinds of visible behavior occur during face-to-face interaction. In discussing floor regulation, I mentioned eye contact and gesturing. There are also facial expressions, such as color changes as in blushing or blanching, pupil dilation (or constriction), eyebrow movements, eye movements, mouth movements (smiling, frowning, pursing the lips), and then hard-to-describe combinations as in general tension, sneering, and so forth. There are head and body movements apart from what is going on in the face: movements toward or away from the other, nods or shakes of the head, sudden cessation of movement (as in rapt attention). And there are global visual characteristics: attractiveness, neatness, posture, "spread" (sitting or standing too close to another, or with arms outstretched, taking a lot of room), among others. Some of these are readily interpretable; some can be interpreted only by some people after special training; some perhaps are meaningless (see Scheflen & Scheflen, 1972).

If we are strict in our application of the criteria for communication to human interactions, most of these situations do not constitute a high level of interaction. Vocal or visual cues to speaker identity—myriad signals including facial features, idiosyncratic movement, or dress style and vocal tone—may be classed at the vegetable or tonic levels. Emotional state signaling, in tone of voice or facial expression or general body tension, as obvious physical correlates of transitory bodily states, may be classified at the phasic level. (Do not be misled by the arbitrary relation of the expression to the emotion; remember that redness has no obvious relation to sexual readiness but for the stickleback fish is still a physical correlate of that state.) For the most part, as transmitters, we are unaware of these symptoms—not monitoring for feedback about them—and would be unable to change them even if we were.

Under extraordinary circumstances, when we are intentionally trying to convey a particular impression, so that the *message* of the interaction is our appearance, poise, or emotional state (as in an interview), we may attempt to control transmission of these signals, and they may be used as communication. Under circumstances like interviews, the receiver is also actively trying to form a representation of the person or the state and so will be processing these signals or symptoms and perhaps giving feedback about them. But interviews are atypical communication situations. Normally, such behavior serves at best as signals, not messages or symbols, and probably more often as symptoms, which the receiver ignores. These then are not communication because (a) they are not actively, intentionally transmitted; (b) they are not actively processed by the receiver; and (c) there is no feedback or evaluation loop. Moreover, as with the animals and plants we examined, they indicate only the transmitter's being and state, nothing external or distant.

In regulation of interaction, as in whose turn it is to talk, nonverbal vocal and visual signals seem to be communicating. Turn-taking is effective—seldom are there interruptions or long pauses before the other picks up the cue—and this suggests that the speaker and listener must be actively monitoring for turn-taking signals. Thus a feedback loop, a shared situation, exists. Both speaker-surrendering-the-floor and listener-taking-over-the-floor signals seem to be deliberately, actively transmitted also. So this is communication. It is not high level, however, because what is being communicated is current "emotional" state—desire to talk or desire to give up talking.

Now, are there aspects of language itself that may be considered as noncommunicating by our criteria? Idiosyncratic language use, which identifies the speaker in some way, might be one—as our using English identifies us as English speakers, although that is an unintended, passive effect of most messages. Some of our passive language style, our dialect and word choice, may be unconscious but is *intentional* identification with a group (change from above) or separation from one. We may question whether use of particular pronunciations, syntactic constructions, vocabulary, or topics of conversation intentionally or unintentionally transmit our age, sex, place of birth, social class, profession, or social group membership. But these *social markers* (Scherer & Giles, 1979) exist in nonverbal signaling (clothing styles and so on) as well. It is interesting to consider that *language, while communicating, is also, at another level, just an instance of behavior and can serve too as a signal or symptom.*

A second potential candidate for noncommunication within language is in highly stereotyped interactive sequences: (A) Hi. How are you? (B) Fine and you? (A) Fine . . . and then the message. These sequences seem to be passively processed by both A and B: We all have experienced the sudden interjection by one or the other, when the message part starts, of "No, I'm not fine. Actually . . . ," or one or the other giving an atypical response—"sick," "suicidal," "wonderful"—when "fine" was expected and this actual response was ignored. Thus we can infer that usually neither participant is actively or deliberately processing the verbal content of the signal, using it to evaluate the interchange or giving feedback on the content. In fact, here the interchange seems almost at the level of Jack and Jill's interchange, with nothing communicated but turn-taking signals, politeness, and the desire to keep the conversation going.

Given these criteria, what we frequently classify as *poor* communication may in fact be instances of *non*communication, even when syntax or semantics is quite elaborate. Consider, for example, a person reading or giving a lecture, never looking up, actively avoiding feedback from the audience. Is this any different from lecturing by tape recorder? The intent here seems to be to get through the hour, not to change the receivers' mental representations. Therefore, it is not communication—of the lecture content.

A third instance of verbal signaling that is not communicating may be found in some interjections. In English, for example, when hurt, we say, "Ouch"; astonished, "No!?"; comprehending, "Aha"; impressed, "Oooo." These are specific to our language; other noises are used in other cultures, odd as that may seem. However, this is like the dialect features in the white-crowned sparrow; even if learned, they are still very closely tied to basic physical states and are uttered usually only as symptoms of those states. Are statements of state like "I am happy" or "I am in pain" likewise symptoms? I would argue no, because the speaker has chosen to make the statement and is therefore deliberately trying to convey something. In a smile or a grimace of agony or an interjection of "Ouch," the transmission is automatic and therefore a symptom. I admit that this is a small distinction.

The design features described here for communication and their application to animal and human interactions are by no means absolute truths. Scientists and philosophers have been groping for defining and distinguishing characteristics of interactions for generations and, as you may feel, have not as yet arrived at any decisive answers. You are free to disagree with any of the classifications, distinctions, or conclusions made here, but apply your objection consistently: If you feel intention is unnecessary for communication then it follows that inanimate objects could communicate. If you wish to resolve the issue by saying everything is communication, then you must conclude that there is no difference between us and the trees.

### Summary

Communication involves active, intentional transmission of a signal as well as active, intentional reception, effecting a change in the receiver. There must also be feedback from the receiver, creating a closed loop between the interactants. Given this analysis, many of the systems for changing behavior in another that we have examined are not communication because transmission is unintentional or there is no deliberate feedback, at least as far as we, observers foreign to the culture and to the sensory capacities of the interactants, can tell. Moreover, applying these criteria to humans, we find some secondary forms of expression, such as visual art and literature, at times to be noncommunication. Finally, some forms of primary expression, body language, tone of voice, stereotyped language, and social markers in language, are signaling, not communication as such.

## Design Features for Language

As we saw in the last section, human language signals as well as communicates. However, language's primary function is to transmit a mental representation from one individual to another, a communication. Humans transmit mental representations nonlinguistically too, as in maps, visual art, music, dance, and pantomime. (How) Can we define the differences among simple, symbolic, and linguistic communication?

### Modality-Tailored Characteristics

Probably the most comprehensive set of design features for language was proposed by Hockett (1960; Hockett & Altmann, 1968) after analysis of characteristics shared by languages of the world. His features are shown in Box 2.4, together with an analysis of the systems we have looked at with respect to the features. (Note that I have applied these features to some systems differently than Hockett himself did.) Hockett's first defining feature is the *use of the vocal-auditory channel,* which, he argued, was an important evolutionary development in that it freed the rest of the body for other activities, allowing humans to communicate

### Box 2.4.  Characteristic Properties of Languages

| CHARACTERISTIC FEATURES | SYSTEM | | | | | | | | | |
|---|---|---|---|---|---|---|---|---|---|---|
| | Fly-Frog | Stickleback | Cricket | Sparrow | Bee | Whale | Nonhuman Primate | Apes and Language | Human "Body Language" | Visual Art and Music |
| **COMMUNICATION** | | | | | | | | | | |
| Active Transmission | ✓ | ✗ | ✓ | ✓ | ✓ | ✓ | ✓ | ✓ | ☑ | ✓ |
| Active Reception | ✗ | ✓ | ✓ | ✓ | ✓ | ✓ | ✓ | ✓ | ☑ | ☑ |
| Interchangeability | ✗ | ✗ | ✗ | ✗ | ✓ | ? | ✓ | ✓ | ✓ | ✓ |
| Information Rate (Simultaneity and Smear) | ✗ | ✗ | ✗ | ✗ | ? | ? | ? | ? | ? | ? |
| Feedback | ✓ | ✓ | ✓ | ✓ | ✗ | ? | ✓ | ✓ | ☑ | ☑ |
| **PHYSICAL** | | | | | | | | | | |
| Vocal-Auditory | ☑ | ✗ | ✓ | ✓ | ✗ | ✓ | ☑ | ✗ | ☑ | ☑ |
| Rapid Fading | ✗ | ✗ | ✓ | ✓ | ? | ✓ | ☑ | ✗ | ☑ | ☑ |
| Broadcast Transmission/ Reception | ☑ | ✗ | ✓ | ✓ | ✗ | ✓ | ☑ | ✗ | ☑ | ☑ |
| **SYSTEM CHARACTERISTICS** | | | | | | | | | | |
| Specialization (system exists only for itself) | ✗ | ☑ | ☑ | ☑ | ✓ | ? | ☑ | ✓ | ✗ | ✓ |
| Semanticity (association not identity between sign and referent) | ✗ | ✗ | ✗ | ☑ | ✓ | ? | ☑ | ✓ | ✓ | ☑ |
| Arbitrariness (sign and referent arbitrarily related) | ✗ | ✓ | ✓ | ✓ | ☑ | ? | ☑ | ✓ | ☑ | ☑ |
| Discrete (vs. continuous) | ✗ | ? | ? | ? | ☑ | ? | ☑ | ✓ | ✗ | ☑ |
| **TOPIC** | | | | | | | | | | |
| Displacement (time and space) | ✗ | ✗ | ✗ | ✗ | ✓ | ? | ✗ | ✓ | ✗ | ☑ |
| **COMBINATION** | | | | | | | | | | |
| Productivity | ✗ | ✗ | ✗ | ✗ | ✓ | ✓ | ✗ | ✓ | ☑ | ✓ |
| Duality of Patterning (awareness of levels element is in) | ✗ | ✗ | ✗ | ✗ | ✗ | ? | ✗ | ✗ | ✗ | ✓ |
| Metalanguage | ✗ | ✗ | ✗ | ✗ | ✗ | ? | ✗ | ? | ✗ | ✓ |
| Recursiveness | ✗ | ✗ | ✗ | ✗ | ✗ | ? | ✗ | ✗ | ✗ | ✓ |
| Prevarication | ✗ | ✗ | ✗ | ✗ | ✗ | ? | ✓ | ✓ | ✓ | ? |
| **LEARNING** | | | | | | | | | | |
| Learnability | ✗ | ✗ | ✗ | ✗ | ✗ | ? | ☑ | ✓ | ✓ | ✓ |
| Traditional Transmission | ✗ | ✗ | ✗ | ☑ | ☑ | ? | ☑ | ✓ | ☑ | ✓ |

NOTE: This table is a summary of features for communication and language, with indication of how the nonlanguage systems distribute with respect to them. ☑ means some or sometimes.

while doing other things. Establishing the vocal-auditory channel as a necessary characteristic for language automatically rules out systems such as the bees' waggle dance and, significantly, sign language, visual art, music, pantomime, and writing, for an ad hoc reason. I do not consider it a requirement for language (and many have eliminated it), but note it here in part for historical reasons and in part because it is the primary modality for most human communication.

Five characteristics of the vocal-auditory channel (and perhaps other channels as well) were listed by Hockett as design features and are significant language characteristics. These are rapid fading, broadcast transmission and reception, interchangeability, total feedback, and specialization. Rapid fading refers to the transitory nature of the speech signal; we cannot keep studying it but must encode it rapidly because it disappears. (Indeed, one argument for using artificial language systems with the apes was that this could override the rapid fading characteristic, providing a memory aid; the chimpanzee could study the board or monitor as long as needed to decode the message.) Pantomime, music, and sign languages are also rapidly fading signals, but writing, visual art, many forms of chemical communication, red spots on the stickleback, and so on are not.

*Broadcast transmission and reception* means we can produce a signal that anyone within hearing distance can receive. This is different from a handshake, for which transmitter and receiver must be in direct contact, or from the tactile mimicry of the bees. For humans, visual signals can be broadcast less than can auditory ones because hearing is roughly omnidirectional, while we must be looking at a visual signal to notice it.

*Interchangeability* is a feature we have already discussed with respect to general communication: In our system, an individual can serve equally well as transmitter or receiver, speaker or listener. This is in part because we are all endowed with the same auditory and vocal systems; we do not have sex-specific, specially developed markings like the red spot or male songs. (Here we should note that while female white-crowned sparrows do not sing the male song, they *can* if stimulated hormonally—so the neural potential for the interchange is there. And the males, of course, receive the song as well as sing it when they duel for territory.) Interchangeability is a feature also of the bee system and of sign language and, talent aside, of music, visual art, and literature. Interchangeability is, of course, missing in the dolphin language project but was increasingly encouraged with the apes.

*Total feedback* relates to interchangeability and the vocal-auditory system: We hear ourselves speak and so monitor our own signals as well as those of others. This contrasts with signals like the stickleback's red spot, which cannot be seen by the transmitter. We can also watch ourselves sign, read what we write, and listen or watch ourselves perform, so the monitoring function applies to all human message transmissions.

*Specialization* entails the distinction we made between symptoms and signals— some interaction systems use a by-product of normal function as a signal (as in a dog's marking his territory by urinating); their communication medium is not reserved only for communication. In contrast, our speech and gesture systems seem to be specialized only for communication. A similar argument may be made for music and visual art.

### Semantics, Syntax, and Acquisition Characteristics

The six properties just discussed describe communication features of language systems but not features of language itself. Hockett's remaining features define linguistic systems in particular. There is *semanticity:* The relation between a signal and its referent is learned through association. Smiling, in many instances, contains no semanticity but is part of being happy. The word *happy,* on the other hand, signifies happiness only through association. Most of the natural animal communication systems do not have semanticity: The monkey scream for a particular predator is specific, but unlearned, like our reflexive smile. Ditto for the bee dance and even the deceptive flirting behavior of the sea lion. The dialect features in the birdsong, while learned, are not semantic; they signal no relation between song and its referent, readiness-to-mate, beyond the generic song itself. In contrast, probably all of the human-like language projects reflect semanticity, by design.

Most associations in language are *arbitrary;* there is no external connection between the sounds and the things they signify. Note that a word like *bow-wow* for "dog" employs semanticity—the sound of the animal must be associated with it, but it is nonarbitrary because the sound is connected concretely with the object it represents. Visual arts and pantomime are nonarbitrary. They may exhibit semanticity when a particular thing may be depicted because it stands for something else in the culture, as when Warhol uses a Campbell's soup can for commercialized, mass-produced cooking. The symbol is semantic, but the depiction is nonarbitrary because it is a direct, if conventionalized, portrayal of the object. Most of the natural animal communication systems are arbitrary (there is no direct relation between a scream and a predator, or a song and mating readiness), if not semantic. The bee system is an exception here because the angle of the dance nonarbitrarily relates to food direction. Again, the language projects all either designed their languages or used a human language with arbitrary symbols.

The relation of sounds to meaning is *discrete* (as opposed to continuous or graded): The words *loud* and *soft* signify opposite ends of a continuum, but the difference in sound between *loud* and *soft* does not mirror that difference; *soft* is not softer sounding than loud. When we wish to signify that there is more of something, we add discrete morphemes: "more x," "xier," "very x"; we do not usually signify it by raising our voices (matching the increase with intensity) or increasing the word length. Note that here again the bee system diverges from human language: The better the quality, the more intense the dance. We might consider the reduplication in pidgins and creoles to reflect a less discrete system than full-blown language, as greater intensity or "more" is indicated by more of the same words. Likewise, most of the spontaneous combinations of signs in apes are reduplicated for emphasis, grading a discrete system.

The next feature Hockett suggested refers to what we talk about rather than the kind of association that is made. He called the feature *displacement,* referring to our ability to talk about things that are displaced in time (future or past) or in space (things not immediately in front of us or perhaps even nonexistent). With respect to displacement, others have proposed that a unique aspect of language is its ability to describe the environment, not the signaler—displacement from the transmitter's state (Hinde, 1972). This seems to be a feature shared by many forms of human communication: visual art, pantomime, and music as well as language. None of the animals other than the bee used language to discuss things displaced in time or space, regardless of whether they were taught a language that had that capability.

The bees' language focuses on describing the location of a distant resource needed to fulfill a present need.

These distinctive characteristics of language are aspects relating to meaning and meaning representation. Two additional features, productivity and duality of patterning, refer to the peculiar characteristics of phonology and syntax. Human language, by virtue of its rules, is *productive,* open-ended, and continuously creative: There is no limit (other than our imaginativeness) to what we may talk about and how we may express it. Our "body language," in contrast, is nonproductive; we have "symptoms," like blushing, that are rigorously tied to a state, and new symptoms cannot be created for new messages. Syntax (which combines words to form new meanings), morphology (which combines meaning elements to form words), and phonology (which combines phonemes to form words) join elements to give a new representation. This leads to *duality of patterning,* where a single aspect of language has a representation on several levels. Thus, in constructing rhymes, we attend to a word simply as a sound pattern; when we use it in poetry, we look at both the sound pattern *and* the meaning. Note that there is duality of patterning also in acting (where a gesture represents itself as well as indicating an aspect of character), in visual arts, and in music.

Productivity *is* exhibited in nonhuman communication: Bees describe new location-distance-quality combinations; Kanzi at least, if not Washoe, Koko, and Nim, created new symbol combinations. However, there is little evidence of duality of patterning for nonhumans, of an animal, say, playing with the shape features of a lexigram or sign *and* interpreting the meaning of it. (Brown [1958] tells a story suggestive of discreteness, duality of patterning, and productivity in at least one jackdaw. Jackdaws, monogamous birds, have different songs for different events: a mating song, a baby song, a danger song, a flight song, and a come-home song. Once united, a couple "flirts" with each other: They talk in the baby song to each other, the female makes submissive postures, and the male feeds the female special delicacies. The anecdote is that the female of one pair, after the male had died, composed a new song, consisting of elements of all the other songs of the jackdaw life, with the dominant theme being the come-home song. As Brown observed, this is reminiscent of human ballads. It also shows that the songs themselves can act as elements in a combination with new meaning.)

Note that duality of patterning is a commonplace in human culture, within and apart from human language. As we have observed, for instance, in "change from above," we use language to communicate meaning *and* social group membership. We also use clothing to keep warm *and* communicate style and group membership.

The final feature Hockett (1960) discussed is *traditional transmission,* referring to how language is acquired. *Traditional* means it is passed from one generation to the next through learning, and is not completely innately specified as in many of the signal systems. Nevertheless, Hockett noted that there are genetic influences on our capacity to acquire language.

More recently, Hockett and Altmann (1968) added three characteristics to the list: prevarication (lying), ability to learn other languages *(learnability),* and ability to talk about the communication system itself. We briefly discussed prevarication when we discussed animal deceptions. It is important because in a sense it indicates greater displacement of the transmission from the immediate context, and greater awareness of the receiver's likely response. Traditionally, language has been seen as uniquely giving us a way to pray, and humanness as a unique ability to recognize God. It is ironic, perhaps a true symbol of our deconstructionist times, that we now invoke instead of prayer the power of language to lie as a sine qua non of language.

The ability to learn other languages is self-explanatory and indicates a continuous flexibility of the language systems. Naturally it does not appear that animal communication systems exhibit learnability, but it is clear from the ape and dolphin studies that the animals may learn a human-sponsored system that has at least some languagelike characteristics.

The ability to discuss the communication system using the communication system is probably the highest level of duality of patterning. Words used to describe characteristics of words are called *metalanguage;* communication about communications is called *metacommunication.* The only evidence of metacommunication in the ape language projects is in the symbol translated "name of" taught to Sarah and Lana. If you accept that they understood the concept underlying naming, then they may be considered to be able to metacommunicate. (I wonder, however, whether Sarah would appreciate the irony in the sentence "the name-of red is blue," as we might in whispering the word *loud.*) I have already suggested that there may be no "meaning" in these metalinguistic utterances other than the instruction to associate the object on either side of them; an equal sign for us would not constitute a metalinguistic symbol, and it is not clear that "name of" means anything more than "=" to them.

The three new features apply not just to human language but to other forms of human expression. We must learn the conventions of an art form to understand it; we may use art to create a false mood and we may refer to other artistic expressions within a given artistic expression.

In addition to Hockett's thirteen plus three design features, others have proposed critical distinguishing characteristics of language that we should consider. Thorpe (1972) suggested that to be language, there must be a combination of two or more elements purposefully for a single effect, the same elements able to recombine in different ways for different effects. As you may recall, the absence of syntactic combinations is what Terrace et al. (1979) found nonlanguagelike in the chimpanzees' signing behavior. Again, the bee alone of the natural language systems uses such element combinations to create new messages.

Lyons (1972) proposed that language is characterized by *medium transferability:* We can communicate the same message in speech, lipreading, writing, and so on; there is no fixed symbol type. Kanzi seemed to be able to transfer media, using lexigrams, photographs, and speech to understand messages.

*Information Rate Properties*

A final characteristic that has been proposed is the amount of information transmitted:

Communication proceeds in the face of a number of uncertainties and has the character of, or may be described as consisting of, numerous inductive inferences being carried out concurrently. The number and variety of these uncertainties is particularly apparent in the case of speech. For instance:

(1) Uncertainties of speech sounds, or acoustic patterning. Accents, tones, loudness may be varied; speakers may shout, sing, whisper, or talk with their mouths full.

(2) Uncertainties of language and syntax. Sentence constructions differ; conversational language may be bound by few rules of syntax. Vocabularies vary; words have many near-synonyms, popular usages, special usages, et cetera.

(3) Environmental uncertainties. Conversations are disturbed by street noises, by telephone bells and background chatter.

(4) Recognition uncertainties. Recognition depends upon the peculiar past experiences of the listener, upon his familiarity with the speaker's speech habits, knowledge of language, subject matter, et cetera.

There are many sources of uncertainty, yet speech communication works. It is so structured as to possess redundancy at a variety of levels, to assist in overcoming these uncertainties. (Cherry, 1957, p. 277)

On the basis of analysis of semantic, syntactic, and phonological structure, we may further analyze the information requirement. The amount of information is partly determined by the way information is packed in the speech signal, the lack of invariance, or one-to-one relation between aspects of the speech signal and the message. Thus one "discrete" segment is packed with information about many layers of language and communication—speaker identity and emotion at the lowest, signal level; phonetic identity of several "segments"; semantic or morphemic identity and syntactic identity at the higher, linguistic levels.

At the same time, if a particular segment is eliminated, because its cues to any one aspect are smeared across adjacent segments, there may be no information loss; the message(s) (and signals and symptoms) may still be recovered. Marler (1975), in fact, described the human speech signal as *graded* because of this simultaneity: As we saw in our discussion of speech perception, the signal continuously changes and the hearer imposes perception of discrete segments (categorical perception) on the changing signal. That is, language perception entails discrete elements, as Hockett noted, but the signal itself is graded. The graded signal, Marler argued, allows more subtle information to be transferred; the discrete perception allows the signals to be used in isolation or novel combination because they may be matched with discrete patterns in memory and not just compared with the other portions of the signal in which they are embedded.

We see analogous instances of simultaneity and smear at higher levels. For example, co-occurrence rules, argument specification, and syntactic structure generally all provide redundancy, allowing us to miss a word and still recover the message from other parts of the sentence.

Thus at all levels of language we see simultaneous transmission of many "segments" and smear of the "cues" for one segment across many. We propose simultaneity and smear as additional defining characteristics of language.

Simultaneity and smear, together with duality of patterning, allow for poetic devices: We can focus attention simultaneously at the meaning level and the sound level (because they are simultaneously transmitted) to produce appreciation of alliteration or rhyme; we can focus attention simultaneously at many meaning levels because they are simultaneously transmitted to make metaphors and puns; we can focus attention on meaning and structure simultaneously for rhetorical devices such as rhetorical questions, or structure repetitions (I came, I saw, I conquered) to show similarities in meaning.

Probably related to simultaneity and smear is the rate at which we transmit information through language. I will not quantify it and therefore cannot compare language with other forms of expression in this respect but propose that there is a rate characteristic of language, although this characteristic may be uninteresting with respect to what it tells us about language as symbol system. It does indicate systems that could not be used as language, for us, however. Try to communicate an understandable message by spelling out loud: It is nearly impossible to keep track of the thought and spell at the same time; as transmitters, we get slowed so much we lose the message. Similarly, if someone spells at you, by the time you have put the letters together into words, you have forgotten previous words and lost the point of the message. (I am not sure whether this means we are getting information too fast—each letter is its own signal and there are too many of them per word—or too slow—fewer words get said per unit time.)

Altering information rate in other ways also disturbs our natural communication, as in inserting *long* pauses between spoken words or very short pauses between complex sentences, or organizing a paragraph so that we are not getting continual small information increments on a theme. As Pierce (1972) observed,

> Beethoven is said to have declared that in music everything must be at once surprising and expected. That is appealing. If too little is surprising, we are bored; if too little is expected, we are lost. Communication is possible only through a degree of novelty in a context that is familiar. (pp. 37-38)

To be recognized as language, the message rate and rate of old (redundancy) to new must fall within a certain range to keep us attending to the message; this range is characteristic of language. This relates to simultaneity and smear in that they give a way of packing old and new together and of transmitting information at a high rate without concern for loss.

Now, I believe that simultaneity, smear, and the characteristic information rate are human perceptual constraints on fluent language. Because they reflect our perceptual capabilities and needs, the identity or nonidentity of transmission rate in an animal system is no more relevant than was the apes' inability to speak because of their vocal anatomy. Therefore, I will not attempt to evaluate nonhuman or nonlanguage systems with respect to these characteristics. However, I also believe that they are critically important in determining the shape of language: In no human language do speakers spell at one another. No human language could use an absolute one-to-one map between communication elements and referents; that is, we don't spell out words letter by letter but say them syllable by syllable, and so on.

Related to this is our use and reuse of elements and rules, another design feature I propose. Do you think it would be possible to find a language organized so that each word consists of a different number of the same elements: one word being A, for instance, and another AA, a third, AAA, and so on (Hockett, 1960)? Although this would have the advantage of there being few elements to learn and to recognize, it has the disadvantage of having words too similar, too easy to confuse. To avoid this, languags use many elements in combination. Again, though, there must be a boundary on this: If each word or sentence shares no feature with any other word or sentence, there are too many elements to memorize. Thus we see languages each having some number of elements that get used repeatedly within the bounds of easy discriminability and easy learnability. This occurs at all levels of language: If the nasal stop (e.g., m-b) distinction is employed in a language, it is likely to be used for several places of articulation (also n-d), which makes the learning of that feature efficient. If a plural is made one way for one word, that method of pluralization is likely to be generalized to many words, again for efficiency of learning. Thus, again without quantifying it, I propose that a distinguishing feature of language is the number of elements or rules used at each level and their efficient reapplication; the number and reapplication are determined by constraints on human memory and perceptual discriminability (see Miller, 1956). Because this is our specific capability again, I will not rate animals on this dimension.

A striking, and in my view, necessary feature of language related to the reapplication of elements and rules is recursiveness. Recursiveness occurs in sentence embedding when a sentence is rewritten as a sentence containing a sentence, and, again, this "feature" occurs at many levels. At the overall communication level, as stated earlier, we may perhaps be the only beings for whom A is aware that B is aware that A is aware that B is aware, and so on, of what A means. In semantics, because of recursiveness of reference, we appreciate paradoxes like "This statement is false" or "I always lie" (Hofstadter, 1979). At the syntactic level, recursive application of rules permits imagining infinitely long sentences—a sentence that contains a sentence that contains a sentence and so on.

Recursiveness is related to productivity but as a special, interesting case. It is possible to have a productive system without altering the basic productive units— for example, apple and banana and pear and so on. In this case, each word, or at least each noun, does not change in syntactic function or actually modify the meanings of another. Kanzi's compound verb "tickle bite" is such a nonrecursive compound. Sentence embedding or connecting sentences through production of subordinate and main clauses does change the units. A sentence (e.g., The cat chased the rat) that before was an end in itself becomes a unit (an NP—the cat that chased the rat), which can build with other units-that-had-been-end-products in the same way that each of them had been composed by smaller units.

As a characteristic property of language, recursiveness thus produces or refines other characteristic properties: There is not just combination of symbols but a certain kind of combination, *hierarchical combination;* there are not just discrete elements but discrete elements of variable size. This property of recursiveness is not restricted to language but appears in other forms of human expression (see Hofstadter, 1979, for innumerable elating examples) when we embed themes within themes in music, when we draw a self-portrait looking in a mirror drawing a self-portrait looking in a mirror, and so on.

These last properties are, in my view, what separates pidgins from creoles, placing pidgins at a "primitive" level. Both emergent languages exhibit important design features tied to human communication, like broadcast transmission, semanticity, duality of patterning (at least of sound and morpheme), and the like. Pidgins use fewer elements than creoles or full languages, less hierarchical ordering, and less recursiveness, although they do evidence instances of each. Creoles use more units in more productive hierarchical combinations than pidgins, employing function words created from content words, and fully embedding clauses. Objectively, this is what makes the pidgin more primitive. It stands in marked contrast to nonstandard dialects like AAEV, which have a full complement of units, hierarchical ordering, duality of patterning, and recursiveness. (See Chapter 8 in *Language and Its Normal Processing* for a richer description of pidgins, creoles, and AAEV, complete with examples.)

## Summary and Conclusions

In this section, we reviewed and proposed characteristic and defining features of language and rated the animal communication systems relative to them. The features and ratings are summarized in Box 2.4. It is reassuring to note as we look over Box 2.4 that, as each of the systems seems to be more like what we think of as human communication, more of our language criteria apply. Generally the criteria fall into three broad categories: characteristics that arise from the human makeup such as information rate, characteristics of language as a symbol system, and characteristics of language learning. The first type may be uninteresting with respect to whether language provides us with, or is indicative of, special cognitive skills, but it will help us to recognize language apart from the communication of other organisms. The other types are more interesting in relation to the question of how language enables us to process the world differently from others. It is important to note that none of these characteristics alone is sufficient to define language; the constellation of characteristics forms the definition.

## Summary and Conclusions

This section attempted to establish that language (a) may be characterized; (b) is, at this time, unique to humans; and (c) is unique, in at least some respects, among human activities. This should not be an astounding statement, given that it was derived circularly—our purpose was to establish what separates human language from other signal systems and other human activities.

There are, of course, features of white-crowned sparrow song that make it unique from the systems of all other animals (that is how we recognize a bird from its song alone), from any other white-crowned sparrow activity (or we would call that activity sparrow song), and features of bees' hive building that make it unique from any other bee activity and from any other architecture system, and so on. The use of critical information rate, reapplication of features and rules, and the like, as part of the human cognitive and perceptual constraints on language, are analogous to beehive construction being peculiar to bees. In this sense, the claim that language is unique is not a strong one with deep philosophical implications assuring our place next to angels. Establishment of these characteristics for language *is* the strong claim because they provide a means for separating language and humanness from nonlanguage and nonhumanness.

Some of the characteristics are more interesting than others: Recursiveness, for example, is a feature of the system that makes it a powerful tool for thought and is thus more interesting than a human-tailored information rate, which is a property of the producer, not the system. However, it is my contention that language looks the way it does because of human processing constraints, and that one way in which we can reject a system as language is if it deviates from these constraints.

Let us examine this contention and its implications further. Consider the flight of birds, also likened to angels historically. There is no being that flies naturally as birds fly. There are analogues to wings—our hands or a seal's flippers. Examination of the anatomy of these limbs shows profound similarities, which do not result in anything like the same skills. Analogous to this similarity and difference, communication systems may use the same organs, and social and cognitive structures, but be differentially tuned to achieve far different results. This evolutionary tuning may entail a perceptual constraint like information rate.

We may also note that, using nonanalogous structures and abilities, other living things fly—insects and us (in planes). Here we may talk of features like aerodynamics, lift, and so on, intrinsic to flight apart from the organ, natural or not, that produces it. These features, which are characteristic of the result, I see as analogous to features like recursiveness, which may lift our symbol system to a different plane than other animals'. We may explore the two types of features for different reasons: to determine biological continuities or the power of the system. Building a prosthesis with that power (an airplane is a prosthesis for flight), either in an intelligent computer program or in a specially trained animal model, will not change our uniqueness because we will still do it differently but will increase our understanding of the ability.

We should also note that as animals may be constrained from processing our communication as we do, lacking such things as our peculiar information rate, we may be constrained from appreciating the power of their communication systems because of human perceptual blinders. Chemical communication systems used by ants to organize their complex social structure automatically seem like they "must" be more primitive than language because *our* (outsiders to the system) chemical senses are too primitive to allow appreciation of their richness and coding schemes.

It is important to emphasize that rejection of another system as language on the basis of this type of property does not indicate that the system's users cannot think abstractly or symbolically, just that they do not express their thoughts as we do. In the next section, we will examine some aspects of human biology and evolution that may underlie even the subtle, more interesting system characteristics of language.

## LANGUAGE: BIOLOGICAL AND EVOLUTIONARY MECHANISMS

Language is the way it is partly because of general human information processing capacities that have shaped language and partly because of special structures that may have evolved for the purpose of human communication. (It may be, of course, that structures we use for communication evolved for other purposes and are now subserving language.) With respect to general human information processing capacities, among others we have noted

1. the information transmission rate (which seems to be constant across languages, although accomplished by different means, like order versus inflection for syntax),
2. the redundancy of transmission (which is necessary for imperfectly attending organisms),
3. the use of features to maximize discriminability (as constrained by our perceptual systems), and
4. the reuse of features to minimize learning and memory.

We may add the fact that

5. speech frequencies fall within the most sensitive frequency range of the human ear.

We next discuss hypotheses concerning special structures that may have evolved for the purpose of human communication.

### Review of Mechanisms Already Noted

The assumption that special structures have evolved for human communication is quite controversial. Because it is a very strong assumption, I will begin by buttressing it with reminders that we have observed biological structures for communication in the animal kingdom that are under genetic control and may have been subject to evolutionary pressure. These can serve as analogies for such development in humans.

In this regard, we have already seen genetically controlled song centers for transmission and reception in the cricket, similar song centers (which presumably are also under genetic control) in the white-crowned sparrow, and neurons specifically tuned to call production and reception for features of either in the cricket, bird, and monkey. And Deacon (1997) notes that corresponding regions of the brain across vertebrates including us and other primates seem to be responsible for vocalization. We have also proposed a simple model to interrelate biologically determined song characteristics and learning, allowing flexibility in communication—the tunable blueprint model (Marler & Mundinger, 1971).

There is biological evidence for tunable blueprints at the single-cell level, at least in developing visual systems. Allowed normal exposure to light during a critical period, neurons in the cat visual cortex have predictable innately specified light sensitivities. However, if visual stimulation of the kitten during the critical period is severely abnormal, confined experimentally to viewing of a single pattern pasted on glasses in front of the eye, the neurons' sensitivities conform, within limits, to this overexposed pattern. This indicates that they are "tunable" (see Eimas & Tartter, 1979; Hirsch & Tieman, 1987, for review). Although this is not a tunable blueprint for *communication,* the tuning of the white-crowned sparrow male song could be served by the same type of biological mechanism.

Thus we have reasonable analogies for biological control of transmission and reception of a communication system and for learning of characteristics of a specific input (a particular language or dialect). Marler (1970, 1975) proposed similar blueprints in humans for speech sounds. These evolved to allow discrete, categorical perception of a continuous speech stream.

We also have observed analogies for development of complex systems where simple ones will do—as in the elaborate vocal repertoire of the marsh wren. Sexual selection is a potent force in developing such communication skills in birds and maybe in us. Finally we should note that within the natural selection framework, it is possible for a skill to propagate itself. In *Baldwinian evolution* (Deacon, 1997), a particular behavior modifies an environmental niche to favor particular species traits over others. So, we see lactose tolerance developing in those cultures that have the longest history of dairy-animal husbandry: Domestication of this rich and reliable food source favored those genetically able to take advantage of it. Likewise, Deacon proposes, brain development toward greater symbolic activity would have allowed our ancestors to create "civilization," which in turn would have increased resources necessary for survival *and* favored those who could better fit the civilized niche—those with symbolic capabilities in communication.

## Specially Evolved Human Communication Mechanisms?

Two structures specially evolved for human language have been proposed, and hinted at, in this chapter. One is a specially developed articulatory system, specialized for speech, and the other is a specially developed neural structure for language comprehension and production.

To support a specially developed mechanism for speech, note the following:

1. Speaking, especially at great length, requires an adaptation of normal breathing.

2. Our facial musculature differs from that of other animals and allows greater control of both articulation and facial expression.

3. Our glottis is distinct from that of other species, vibrating easily only during exhaling (Lenneberg, 1967).

4. There is a significant difference in the shape of the adult human vocal tract as compared with infants, chimpanzees, and Neanderthal man (Lieberman, 1987, but see Arensburg & Tillier, 1991, for contradictory data for the Neanderthal).

This last difference has two effects, according to Lieberman, one an evolutionary disadvantage—we are more likely to choke—and the other, a possible compensating advantage—we alone can produce the point vowels /i, a, u/. However, it is not clear how important the point vowels are to language, and consonant production would not be affected by the vocal tract change. Moreover, at least for the Neanderthal, recent fossil finds indicate that they were anatomically as likely to produce vowels as we are (Arensburg & Tillier, 1991).

We also see evidence for specialized neural development, which I will discuss in greater detail in Chapter 5. Already we have noted that there is a language center, lateralized primarily in the left hemisphere of the brain. This area is larger than the corresponding area on the right side, even in newborns, suggesting perhaps an innate specification for language function (LeMay & Geschwind, 1978). Further, there is differentiation of function within that language center: The anterior portion seems to govern motor aspects of language (production), while the posterior governs comprehension. And we also see increased cranial capacity in modern man as compared with fossil man and many existing species (see Lenneberg, 1967; see also Deacon, 1997, for amplification and critique of brain size arguments).

Finally, there are critical changes in brain growth during human development that have been thought to coincide with sudden changes in linguistic capacity, such as the brain's doubling in size during the first two years of life, at which point the child begins to combine utterances syntactically (Lenneberg, 1967). Our small body size relative to a large brain means, moreover, that we use a relatively small proportion of neurons to regulate the body itself (and these are recruited during fetal development). Those not so engaged are free during infancy to be recruited to respond to other inputs; that is, they are *displaced* to new uses. Deacon (1997) argues that the dominant stimulation of those neurons so freed (the prefrontal region of the brain) during infancy has resulted in our symbolic thinking.

The extraordinary brain growth of early infancy has been hypothesized to reflect development of language centers, the unfolding UG, and the activation of a language "reflex." Alternatively, and perhaps more consistently with the continuity implied by evolution, language itself may have evolved to employ optimally the strategic processes or processing styles—symbolism, hierarchical structures, repetition of segments, redundancy—emerging as brain centers sensitive to different stimulation mature (Deacon, 1997).

A final biological influence on the development of language should be noted. We have a very long childhood relative to other species, and this increases the opportunity for traditional transmission, and thus the number of learned rules and elements that can be incorporated into our communication system (Hockett, 1960). And, as different brain centers develop interconnections, or are recruited, at

---

**Box 2.5. Human Biological Predisposing Conditions for Language**

— Specially evolved vocal apparatus and breathing for speech.
— Coincidence of speech production frequencies with auditory sensitivities.
— Lateralized brain function with a "language center," subdivided into, perhaps, production and comprehension regions.
— A tunable blueprint, perhaps, for learning the language's sounds during a critical period.
— Sexual selection constraint, perhaps, to prefer vocal and linguistic complexity.
— A long period of helplessness in infancy and childhood that enables traditional transmission.
— Cognitive and perceptual abilities constraining the number of critical features in language, their reuse, the amount of redundancy, and a preferable information transmission rate.
— Cognitive abilities to organize and reorganize information hierarchically and recursively in language and other cognitive domains.

---

different times, at each level of maturity we may regard the language model through a different cerebral lens, of which the less-is-more process mentioned in the last chapter is only one. As we will explore in the next chapters, during childhood there may be critical periods for language acquisition analogous to those observed in bird song acquisition or visual development. These critical periods could reflect general cognitive changes (movement to or from a "less-is-more" state), or the unfolding of a specific language acquisition device. In either case, we see in development of language evidence of biological control.

---

## SUMMARY AND CONCLUSIONS

In this chapter, I attempted to define characteristics of language that make it distinct from, although at times analogous to, other forms of human communication and other communication or signal systems in nature. This was not undertaken to argue that language is in any way better than other forms of interacting, just that it is different, and that the differences are definable. Language is different from other signal systems because we are different from other species (as they are from one another), and these differences constrain and shape language.

In the next chapters, we will look at the effects on language of changing these constraints—first in conditions of social or linguistic deprivation, where traditional transmission is abnormal; then in language-learning disability or in retardation where genetic control of cognitive or language development is abnormal; then in the deaf, where the constraints of the vocal-auditory channel are replaced with the constraints of the visual-gestural channel; then in brain-damaged adults, where the neural structures supporting language are disrupted; and, finally, in psychopathology, where social and perhaps neural-cognitive structures differ from normal. From the perspective of this chapter, we look at these communication systems (a) to determine if they have the characteristics we have defined as necessary for language (Or are they more primitive, similar to, or different from, the chimpanzee's performance with human language?) and (b) to determine how the difference in biology or environment constrains the shape of language.

Before studying these atypical human populations, it is perhaps useful to consider normal human populations who nevertheless may deviate from typical adults in cognitive, perceptual, and social constraints on language as well as in language experience. Do all languages meet our language criteria? Are developing languages—pidgins, creoles, and child language—primitive in the sense of failing some criterion?

In several instances in this chapter, I pointed out that dialects, even a discriminated-against nonstandard one like AAEV, have the full complement of language features, including the higher-order ones of metalanguage, hierarchical structure, word play, and so on. This appears to be true even of the creoles that are developed by children exposed to pidgin language as a primary language: Creoles have a regular syntax, recursively embedding sentences, symbolic use of words, and function words (recruited from the content word vocabulary but regularized for this purpose). It is not true of pidgins, which, with no inflection or function words and irregularly applied syntactic ordering, lack duality of patterning, hierarchical structure, and metalanguage.

How about normal child language? (See Chapter 9 in *Language and Its Normal Processing* for the background for the data alluded to here.) Clearly, children are not born producing or understanding language as we know it. Applying our criteria to them rigorously as we did to the apes, at what point can we say that they have moved from a signal system to a symbol system and from a symbol system to a linguistic system, only then distinct from the animal systems we critiqued?

Between 1 and 2 years of age, children generally utter single words—to name, request, or draw attention to the referent. "Language" as such is not evident here because there is no apparent productivity (syntax), let alone hierarchical structure, and so on. In the one-word stage, we do see rapid fading, broadcast transmission and reception, interchangeability, and total feedback. (Indeed, these features appear before the child says any words; they are properties of crying and cooing.) Of more interest, at the one-word stage, there is evidence of specialization, semanticity, arbitrariness, and discreteness, as children control vocalization for speech and learn to apply the sounds of their language to unrelated referents.

At around the age of 2, children begin to produce two-word phrases, a rudimentary syntax perhaps missing in the ape language. To the extent that the combination of words does not create a new meaning, a semantic relation that extends beyond the meanings of the individual elements, this does not increase the languagelike features. Once the child combines more elements, however, we see the emergence of real language. Children begin to talk about things that are not currently occurring, indicating displacement. They seem to be regularly applying syntactic rules, indicating productivity. And they seem to be creating new, hierarchical units by combination, showing duality of patterning.

The other language features we discussed are either inapplicable or harder to assess. Traditional transmission, learnability, and simultaneity and smear clearly apply to the language acquired but not to the acquirer, and so are irrelevant. The folk wisdom is that children are less likely to lie (leading to embarrassing situations when a white lie would be expected), but there is no question that sometimes they cry for attention, deliberately implying a physical problem when there is none. Metacommunication is acquired in part by the three-word stage because children can respond to questions for names and ask such questions. But abilities to comprehend metaphors fully, to respond like adults to questions about segmentation of sentences or words, or to respond to linguistic aspects of words apart from their referents do not appear fully until much later, between school age and adolescence, depending on the skill.

Children transmit less information than adults, at least in our adult view, perhaps because they see less common ground and so provide details that we easily infer. When we respond to another's statement, we do so less redundantly with the previous utterance than does a child, but if children do not observe the redundancy, they are transmitting more information than we would be with the same utterance. Certainly, phonetically, children and adults transmit information at similar rates.

Finally, once children start forming higher-order units, after the two-word stage, they exhibit recursiveness: Sentences may contain conjoined sentences. Thus, with the possible exception of the metalanguage criterion, once children combine more than two elements, we may conclude that a child "has language"; with the metalanguage criterion, we have to say that children do not "have language" fully until adolescence.

Now, you may have been tempted to conclude that infants have language, because you know they will eventually. Such intuitive conclusions may have likewise biased you one way or the other with respect to the apes or to nonstandard human languages. I hope to have demonstrated that objective consideration is possible, as you evaluate the language produced against each criterion. You may reach conclusions different from mine by rejecting or adding particular criteria, but then do so consistently, for adults, animals, and children.

This is especially important as we examine the communications of the exceptional human populations, the brain damaged, learning disabled, psychotic, and deaf in the next chapters. Some will meet our criteria and will thus demonstrate the adequacy of language in the absence of a typical characteristic. Others will not, and will illustrate how changing that constraint critically alters language.

Indeed, young, prelingual children may fail to meet our language criteria because of limited memory or analytic skills (cognitive constraint), limited exposure to language (environmental constraint), or limited understanding of the needs and perspectives of others (social constraint). I suggested (in Chapter 9 in the companion volume) in fact that child language acquisition may be accomplished through a seamless coordination of the child's initially primitive and innate sensory, social, and communicative skills, with adults' innate caregiving responses, both gradually developing in tune with the child's developing cognitive skills and increasingly complex social and communication needs.

Deacon (1997) says in addition that what appear to be innate language-learning strategies may arise as different brain regions with different processing approaches develop and work on the language input. The same data will not distribute in the same way over a matured brain; thus child language acquisition may also instantiate a seamless coordination of language properties with brain development.

We turn next to consider the constraints of nature and nurture in language acquisition: What happens to children deprived of social contact or language during childhood? Does the developing human brain create language instinctively? Can *primary* language be acquired in adulthood? Can children suffer genetic impairment of language alone, or conversely, can language processing escape the ravages of cognitive retardation?

## REFERENCES

Ape language. (1981). *Science, 211,* 86-88.

Apfelbach, R. (1972). Electrically elicited vocalizations in the gibbon *Hylobates lar (Hylobatidae),* and their behavioral significance. *Zeitschrift für Tierpsychologie, 30,* 420-430.

Arensburg, B., & Tillier, A. M. (1991). Speech and the Neanderthals. *Endeavor* (New Series), *15,* 26-28.

Baker, M. C., Spitler-Nabors, K. J., & Bradley, D. C. (1981). Early experience determines song dialect responsiveness of female sparrows. *Science, 214,* 819-821.

Baptista, L. F., & Petrinovich, L. (1984). Social interaction, sensitive phases and the song template hypothesis in the white-crowned sparrow. *Animal Behaviour, 32,* 172-181.

Bentley, D. R., & Hoy, R. R. (1972). Genetic control of cricket song patterns. *Animal Behavior, 20,* 478-492.

Brines, M. C., & Gould, J. L. (1979). Bees have rules. *Science, 206,* 571-573.

Brown, R. (1958). *Words and things.* New York: Free Press.

Bruemmer, F. (1983). Sea lion shenanigans. *Natural History, 92,* 32-41.

Cheney, D. L., & Seyfarth, R. M. (1992). The representation of social relations by monkeys. *Cognition, 37,* 167-196.

Cherry, C. (1957). *On human communication.* Cambridge: Technology Press of MIT; New York: John Wiley.

Darwin, C. (n.d.). *The descent of man.* In *The origin of species and the descent of man* (pp. 445-495). New York: Modern Library. (Original work published 1871)

Deacon, T. W. (1997). *The symbolic species: The co-evolution of language and the brain.* New York: Norton.

Delgado, J. M. R. (1977). Hell and heaven within the brain. In P. Zimbardo & C. Maslach (Eds.), *Psychology for our times* (pp. 81-90). Glenview, IL: Scott, Foresman.

Dore, J. (1975). Holophrases, speech acts, and language universals. *Journal of Child Language, 2,* 21-40.

Duncan, S., Jr., & Fiske, D. W. (1977). *Face-to-face interaction.* Hillsdale, NJ: Lawrence Erlbaum.

Eimas, P. D., & Tartter, V. C. (1979). On the development of speech perception: Mechanisms and analogies. In H. W. Reese & L. P. Lipsitt (Eds.), *Advances in child development and behavior* (Vol. 13, pp. 155-193). New York: Academic Press.

Epstein, R., Lanza, R. P., & Skinner, B. F. (1980). Symbolic communication between two pigeons *(Columba livia domestica). Science, 207,* 543-545.

Fouts, R. S., & Fouts, D. H. (1989). Loulis in conversation with the cross-fostered chimpanzees. In R. A. Gardner, B. T. Gardner, & T. E. Van Cantfort (Eds.), *Teaching sign language to chimpanzees* (pp. 293-307). Albany: SUNY Press.

Fouts, R. S., Fouts, D. H., & Van Cantfort, T. E. (1989). The infant Loulis learns signs from cross-fostered chimpanzees. In R. A. Gardner, B. T. Gardner, & T. E. Van Cantfort (Eds.), *Teaching sign language to chimpanzees* (pp. 280-292). Albany: SUNY Press.

Gallup, G. G., Jr. (1979). Self-awareness in primates. *American Scientist, 67,* 417-421.

Gardner, R. A., & Gardner, B. T. (1969). Teaching sign language to a chimpanzee. *Science, 165,* 664-672.

Gardner, R. A., & Gardner, B. T. (1975). Early signs of language in child and chimpanzee. *Science, 187,* 752-753.

Gardner, R. A., Gardner, B. T., & Van Cantfort, T. E. (Eds.). (1989). *Teaching sign language to chimpanzees.* Albany: SUNY Press.

Gautier, J. P., & Gautier-Hion, A. (1982). Vocal communication within a group of monkeys: An analysis by biotelemetry. In C. T. Snowdon, C. H. Brown, & M. R. Peterson (Eds.), *Primate communication* (pp. 5-29). Cambridge: Cambridge University Press.

Gould, J. L. (1980). Sun compensation by bees. *Science, 207,* 545-547.

Griffin, D. R. (1984). *Animal thinking.* Cambridge, MA: Harvard University Press.

Heffner, H. E., & Heffner, R. S. (1984). Temporal lobe lesions and perception of species-specific vocalizations by macaques. *Science, 226,* 75-76.

Herman, L. M., Kuczaj, S. A., II, & Holder, M. D. (1993). Response to anomalous gestural sequences by a language-trained dolphin: Evidence for processing of semantic relations and syntactic information. *Journal of Experimental Psychology: General, 122,* 184-194.

Herrnstein, R. J., & Loveland, D. H. (1965). Complex visual concept in the pigeon. *Science, 146,* 549-551.

Hinde, R. (1972). Comments on Part A. In R. Hinde (Ed.), *Nonverbal communication* (pp. 86-98). Cambridge: Cambridge University Press.

Hirsch, H. V. B., & Tieman, S. B. (1987). Perceptual development and experience-dependent changes in cat visual cortex. In M. H. Bornstein (Ed.), *Sensitive periods in development: Interdisciplinary perspectives* (pp. 39-79). Hillsdale, NJ: Lawrence Erlbaum.

Hockett, C. F. (1960). The origin of speech. *Scientific American, 203,* 88-96.

Hockett, C. F., & Altmann, S. A. (1968). A note on design features. In T. A. Sebeok (Ed.), *Animal communication* (pp. 61-72). Bloomington: Indiana University Press.

Hofstadter, D. R. (1979). *Gödel, Escher, Bach: An eternal golden braid.* New York: Basic Books.

Hoy, R. R. (1974). Genetic control of acoustic behavior in crickets. *American Zoologist, 14,* 1067-1080.

Hoy, R. R., & Paul, R. C. (1973). Genetic control of song specificity in crickets. *Science, 180,* 82-83.

Jurgens, U. (1982). A neuroethological approach to the classification of vocalization in the squirrel monkey. In C. T. Snowdon, C. H. Brown, & M. R. Peterson (Eds.), *Primate communication* (pp. 50-67). Cambridge: Cambridge University Press.

Kroodsma, D. E. (1983, September). Marsh wrenditions. *Natural History,* pp. 43-46.

Labov, W. (1972). *Language in the inner city: Studies in the Black English vernacular.* Philadelphia: University of Pennsylvania Press.

LeMay, M., & Geschwind, N. (1978). Asymmetries of the human cerebral hemispheres. In A. Caramazza & E. B. Zurif (Eds.), *Language acquisition and language breakdown* (pp. 311-328). Baltimore: Johns Hopkins University Press.

Lenneberg, E. (1967). *Biological foundations of language.* New York: John Wiley.

Leppelsack, H. J., & Vogt, M. (1976). Responses of auditory neurons in the forebrain of a songbird to stimulation with species-specific sounds. *Journal of Comparative Physiology, 107,* 263-274.

Lieberman, P. (1987). *The biology and evolution of language.* Cambridge, MA: Harvard University Press.

Linden, E. (1986). *Silent partners: The legacy of the ape language experiments.* New York: Times Books.

Lyons, J. (1972). Human language. In R. Hinde (Ed.), *Nonverbal communication* (pp. 49-85). Cambridge: Cambridge University Press.

MacKay, D. M. (1972). Formal analysis of communicative processes. In R. A. Hinde (Ed.), *Nonverbal communication* (pp. 3-25). Cambridge: Cambridge University Press.

Marler, P. (1970). Birdsong and speech development: Could there be parallels? *American Scientist, 58,* 669-673.

Marler, P. (1975). On the origin of speech from animal sounds. In J. Kavanaugh & J. E. Cutting (Eds.), *The role of speech in language* (pp. 11-37). Cambridge: MIT Press.

Marler, P., & Mundinger, P. (1971). Vocal learning in birds. In H. Moltz (Ed.), *Ontogeny of vertebrate behavior* (pp. 389-449). New York: Academic Press.

Marx, J. L. (1982). How the brain controls birdsong. *Science, 217,* 1125-1126.

Miller, G. A. (1956). The magical number seven plus or minus two: Some limits on our capacity for processing information. *Psychological Review, 63,* 81-97.

Mistler-Lachman, J. L., & Lachman, A. (1974). Language in man, monkeys, and machines. *Science, 185,* 871-872.

Morris, C. (1964). *Signification and significance.* Cambridge: MIT Press.

Newman, J. D., & Wollberg, Z. (1973a). Multiple coding of species-specific vocalizations in the auditory cortex of squirrel monkeys. *Brain Research, 54,* 287-304.

Newman, J. D., & Wollberg, Z. (1973b). Responses of single neurons in the auditory cortex of squirrel monkeys to variants of a single call type. *Experimental Neurology, 40,* 821-824.

Nottebohm, F. (1970). Ontogeny of birdsong. *Science, 167,* 950-956.

Patterson, F. G. (1978a). Conversations with a gorilla. *National Geographic, 154,* 438-465.

Patterson, F. G. (1978b). The gestures of a gorilla: Language acquisition in another Pongid. *Brain & Language, 5,* 72-97.

Payne, R. S., & McVay, S. (1971). Songs of humpback whales. *Science, 173,* 585-597.

Pepperberg, I. M. (1981). Functional vocalizations by an African grey parrot (*psittacus erithacus*). *Zeitschrift für Tierpsychologie, 55,* 139-160.

Pepperberg, I. M. (1983). Cognition in the African grey parrot: Preliminary evidence for auditory/vocal comprehension of the class concept. *Animal Learning and Behavior, 11,* 179-185.

Pepperberg, I. M. (1987). Acquisition of the same/different concept by an African grey parrot (*psittacus erithacus*): Learning with respect to categories of color, shape, and material. *Animal Learning and Behavior, 15,* 423-432.

Peterson, M. R., Beecher, M. D., Zoloth, S. R., Moody, D. B., & Stebbins, W. C. (1978). Neural lateralization of species-specific vocalizations by Japanese macaques *(Macaca fuscata). Science, 202,* 324-326.

Pierce, J. R. (1972). Communication. *Scientific American, 227,* 31-41.

Premack, D. (1971). Language in chimpanzees. *Science, 172,* 808-822.

Premack, D. (1976). Language and intelligence in ape and man. *American Scientist, 64,* 674-683.

Premack, D. (1979). *Trivial language in a nontrivial mind.* Paper presented at the Western Psychological Association meeting, San Diego, CA.

Premack, D. (1986). *"Gavagai!" or the future history of the animal language controversy.* Cambridge: Bradford Books of MIT Press.

Premack, D., & Woodruff, G. (1978). Chimpanzee problem-solving: A test for comprehension. *Science, 202,* 532-535.

Rumbaugh, D. M. (1977). *Language learning by a chimpanzee: The Lana project.* New York: Academic Press.

Rumbaugh, D. M., Gill, T. V., & von Glaserfield, E. C. (1973). Reading and sentence completion by a chimpanzee *(Pan). Science, 182,* 731-733.

Savage-Rumbaugh, E. S. (1986). *Ape language: From conditioned response to symbol.* New York: Columbia University Press.

Savage-Rumbaugh, E. S., & Lewin, R. (1994). *Kanzi: The ape at the brink of the human mind.* New York: John Wiley.

Savage-Rumbaugh, E. S., & Rumbaugh, D. M. (1980). Requisites of symbolic communication—or, are words for birds. *Psychological Record, 30,* 305-318.

Savage-Rumbaugh, E. S., Rumbaugh, D. M., & Boysen, S. (1978). Symbolic communication between two chimpanzees *(Pan troglodytes). Science, 201,* 641-644.

Savage-Rumbaugh, E. S., Rumbaugh, D. M., & Boysen, S. (1980). Do apes use language? *American Scientist, 68,* 49-61.

Scheflen, A. E., & Scheflen, A. (1972). *Body language and social order.* Englewood Cliffs, NJ: Prentice Hall.

Scherer, K. R., & Giles, H. (Eds.). (1979). *Social markers in speech.* Cambridge: Cambridge University Press.

Schultz, J. L. (1983). Tree tactics. *Natural History, 92,* 12-25.

Snowdon, C. T. (1982). Linguistic and psycholinguistic approaches to primate communication. In C. T. Snowdon, C. H. Brown, & M. R. Peterson (Eds.), *Primate communication* (pp. 212-238). Cambridge: Cambridge University Press.

Stevens, K. N. (1989). On the quantal nature of speech. *Journal of Phonetics, 17,* 3-45. (Reprinted in R. D. Kent, B. S. Atal, & J. L. Miller, Eds., 1991, *Papers in speech communication: Speech production,* pp. 357-400. Woodbury, NY: Acoustical Society of America)

Terrace, H. S., Petitto, L. A., Sanders, R. J., & Bever, T. G. (1979). Can an ape create a sentence? *Science, 206,* 891-902.

Thompson, C. R., & Church, R. M. (1980). An explanation of the language of a chimpanzee. *Science, 208,* 313-314.

Thorpe, W. H. (1972). The comparison of vocal communication in animals and man. In R. A. Hinde (Ed.), *Nonverbal communication* (pp. 153-175). Cambridge: Cambridge University Press.

Tinbergen, N. (1952). The curious behavior of the stickleback. *Scientific American, 187,* 22-26.

Tinbergen, N. (1955). *The study of instinct.* Oxford: Oxford University Press.

von Frisch, K. (1974). Decoding the language of the bee. *Science, 185,* 663-668.

Wade, N. (1980). Does man alone have language? Apes reply in riddles and a horse says neigh. *Science, 208,* 1349-1351.

Wollberg, Z., & Newman, J. D. (1972). Auditory cortex of squirrel monkey: Response patterns of single cells to species-specific vocalizations. *Science, 175,* 212-214.

Woodruff, G., & Premack, D. (1979). Intentional communication in the chimpanzee: The development of deception. *Cognition, 7,* 333-362.

Zaretsky, M. D. (1971). Cricket song-patterned response in a central neurone. *Nature, 229,* 195-196.

## STUDY QUESTIONS

1. Discuss the genetic control of transmission-reception, tunable blueprint model, call detector model, and sexual selection with respect to their potential influences on human communication. For each, explain the phenomenon with respect to the organism it was described in, and then explain how it might also (have) work(ed) in humans.

2. Briefly describe body language and paralanguage in human signaling. Are these communication? Why or why not? (Discuss this from the point of view expressed in the chapter, but critically; if you disagree, indicate why, how, and the implications.) Is body language language? Again, why or why not? Be critical!

3. Critically discuss the design features for language. Do you think the chimpanzees have demonstrated human language capability? Why or why not?

4. Discuss biological mechanisms that may have specially developed in humans to subserve our communication system. Consider their analogues in the animal kingdom and whether they confer a "special" capacity for symbolic thinking in us.

5. Take the design features for language and communication presented here and, for each, discuss when and how it appears in child language acquisition. At what age do you think children "have language"? Which (if any) design features do you therefore consider noncritical? (Be sure in your answer to present data from language acquisition, such as when and in what form children first use the vocal-auditory channel or exhibit displacement.)

# Genetics Versus Environment: Nature's Experiments in Language Learning

What happens if children are neglected for 13 years or so and thus are exposed neither to the human social contact usual for developing language nor to specific language structures during early maturation? Can they learn language? Does the acquisition process at a later age look "normal," or have some critical periods for learning passed so that new techniques must be used for language learning? Do adults talk to alinguistic *adolescents* in the same way as they do to alinguistic *infants,* or do they naturally model different language? Does it matter for how long the child has been language-deprived?

Suppose the children are treated lovingly but are not exposed by parents to appropriate language—say, if the children are deaf? In this case, the social situation should be appropriate to stimulate communication rather than suppress it, but specific language experience is removed. Do children spontaneously activate innate language structures? What form do these take given neither the adult example nor auditory feedback from the child's own productions?

Finally, consider children who are raised normally but who do not learn language, literacy, or other skills as normal children do. Do the disability and compensatory interventions suggest a range of individual difference, a general cognitive deficit subsuming language, or a genetically dysfunctional language module?

In Chapter 1, I reviewed the circumstances of the development of human communication normally—a loving, caring home with native-language-speaking caretakers interacting with the infant, if not actively teaching. I questioned whether aspects of language acquisition might be innate and reflexive or innate and requiring environmental interaction to prime, perhaps during critical periods (as we saw in the last chapter for white-crowned sparrow song acquisition), or whether language is learned similarly to other statistically regular occurrences. I also questioned the effect of parental interaction on language development: Do parents tailor their language to children and provide them with feedback? Does this help the child learn?

As we have noted, study of normal language acquisition cannot yield definitive answers to these questions because in normal acquisition all factors are confounded: The child is cared for and given appropriate stimulation; the child receives language input from birth so it is difficult to tell whether there is a critical period; and the parents are appropriate interactive responders so we cannot tell if the child is being shaped by them or would learn language anyway. In this chapter, we will look at some cases of abnormal language acquisition that can help separate these individual potential influences. Three types of abnormal development will be examined: (a) neglected, abandoned, or abused children deprived both of social contact generally and of language specifically; (b) congenitally deaf children raised normally by hearing parents but without specific training in manual language (children raised by signing parents who provide a language model will be discussed in the next chapter); and (c) children with language learning abnormalities seemingly independent of other cognitive abnormalities.

## INTERPRETING THE EXPERIMENTS: SOME CAUTIONS

The data we will be discussing derive from case histories, which are *not* experiments. In an experiment, the experimenters control potential outside influences and manipulate the factor(s) they are interested in studying. An ideal, although horribly unethical, experiment would be to take identical triplets, raise one with normal language, one with love but no language, and one in isolation with only physical needs attended to (à la Psammetichus—see Chapter 1). We would thus know that the subjects were genetically identical and so could confidently attribute language learning differences to their environments.

In the case histories we will be examining, we have in many instances no knowledge of whether the child was normal at birth or what its experiences were before its discovery by civilization. Therefore, if the child does not develop language normally, we do not know whether that was because the child had an innate learning disability (which might have led to its neglect or abandonment) and would never have learned language, or was too old to learn language at the point of discovery.

A second problem of interpretation lies in the fact that 13 years of neglect does not mean 13 years of no experience. Aside from the lack of social stimulation, which might deter language learning, an adolescent will have learned how to survive in whatever bizarre world has been created for it. For example, one of the children we will study, Genie, upon discovery at age 13 displayed an unnatural love of plastic objects, preferring them to other toys or objects provided for her entertainment, collecting not only plastic jewelry and toys but also plastic plates, trash cans, and so forth. One interpretation of this could be that all children innately like plastic, but most deflect this interest given exposure to, say, stuffed animals. A second interpretation might be that at the age of 13 a love of plastic unfolds in all children but is not normally noticed because so many other interests are still being pursued from earlier development. The third, and in this case obviously most likely, explanation is that something happened in this child's experience that caused an abnormal interest in plastic. In Genie's case, the only objects in the room where she was confined for many years were plastic raincoats and plastic cottage cheese containers. Although in this case the cause is obvious, we cannot always clearly attribute a learning abnormality to particular prior experience, its absence, or an unfolding blueprint.

A similar, if less dramatic, difficulty appears in interpreting language acquisition data from deaf children raised in homes where the parents deliberately suppress gestural communication to encourage or force the child to learn to speak and lipread. Although the motive is benign, the suppression may "teach" the child not to try to communicate at all.

Another problem in interpreting data on language development in older children is that the "teaching" techniques are probably not identical. When talking to an infant, adults use simpler sentences, redundant with nonverbal context, and exaggerate facial expressions and intonation. It is not clear that beyond speaking more loudly and slowly, we simplify our language in talking to adults who do not understand us. It is quite possible that part of our innate response as adults to "babyishness" (in addition to finding it cute and wanting to care for it) may be a simplified language pattern. Older children will not elicit sympathy for crying or wetting themselves; likewise, they may not elicit the same solicitous parental language model. Thus the older child's different learning pattern could arise either from a different teaching program by the caretaker or from a different set of skills acquired by maturity or prior experience.

Finally, we must consider the systematic differences, "social/expressive" or "analytic/referential" (mentioned in Chapter 1), in learning styles that many investigators have found in children initially learning language. Language is sufficiently redundant to allow full learning regardless of which approach is taken to it. Thus, children who appear very retarded with respect to learning abstract cognitive skills may be unable to analyze in general and show some language disturbance but have language relatively well preserved, having taken the social tack of mastering it. A particular pattern of skill loss and preservation may therefore reflect a *preserved general cognitive learning style, not a preserved module*. Indeed, failure of a brain region to develop normally may result in hypernormal activity (due to neural displacement) of other regions with a distinctive mark on particular cognitive processes, creating idiot savants perhaps (Deacon, 1997).

## FERAL CHILDREN

From time to time, adults have found children surviving alone in the wild, and assumed they were cared for by animals. Probably the best known of such stories in Western culture is the legend of Romulus and Remus, typical in many respects except for the ultimate stardom of the abandoned children. Romulus and Remus were twin heirs to an ancient throne, ordered drowned by a usurping uncle. Rather than drown them, their executioner set the infants in a basket on the flooding, turbulent waters of the Tiber. A pair of healthy, if grubby, infants were later found downriver, in the den of a she-wolf, apparently suckled by the animal. Restored to civilization, the infants lived to found Rome. Similar stories, occasionally based on stronger evidence of animal rearing, have arisen in many parts of the world.

### *Credibility of Reports*

Whether such children are in fact reared by animals or manage to survive by themselves in the wild is a moot question. As several investigators (for example, Dennis, 1941; Tyler, 1863; Zingg, 1940) have noted, there is a bias on the part of observers to attribute rearing of wild children to animals. Such children act barbarically, and it is assumed that they have acquired their "manners" from animals. Small children are not believed able to fend for themselves in the wild, and so it is surmised that they have been helped by animals. And the children are often discovered in animal dens or in the company of animals, suggesting to the discoverers that the association is customary.

There is reason to be skeptical of these reports, however. If animals do rear human children, we would expect to hear stories about the same animals in that role around the world. In fact, the animals assigned the role of foster parents vary predictably in different regions depending on the prevailing mythology of the region. If wolves are seen as near-human—think about our concept of were-wolves—they seem to be frequent adopters. In parts of the world where bears are seen as humanlike, bears seem to rear abandoned infants more than wolves. This suggests *bias* on the part of the observers. Moreover, discovery in an animal den or in the company of animals does not necessarily imply rearing by those animals. The child may have fled from human pursuers and taken shelter in the cave of an animal but not permanently live there. Finally, reports of the suckling of children for several years are incredible because most mammal mothers wean their own young after a few months and would likely generalize those habits to their human adoptee.

### *Review of Early Cases*

It would be good to know whether the wild children had indeed been raised with the benefit of the social company of animals or had lived in isolation. However, even without that knowledge, we can look at their behavior before and after rehabilitation to society to see what deprivation of human contact in the early years produces. There is no doubt that there have been children who have suffered extreme neglect and survived, and these children, interestingly, seem to show similar perceptual, social, linguistic, and cognitive capabilities on initial rescue. Some have been totally rehabilitated to society; others have never completely recovered from their early experience. The chances of rehabilitation may depend on individual differences among the children, different prewilderness or wilderness experience, and/or the age at which they were discovered and rehabilitation began.

Zingg (1940) reviewed 31 such reported cases beginning in the fourteenth century. The common characteristics (aside from observer bias) were insensitivity to heat and cold, unwillingness to share, repressed sexual expression, keen eyesight, especially at night, and beastlike eating habits such as sniffing food before eating, killing and eating animals raw, eating raw starches and vegetables (like potatoes), and having a distaste for normal human foods like bread. Many of the children were also reported to run on all fours and to be quite scarred and calloused. Most were mute when discovered and made at most animal-like sounds. Of these 31 children, 4 learned to talk reasonably fluently (1 became a nun), and 1 acquired 50 words after recovery. For 2 of those who acquired fluent speech, there are no data about the age of rescue or methods of teaching language (this includes the nun); another of them was recovered at about age 10; the last, Kaspar Hauser, was not a wild child but one imprisoned with human caretakers, and so his recovery is not as remarkable. He will be discussed in the next section.

Given the paucity of data on the children, as Zingg decided, drawing conclusions about their capacities is unwarranted. However, we should note that most of the children who could not be rehabilitated to speak were discovered at 8 to 12 years of age.

The child who learned 50 words is a documented case of a child reared by animals. She was discovered in 1920 in India at about age 8. Rumors had been reported of children running with the wolves. Tracks led to a den in which were discovered two children, one about 8 years and one about 18 months, clasped together in a ball with two wolf cubs (Brown, 1958). The younger child, named Amala, died within a year after rescue, after having begun to utter some sounds. The older child, Kamala, lived for about 10 years, developed social skills, and learned 50 words.

## Victor: A Well-Documented Case

The wild child for whom there are the most data, Victor, was discovered more than a century before Amala and Kamala, roaming the fields of France (see Lane, 1979). He was about 13 at the time of his final rescue and return to civilization. He was entrusted to the care of Dr. Itard, who "experimented" with the child to see (a) what the condition of a man-of-nature actually was (an important philosophical issue of the time) and (b) whether such a person could be rehabilitated to a "normal" life.

*Perceptual Sensitivities*

The same reports were made of Victor, "the wild boy of Aveyron," as were made of most wild children—insensitive to temperature, uncivilized appetite, running on all fours, and so on. Some of these Dr. Itard substantiated and some he refuted. Victor was able to thrust his hand into a fire to retrieve potatoes and he would eat them directly, making noises of pain, indicating that he did feel, but ignored, the heat. He was able to run naked—in fact, preferred to do so—in the dead of winter and showed no sensitivity to the cold. Generally, he sniffed his food before eating and preferred potatoes and nuts (raw) to cooked meats, bread, and vegetables. But Dr. Itard never observed him going around on all fours, nor were his palms and knees particularly calloused as they would have been if this had been his usual mode of locomotion. Dr. Itard wrote that he doubted it was possible for a human to assume such a stance comfortably or efficiently.

*Training Victor*

Victor was trained by Dr. Itard for five years, during which time he showed considerable progress in sensory, emotional, moral, cognitive, and linguistic development. Of as much interest as Victor's progress are Dr. Itard's teaching methods, which often foreshadow the behavioristic techniques (discussed in the previous chapter to teach the plastic language to Sarah) of shaping, fading, reinforcing, and punishing. His procedure has influenced current educational programs for the deaf, mentally disabled, and psychotic as well as the Montessori program of education.

*Developing the Experience of Punishment and Reinforcement*

The first problem was that Victor seemed relatively insensitive to outside stimulation, so that little could serve to reinforce or punish a behavior. Moreover, Victor seemed to have very short visual and auditory attention spans. His main motivations were to escape and to address physical needs such as hunger. To increase Victor's sensitivities, Dr. Itard began a program of tactile stimulation, giving the boy long hot baths and massages. This increased not only his temperature and tactile awareness (he began to dislike going out in the cold, would test his bath water before entering it, and enjoyed stroking velvet) but also generalized to all forms of sensory stimulation.

The next task was to develop, in modern terminology, *secondary reinforcers,* so that social praise might serve as the reward (it is initially paired with a primary reinforcer, which is then faded) removing Victor from the beastlike interest in food. Dr. Itard accomplished this while improving Victor's visual attention. He placed a nut (the primary reinforcer) under one of three cups and rewarded Victor with the nut if he was able to keep track of it when he moved the cups. Eventually the "shell game" became fun for itself and the primary reinforcer was gradually removed. Similarly, secondary reinforcers were mapped to trips outside and so on. Social reinforcement (praise) or punishment (dismay) became sufficient to control behaviors.

## *Developing Emotions*

Dr. Itard was also interested in measuring and training emotional responses. At first Victor was never seen to cry, although sometimes he smiled or laughed. After some time in civilization, he would shed tears (even tears of joy on reuniting with his governess after an escape, and then again, when she reproached him, in sadness, at the tone of her voice). Victor also began to exhibit more "refined" emotions. Shortly after his governess' husband had died, he set the table with a place setting for the man, as had been customary. This caused an outburst of grief from the widow, which seemed to cause Victor considerable pain. He cleared the place setting and never again made that error. Another time, Dr. Itard pretended to be about to punish Victor after a correct performance, to see how he would respond to the injustice. Normally, Victor submitted passively to punishment, but this time he resisted, biting the doctor, who was pleased nevertheless at the exhibit of moral awareness.

It might seem that we have digressed considerably from a discussion of language, but it is important to remember that *language serves a function of human communication in human social settings.* As such, the child must understand that communication is possible and enables participation in a social group, and, second, that interaction in the group depends on a shared understanding of "rules" within the culture. For children to learn language through a social/expressive style, they must experience it socially. We have also seen that communicating meaning requires establishing common ground and inferring the speaker's intent, the utterance's *illocutionary force,* dependent on "cooperative principles." Both language and nonverbal communication depend on such shared understanding. They do not develop in a social vacuum. Thus, for someone whose "culture" is 13 years of isolated living in the wild, the first step is socialization, to understand the speakers' culture.

Language depends not only on the mutual understanding necessary for communication but also on specific cognitive and perceptual skills. To understand speech, for example, hearing must be good, differential attention must be paid to vocal and other noises, some variations in speech sounds must be ignored and others attended to (categorical perception), and memory must be adequate for storing the rapidly fading signals. After socialization, therefore, it is necessary to assess and develop cognitive and perceptual abilities before training language itself.

## *Teaching Speech*

With respect to language development and language training, Dr. Itard noted first that Victor was neither deaf nor mute. Victor would turn when there was a sudden loud noise or the softer noise produced by cracking a nut. Victor made laughing sounds spontaneously and was induced to imitate some speech sounds. The process of teaching imitation was to strike one of three noisemakers (a bell or drum, for example) and then allow Victor the opportunity of reproducing the action. After Victor learned this task, Dr. Itard moved to reproduction of sound in the vocal tract, which took a long time and resulted in the acquisition of only a few vowels.

Lane (1979) pointed out that Victor might have learned more speech had Dr. Itard not trained speech using the letters of the alphabet, which do not map to speech sounds uniquely (consider all the ways "e" may be pronounced, and that the sound of "f" may also be written "gh" and "ph," for example). A better choice would have been to teach through phonetic features, which map more directly to the vocal gestures Victor would have been trying to make, or phonemes, for which, unlike letters, there is a direct sound association.

### Teaching Visual Speech

Despairing at last of teaching Victor speech, Dr. Itard began to teach him language through vision, using gestural communication and written words. Victor spontaneously "gestured"—fetching his coat to indicate he wanted to go out, or other people's coats to indicate that it was time for them to go, understanding when handed a pitcher that he was to go fetch water. Unfortunately, this was never worked into a sign system.

Instead, Dr. Itard trained written language, using a method of shaping. First, Victor was required to select for each of several objects the picture of that object. Victor would not do this spontaneously. Dr. Itard had noticed that Victor liked things to be neat, and used this to train him. He placed some objects in a row with their pictures behind them and then scrambled the objects, indicating to Victor that he was to put them back in order, still indicated by the pictures. Victor complied, but Dr. Itard noted that the correct performance could have been due to his remembering the original order or matching the objects to the pictures. To test this, he changed the order of the pictures; Victor still returned the objects to the original order. By increasing the number of pictures and objects and the frequency of their scrambling, Dr. Itard succeeded in getting Victor to attend to the pictures as representations of the objects.

Then the second stage began: mapping the letter names (written words) to the pictures. This also initially failed because Victor did not know the alphabet. Backtracking, Dr. Itard taught him the alphabet by using a *matching-to-sample* technique, where one cutout letter was given as a sample and Victor had to select the matching alternative from a set of cutout letters. This technique was used to train finer and finer discriminations until Victor had learned the alphabet.

Then, again using matching-to-sample, Dr. Itard taught spelling—with a board on which letters could be mounted, anticipating Premack's technique with Sarah more than 150 years later. Victor was taught how to spell the names of objects he frequently requested such as *lait* (French for milk) so that he could use his written language to make such requests. Several such words were taught, ending the first nine months of Victor's return to civilization. At that time, Dr. Itard made his first report on Victor's progress. He concluded that man's nature when deprived of civilization is nonintelligent, amoral, and savage; that social responses and social needs must be learned; that individualized training could overcome previous experience; and that this imitative force, whose purpose is the education of his organs and especially the apprenticeship of speech, and which is very energetic and active during the first years of his life, wanes rapidly with age, with isolation, and with all the causes which tend to blunt nervous sensitivity. We may conclude that the articulation of sounds, indisputably the most unimaginable and useful result of imitation, must encounter innumerable obstacles at any age later than early childhood. (quoted in Lane, 1979, p. 129)

### Teaching Words

Dr. Itard continued training Victor for another four and a half years, at the end of which he wrote a second report. During this time, he taught Victor to apply the names of objects he had learned to object classes rather than to individual objects. To do this, he had to teach similarities between objects that had previously been considered different—for example, a knife and a razor could be individual objects that form a class, "cutting tool" or some such. Once the similarity was learned in these disparate objects, the principle of object classes formed by shared function (such as "tool"), visual similarity, or whatever was acquired. Not only did this training give Victor the needed "rules" for forming semantic classes, it also provided a new mental flexibility: Victor in one instance took a small, curved picture down from the wall and held it horizontally as a substitute for a plate, to request food.

Beyond teaching superordinate classes and additional object names, Dr. Itard taught Victor adjectives and verbs. Large and small books were selected and Victor was taught to differentiate them using the appropriate adjective, then the adjective pair was applied to nails to see if the concept generalized; familiar objects were manipulated differently and then their names combined with verbs "naming" the manipulation, and the verbs were then transferred to manipulations of new objects—very much again like Premack did with Sarah (see Chapter 2).

As Victor's vocabulary and grammar grew, placing the word names on the board became cumbersome, so Dr. Itard taught Victor to write by imitation. Ultimately, Victor could write words from memory and use his writing to communicate his needs. The size of his vocabulary or complexity of his grammar were not discussed.

### Summary

There are several fascinating points to be gleaned from Victor's story (together with those of the other wild children). Probably most important is the fact that there is some language recovery even after a long period of isolation. This could be because the wild children did have some language before their life in the wild. As Dennis (1951) observed, to survive on their own in the wild, most of the children must have been abandoned after infancy so that they were already mobile and eating solid foods. This suggests that they were somewhat socialized before their wild lives started. However, their behavior showed no residue of early socialization, arguing *against* a hypothesis of durability of early experience. On the other hand, most were not able to shed the effects of years in the wild to learn language, which investigators use, illogically and inconsistently, to support the notion of permanence of early experience.

If Victor knew no language when abandoned, we could conclude that the critical period for such things as symbolic naming or forming simple sentences extends to the teens, if it ever ends. On the other hand, *spontaneous* naming, *spontaneous* vocal imitation, and vocalization itself seem to require early stimulation to emerge. (If Victor had some language, we would make a similar argument and say that functions like symbolic naming do not need stimulation to be maintained but those like vocalization do.)

It is interesting to note also that basic social and perceptual responses need encouragement in early childhood or they either die out or are never formed. Note too that writing may be acquired in the absence of speaking. However, his speech perception and analysis skills may have been intact and employed to this end. (As I reviewed in Chapter 1, phonological decoding provides an important route to interpreting print.)

Finally, we must note the parallels and relative effectiveness between Dr. Itard's teaching techniques and those used to train chimpanzees to communicate or to train "normal" children. There is no question that operant procedures can be effective tools for teaching language and can work as well for humans as for chimpanzees. Whether Victor learned more (or less) than Sarah as a result of his human nature (or years in the wild) is impossible to say, given the information we have available on his language. But there is no question that he received different and more rigorous language training than do most children, with a less beneficial effect. His poorer performance may be due to his age at first exposure, the years of neglect, the differences in training technique, or some combination of these causes.

In sum, although we are not sure about Victor's earliest experiences, the advances that he made after rescue suggest that the effects of early experience are not immutable: Either he changed twice, losing early socialization in the wild and then losing wild behavior back in civilization, or only once, with the latter. Language did not "unfold" in Victor or the other children once they were exposed to it, either because UG does not exist as a language-learning aid or because it had turned off already. However, at late ages, vocabulary, concepts, and perhaps syntax seem to be teachable by behaviorist techniques. This does not prove that such techniques are used in natural language acquisition, because it is conceivable that natural language learning may make use of UG, the critical period for which had passed in these children, or that language processing may distribute differently across the developing brain (aiding its analysis as in less is more; see Chapter 1) than across the mature one. Finally, Victor's case and Dr. Itard's success point to the importance of social environment in developing language.

## DEPRIVED CHILDREN

In the last section, we looked at language development in children socially isolated from human culture. To rehabilitate isolates, the effects of absence of appropriate

---

**Box 3.1. Feral Children**

Caveats

Reports of children raised by animals are likely overstated because the animal varies depending on the cultural view, unlikely if it was an unbiased observation.

We cannot know the early experience of an "abandoned" child, or whether the child was abandoned because it was cognitively or socially abnormal.

Common Characteristics of Confirmed Cases
— Inattentive to tactile sensations
— Mute
— Hypersensitive to smell
— Eats uncooked food
— Antisocial

What Can Be Learned

Using behavioristic techniques, social interests can be established and then used to reinforce language, but not speech, acquisition. Spontaneous imitation of language is nonexistent.

The different learning style may result from the passing of a critical period for language acquisition per se, or from the approach to language processing taken by a mature, not developing, brain.

---

social stimulation and social contact and of lack of specific language models both must be overcome. In the feral children, we cannot tell if learning failures result from either or both.

There are several reported cases of children who were raised without a language model or normal cognitive and sensory stimulation but who still have contact with some semblance of human society, so they do not have to fend for themselves, do not acquire savage mannerisms, and are not forming their first human affectionate contacts in their teens. Rehabilitation of these children has been more successful than of the wild children.

## Early Cases

An early such case is that of Kaspar Hauser, found in 1828 at about the age of 17, referred to in the previous section as one of the cases restored to fluent speech. He has been assumed to have been the heir to the throne of a small state in Germany, imprisoned at a young age in a dungeon, and hidden from view so the usurpers' plot would not be discovered. His recorded memories after discovery indicate some contact with human beings: He had two hobbyhorses and a toy dog to play with and was fed on bread and water. There are some discrepancies in the literature about his case, but it appears that he had some language when he was found: According to Zingg (1940), he spoke one sentence on discovery, quite garbled; according to Marcus (1996), he could neither speak nor understand speech upon discovery but could write his name. Either indicates some human contact in prison, or some language before (which he *forgot* during confinement). He was stabbed to death five years after rescue, before which time he had learned enough to attempt an autobiographical account (Marcus, 1996), achieving sufficient speech and literacy to become a legal clerk (Zingg, 1940).

Within this century, there have been several cases of similarly deprived children (in the United States) for whom we have more data on their initial condition, their training, and their ultimate condition. Anna (Davis, 1940, 1947) was "found" when she was 5 years old. She was illegitimate, which infuriated her mother's father. He had tried to farm her out to several foster homes, but the social welfare agency decided ultimately that she should go home. Her grandfather then kept Anna and her mother confined in the attic. Note that although deprived, she still had the social company and care of her mother (who was similarly deprived).

Anna was visited by Davis three days after her removal to an orphanage. Davis reported that her reflexes were good, that she was able to localize to sound, that she showed good touch sensitivities, and that she was able to grasp and manipulate objects with her hands. However, she was apathetic and did not engage in social play but in asocial ritualistic play with her own fingers. (*Ritualistic* means repetitive—where the same movement or movement sequence is performed over and over again. Finger-drumming is ritualistic as is hair twirling, both ritualistic behaviors observed in many normal adults.) A year later, she was able to walk alone and to respond to verbal commands and recognize people. She displayed some interest in getting attention from others. She was still relatively insensitive to outside stimuli, barely wincing when a blown-up paper bag was popped. Of interest, a clinician who visited her at the time reported that her spontaneous speech was in the "babbling stage" (Davis, 1947, p. 433). It is unclear whether this means that the 6-year-old was now engaging in the same kind of behavior found in 6-month-olds (babbling many sounds from different languages) or was speaking unintelligibly; there are no other reports of babbling in isolated children.

On Davis's last visit in 1941, Anna had regained considerable physical coordination: She was able to bounce and catch a ball and eat with a spoon. She also spoke like a 2-year-old, using some simple sentences. She died the following year, so whether her language would have continued to progress will never be known. Nevertheless, she, like Kaspar Hauser and unlike the wild children, showed gains in recovering speech. This could be because of her relatively young age or because of her incomplete isolation from human society.

Anna had not been given specific, individual training as had Victor; she was placed in an orphanage and given only physical care. She might have more fully and quickly recovered had language been specifically trained. Another child discovered at about the same age and same time, Isabelle (Mason, 1942), made considerably greater progress, but with specific training.

Isabelle was imprisoned, with her mother, by her maternal grandfather. Her mother seems to have done her best to care for her, so she was less socially deprived than the other cases. However, her mother could not model language, being both deaf and mute from 2 years of age as a result of brain damage from a traumatic accident. Therefore, Isabelle spent her first six and a half years in silence; then her mother escaped with her and had her admitted to a hospital. Isabelle spent her first few days in the hospital in tears and then displayed a generally flat, apathetic affect, not uncommon for young children separated from parents.

Mason was able to capture Isabelle's interest by lavishing attention on another child on the ward; Isabelle began to imitate what the other child was doing to get attention for herself. Mason then initiated a game of labeling body parts and jewelry to which Isabelle could point, beginning language training. Although Isabelle attended to sounds, learned to respond to words, and readily imitated gestures, she did not spontaneously imitate speech. This had to be shaped. After one month, she produced single words: "mama," "fat," "pretty," and "bye," in appropriate contexts. Two months later, she had progressed to short sentences, also appropriately: "That's my baby [doll]," "open your eyes," "'top it [stop it]," and "'at's mine [that's mine]." At the same time, she could read some printed words. A year after rehabilitation began, she was able to write, count, add tens, listen attentively to, and paraphrase, stories with her own small vocabulary.

Eighteen months after initial training, her vocabulary was estimated to be 1,500-2,000 words and her sentence structure was complex. The following are examples of spontaneous questions she asked: Why does the paste come out if one upsets the jar? What did Miss Mason say when you told her I cleaned my classroom? Do you go to Miss Mason's school at the university? These illustrate knowledge of correct inflectional morphology, pronouns, and prepositions, and, more impressively, good grasp of linguistic meaning, world knowledge, and complex syntactic structure like question formation, sentence conjunction, and embedding.

It is obvious that Isabelle's recovery was spectacular, compared with that of other children we have discussed. Moreover, in her case, it is likely that she had little, if any, early exposure to language, given that her mother's condition precluded that. (It is possible that her grandfather talked to her but, given his general neglect, not likely.) We can attribute the extent of her recovery to several factors: her lack of social isolation given her strong relationship with her mother, her young age on discovery, and the specific individual training she received. Her social contacts meant that social needs did not have to be taught: Isabelle cried (recall that tears were rare in wild children until after socialization) and sought human attention; therefore, attention and its removal could be used immediately as social reinforcers and punishers. Her age and training enabled her to learn speech, impossible for Victor. Still, speech acquisition seems markedly different at $6\frac{1}{2}$ years than at 1 year: There is no spontaneous imitation and no play with sounds, once produced. Syntactic and semantic skills are recoverable, and Isabelle went from single words to sentences (and learned to read!) about 12 times faster than normal.

### Conclusions

Comparing Isabelle and Anna with the wild children, we can see the benefits of early exposure to language as well as early exposure to some society. There are several reasons that these children may have advanced beyond Victor. They were younger; thus from the standpoint of UG or critical periods, the innate guide or blueprint for language learning may still have been operative. From a learning standpoint, they had less experience before socialization, which would have meant less to overcome to acquire new habits. And, finally, because they were younger, what was expected of them may have better matched their capabilities.

To clarify this last point, consider the 6½-year-old Isabelle, who, from a Piagetian standpoint, should be either *preoperational* or in the *concrete operation* stage. Thus she should be developing and modifying *schemes* (mental structures or concepts) for concrete objects, which would also be what her teachers would be providing labels for. Victor, at 13 and a survivor, would no longer be studying objects like potatoes and nuts to produce complete schemes for them because he already would have such schemes. Therefore, when Dr. Itard would try to direct attention back to those objects to teach a label, there would be a mismatch that could retard learning.

Thus the facile language learning we see in younger children could lie in their getting labels for things that are uppermost in their thoughts. The advanced development of Isabelle over Victor can thus be explained by a bioprogram for language, by cognitive/social constraints affecting language learning, or by different (tacit) teaching/modeling techniques. By contrast to Victor's, her case supports, for whatever reason, the advantage of early language learning. The two cases together emphasize the importance of social contact in language acquisition.

## A Well-Documented Case: Genie

The isolated child for whom we have the most data is known as Genie (Curtiss, 1977; Curtiss, Fromkin, Krashen, Rigler, & Rigler, 1974; Fromkin, Krashen, Curtiss, Rigler, & Rigler, 1974). Discovered in 1971, she has been tested and trained according to current psycholinguistic theory and procedures. Thus her skills are the most easily compared with normal acquisition and normal adult language.

### History

Genie's history resembles that of Anna and Isabelle. She was born to a weak mother and an abusive father who hated children. They had had two children previously: The older had died of pneumonia from being kept in the garage; the younger was saved from a similar fate by the father's mother. Unfortunately for Genie, this woman died about a year after Genie's birth, unleashing the father's full abuse. The father preserved his mother's room as a sanctuary, and Genie was confined in the only other room on that floor. Strapped to a chair by day and bundled in a special harness at night, Genie was severely restricted in both movement and sensation. The only visible "decorations" in her room were two plastic raincoats hanging on the wall. A single window allowed light but was too high for her to see out of. She also heard few sounds because the room next to hers was empty and her father, hating noise, did not allow either a television set or a radio in the house and beat Genie for any sound she made. Her food was restricted to baby foods, fed to her by spoon.

Hospital records indicate that Genie was probably normal at birth; she weighed 7½ pounds and appeared alert. She had a congenital hip dislocation, which was treated, and she was seen twice by the doctor who put on and removed the splint. Both times she seemed normal, although at the second visit, when she was nearly a year old, she was somewhat underweight.

She was not discovered until she was 13½ when her mother, who was nearly blind, was allowed to go to an eye doctor for treatment. Genie accompanied her and as soon as she was seen in public she was recognized as highly abnormal and taken to a social welfare agency. The father committed suicide the next day.

### Condition on Discovery

Suffering from severe malnutrition, Genie was admitted to a hospital. Like the wild children, she was insensitive to temperature and touch. She was also completely silent, even throwing tantrums without making a sound—not surprising considering that she had been punished for every whimper. Unlike the wild children, her attitude was social: She made good eye contact and gave the impression of understanding to the hospital staff. Within one month after her removal to the hospital, she recognized the words "Genie," "mother," "walk," "go," "no," "don't," "door," "jewelry," "box," "rattle," "bunny," "red," "blue," "green," and "brown." She attended to mouth movements and tried to imitate them, soundlessly. Seven months after admission to the hospital (age 14 years and 2 months), her doctor recorded this conversation:

Dr. We have to put it back now.
G. Back.
Dr. That's hot.
G. Burn.

### Language Tests

*Sound skills.* Genie was first tested formally in 1973, three years after her rescue (age 16½). She had in the meantime been discharged from the hospital and placed in a foster home, where she received informal "training" from her foster family in communication, much as any child would. (Note, however, that Genie was a teenager in appearance, therefore likely to elicit different communication behaviors from the family than would an infant.) The tests she was given were designed to measure various linguistic skills. Speech perception was measured by use of a picture selection task in which the picture names differed in only one phoneme, for example, "lamb" and "lamp." Both initial and final consonant discrimination were measured, as was consonant cluster (e.g., "sp") perception. In the entire battery, Genie made only two errors. Another test measured her mental representation of sound, not just immediate discriminations. She was presented with two pictures and an unrelated word. Her task was to select the picture whose name rhymed with the word. This task, too, presented no problems.

Imitation was good except for pitch and volume control. In spontaneous speech, however, her pitch was abnormally high and her voice very breathy, and she tended to distort the sounds, simplifying consonant clusters (by deleting a consonant or by inserting schwas between the consonants), *neutralizing* vowels (i.e., making them more like the schwa, with less extreme articulation), dropping final consonants, deleting unstressed syllables, and "reducing" consonants of other manner classes to stops of the same place of articulation (e.g., m → b, or f → p). Examples of her spontaneous utterances are as follows (written phonetically as indicated by the brackets; a = ah; ɪ = short i):

all → [ ɔ ] ("aw")            blue → [bəlu]
touch → [tʌ] ("tuh")         stop spitting → [tapapɪtɪ]
soup → [su]                   little → [lɪə]
blouse—[bæ ͧ] ("bow")

In addition, at times, /z, s, ð, θ, h/ (ð = the "th" in "the," θ the "th" in "theta") were reproduced as /d/ or /t/ and /m/ as /b/. None of the alterations Genie made were hard and fast; sometimes she would produce a word perfectly and at other times transform it.

*Comprehension skills.* More important for *language* acquisition than sound production or perception are the higher-language functions: syntax, morphology, and semantics. As I noted, Genie was attentive and responsive to the hospital staff from the first. Her comprehension of their instructions was dependent on pantomime and gestures; words alone did not suffice. One month after admission, for example, her doctor asked with appropriate context, "Do you want to look again?" and Genie looked, and subsequently, again with the nonverbal situation clear, "Look at Mrs. M. now; do you see her?" and Genie went up and touched her. Her response also included at times a vocalization, either imitative ("Is that fun?" → "[fʌ]") or unintelligible.

*Grammatical skills.* A year after placement in the foster home, specific grammatical comprehension tests were administered. Genie was tested for comprehension of negative versus affirmative sentences, adjectives, prepositions, singular versus plural nouns, conjunctions (e.g., *and* versus *or*), pronouns, comparatives (e.g., *bigger* versus *smaller*), superlatives (e.g., *biggest* versus *smallest*), tenses, active versus passive voice, questions, and relative clauses. The tests required either selection of the appropriate picture (e.g., "Show me the bunny that does [not] have a carrot") or manipulation of objects to fit the sentence (e.g., "Put the blue fox in [on, next to . . .] the white box").

From the first, Genie was perfect or nearly perfect at differentiating affirmative from negative sentences, polar (e.g., *hot* versus *cold*) and comparative (e.g., *hotter*) adjectives, the pronouns *all, one, they, each other,* and *themselves,* and color words. The particular words *big* and *little* she interpreted first as absolute quantities, but once she realized they were relative measures, her performance was perfect. She understood superlatives about 70% of the time, except for *biggest,* which was always correct. She confused *some* at first with *all,* then with *one,* and never understood it properly. With the exception of those mentioned, she could not distinguish or use most personal pronouns properly. She perfectly understood *and* but consistently interpreted *or* as *and.* Her performance on prepositions showed relatively steady improvement but was never perfect, with great variation between individual items. She was almost 98% correct on *in* from the first but only 40% correct on *under.* Curtiss (1977) observed that opposite prepositions like *behind* and *in front of* were acquired as a pair rather than in the normal pattern of using both interchangeably for one concept. Similarly, she seemed to learn polar adjectives as a pair rather than first acquiring the positive form and then the opposite, the *marked* (more cognitively nonneutral) form.

Looking at the morphemes frequently studied in English acquisition (Brown, 1973; see *Language and Its Normal Processing,* Chapter 9), we find some similarities but many differences between Genie's performance and normal children's. Without specific drilling, Genie performed at chance in differentiating singular and plural items. Curtiss trained all morphophonemic variants (e.g., /s/, /z/, /əz/) of the plural, repeating them with appropriate pictures, after which Genie performed perfectly. The tenses tested were the future (will, going to), the present progressive (is -ing), and the past (regular, irregular, and finish + VP). Genie's performance was good only on the "going" form of the future and the "finish" form of the past, indicating that she did understand the meaning behind tenses but not the morphemes marking them. Her performance after four years of experience contrasts with that of normal children, who acquire the present progressive first, at about 2½ years, and the rest of these forms by age 4. Her performance also contrasts markedly with the 6½-year-old Isabelle, who clearly surpassed her with respect to complexity of sentence structure and syntactic relations expressed.

Genie's performance was, not surprisingly, worse with complex sentences, the next level of grammar. Her comprehension of subject and object in testing was poor for *both* actives and passives; her best performance on the final tests was 74% on nonreversible actives (e.g., the boy watered the plant, where interpreting the plant as subject is nonsensical). Similarly, her performance was poor on answering wh-questions such as "What is the blue box on?" (a subject-question) or "What is on the blue box?" (an object question). Her performance was poorer on object questions than subject questions, as is found in normally reared children. She also had difficulty with relative clauses and, as is normally found, the greatest difficulty with *center-embedding* (as in "The rat the cat chased ate the cheese" where the relative clause is in the middle of the sentence, not at an end as in "This is the house that Jack built"). The only complexity that she understood well was negation—in simple sentences, as already mentioned, and also in complex sentences such as "The book that is (not) red is on the table."

*Discussion of performance on the tests.* It is important to observe that although her performance was poor on these tests, the testing situation was constrained. Comparison of her performance on these tests with normal children's performance in spontaneous conversation (which is how Brown inferred morpheme acquisition) from transcriptions automatically puts Genie at a disadvantage. Genie's spontaneous performance exceeded her test scores as well. In real life, there are additional cues—the context usually indicates who the agent and who the patient really are. In the test situation, one is presented with two pictures of agents and patients, either of which might be described by the sentence to be presented.

One reason to attribute a greater competence to normal children than to Genie is that their abilities to comprehend in natural situations are supplemented by their spontaneous productions. Genie's spontaneous speech was quite limited, perhaps reflecting her history of punishment for sound production but perhaps also reflecting a limited competence. Also because her sound production was abnormal, it is hard to interpret omissions and additions in her speech. For example, because she frequently simplified consonant clusters by deleting a consonant, omission of the plural marker could reflect either a lack of internalization of the morphological rule for plurals or the application of a supplementary phonological rule deleting the /s/ (as we have in writing possessives: If a word ends in "s," possession is marked by an apostrophe and no added "s"). Or, because she frequently broke up consonant clusters by schwa insertion, if the most common plural form in her speech was "-es," it would reflect her own idiosyncratic rule, not knowledge of the convention to add / z/ to words ending in /s/ or /z/.

*Production measures.* Initially Genie's speech consisted of single-word utterances and uninterpretable sounds. (Could the uninterpretable strings be what was called "babbling" in Anna?) Eight months after her discovery, she began to produce two-word utterances. Her vocabulary at the time was about 200 words, many more than normal at the beginning of the two-word stage. Her first two-word utterances look normal (Curtiss, 1977).

> Jones['s] shampoo.
> Yellow poster.
> D. hurt.
> Like powder. (p. 144)

These reflect, respectively, a possessive-noun, modifier-noun, noun-phrase (NP)-verb (V), V-NP structure. Like normal children, possessor-possessed was one of the first *case* relations (or syntactic relation) relations to appear in her speech.

A year after her admission to the hospital, she began spontaneous production of three-word utterances, like normal children's, of the structure NP-V, V-NP, or N-V-N. Examples (Curtiss, 1977) are

> Genie love M.
> Spot chew glove.
> Four teeth pull. (p. 145)

She also produced long NP strings such as "little white clear box" or "Sheila mother coat." More interesting was her production four months later of two two-word sentences, "Cat hurt. Dog hurt," followed immediately by "Cat dog hurt" (Curtiss et al., 1974), suggesting an understanding of compounding. During this same period, she began constructing negative sentences, as young children do, with a preposed negative particle. Her first was "no more" and later she added "not" to distinguish between refusal and other types of negatives. Unlike most children, she never learned to move the negative into the sentence.

In the two-word period she learned to signify locations as in "play gym." As her grammar developed, she would convey the same sense in prepositional phrases such as "Mama wash hair in sink."

By the following year, she began using embedded sentences in her spontaneous speech (two years after rehabilitation began, at about age 15), demonstrating the acquisition of recursion. Examples are as follows (Curtiss, 1977):

Tell [M] door was locked.
See I want you open my [your] mouth.
I want mat [which] is present.
Father hit Genie [who] cry long time ago. (pp. 158-160)

Conspicuously absent from her speech were questions. Her foster family tried to drill those by modeling transformation of her spontaneous sentences into questions, but this caused tremendous confusion and random preposing of wh- forms in sentences. After the family stopped, these strange sentences disappeared. Genie never learned the question form. In Bloom's (1991) taxonomy of the pragmatics of questioning in discourse, questioning others is the most complex form; earlier are simply stating feelings and responding to others' questions.

As you may have observed, also absent from Genie's speech were most grammatical morphemes, pronouns, *affixes* (prefixes and suffixes), and articles; her sentences, even the complex ones, look very *telegraphic* (a descriptive label for children's early sentences, omitting function elements). The first morpheme she used consistently, like most children, was "-ing," which appeared after about two years. Six months later plural markers appeared, but only occasionally. At the same time, she introduced "the" into some NPs and started to use the possessive morpheme. Past markers appeared sporadically the following year, and the third person marker on verbs (e.g., he gives) was not used even after five years of rehabilitation (age 18). The only pronouns she used reliably were "I" and "you."

Genie never engaged in language games, playing with sounds or syntactic frames, as children (or adults) do when they learn a new form. Some of her spontaneous creations were stereotypical, fitting words into set formulae such as "Help me -" or "I want -." However, some of her productions seemed creative or productive. Protesting being taken on a trip, she wished "Little bit trip"; instructed that her mother was not old, she claimed "Mother new." She also seemed aware of the syntactic paradigms used by others (strict subcategorization rules). Her response to a question of the form "What did you do?" was always a verb; to "What kind -?" a noun or adjective, as appropriate.

*Summary and interpretations.* Compared with Isabelle's or with normal children's, Genie's language skills are both poor and different. Abnormalities include a retarded rate of development, failures to acquire certain syntactic forms, a marked discrepancy between comprehension and production, deviant order of acquisition, and abnormal variability in applying what she had learned.

It is tempting to attribute her deviance to the late age at which she began learning language, 13½ years as opposed to 6½ years or 6 months. If there is a critical period for learning language and if this precedes puberty, then Genie's acquisition pattern may reflect language learning in its absence, without the benefit of UG. Again note that what may be missing is either blueprints for language specifically, or a match between Genie's cognitive and brain structure at 13 and basic language input or instruction. Because Genie was so deprived compared with Victor, it seems unlikely that she would have already formed schemes for many real world objects or ideas. She may, however, be missing the blueprints for developing some of these schemes—these would be general cognitive blueprints, not language-specific ones—if these unfold early in maturation.

*Physiological tests.* One striking fact suggests that there may be language-specific structures that Genie lacked. Genie was strongly right-handed but tests showed that she processed her language in the right hemisphere. As you may recall, right-handed individuals usually show a right-ear advantage for dichotically presented speech, believed to reflect specialization of the left-hemisphere language center in the brain. As we will see in detail in Chapter 5, more than 95% of right-handed individuals afflicted with damage to areas of the left hemisphere show severe language impairments, as compared with right-handers with damage to the same areas in the right hemisphere. (This suggests the left-hemisphere injury affected a "language center.")

Because Genie was right-handed, there is a greater than 95% chance that she would have language in the left hemisphere. Genie was given several dichotic listening tests, equivalent tests in vision, *evoked potential* tests (which measure brain activity), and a battery of cognitive tests used to distinguish right-brain-damaged from left-brain-damaged patients. *On all, she responded like a person with left-brain damage.* When presented with speech in only one ear, she performed equally well with her left and right ears, indicating no hearing loss. Under dichotic competition, however, her left-ear score was perfect while her right-ear score never exceeded 20% correct. Both the direction and the magnitude of the difference are highly unusual; normally, individuals make some errors in both ears with a slightly better performance in the *right* ear. Evoked potential studies showed a greater activity in Genie's right hemisphere than in her left when she performed linguistic tasks, the reverse of what is found in normal right-handers. The visual tests showed an advantage for language presented to the right hemisphere, as opposed to the left-hemisphere advantage normally found.

Genie also excelled at tasks that normally require right-hemisphere involvement, such as face recognition, holistic recall of unrelated objects, and number perception without counting; she scored better than normal adults, frequently the highest score ever recorded. For nonlinguistic left-hemisphere tasks, like counting or sequencing, she was well below average. The results are consistent with right-hemisphere dominance, which would bring different strategies to language processing than the normal left-hemisphere (language-specific?) strategies.

With respect to Genie's performance and the critical period hypothesis, we may tentatively draw several conclusions. Genie's language is processed in the right hemisphere, unlike most right-handers, and therefore the right hemisphere may have imposed its own processes, different from those of the normally used left hemisphere, on language acquisition. This would account for her deviant perform-ance (and competence?). The left hemisphere may normally process language only if it is stimulated during a critical period, which could end some time before puberty (possibly as early as 5 years of age when brain lateralization is completed; Krashen, 1973). If the left hemisphere is not stimulated during the critical period, not only is it unable to learn language but it becomes less effective relative to the right hemisphere on all cognitive tasks.

Indeed, what seems to be missing from Genie's language is analytic skills: analysis of words into productive morphemes, of sentences into rule-governed structures. She seems to have learned language holistically, substituting words into frames, and *semantic* concepts like negation into unanalyzed sentences. As men-tioned in Chapter 1, Newport (1990) argues that a hallmark of *late* language acquisition is holistic, rather than analytic, processing, with particular problems for morpheme acquisition.

### A Sad Footnote to Genie's Story

In April 1992, Russ Rymer published an inflammatory history of the Genie case in the *New Yorker* magazine, describing Genie's history before and after her discovery and language testing. As he reports the story, there was a conflict between the primary psychologist and a teacher responsible for Genie's rehabilitation. Both had formed attachments to the child (and the child to the adults), and both may have been interested in the fame and fortune that study and rehabilitation of Genie might have offered. The psychologist won "custody": His was the foster family Genie was assigned to and his was the research plan that was undertaken and federally funded. Perhaps out of concern for Genie, or for revenge, the teacher maintained contact with Genie's mother and ultimately persuaded her to sue the research team for loss of privacy and loss of control of Genie.

Rymer's article raises the question of whether the interests of "science"—obtaining evidence on the nature versus nurture issues in language acquisi-tion, which we are discussing in this chapter—may have superseded Genie's rehabilitation—a serious ethical concern. To me, it does not appear that Genie's interests were superseded. The research team concentrated on language development, which as we have seen involves social training, cognitive and category development, and syntax training. She was tested a lot but only trained specifically on the plural and questions; language was to be acquired "naturally." Note that this is the approach that has been used with "feral" children through the ages and was the approach that appeared best in providing the apes with language. It was *not* an experiment, in lieu of a proven, standard course of rehabilitation: There was and is none. It is only through careful documentation of what is done and how successful it is that a rehabilitation method can be developed. The focus on success at language acquisition is also reasonable. Had language been successfully acquired, the door would have opened to all manner of cognitive growth, human interaction, and social potential; without "normal" language, Genie would always be a fringe, handicapped member of society. The focus on language therefore is not misplaced.

As we saw with many of the ape language projects, and with Victor, language "instruction" is given in a warm, family environment, along with conventions of daily living, like dressing, teeth-brushing, and toilet use. Because of the scientific interest in Genie's case, she became the recipient of state-of-the-art, individualized training and care, an unlikely happening for a child of poverty and neglect. She also became a member of an affluent family for a time; Genie remained in the psychologist's family for four years (until the federally funded study ended), and then was returned to her mother, with the psychologist attempting to maintain contact and support, offering to send her to camp, for instance. (Her mother declined and moved Genie to foster care.) As long as permitted to, Curtiss visited, both to maintain the relationship and to continue the research.

We need to be vigilant in ensuring ethical treatment both during study and, as we saw with the linguistic apes (Chapter 2), once the study ends. Was the psychologist's family ethically obligated to keep Genie? Certainly no more so than her mother, who turned her over to foster care when tending her became too much. The scientists here seem to have fulfilled both their scientific obligation and also their humane one, in attempting to continue the treatments—here, testing and assisting Genie.

Unfortunately, they were not allowed to realize that end. The UCLA research team (Fromkin & Curtiss, 1992) responded to Rymer's story, noting that the suit was ultimately thrown out of court; none of the researchers benefited monetarily from their work; and, indeed, all royalties were placed in a trust fund for Genie, contractually agreed to well before the lawsuit. And the teacher, who claimed to have Genie's interests and affections at heart, never visited her. In fact, she "created a nightmare for everyone concerned with Genie, herself, and with the study."

This was a second nightmare for the girl who had had a nightmare childhood. The consequence of being sued was that the research team was denied contact with Genie during the battle. So Genie suffered sudden loss of her adoptive friends and family. When the suit was dismissed in 1984 and the medical and research team "ordered" to resume the treatment they had never wanted to stop, according to Rymer, Genie's mother hid her away, leaving no address for the scientists to find her. As of 1992, Genie was in a home for retarded adults, visiting her mother one weekend each month. She received no further language training or testing. Curtiss (personal communication, April 1996) has not been allowed by Genie's mother to see her but has learned that she is "in a warm, fun board-and-care home, where she appears to be content, although pretty nonverbal. She participates in the Special Olympics."

## Summary and Conclusions

In this section, we examined the language-learning capabilities of children raised with little stimulation, especially linguistic, but with some human contact. Unlike the wild children discussed earlier, recovery of speech and language is possible for these children provided they are given individual training and it is started at an early age. Comparing the wild children with these children suggests that some early social contact is necessary for the development of language, even if it is not very nurturing or specifically language-supporting. Comparison of both groups with normal children suggests further that specific social reinforcement for speaking may be necessary at ages under 5 years for sounds to be spontaneously imitated.

The difference between Isabelle's and Genie's language development indicates that exposure to language probably needs to begin before puberty for relatively normal development. In that case, syntactic markers, complex sentences, and the full complement of syntactic constructions are acquired, probably using the normal left-hemisphere language mechanism. (This is more a guess than a conclusion; we do not know whether Isabelle processed language in her left hemisphere or her right.) Otherwise, language is acquired in the other hemisphere, and perhaps because of its processing approach or the absence of some innate language guides, there is general inattention to syntactic and morphemic rules (subject versus object, tense markers, movement transformations) as compared with general semantic functions (adjectives, negation, locatives).

## DEAF CHILDREN IN HEARING HOMES

The children discussed in the previous two sections were deprived sensorily and socially as well as linguistically. There is another group of children who may provide data from rearing under conditions not so deprived: profoundly deaf children raised by hearing and speaking parents (and some deaf parents) who fail to learn language normally because they can hear neither their own productions nor those of their parents.

## General Social Histories

It is important to distinguish profoundly deaf children from hearing-impaired children, deaf children raised with sign language, and the earlier groups. *Deafness* is defined as the inability to hear sound in the frequency ranges of speech, below

---

### Box 3.2. Language Development in Isolates

— Three early cases of isolated children, recovered to society before puberty, suggest the possibility of complete recovery. An important condition is socialization and human contact during the isolation, even if there is no speech.

— Genie, a neglected and abused child, recovered to society after puberty and, provided with intense language instruction, demonstrated some language mastery, but abnormally.

  — She learned speech but erratically applied phonological rules. Speech perception and phoneme discrimination were excellent.

  — She learned a large number of words and spontaneously combined them.

  — Morphology was also erratically acquired, with semantically transparent morphemes, like "not," "finish" for the past tense and "will" for the future, much more consistent than regular inflections.

  — Syntax was deviant and erratically applied: Semantics was used to determine case relations; questions were never asked; relative clauses were poorly understood; the only complex form consistently used was negation.

  — Physiological testing revealed her language was processed in her right hemisphere—statistically very unusual for a right-handed person like Genie. Other cognitive tests also suggested a strong right-hemisphere dominance and unusually poor abilities in left-hemisphere-controlled tasks.

  — The implication is that there is a critical period for left-hemisphere-based language-learning schemes that ends before puberty. These schemes may be syntax-specific, either by providing the principles by which language input is parsed or by providing general analytic skills needed for parsing.

---

3,000 Hz. We do not need both ears nor is the full frequency range of speech necessary to distinguish most speech sounds (see Chapter 7 of the companion volume), so deafness in one ear, or deafness at frequencies above 1,000 or 1,500 Hz, will not profoundly affect speech comprehension. A child with such problems usually learns speech in the normal way, perhaps assisted by a hearing aid. Children who are *binaurally* deaf, deaf in both ears, will have difficulty learning speech through traditional transmission. If the parents are deaf, sign language may be taught traditionally because this is what most deaf parents are likely to use in their everyday communication with each other and with the children. (Language acquisition of sign will be discussed in Chapter 4.)

If the parents are hearing, they may opt (as done frequently in the past) for a method of *oral education:* treating their children as though they were hearing, minimizing gestures to force them to attend to lip movements for lipreading and to whatever sounds they can also manage to hear. When the children are old enough, they may be sent to a school for the deaf where speechreading and speaking skills are taught more formally.

These deaf children are not deprived except for the delay in experience with a native language and their inability to hear. They live in normal homes with appropriate visual, tactile, and taste stimulation. They also have the advantage of more communication with their parents than the children in the last section did. Parents are likely to use gesture for important concepts like "Don't touch the hot stove," so that there is little chance of misunderstanding.

Although there are reports of complete "oral successes" in the profoundly deaf, the instances are rare. More typical, around the world, are the children who struggle with the spoken language of their parents and surreptitiously sign to other children in their school. As Tervoort (1978) describes it,

> Anyone who has ever visited a school for the deaf and observed its pupils, especially the younger ones, more than very superficially must have noticed the striking difference in their behavior in situations in which so-called "good" language, to be used on behalf of the hearing partner, is requested from them, and their behavior in circumstances where they are left free to communicate as they please among themselves. *In the first instance, their behavior is awkward, inhibited, and hesitant; it reminds one of a foreigner, unfamiliar with the language, who tries to utter something which he has to put together by thinking hard and using the little he knows.* In the latter case, however, the deaf children's behavior is that of partners at ease who focus upon the subject matter at hand, to be dealt with in a communicative code the use of which is a matter of course. (p. 173, italics added)

Tervoort contends that the deaf child who succeeds orally is one who merges the sign language of peers with the spoken language of teachers, losing the former—not one who never signed.

Other investigators have similarly concluded that deaf children born to nonsigning, hearing parents usually show a language delay in speaking. Many youngsters do not acquire even the beginnings of language, whereas others acquire the basics, but not the fine points, of syntax. Few orally educated deaf individuals learn to read at better than the fifth-grade level, only 12% are considered linguistically competent, and only 4% are rated as proficient lipreaders or speakers (Schlesinger, 1978). Compared with deaf children raised by signing parents, orally raised deaf children, even those given intensive preschool academic training, are significantly poorer academically than manually trained children (Stewart, 1993; Vernon & Koh, 1971). Most deaf adults do become proficient in a language, not the drilled oral language but the sign language used by the deaf community (Schlesinger, 1978).

Of course, in interpreting the acquisition of spoken language by deaf children, we must keep in mind that these children are not only learning language late and doing so in classroom drills, not "traditional transmission," but also that they are receiving a highly impoverished signal. It is estimated that only 16 of the 40 phonemes of English are distinguishable from lipreading (Erber, 1974). Given the perceptual difficulty, it is not surprising that language acquisition is abnormal.

## Spontaneous Signed Language

More interesting for our purposes than the deaf child's success (or failure) at mastering speech and language from oral education is that orally trained deaf people sign. Signing either occurs surreptitiously in schools for the deaf or is acquired by orally trained deaf adults when they join the deaf community. Where does the sign come from, and does it look like language?

Goldin-Meadow has examined the structure of sign spontaneously invented by deaf children (Goldin-Meadow, 1982; Goldin-Meadow, Butcher, Mylander, & Dodge, 1994; Goldin-Meadow & Feldman, 1977; Feldman, Goldin-Meadow, & Gleitman, 1978) and its relation to the communication patterns of the parents (Goldin-Meadow & Mylander, 1983). As of 1994, the researchers had studied 10 deaf children of hearing parents, aged from 17 to 49 months at the initial visit. The children were videotaped in one- to two-hour sessions for eight weeks. Interviews were unstructured: A child was given toys to play with and encouraged to interact freely with the toys, the parent, or the interviewer during the session.

Analysis of the videotapes by two coders yielded substantial agreement on communicative gestures, gesture boundaries, and gesture combinations, as well as gesture meaning, using *rich interpretation* (making inferences about what was said using the nonverbal context). The children use two types of gestures predominantly: pointing gestures, signifying objects in the environment, and iconic gestures, signifying actions or attributes. Pointing may be an instance of *deixis*—pointing through language (as with the English *this*); *iconic* gestures look like what is described (like onomatopoetic words sound like their referents).

It is important to note that characterizing a "language" with no rigid conventions, used by only one "speaker," is fraught with difficulties, including potential observer biases with no built-in means of determining whether interpretation is correct. It is only an interpretation, for instance, that deictic gestures signify objects and iconic gestures signify actions or attributes; we cannot look them up in a "dictionary." As in studies of normal child language interpreted through rich interpretation, correctness is in part established by agreement among observers, as when the mother and the experimenter independently understand a production the same way. It is also established in part by negotiation with the producer; the observer responds to the child and sees if the child accepts the response as appropriate or not. Finally, Goldin-Meadow and her colleagues conservatively assigned gestures to linguistic units: The gestures had to be produced with little variation from utterance to utterance, or a variability predictable with context, like an action gesture moved toward locations depending on the location of the patient.

One child was studied particularly to determine if his gestures signified conventional noun-verb, subject-predicate categories (Goldin-Meadow et al., 1994). As in oral language, a word (here a gesture) used to direct the observer's attention was taken to be the "topic," "subject," or "noun." A word commenting on the topic was categorized as a "predicate," a "verb," or an "adjective." When the child was 2, most of his nouns were deictic gestures, and his predicates were iconic or characterizing gestures. As he matured, characterizing gestures were used as nouns 40% of the time, although they still predominantly served as predicates. (Note that this occurs in English too: A *gerund* is a noun-form of a verb, as in "*swimming* is great exercise.") When older (3¼ years), for a small proportion of gestures, he used the same gesture as both noun and verb, a developmental sequence seen in hearing children of hearing parents as well (as we do with *brush,* for example). Importantly, he often produced the two forms differently, abbreviating (using one hand rather than two, for instance) the noun version, but not the verb version (similarly, English uses stress to differentiate noun-verb pairs like "contrast"). He also distinguished nouns and verbs inflectionally. A characterizing gesture located near or moved toward the patient (for a transitive verb) or recipient (for an intransitive verb) was always a verb; nouns did not move in space relative to their argument structure.

Note that for the children Goldin-Meadow has studied, unlike the apes taught sign, gestures spontaneously combined into "sentences"—a point at a shoe and then at the table indicates "put the shoe on the table"; at a jar and then making a hand twisting motion, that the jar is open. Sometimes the children rigidly ordered sentential relations; the child described above, for example, preferentially used patient-action ordering for transitive sentences, but noun-adjective ordering for descriptive sentences like "The block is curved." The children also spontaneously produced complex sequences of gestures as in one child's gesture at a shovel, then downstairs (where it was usually kept), then a digging motion (what it was usually used for). These complex sequences were considered a single sentence because there was no appreciable pause between gestures or return of the hands to neutral position.

Another individual extensively analyzed by Goldin-Meadow (1982) showed a further important syntactic creation indicative of recursiveness. This child produced two types of sentences: one to request an action or to comment on an action, and the other to comment on a perceived attribute of an object. These two sentence types were conjoined in all possible ways. For example, two actions performed sequentially were gestured: TAKE-OUT GLASSES [and then] I [will] DON [them]. (Note that it is customary to write the English translation of signs in capital letters.) An action sentence conjoined with an attribute sentence produced a relative-clause-like construction, as in [you] MOVE-TO [my] PALM GRAPE [which one] EATS. In the second sentence, the relative clause was not redundant because the grape in question was a toy grape and would not be eaten. The relative clause developed the pretense.

## Parental Gestures

Of interest, the parents' use of these gestures was well behind the children's—the mother of the child who differentiated noun and verb gestures shared only 18 gestures with her son (approximately 10% of their gesture vocabularies) and did not mark her grammatical categories with inflections to form a consistent system. This indicates that the parents do not teach the gesture language. In fact, it seemed more likely that the children taught their parents given that the parents generally used the objects themselves as props, rather than referring to them as the children did, by pointing, a form of *pronominal* (pronounlike) reference.

Parents produced two different types of responses to the gestures: reinforcement, by smiling or complying with a request, or "punishment," by not understanding, asking for clarification, frowning, or ignoring a request. Attempts to correlate these responses with the frequency of occurrence of the gestures in the children yielded no relationship, further suggesting that the parents were not shaping the children's language.

## Summary and Interpretation

It seems that children spontaneously develop language-like behavior given a supportive although nondirective social background. In the child productions, we see some few defining features of language as described in the last chapter. The children actively transmit and receive, can serve in either role (interchangeable), and can monitor their own productions as well as those of others (feedback). The signals produced disappear as they are made (rapid fading) and are discrete. The signals may refer to objects not in view (displacement) and are combined productively and, at least for one child, recursively. Because the gestures in combination specify case or syntactic relations (like the patient of the action) that they do not in isolation, they show duality of patterning. They are clearly learnable, and when the children enter school and begin formal oral training and writing, they will exhibit medium transferability. Finally, because the gestures may occur together with emotion in facial expression, they show some simultaneity.

However, many of our design features are missing from this communication system. Some are trivial: those that deal directly with characteristics of sound such as "sound" or "broadcast transmission and reception." But to the extent that the gestures mirror the event they describe, they exhibit neither arbitrariness nor semanticity. (This may be an overstatement because frequently the parents did not understand, so the gestures cannot have been as transparent as they may seem.) There is also no evidence of metalanguage, although there is not much metalanguage in any average 4-year-old.

Given what is missing, I would not want to call this language, in this form, but it is still strikingly different from the behaviors we reviewed in animals. Moreover, as we shall see in the next chapter, this kind of system may grow into a complex, full-blown language—given time, an adult conceptual system, and the general force of change in language through use. It is striking that these children, unlike animals, seem to have an instinctive need to communicate about the environment for reasons other than for direct reinforcement. Given no barrier, they invent a symbol system enabling them to so communicate, and they spontaneously combine their symbols to form propositions.

## Acquiring Sign Language as Adults

What happens to children such as the ones described if they get no formal sign language training in childhood and are not some of the few oral successes? On the basis of stories like Genie's and recovery patterns from brain damage in childhood and adulthood (to be discussed in Chapter 5), the psycholinguistic position has been that, as adults, they would never be able to learn fluent language. In a recent, moving story, Schaller (1995) confirms the psycholinguistic *bias* but dispels its conclusion: She taught a 27-year-old congenitally deaf Mexican illegal immigrant to communicate in sign. He became a proficient signer, surpassing her sign-as-a-second-language signing skills.

When Schaller met Idelfonso, he was alert, aware, intelligent, and motivated to communicate and learn but did not see words as symbols, as anything beyond an action to imitate. Schaller began by making different actions for him to imitate, including the action of making a symbolic representation (a blackboard drawing of a cat and the sign CAT). She also demonstrated different behaviors toward the referent and the symbol, petting the drawing but not the sign. After repeated attempts at this, Schaller (1995) observed,

> Suddenly he sat up, straight and rigid, his head back and his chin pointing forward. The whites of his eyes expanded as if in terror. He looked like a wild horse pulling back, testing every muscle before making a powerful lunge over a canyon's edge. My body and arms froze in the mime-and-sign dance that I had played over and over again for an eternity. I stood motionless in front of the streaked *cat* [the blackboard version], petted beyond recognition for the fiftieth time, and I witnessed Idelfonso's emancipation. . . .
>
> Slowly at first, then hungrily he took in everything as though he had never seen anything before: the door, the bulletin board, the chairs, tables, students, the clock, the green blackboard, and me. He slapped both hands flat on the table and looked at me, demanding a response. "Table," I signed. He slapped his book. "Book," I replied. My face was wet with tears, but I obediently followed his pointing fingers and hands, signing "door," "clock," "chair." (pp. 44-45)

With difficulty, Schaller succeeded in teaching him other-than-name words, verbs and adjectives, and he combined them. He strove to communicate answers to her questions about his languageless life: where he had come from, how he had survived, and so on, and through mime and sign succeeded—clearly having encoded the thoughts without language. He also strove to learn answers to haunting questions, about property ownership, laws, racism, culture—clearly having had deep thoughts and a deep moral sense without language.

After less than a year, he left the school where Schaller had been a part-time instructor, and she shortly thereafter also left. More than seven years later, she returned to the region, in a quest to find Idelfonso and to document that his case was not rare, that there are many languageless adults and they can learn language as adults. Her book provides compelling evidence of the last—there are many languageless adults learning language—but her relationship with Idelfonso is as a friend and teacher, so we do not have scientific language tests comparing his skills and strategies with signers who learn language as children. However, when she meets him, he has earned a green card, a driver's license, and is holding a regular job as a gardener in a hospital. He has friends who sign, and she feels he outsigns her and is proud of his fluency. She reports the following observation by Idelfonso:

> Whenever I can, I find an interpreter to interpret the television news. It's important to know what's happening in the world. I don't understand why there's so much killing and war and stealing, people arguing about who owns what all the time. I think it's because some people are greedy, and they want more than they need. I want some land and a place to live, but just a small place and a little land, so I can have my own garden. There is enough in the world for everyone to have a little garden. Everyone could be content. But some people want gigantic houses and gigantic gardens, so they fight and steal and buy up all the land and others can't have anything.
>
> . . . I tried to put the nameless, languageless man with the folded arms together with the confident living-room conversationalist. I agreed with what he said by nodding my head and signing "yes," but the only comment I could make was that his signing was now better than mine. (p. 164)

In this aftermath, Schaller is introduced by Idelfonso to his younger brother (also deaf) and other deaf languageless Mexicans living in California, all emanating from the same village. Idelfonso is the only one who at that time knew sign, and he is clearly the leader, at least in the interaction with Schaller and another signing and English-speaking friend. He serves as interpreter from the signers to the languageless deaf, and conversely, but the deaf friends successfully mime-gesture-enact their life stories, communicating with one another.

In my view, it is likely that Idelfonso's motivation to learn language was nurtured through his ability to socialize and communicate with his deaf brother and friends; while isolated from the hearing world, and the sign-languaged deaf world, he was not isolated from humanity or from normal perceptual and cognitive experiences as Genie had been. Perhaps his language is processed in the left hemisphere like normal, or perhaps in the right, because it was learned after the critical period. Perhaps his language lacks some abstract analytic processes for the same reason. We do not know because these tests were not carried out. But certainly it conveys all that one would want language to convey and seems to fluent observers to be language. It appears abstract, symbolic, arbitrary, recursive, hierarchical, and so on.

So it is not necessary to learn language before puberty to acquire language. But it appears necessary to have supportive cognitive, perceptual, and, above all, social experiences to establish a language base.

---

### Box 3.3. Features of Spontaneous Gesture Languages

— Orally raised deaf children have difficulty learning spoken language because less than 40% is visible from lipreading. They are exposed to nurturing, social families who do use gesture communicatively with them but not in a regularized system.

— Such children's gestures do not resemble their parents'. Both parent and child gestures show deixis and iconicity.

— The children evidence more advanced language features, when carefully studied. These include
   — abstract gestures, less likely than parents' gestures to actually touch the object;
   — spontaneous combination of gestures into sentences expressing different case relations;
   — use of order or inflection to mark case relations and parts of speech;
   — conjunction of simple propositions into complex sentences, in one case with recursion;
   — regularization of gesture creating a coherent system; and
   — a similar developmental pattern to hearing children acquiring speech or deaf children acquiring sign from their parents from birth.

— Children raised without formal language, but with social support and the opportunity to communicate through pantomime, can learn language, with all its higher-level features, *as adults*. It may be processed in the brain differently or be simpler morphologically: This has not been studied.

---

## CONGENITAL LANGUAGE ANOMALIES

Thus far we have examined language development in people for whom, for all intents and purposes, the biological substrate(s) for language and cognition was intact but social and/or perceptual conditions were abnormal. The patterns of language development in these individuals strongly suggest that language is social and will not develop in the absence of human bonds. The presence of human social interchange seems to enable language-like expression to emerge, even without a language model. Such rudimentary expression includes naming, predicating, combining forms perhaps recursively, and systematizing forms and labels, creating a regularized, coherent communication base. *These may be the principles of UG.* The data suggest that language learning after childhood is possible but may be very different.

What we cannot conclude so far is whether the "principles" are language-specific or general cognitive. Genie, our strongest case for a critical period, showed language abnormalities and an unusual brain-lateralization pattern but also displayed general cognitive abnormalities consistent with relative loss of left-hemisphere cognitive functions (including, but not exclusively, linguistic ones) and relative preservation of right-hemisphere functions. We next examine individuals whose histories might indicate whether language and general cognitive functions are indeed separable. We will look at the language acquisition of "language-impaired" (including reading-impaired) children, at a family with a particular language deviance, and at some cases of severe retardation with relative preservation of language.

## Language-Impaired (LI) Children

Children are classified as *language-impaired (LI)* when they show a significant delay in acquiring language, needing therapy and intensive focus for what normally seems to happen casually. Children diagnosed as LI may constitute a single group, with a single disorder or, more likely, may encompass a number of different deviant patterns of language acquisition. Bloom and Lehey (1978) describe language disorders that show impairment of form, content, or use or some combination of them. One 7-year-old child, for example, used single words with gestures to communicate intent perfectly: "Hi"—points to self, then down the hall—"milk," indicating she is going down the hall to get some milk (p. 293). Another child used fluent speech with little conceptual connectivity: A 6-year-old who was asked to describe a button produced the following: "this is a button/it has two holes in it/it's like a lady has/it has a shape/it is round/this is a button/you put it on your blouse or an apron in case an apron has a button" (p. 296). And some children may have form and content more or less intact but miss the cooperative principles, as with a 10-year-old who responded to the therapist's commenting on snow outside precluding their going out by saying, "that's okay/yeah/I can stay inside with Joe/yeah/okay I can stay inside with Joe/okay/I do some work inside with Joe/oh I can work with Joe/Joe big Joe gonna stay inside" (p. 298).

The three examples indicate the need for special language intervention, but it seems unlikely that they stem from the same language-learning difficulty. It is also unclear whether these children suffer from a language-specific disorder(s) or from a more general cognitive disorder(s) with evident manifestations in language acquisition. At least some of the children studied have been shown to have cognitive/perceptual problems as well as language problems, which, when corrected, help both.

Fletcher (1991), using standard test batteries, studied 160 three- to ten-year-old children diagnosed as language-impaired but who had no general IQ or emotional impairment. Their spontaneous speech showed similar "errors" to those of normal children, but more frequent ones, along with a lower frequency of spontaneously self-correcting, or *repairing*. The language samples of children over the age of 6 were difficult to distinguish syntactically from samples from normal 5-year-olds, indicating a language delay, but had quite complex syntactic structures (as did all but the first example cited from Bloom and Lehey). As examples of the "deviance," consider these utterances:

my mum was take me a picture
he give the milk out
she's sitting on a table getting some milk
do writing a picture (p. 178)

Note the violations of inflection ("was take" or "he give"), argument structure ("picture" should have "me" as an argument, which is not so marked by either word order or the preposition "of"), and semantics (chairs, not tables are sat on; pictures are drawn, not written). Note also, though, how much is correct: Inflections are often marked, word order and syntax are more often correct than not, and semantic errors are not random but are substitutions from the same semantic category or a similar slot. Thus, for these children, language is perhaps acquired similarly to normal—certainly these sentences are not as deviant as Genie's!—but perhaps more laboriously, requiring greater attention.

Also suggesting that language acquisition is quantitatively, not qualitatively, different are language comprehension data for some LI children (those with no apparent cognitive or social problems apart from language delay). Curtiss and Tallal (1991) studied preschool children with nonverbal IQs above 85 and no emotional problems, comparing those with language performance at least one year below their mental age (the LI group) with a group whose language performance was better than six months below their mental age (the normal comparison group). Both sets of children were given forced-choice language comprehension tasks, for example, a picture verification task for a reversible active sentence like "The boy is pushing the girl" (i.e., the subject must match the sentence to a picture from among a set showing the boy pushing the girl, the girl pushing the boy, a boy and a girl doing something else, and so on). On most such tasks, the LI children made more errors than the normal children, but the *pattern* of errors was the same. So, for the example given, both groups were most likely to err by selecting a picture showing a girl pushing a boy, and next most likely to select a picture of a girl and a boy both pushing. And looking at both production and comprehension of morphological and syntactic constructions, like negation, regular past tense, passive voice, and so on, Curtiss and Tallal found identical acquisition order in the LI and normal group. The difference again lay in the absolute age of acquisition, not the pattern.

There were two significant differences between the LI and the normal group, both suggestive of a general cognitive deficit with impact on language, not a language-specific deficit. The first is that the LI children had difficulty perceiving and repeating sequences of (nonverbal) stimuli in many modalities, requiring longer durations of presentation or longer interstimulus intervals (ISIs) to be correct. For the LI children, but not the normal children, nonverbal sequencing abilities were significantly correlated with the ability to understand the reversible sentences. That is, to attend to the order of the words in the sentence, the children needed to be able to attend generally to order. For nonreversible sentences, where order is redundant with semantics, the correlation was not significant for the LI children either. Curtiss and Tallal suggest that abnormalities in acquiring syntax and morphology in an order-dependent language like English may derive from a basic cognitive deficit in sequencing. This may retard isolation and ordering of the parts. The greater cognitive load needed to sequence language may result in less attention to monitoring or semantic selection, allowing more than normal "normal" errors to slip through.

The second difference between these LI and the normal children can also be explained as a sequencing failure. The abilities of both sets of children to comprehend sentences with redundant markers (like "that" or "who" introducing relative clauses) were measured. As I reviewed in Chapter 1, these syntactic markers speed processing normally (at least for some verbs). For both LI and normal control subjects, there was a small effect of the redundant marker, but in opposite directions: The normals did slightly better with the extra "cue"; the LI children did slightly worse with the extra "word(s)." Note that I switched from "cue" to "word." For the normal children, the "that" indicated the syntactic structure; for the LI children, it was only an extra item to deal with. With the extra cognitive load needed to sequence, tracking one more item hurt their extracting the probable sense from the semantics and overall word order.

Recent work by Tallal and colleagues (Merzenich et al., 1996; Tallal et al., 1996) supports the idea that, at least for some LI children, it is a cognitive deficit underlying the linguistic one. The authors developed computer games that intensively (8-16 hours over a couple of weeks) practiced the sequencing of increasingly rapid acoustic inputs. The games began with long stimuli and interstimulus intervals (ISIs) and the child had to repeat the order. If the child was correct, successive trials reduced both duration and ISI until normal response levels were achieved. Another training task involved the children practicing with speech "slowed" by computer. Both resulted in rapid growth of auditory sequencing and language processing skills, pushing them *two years* ahead of where they were before training in as little as *four weeks.* Such rapid learning suggests "there may be no fundamental defect in the learning machinery in most of these children" (Merzenich et al., 1996, p. 80);

> that the symptomatology of LLI [language-learning impaired] children may reflect primarily bottom-up processing constraints rather than a defect in linguistic competence per se . . . it appears that they had developed considerably more language competence than they were able to demonstrate or use "on line" under normal listening and speaking conditions. (Tallal et al., 1996, p. 83)

LI children may congenitally suffer from specific cognitive deficits, like sequencing, which affect extracting some of the regularities of language. Given how important language is in human life, the language impairment/delay stands out more than other manifestations of the cognitive deficit. And given the redundancy of language, and that there are many ways to observe its regularities, the usual path to the linguistic goal may be circumvented using a still available, but perhaps more laborious, route. Of course, because it appears that there are many types of language-learning disorders, ranging from abnormal vocabulary to abnormal pragmatics, it is unclear that a single cognitive problem or therapeutic approach will be successful for all.

## Developmental Dyslexia

Learning disabilities involving reading (*developmental dyslexia*) affect up to 20% of schoolchildren in the United States (Roush, 1995). Reading and writing are likely to be problematic if there is a language-learning disability because (a) they depend on a sophisticated model of spoken language (grammar, vocabulary, and the phonology), (b) any general cognitive dysfunction, say, in sequencing or analyzing into component morphemes or phonemes should likewise affect analysis of written materials into graphemes, and (c) literacy itself requires considerable exposure to stories and their cultural conventions, which may not be well attended to by children with language difficulties. In addition, reading and writing require motor and visual skills distinct from those of speech and hearing, so they may yield difficulties in some children for whom oral language poses no problem.

Some forms of developmental dyslexia appear to have a biological substrate. Dyslexias are more common in boys than in girls, suggesting a sex link, although they can occur in either sex. They can run in families (S. Richardson, 1992), as can some forms of LI (as we will see in the next section). A specific chromosome has been implicated in phonological processing deficits associated with the most common dyslexias (Roush, 1995). Finally, anatomical and metabolic studies of dyslexic brains indicate abnormalities in regions suspected of involvement in visual information processing, temporal processing, and language generally (Roush, 1995; Shaywitz & Waxman, 1987).

Like LI, dyslexia is diagnosed by delay, when a child's reading skills lag substantially behind other intelligence performance measures—say, a normal IQ but a reading level 18 months below normal (Castles & Coltheart, 1993). Note that such a diagnostic definition precludes early treatment, which would be desirable if there were a "critical period"; by definition, we must delay 18 months to make the diagnosis. As we saw with LI, it is critical to differentiate a disability—a deviant learning style—from slow progress, that is, dyslexia apart from poor reading.

*Dyslexic types.* Of those children diagnosed with dyslexia, 80% or more have difficulty with phonological processing in the auditory modality as well as with reading (E. Richardson, 1984). The phonological processing difficulty or whatever underlies it in "classic" dyslexia (Frith, 1985) prevents children from progressing beyond the *sight word* or *logographic* stage of reading, where a word is recognized as a whole pattern. These children can develop an impressive sight vocabulary but do not learn to segment a word into components fluently, although such *alphabetic* strategies can be successfully drilled. Frith also describes a second type of dyslexia with phonological processing problems, "developmental dysgraphic." These children master alphabetic strategies but not *orthographic* ones, never learning morphemic regularities like "tion." While better readers, they have severe spelling problems.

Some dyslexics find reading regular, pronounceable nonwords (like *brank*) unusually difficult, suggesting they recognize sight words but not *grapheme-to-phoneme correspondences (GPCs)* (Castles & Coltheart, 1993). They often read a nonword as a visually similar real word (Seymour & MacGregor, 1984). Other dyslexic children have greater difficulty with irregular words (like *have,* which, by GPCs, should have a long "a"), suggesting that they are not recognized as a unit but are erroneously assembled using a GPC strategy (Castles & Coltheart, 1993). As we will see in Chapter 5, literate adults with different kinds of brain damage are differentially able to pronounce nonwords and irregular words also. The difference in the children, as in the adults, suggests a differential impairment of one of the processing routes for printed information.

Seymour and MacGregor (1984) diagnosed other types of dyslexia, occurring more rarely. Some of the children they tested seemed to be particularly impaired by letter distortions (like writing the word diagonally) and matching visual sequences of letters; these were classified as *visual-analytic dyslexics.* Other dyslexics became more impaired as word length increased, suggesting that they failed to chunk regular alphabetic sequences (like "tion") into a single unit.

*Visual processes in dyslexia.* While we have just seen that dyslexics comprise a variety of different subtypes, many studies have perhaps naively examined cognitive and reading processes in dyslexics as a homogeneous population (Martin, 1995). By and large, these have found that dyslexics are slower and less automatic than normal readers, that they do not necessarily read differently but that they may differentially use visual information coming to different parts of the eye: the center or *fovea* and peripheral to it.

Dyslexic children's eye movement patterns are not highly abnormal, although they fixate longer with shorter *saccades* (controlled "jumps" from one fixation point to the next) and more backtracking movements than normal. Like normals, they look longer for low-frequency and longer words, and look ahead for help with difficult words (Hyona & Olson, 1995). And their longer looking times and so on disappear with reading material targeted to their reading level as opposed to their age level (Rayner, Pollatsek, & Bilsky, 1995). Thus their reading eye-gaze pattern is like that of a normal reader reading difficult material, not of a reader using a deviant strategy.

There is some evidence that dyslexics do not use information peripheral to the fovea efficiently, as do normals. Normal readers use this to preprocess before they focus. Rayner (1986) improved dyslexic's performance by controlling their viewing field, their attention to foveal and peripheral letters, with a window that moved across the page. Also, for normal readers, letter identifiability falls off markedly between the fovea and periphery, but for some dyslexic adults it does not, impeding their attention to the foveal information. Geiger and Lettvin (1987) used this observation to "cure" a severely dyslexic adult, training him to concentrate on his supernormal peripheral vision rather than the foveal vision. This improved his reading seven grade levels within four months and, as he put it, caused him, at 25, "at last [to] see the form of the words clearly" (p. 1242).

*Cognitive deficits in dyslexia and its remediation.* There have been two general cognitive skills investigated with respect to dyslexia: naming automaticity and temporal processing. Both have shown some diagnostic reliability. Wolf (1991) conducted a five-year longitudinal study of children, beginning in kindergarten, investigating their speed at naming letters and pictures of common objects. She found that naming speed in kindergarten was significantly related to reading skills in second grade. By second grade, there was a significant difference in a child's speed at naming numbers and letters and that of naming an object. Number and letter naming skill only (!) correlated with reading skills in second grade: Presumably, if letter recognition were automatized, attention in reading could focus on higher levels of meaning. Relative to "poor" readers, dyslexics were slower on all forms of naming and were less able to select the word's meaning in a multiple-choice format.

Wolf argues that the dyslexic is impaired particularly in retrieving items from the lexicon given the graphic symbol. And S. Richardson (1992) notes that the factor most characteristic of children clinically referred for reading problems is a naming deficit or *dipnomia*. Thus both phonological deficits and naming problems in oral language are reflected in reading.

As we have seen, Tallal has implicated temporal processing deficits in LI; she has also instigated research into their causing dyslexia (see, for example, Tallal, Galaburda, Llinas, & von Euler, 1993). "Temporal processing" has been investigated in tasks as diverse as auditory sequencing and maintaining a finger-tapped rhythm (Farmer & Klein, 1995). Because a range of skills is encompassed in the term *temporal processing disorder* and because the deficits may either span several modalities or be confined to one, some researchers have seriously questioned the validity of the concept (e.g., Studdert-Kennedy & Mody, 1995).

Nevertheless, Tallal et al. (1993) present evidence that the part of the brain responsible for processing rapid, transient visual signals is more disorganized in dyslexics than normals, and their visual evoked potentials to short, rapidly changing *(transient)* signals are reduced relative to normals. Farmer and Klein (1995) review research showing that dyslexics require longer silent intervals than normal to separate two auditory or visual events, and that they also require longer stimuli and silent intervals to judge the temporal order of a sequence correctly.

There is some question as to what the temporal order deficit, if it is real, means for the dyslexic. It may signify a correlated problem with the reading problem, and one that could predict the reading problem and be amenable to earlier diagnosis. Alternatively, it might "cause" the reading problem by creating some specific difficulty in abstracting GPCs and in phonological processing generally (Studdert-Kennedy & Mody, 1995).

Phonological processing problems have been implicated in poor—not dyslexic—reading, which phonological training has been shown to improve (Bradley & Bryant, 1983; Chapter 11 of *Language and Its Normal Processing*). Likewise, E. Richardson (1984) improved dyslexic children's performance by presenting words in isolation and teaching the sounds of letters as well as how to segment the words into onset and rime. From there the children were trained to pronounce unknown monosyllables and, ultimately, multisyllabic words. He found rapid progress in developing age-appropriate reading scores in three-fourths of the children so prepared. A recent report by the National Institutes of Health also recommends " 'highly structured, explicit, and intensive instruction in phonics rules and [their] application to print' " (quotation cited in Roush, 1995, p. 1896).

I should also note that the dyslexic's difficulty may be a general cognitive inattention to print. S. Richardson (1992) advocates a multisensory approach (akin to Dr. Itard's technique with Victor) to teaching reading, which may in part slow input of visual information, and may in part enrich its processing. In the *VAKT* (visual-auditory-kinesthetic-tactile) approach, children trace the graphic inputs with their fingers, saying each word as they trace it, and then write the words they are speaking. The stories they write are typed for them, and these are the materials with which they practice reading. The approach reinforces existing language connections through each of the modalities, and also explicitly relates for the child the printed word to the concept—the concept of the child's own creation. This may help focus attention on the meaning of print and the different appropriate units of language analysis, to help the dyslexic model language through print.

Reviewing the language-learning and reading disability literature does not provide a clear answer as to whether there is a language-specific biological disturbance. On the one hand, there is no question that there are familial trends and that a failure to acquire language or segmentation strategies without a focused, overt drill is abnormal, and so could indicate the failure of some "automatic" module to kick in. On the other hand, the language-learning or reading acquisition failures do not seem to be "pure," encapsulated from other cognitive functions like sequencing and visual acuity thresholds, and the deviances they produce seem to be on a continuum with poor or slow skills, not a wholly different way of processing language. It may be that one of the many routes to the multiply determined language signal is genetically impaired, and the LI child must be more explicitly guided to alternatives than a child with the full set of possibilities.

## Familial Transmission of a Language Disability

The evidence just reviewed does not strongly support a genetic defect in language learning per se, but it does suggest genetic influences on language learning. That is, there is no reason to assume an environmental cause for either an underlying nonverbal sequencing problem or the language delay, or both; rather, there may be a biological basis for a different cognitive "strategy" that affects language. However, LI children constitute a heterogeneous population, each with a language disorder but not necessarily the same one from the same cause.

One form of LI appears to be genetic and may be specifically linguistic (Gopnik & Crago, 1991). This language impairment runs in families, and its distribution is consistent with inheritance from the mother of a dominant trait. Neurological studies of some familial LI families suggest atypical asymmetries of the brain, with the left-side language area no larger than its counterpart on the right.

Gopnik and Crago systematically tested language skills in six adult members of a family of which about half its members over three generations had the disability

---

**Box 3.4. Congenital Language Abnormalities**

— Language-impaired children suffer from developmental delays in language acquisition. Morphological and syntactic structures in production and comprehension are acquired in the normal order but more slowly. Speech errors are distributed normally but occur more frequently.

— Language-impaired children also suffer from nonverbal deficits, in sequencing in particular, which may underlie their language performance. Difficulty perceiving temporal order is likely to affect acquisition of order-dependent languages like English, where inflections are few and part of speech and case relations are marked by position in a constituent.

— There is no clear evidence from LI children of a defect in a language "module" or of a defective "principle" of UG.

— Developmental dyslexia selectively impairs learning to read. It often occurs with LI. It may have a genetic base, running in families and affecting males more often than females. Most cases are impaired in phonological processing and naming and have associated oral-language deviances.

— Some developmental dyslexics may have an underlying or associated cognitive processing problem in automaticity of naming, chunking segments into higher units, or temporal processing. Some have specific visual abnormalities.

— Slowing reading, directing attention and eye gaze, stressing phonological models, and encouraging multisensory, active involvement in reading have helped different dyslexics.

---

(all attended special schools). That it did not appear in some family members suggests that it occurred independently of input, because all family members would have heard the same language. The investigators did not report looking for general auditory or nonlinguistic cognitive impairments in these subjects.

The pattern of language skills and impairments they did find strongly suggests a language-specific problem. For example, the subjects were asked to perform simple commands like "touch the book" versus "touch the books," with a stack of three books and one book in front of them. They discriminated the "-s" ending at least as well as normal control subjects, suggesting they had no problem hearing it or remembering its position. However, when asked to pronounce the plural for a singular nonsense word (e.g., *wug*), they were much poorer than normal. One subject, confused, whispered to herself under her breath, "Add an s." Another laughed, challenged with "How should I know?" and left it unchanged; to the next one, "zat," she gave "zacko" as the plural.

A particular disturbance on regular morphemes was noticed in many instances. These family members correctly produced irregular past tenses more often than regular ones. Notebooks of their school compositions suggested that regular past tenses were acquired *individually,* after a teacher corrected a particular form; no general pattern was abstracted from the examples and applied. Likewise, the family was impaired on derivational morphemes, as in converting "There is a lot of sun today" to "It is ___." But they had no trouble performing sequences of simple commands given verbally and retained in memory, or in correcting sentences with missing arguments like "The nice girl gives" to "The nice girl gives him a ball." They did have difficulty understanding pronouns, and their spontaneous speech and narrative descriptions avoided pronouns, instead repeating the entire noun phrase.

Gopnik and Crago point out that all the deficits reflect a difficulty in productively using abstract grammatical morphology, in representing the morpheme and its combinatorial rules. First, most of the deficits overtly are deficits in morphology. When morphology is correct, it is as an unanalyzed form, as with the irregular past tenses and the individually learned regular past tenses. Second, this may even apply to the correctly discriminated plural: It may be that *book* has been learned as a single item meaning one reading material, and *books* as another semantic entry meaning several reading materials. Finally, note that pronouns provide a problem precisely because they are abstract variables (she = mother, daughter, girl, professor, mare, car . . . ), which must be selected on the basis of gender, number, and case—inflectional morpheme "meaning."

This suggests that the deficit in analyzing and applying morphology productively may be overcome by other intact language and cognitive abilities: Semantics, pragmatics, and a considerable number of syntactic operations seem to be available. Nevertheless, the strong inheritance pattern and coherent linguistic pattern suggest that there may be a genetic, language-modular, UG specification of analysis and productive use of grammatical morphology. Again, it is interesting to note that analytic morphology provides a specific language-learning problem: Newport (e.g., 1990) finds that this analytic ability is less available to late language learners, that is, people learning a second language as adults (see Chapter 10 in the companion volume and Chapter 4 in this volume for sign acquisition).

## Language Preservation in General Retardation

We have just looked at what seems to be a heritable pattern of abnormal morphological processing, suggesting, in the absence of any other cognitive deficits, that some specific language-learning tasks may be relatively insulated—part of a genetically specified language module. There are individuals who show the converse pattern, relative language preservation but severe cognitive deficits. To the extent that these individuals process language normally, they too constitute evidence for a language module, independent of other cognitive functions.

### Williams Syndrome

Williams syndrome is a rare (one of 25,000 live births) genetic disorder that results in a characteristic facial appearance, abnormalities of many organ systems (heart, kidney, and so on), mild to moderate retardation, hypersensitivity to auditory stimulation, and a " 'friendly and loquacious' personality" with " 'unusual command of language' " (Bellugi, Wang, & Jernigan, 1994, p. 24, quotation of early writers on the syndrome). As an example of the loquacious style, Bellugi, Bihrle, Neville, and Doherty (1992) quote a 15-year-old with the syndrome, who, describing herself, states: " 'You're looking at a professional book writer. My books will be filled with drama, action, and excitement. And everyone will want to read them. I'm going to write books, page after page, stack after stack . . . I'll start on Monday' " (p. 205).

She uses language with sophistication: a meal is "a scrumptious buffet," an older friend is "quite elegant," her boyfriend is "a sweet petunia," and the request for a loan of her watch is answered with "my watch is always available for service." At the same time, spatial skills like drawing, and normal motor skills like tying shoes, are profoundly impaired.

Bellugi, Neville, and colleagues have undertaken the systematic study of the cognitive, neurophysiological, and linguistic characteristics of individuals with this syndrome (Bellugi, Bihrle, Jernigan, Trauner, & Doherty, 1990; Bellugi et al., 1994; Neville, Mills, & Bellugi, 1994). They compared Williams syndrome adolescents with age- and IQ-matched (mean IQ about 50) Down's syndrome subjects, revealing strikingly different patterns of abilities and deficits' particularly in language, even though the two groups demonstrated equivalent verbal scores on IQ tests. Sensitive psycholinguistic scrutiny reveals that the poor performance arises from very different reasons.

For example, one of the verbal IQ measures requires the subject to define words, and then scores how good the definition is. Asked to define *hazardous,* four of the six Down's syndrome children who were tested responded that they did not know, and the others gave fragmentary definitions like "don't touch books not belong to you." The Williams syndrome children, in contrast, produced long, convoluted examples of situations in which they might have encountered the word, such as the following:

> Hazardous. Oh I know. Hazardous means that you have trash and the air is not clean. There's smoke coming out of chimneys. There's lots of stuff going on, like you can smell oil, and you can have terrible things happen . . . A lot of trash hanging around and you would have to clean it up and that's hazardous. (Bellugi et al., 1992, pp. 206-207)

As you can see, neither response constitutes a well-formed definition. The Down's syndrome children's definitions were either semantically impoverished (they did not have the vocabulary item) or were poorly formed linguistically. The Williams syndrome children's responses appear poorly formed almost at a pragmatic level—they know the word and how to use it but cannot abstract a definition appropriate for the task at hand.

On both spontaneous production and controlled production and comprehension tasks, Williams syndrome children showed remarkable preservation of language, albeit with some deviances. For example, most of the subjects scored between 80% and 100% correct in comprehension of (reversible) passive and conditional (if-then) sentences and in correcting sentences with errors like "I hope you to eat all your supper." In contrast, most of the Down's children scored less than 50% on such tasks. In a recognition vocabulary test in which they had to match the word to a picture, the Williams syndrome children scored *at least* at their age level, while all but one of the Down's syndrome children scored below their age level. Finally, on a production task (name as many examples of the category "animal" as you can), the Williams syndrome children often named as many instances as normal children their age do, while the Down's syndrome children named fewer. More important, however, the Williams syndrome children produced correct, but atypical and infrequent examples, like "brontosaurus, tyranadon, brontosaurus rex, dinosaurs, elephant, dog, cat, lion, baby hippopotamus, ibex, whale, bull, yak, zebra, puppy, kitten, tiger, koala, dragon." While all these productions are related to animals, they include unusual entries like ibex and yak, and are abnormal in including imaginary animals, separate listings for an adult and baby (cat and kitten), repetition of brontosaurus and/or erroneously substituting it for tyrannosaurus. The results from this controlled production task are consistent with the children's spontaneous use of infrequent, sometimes slightly incorrect words like "evacuate" for "empty" in "I'll have to evacuate the glass."

Apart from their language symptoms, there are two other deviances of Williams syndrome children that are interesting for our purposes. The first is an extreme auditory sensitivity: awareness of sounds in the environment before other people, and an aversion to sounds not usually considered aversive (Bellugi et al., 1994). The second (see Neville et al., 1994, for elaboration) is (perhaps a manifestation of that sensitivity) in the brain wave associated with auditory processing, the auditory evoked potential (EP). In Williams syndrome patients, the early components of these waves are larger than normal, particularly when auditory stimuli, tones, or spoken words are presented in rapid succession. Normally, there is a *refractory period,* a time right after stimulation when the system is unable to respond or respond as vigorously; this seems absent in these subjects. Apart from the amplitude difference, tone-generated EPs look normal; that is, they suggest that the normal brain centers are producing them. In contrast, the EPs for words have a very different *morphology* or shape, indicative of origin in different-from-normal brain centers. The word-produced EPs for Williams syndrome subjects also show greater-than-normal effects of semantic priming. It is interesting to note, however, that their visual EPs appear normal.

Neville et al. (1994) suggest the following from this pattern of results:

1. The hypersensitive auditory processing may underlie "the sparing of and the precocious and hyperfluent nature of the Williams subject language" (p. 82).

2. The lack of refractory response may underlie the production of infrequent and somewhat inappropriate words as "spreading activation" spreads farther with greater intensity than normal.

3. The abnormal morphology of the EPs to spoken words, but not tones or visual words, implicates different systems in the "mediat[ion of] the preserved language

in Williams [children from] those that operate in normal control subjects [consistent with] the fact that this development occurs following abnormal delays in the acquisition of auditory language" (p. 81).

Deacon (1997) explains the relative skills of Williams syndrome children as resulting from underdevelopment of much of the brain with the notable exception of the prefrontal cortex. The underdeveloped regions specialize in making conditioned associations, say, of an object to a word. The *prefrontal cortex* is a region that normally then draws connections between these conditioned associations, moving from associative to symbolic thinking, separating the word from individual instances. For the Williams syndrome child, the prefrontal cortex's mode of thought is operating relatively independently of the basic real world anchors, forced to "define" the language symbols not from instances experienced but exclusively from how they interact with other symbols linguistically. It also becomes the dominant mode of thought in development, because "competitive" processes from other brain regions are not available. So the Williams syndrome child does not have "language" preserved, but some characteristic (perhaps defining) qualities associated with it: symbolism, hierarchical structuring, and so on. As Deacon points out, these "higher-level" features paradoxically can exist independently of what we consider intelligent behavior. For normal functioning language, we need both the low-level associative skills and the higher ones.

It is not clear whether these symbolic and hierarchical structuring abilities are language-specific or are a general cognitive skill that a Williams syndrome child hyperextends to produce normal-looking language. (As mentioned in the last chapter, Deacon argues that language has evolved to optimize the brain's changing processing capacities during development—and we do see these skills evident in music, art, and mathematics—human cognitive nonlinguistic behaviors.) Williams syndrome children are social and therefore, in addition to a special reasoning ability, they may have preserved the underlying need to communicate and to copy social behaviors of adults. And they seem to be auditorily hypersensitive, which may make input in the auditory modality especially available so that they can imitate, remember, and respond to great chunks of words. Their syntactic abilities suggest that they also can analyze these chunks to derive the rules for word combination, but thus far no tests have been published of their competence in morphology so it is not entirely clear that they have analyzed forms and use rules productively.

So, to the extent that Williams syndrome children do language normally and fail at other cognitive tasks, they support a language module. But to the extent that they do it abnormally, they indicate that the language module is not a monolith: Normal language structure is complex and overspecified, achievable at least in part from many angles. As discussion of all the language learners in this chapter indicates, normal syntax, semantics, analysis, productivity, and pragmatics depend on many intact perceptual, cognitive, and social skills but may emerge from different individual applications of skills in these areas.

*Laura*

It is interesting to note that in addition to Williams syndrome, there are other cases of severe retardation with language relatively well preserved. Laura, who was studied by Yamada (1990) and whose drawing and discourse on hoarse voice were displayed in Chapter 1, is one such child. Like the Williams syndrome children, her language milestones were delayed (she had only 15-20 words at 2½ and did not talk in whole sentences until after 4), but then her language took off so that she even acquired some French when the family moved to France temporarily when she was 8. Like the Williams syndrome children, she was loquacious and pragmatically incorrect, circumlocutory in defining words, defining them with regard to specific experiences. She too was morphologically sensitive, repeating "Laura was eaten by an apple" with corrected syntax, "Laura was eating an apple."

For Williams syndrome children and Laura, different cognitive functions appear impaired, but nevertheless language developed well, although delayed. This suggests that it is not a genetically specified, preserved UG unfolding (which it should then do at the normal time), but a set of preserved, though incomplete, heuristics that act on language and other cognitive inputs, perhaps more successfully on language because of its redundancy and accessibility through social, semantic/conceptual, *and* analytic approaches. Note that for both Laura and the Williams syndrome children, the characteristic features of language—semanticity, arbitrariness, interchangeability, hierarchical structure, and so on—are mostly present. Thus, despite their severely impaired cognitive functioning, they have language in a way that none of the animals we examined in the last chapter achieved it.

## SUMMARY AND CONCLUSIONS

I began this chapter urging caution in interpreting the data to be presented in it. As we have seen, language data and data on the living conditions of abandoned, neglected, and abused children are incomplete and subject to much bias in the telling and retelling. Moreover, they are experiments of nature and as such are not rigorous; many factors may not be controlled, such as the child's starting point, previous experience in the environment, training after discovery, and so on, so we never can be sure of our conclusions. We next looked at three groups of children, those left to fend for themselves in the wild, those confined but with some human contact, and those deprived of language by a sensory deficit but not deprived of human social contact. Finally, we looked at children with congenital abnormalities in either language learning or cognitive functioning, to see the extent that linguistic and cognitive behaviors are modular.

Keeping in mind that our conclusions can at best be tentative because of the problems in interpreting the data, we can suggest the following:

1. Complete isolation from human society suppresses the urge to communicate, the spontaneous imitation of other human behavior, and particularly the imitation

---

**Box 3.5. Genetic Language Impairment and Preservation**

— There is a genetic familial language impairment. It is characterized by failure to abstract morphological regularities, with correctly marked forms learned as unanalyzed wholes.

— The familial disorder may differentially implicate the ability to analyze and generalize morphological rules, allowing language to be processed only holistically, as may be the case in adult language acquisition. Language acquisition may be facilitated by this childhood analytic ability, whether general-cognitive or a property of UG.

— There are forms of retardation that seem to leave language relatively well preserved. Williams syndrome is characterized by
  — auditory hypersensitivity, reflected both psychophysically and in the auditory evoked potential;
  — good vocabulary but use of infrequent or slightly deviant words, perhaps because of hyperarousal of spreading activation, reflected also in semantic priming effects in the auditory evoked potential;
  — pragmatic deviances like circumlocution or definition of words by examples of specific encounters with them;
  — use of, comprehension of, and metalinguistic awareness of complex syntactic structures, like reversible passives, embeddings, and if-then sentences; and
  — use of correct morphology.

— It is unclear whether this represents analysis of linguistic structures into fundamental units, and application of rules, or excellent auditory memory and production of, recognition of, or correction to familiar sequences.

---

of speech. Some contact with human society allows for the continued urge to communicate and imitate, allowing a better prognosis for recovery.

2. For recovery of language to be good, it is desirable, but not necessary, that training begin before puberty. Then the child may bring to the task special left-hemisphere analytic, perhaps language-specific, skills and the less mature, more flexible brain, accelerating the normal course of language learning.

3. If training begins after puberty, communication and language skills can be taught, but successful methods seem more akin to operant conditioning of language (or other behaviors) in animals than the relatively passive modeling that is the normal linguistic input to children.

4. If training begins after puberty, the language may have a radically different form from normal language, omitting syntactic fine points like inflections, and may be processed differently from normal, and less analytically, in a different cerebral hemisphere. But a first language can be acquired as an adult!

5. Given an appropriate nonconfining social situation with a responsive parent, if not one able to teach language traditionally, the urge to communicate is sufficiently great that children will invent their own symbol system, with many of the

features that characterize human communication. They have available general principles of naming, predicating, combining units into sentences perhaps recursively, and regularizing unit use into a coherent system. These may be used as a base for establishing more formal language, even late in life.

6. Some language-learning disabilities seem to occur in families, and implicate a general cognitive sequencing problem and/or a problem with abstract phonological and morphological analyses. The resulting language abnormalities may be circumvented with effort but also delay language or reading acquisition and manifest in subtle tests or in greater-than-normal numbers of (uncorrected) errors.

7. Some language-learning abilities seem to be relatively preserved in the face of other deficits in retardation. The relative preservation could suggest a language "module." However, language is acquired after a delay relative to normal, so does not indicate the normal unfolding of a UG, and reflects different processing (more infrequent words, perseveration of a sidetracked theme, definition by context experienced) from normal. A particular cognitive, perceptual, or social approach may be preserved or even overdeveloped relative to normal, selectively favoring one form of language learning.

Thus we saw relatively poor recovery for wild children, with practically no successes at speech recovery and intensive training necessary for recovery of language at all, as in Victor. In the neglected children, we saw poor recovery for Anna, who was not given individual attention. We saw excellent recovery for Isabelle, who received such attention and who did not require painstaking shaping as did Victor, and who took less than two years to learn what most children learn in five. And we saw medium recovery in Genie, who was past puberty and given specific training but who learned a symbol system markedly different from what she was taught, using different brain structures than usual.

In some retarded children, we saw exceptional vocabulary use, complex syntactic structures in both comprehension and production, and heightened auditory sensitivities both perceptually and neurologically. Preservation of their social interests along with exquisite auditory sensitivity and unconstrained abstract cognitive processing enabled compensatory language learning in the absence of fully functioning, appropriately grounded, abstract cognitive abilities.

In the language of Genie, LI children, and the retarded children, we see many of the higher-level design features of language, such as semanticity, arbitrariness, and recursiveness. Conspicuously missing often are duality of patterning and metalanguage, knowing how to define a word, or play on or with words, or when a use is figurative. Perhaps these design features, which require recognizing language as a "thing," in a sense relating to it from the outside and not simply using it correctly, require fully intact cognition, the interplay between concrete associations, and high-level symbolic skills. But without all features, the children's communications still look very language-like and very different from those of the animals taught humanlike language.

This chapter also presented evidence that spoken language acquisition and reading require good auditory sequencing abilities as well as good abilities to analyze and abstract patterns and apply them productively. Without either, we get language delays and deviant phonological and morphological processing. Both may represent general cognitive disorders with particular ramifications for language. Neither appears to significantly affect what we consider design features of language in those afflicted. These data as a whole suggest that for "normal" language, we must have many interacting cognitive and perceptual components in place, but that, absent one, the other components may cover to result in almost perfectly functional language.

Finally, looking at the structure of the communication developed by young deaf children for their own use, we found that it shared many of the communication and symbol characteristics of language, but not those normally attributed to the speech medium or the higher-level characteristics like metalanguage or perhaps arbitrariness. We suggested that these omissions were in part because of the young age of the speakers and in part because of the young age of the language. However, we also saw that adults who have learned no formal, abstract conventionalized language beyond such personal mime languages exist, think symbolically and remember without word and language, and can learn a formal, conventionalized system, beyond "the critical period."

In the next chapter, we will look at these conventionalized, abstract, gestural communication systems, presumably growing out of such "home sign" systems and developing given adult use, language change, and traditional transmission.

---

## REFERENCES

Bellugi, U., Bihrle, A., Jernigan, T., Trauner, D., & Doherty, S. (1990). Neuropsychological, neurological, and neuroanatomical profile of Williams syndrome. *American Journal of Medical Genetics Supplement, 6,* 115-125.

Bellugi, U., Bihrle, A., Neville, H., & Doherty, S. (1992). Language, cognition, and brain organization in a neurodevelopmental disorder. In M. R. Gunnar & C. A. Nelson (Eds.), *Developmental behavioral neuroscience: The Minnesota Symposium on Child Psychology* (pp. 201-232). Hillsdale, NJ: Lawrence Erlbaum.

Bellugi, U., Wang, P. P., & Jernigan, T. L. (1994). Williams syndrome: An unusual neuropsychological profile. In S. H. Broman & J. Grafman (Eds.), *Atypical cognitive deficits in developmental disorders* (pp. 23-56). Hillsdale, NJ: Lawrence Erlbaum.

Bloom, L. (1991). *Language development from two to three.* New York: Cambridge University Press.

Bloom, L., & Lehey, M. (1978). *Language development and language disorders.* New York: John Wiley.

Bradley, L., & Bryant, P. E. (1983). Categorizing sounds and learning to read: A causal connection. *Nature, 301,* 419-421.

Brown, R. (1958). *Words and things.* New York: Free Press.

Brown, R. (1973). *A first language.* Cambridge, MA: Harvard University Press.

Castles, A., & Coltheart, M. (1993). Varieties of developmental dyslexia. *Cognition, 47,* 149-180.

Curtiss, S. (1977). *Genie: A psycholinguistic study of a modern-day "wild child."* New York: Academic Press.

Curtiss, S., Fromkin, V., Krashen, S., Rigler, D., & Rigler, M. (1974). The linguistic development of Genie. *Language, 50,* 528-554.

Curtiss, S., & Tallal, P. (1991). On the nature of the language-impairment in language-impaired children. In J. F. Miller (Ed.), *Research on child language: A decade of progress* (pp. 189-210). Austin, TX: Pro-Ed.

Davis, K. (1940). Extreme social isolation of a child. *American Journal of Sociology, 45,* 554-565.

Davis, K. (1947). Final note on a case of extreme isolation. *American Journal of Sociology, 52,* 432-437.

Deacon, T. W. (1997). *The symbolic species: The co-evolution of language and the brain.* New York: Norton.

Dennis, W. (1941). The significance of feral man. *American Journal of Psychology, 54,* 425-432.

Dennis, W. (1951). Further analysis of reports of wild children. *Child Development, 22,* 153-158.

Erber, N. P. (1974). Visual perception of speech by deaf children: Recent developments and continuing needs. *Journal of Speech and Hearing Disorders, 39,* 178-185.

Farmer, M. E., & Klein, R. M. (1995). The evidence for a temporal processing deficit linked to dyslexia: A review. *Psychonomic Bulletin and Review, 2,* 460-493.

Feldman, H., Goldin-Meadow, S., & Gleitman, L. (1978). Beyond Herodotus: The creation of language by linguistically deprived deaf children. In A. Lock (Ed.), *Action, gesture, and symbol: The emergence of language* (pp. 351-413). New York: Academic Press.

Fletcher, P. (1991). Evidence from syntax for language impairment. In J. F. Miller (Ed.), *Research on child language: A decade of progress* (pp. 169-187). Austin, TX: Pro-Ed.

Frith, U. (1985). Beneath the surface of developmental dyslexia. In K. E. Patterson, J. C. Marshall, & M. Coltheart (Eds.), *Surface dyslexia: Neuropsychological and cognitive studies of phonological reading* (pp. 301-330). Hillsdale, NJ: Lawrence Erlbaum.

Fromkin, V., & Curtiss, S. (1992, April 17). ["Genie log": An e-mail transmission to "Colleagues and friends who have or will read the two part article 'A silent childhood' " by Russ Rymer].

Fromkin, V., Krashen, S., Curtiss, S., Rigler, D., & Rigler, M. (1974). The development of language in Genie: A case of language beyond the "critical period." *Brain and Language, 1,* 81-107.

Geiger, G., & Lettvin, J. Y. (1987). Peripheral vision in persons with dyslexia. *New England Journal of Medicine, 316,* 1238-1243.

Goldin-Meadow, S. (1982). The resilience of recursion: A study of a communication system developed without a conventional language model. In E. Wanner & L. R. Gleitman (Eds.), *Language acquisition: The state of the art* (pp. 51-77). Cambridge: Cambridge University Press.

Goldin-Meadow, S., Butcher, C., Mylander, C., & Dodge, M. (1994). Nouns and verbs in a self-styled gesture system: What's in a name? *Cognitive Psychology, 27,* 259-319.

Goldin-Meadow, S., & Feldman, H. (1977). The development of language-like communication without a language model. *Science, 197,* 401-403.

Goldin-Meadow, S., & Mylander, C. (1983). Gestural communication in deaf children: Noneffect of parental input on language development. *Science, 221,* 372-374.

Gopnik, M., & Crago, M. B. (1991). Familial aggregation of a developmental language disorder. *Cognition, 39,* 1-50.

Hyona, J., & Olson, R. K. (1995). Eye fixation patterns among dyslexic and normal readers: Effects of word length and word frequency. *Journal of Experimental Psychology: Learning, Memory, and Cognition, 21,* 1430-1440.

Krashen, S. D. (1973). Lateralization, language learning, and the critical period: Some new evidence. *Language Learning, 23,* 63-74.

Lane, H. (1979). *The wild boy of Aveyron.* London: Granada.

Marcus, S. (1996, March 31). The wild boy of Nuremberg. *New York Times Book Review,* pp. 11-12.

Martin, R. C. (1995). Heterogeneity of deficits in developmental dyslexia and implications for methodology. *Psychonomic Bulletin and Review, 2,* 494-500.

Mason, M. K. (1942). Learning to speak after six and one-half years of silence. *Journal of Speech Disorders, 7,* 295-304.

Merzenich, M. M., Jenkins, W. M., Johnston, P., Schreiner, C., Miller, S. L., & Tallal, P. (1996). Temporal processing deficits of language-learning impaired children ameliorated by training. *Science, 271,* 77-81.

Neville, H. J., Mills, D. L., & Bellugi, U. (1994). Effects of altered auditory sensitivity and age of language acquisition on the development of language-relevant neural systems: Preliminary studies of Williams syndrome. In S. H. Broman & J. Grafman (Eds.), *Atypical cognitive deficits in developmental disorders* (pp. 67-83). Hillsdale, NJ: Lawrence Erlbaum.

Newport, E. L. (1990). Maturational constraints on language learning. *Cognitive Science, 14,* 11-28.

Rayner, K. (1986). Eye movements and perceptual span in beginning and skilled readers. *Journal of Experimental Child Psychology, 41,* 211-236.

Rayner, K., Pollatsek, A., & Bilsky, A. B. (1995). Can a temporal processing deficit account for dyslexia? *Psychonomic Bulletin and Review, 2,* 501-507.

Richardson, E. (1984). The impact of phonemic processing instruction on the reading achievement of reading-disabled children. In S. J. White & V. Teller (Eds.), *Annals of the New York Academy of Sciences: Vol. 433: Discourses in reading and linguistics* (pp. 97-118). New York: New York Academy of Sciences.

Richardson, S. O. (1992). Historical perspectives on dyslexia. *Journal of Learning Disabilities, 25,* 40-47.

Roush, W. (1995). Arguing over why Johnny can't read. *Science, 267,* 1896-1898.

Rymer, R. (1992, April 13, 20). Annals of science: A silent childhood. *New Yorker,* pp. 41-53, 43-77.

Schaller, S. (1995). *A man without words.* Berkeley: University of California Press.

Schlesinger, I. M. (1978). The acquisition of bimodal language. In I. M. Schlesinger & L. Namir (Eds.), *Sign language of the deaf* (pp. 57-93). New York: Academic Press.

Seymour, P. H. K., & MacGregor, C. J. (1984). Developmental dyslexia: A cognitive, experimental analysis of phonological, morphemic, and visual impairments. *Cognitive Neuropsychology, 1,* 43-82.

Shaywitz, B. A., & Waxman, S. G. (1987). Dyslexia. *New England Journal of Medicine, 316,* 1268-1270.

Stewart, D. A. (1993). Bi-Bi to MCE? *American Annals of the Deaf, 138,* 331-337.

Studdert-Kennedy, M., & Mody, M. (1995). Auditory temporal processing deficits in the reading impaired: A critical review of the evidence. *Psychonomic Bulletin and Review, 2,* 508-514.

Tallal, P., Galaburda, A. M., Llinas, R. R., & von Euler, C. (Eds.). (1993). *Annals of the New York Academy of Sciences, Vol. 682: Temporal information processing in the nervous system.* New York: New York Academy of Sciences.

Tallal, P., Miller, S. L., Bedi, G., Byma, G., Wang, X., Nagarajan, S. S., Schreiner, C., Jenkins, W. M., & Merzenich, M. M. (1996). Language comprehension in language-learning impaired children improved with acoustically modified speech. *Science, 271,* 81-84.

Tervoort, B. T. (1978). Bilingual interference. In I. M. Schlesinger & L. Namir (Eds.), *Sign language of the deaf* (pp. 169-240). New York: Academic Press.

Tyler, E. B. (1863). Wild-men and beast children. *Anthropological Review, 1,* 29-32.

Vernon, M. C., & Koh, S. D. (1971). Effects of oral preschool compared to early manual communication on education and communication in deaf children. *American Annals of the Deaf, 116,* 569-574.

Wolf, M. (1991). Naming speed and reading: The contribution of the cognitive neurosciences. *Reading Research Quarterly, 26,* 123-140.

Yamada, J. E. (1990). *Laura: A case for the modularity of language.* Cambridge: Bradford Books of MIT Press.

Zingg, R. M. (1940). Feral man and extreme cases of isolation. *American Journal of Psychology, 53,* 487-517.

---

**STUDY QUESTIONS**

---

1. Critically discuss the shortcomings of the case histories presented in this chapter. Why is it difficult to draw definite conclusions from these data?

2. Compare Dr. Itard's methods of training Victor with Premack's methods for training Sarah, discussed in Chapter 2. Be specific in making your comparisons!

3. Compare Genie's language acquisition with normal language acquisition. Aside from the age difference, what differences and similarities do you see in her progression of skills?

4. Critically evaluate the critical period notion in language acquisition, given the data presented in this chapter. Discuss whether it is reasonable to assume special language-specific blueprints unfolding at different ages as opposed to general cognitive blueprints.

5. Critically consider the evidence for a language "module" as opposed to a set of general cognitive skills applied to language. Is language its own faculty?

6. Given the data presented in this chapter, which language features seem most vulnerable to disruption by abnormal social, biological, and cognitive constraints. Map the features to the specific deviant constraint.

# 4

# Sign Language as a Primary Language

In Chapter 3, we looked at gesture systems created by deaf children living in a hearing community. The features of these systems were impressive as indicators of native human communication abilities but fell short of our stringent criteria for language. Of course, we were looking at productions of 4-year-old and younger children, and of children who had generated their own system in the absence of reasonable adult models. When these children grow up and have children and grandchildren, will the gesture systems used in their homes as the primary mode of communication show similar impoverishment compared with spoken language? Or will the gesture system take on the semantic and syntactic complexities of human language?

Linguistic complexity could develop from the pressures of dealing with an adult's world or through normal conversation with other deaf individuals who have more sophisticated language. It could also have an innate cause: The putative bioprogram operating on limited input to produce the language observed in the first-generation deaf children of Chapter 3 would not have to start from scratch in the second-generation children.

As I mentioned in Chapter 1, as far back as Aristotle, speech has been imbued with special properties peculiarly conducive to language. To Aristotle, the vocal apparatus was crucial to language, and deafness was the result of atrophy of hearing when cognitive impairment prevented an individual from learning language and exercising the auditory system. More recently, as I presented in Chapter 2, Hockett (1960) began his list of characteristic features for language with vocal-auditory transmission and followed with several features, such as broadcast transmission and reception, that are characteristic of the speech mode of communication. Most languages do use the vocal-auditory channels and so automatically satisfy these criteria. By definition, visual-gestural systems violate the criterion of vocal-auditory transmission and some other criteria peculiar to speech. For example, we must choose to look at a gesture but have no choice except to hear a sound; gestural languages are less able to broadcast than spoken languages.

Does this mean that a visual-gestural system is not a language? Or are the higher-level criteria like arbitrariness, semanticity, or recursiveness more central to our concept of what a language is? If a visual language then meets these standards, we should call it a language despite its modality. Is there something about the vocal-auditory system that enables language to have these special other characteristics? Or is language-as-a-symbol-system a general human cognitive skill relatively independent of the form of the input and output? In either case, how does use of the visual-gestural channel for input and output affect the characteristics of human communication?

To begin to answer these questions, in this chapter we will study the structure and processing of sign languages. Sign languages are used by deaf communities throughout the world. Because of the extensive linguistic and psycholinguistic data available, we will concentrate on American Sign Language (ASL), the system used by the deaf community in the United States. At times, we will compare ASL with other signed languages.

## A BRIEF HISTORY OF ASL

### The Birth of ASL

To understand the evolution of sign language, one has to consider the population using it. For all spoken languages, there is an obvious community of speakers—most people are hearing and it is simple to find people to talk to. Until the eighteenth century in the Western world, if they were wealthy, deaf children were educated on an individual basis. If poor, they were not educated at all. For those educated, instruction was primarily in speech and reading, and communication was necessarily labored. However, the educated deaf person would become integrated into the hearing community. The uneducated deaf person, like Idelfonso (described in Chapter 3), presumably survived within the hearing community by using some *home sign,* a primitive gesture system spontaneously developed, such as those described in Chapter 3. A deaf individual in a large community might meet other deaf individuals with similarly developed systems. Although there are mentions of deaf communities with gestural systems before the eighteenth century, little is known about them (Woodward, 1978).

In 1760 the Abbé de L'Épée opened the first school for the deaf in Paris, initiating group instruction and inadvertently establishing a deaf community. De L'Épée invented gestures to name objects; the deaf students took those "nouns" and invented their own adjectives, adverbs, and verbs to form a language (Lane,

1979). About 50 years later, an American involved in deaf education, Gallaudet, visited de L'Épée's school in Paris and took his most promising pupil, Le Clerc, back to Hartford, Connecticut, to teach in a school for the deaf he was opening there. Le Clerc's arrival and dissemination of French Sign Language (FSL) in the United States marks the birth of ASL. However, arguments have been made that a sign language must have existed before Gallaudet's return because, by 1864, 48 years after the Hartford school had opened, there were enough American deaf educated in sign to establish a college for signing students, Gallaudet College in Washington, D.C. (Woodward, 1978).

It is important to observe that ASL derives from FSL, not from English or the British signing system, BSL. To people unfamiliar with the deaf community, this observation may come as a surprise, in part because nonsigners think there must be a single universal sign language, and in part because Americans assume easy communication with the British. The two sign languages, however, are independent of the spoken languages; a BSL user and an ASL user may need an interpreter to converse together.

## Signed Languages as Creoles

In Chapter 1, I briefly reviewed the conditions under which pidgins and creoles develop (this is described more fully in Chapter 8 of *Language and Its Normal Processing*): A community is perhaps forcibly created, the members of which do not share any full common language, and a common language is imposed by the dominating creators. In this new community, the adults speak a pidgin, a poorly formed sublanguage amalgamated from their native languages and the dominating language, with few regularizations and little syntactic structure. The second generation, with pidgin and perhaps some full parent languages as input, develops structure, function words, and so on, regularizing the pidgin into a creole.

It has been cogently argued that ASL (and perhaps most other signed languages) constitutes a creole and not a full-fledged independent language. As we have seen, FSL was introduced into the United States as the cultured, educated sign language by virtue of its being explicitly taught in a school. This cultured emphasis made it a high-class, dominating form. Presumably, before this introduction there were native American sign systems, perhaps many of them, created in the manner described in Chapter 3. When these multiple-native-language speakers got together for instruction in the high form, FSL, the conditions would have been perfect for development of a creole (Woodward, 1978).

A second creolizing influence is, of course, the language of the dominant community, the hearing people—English. Even when sign is freely taught, instruction is continued in English for reading and writing, and the structures and semantics of English will thus continually influence sign.

The decreolizing process is likely to be slower in sign language than in spoken language because, on the one hand, the modality difference will limit the amount of incorporation of the dominant, spoken language, and, on the other hand, the social pressure from educators and parents trying to integrate the deaf into the hearing community will limit the self-containment of sign as a language. Moreover, given that only 3% to 8% of deaf children have deaf parents, most deaf children learn sign late (in school) after some other communication system has been used (Mayberry & Eichen, 1991). So the process of creolization, to some extent, takes place *each* generation. Continuity and progress in decreolizing can be provided only by the handful of deaf who learn ASL as their native language (Fischer, 1978).

If the argument about creoles applies to ASL, we should expect to see features of ASL common to other creoles—reduplication, few function "words," and so forth. We would not want to use this to argue that the visual modality per se constrains language in this way, given that in spoken creoles we have analogues in vocal-auditory languages.

If the argument that ASL is a creole is correct, it demonstrates an important social constraint on the form of language: Regardless of modality, relatively impoverished exposure to adult language and the necessity of communicating with speakers of different pidgins affect the nature of language. As we saw in Chapter 3, the innate urge to discourse causes children to develop their own "language"; with this language as input, there may also be innate constraints to modify the systems to show more regular features of language. The general thrusts of these language changes indicate the cognitive pressures toward the most efficient type of communication for humans, language.

## THE STRUCTURE OF ASL

## Producing ASL

### The Dimensions of Sign

ASL is produced within a window bounded by the top of the head and the waist and about a foot on either side of the body. It consists of regularly specified movements of the hand(s), arm(s), face, and body. For the most part, it is the movements of the hands and arms that are important in distinguishing signs.

Signs are commonly differentiated along four dimensions: *movement, handshape, location* in signing space (Stokoe, Casterline, & Croneburg, 1965), and *orientation* of the palm (Battison, 1978). For example (see Figure 4.1), the sign THINK (remember, signs are written in capitals to differentiate them from translated English) is produced by moving the hand to the forehead with the index finger pointing to it and the back of the hand oriented toward the observer. The handshape is the index finger extended from an otherwise closed fist; the movement is a touch at the forehead; the location is the forehead; and the orientation is the back of the hand out. THINK differs from WONDER only in movement; in WONDER, the index finger traces small circles on the forehead. THINK differs from IDEA only in handshape; in IDEA, the little finger alone is extended. THINK differs from one sign for GERMAN only in orientation; in GERMAN, the back of the hand contacts

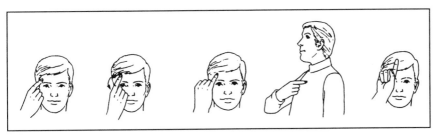

**Figure 4.1.** Five Signs Showing Formational Differences in One Parameter From THINK

NOTE: WONDER changes movement, tracing a circle; IDEA is shaped with the little finger instead of the index finger; ME is located at the chest instead of the forehead; and this sign for GERMAN is oriented with the palm out instead of in.

the forehead. If two signs differ from each other in only one dimension, they constitute "minimal pairs" analogous to words differing in only one phoneme.

Most signs, like most words, differ from one another in several dimensions simultaneously. Battison (1978) estimated that there are 25 distinct locations, 45 distinct handshapes, 10 distinct movements, and 10 distinct orientations. These dimensions do not correspond directly to phonemes or phonetic features but do show hierarchical segmental structure like the units of spoken language. Although sign dictionaries typically show a sign as consisting of a unitary spatial combination of values on the four dimensions, in fact, as Liddell and Johnson (1989) validly point out, signs entail a sequential structure, like speech, in which handshape or orientation necessarily change with the movement, as does location. Like a syllable's consonants and vowels (acoustically, a sequence of changing frequencies or *transitions* as the articulators move and steady frequencies at the target position—see Chapter 6 of the companion volume), a sign consists of "segments," movements, and holds, often with a different dimension value at each hold. The phonological structure of sign places the dimensions of movement and location at the same hierarchical level, and handshape at another one, because, as we will see, handshape alone can represent both an articulatory unit and a free morpheme, a word (Sandler, 1990).

### Fingerspelling

An important subsystem of ASL is fingerspelling, which the uninitiated often erroneously consider to be all of sign. (The letters of the manual alphabet are displayed in Figure 4.2.) In most fingerspelling, handshape is the only changing dimension: The dominant hand is held up, between the shoulder and the cheek, oriented for the most part with palm facing the observer. One handshape corresponds to each letter. "A" is a closed fist, thumb next to the index finger; "b" an open hand with thumb across the palm; "c" an open hand with fingers curved and thumb protruding; and so on. A few of the letters of fingerspelling contain an obvious orientation or movement change; for example, "z" is made with the hand oriented down and index finger tracing a "z" in the air.

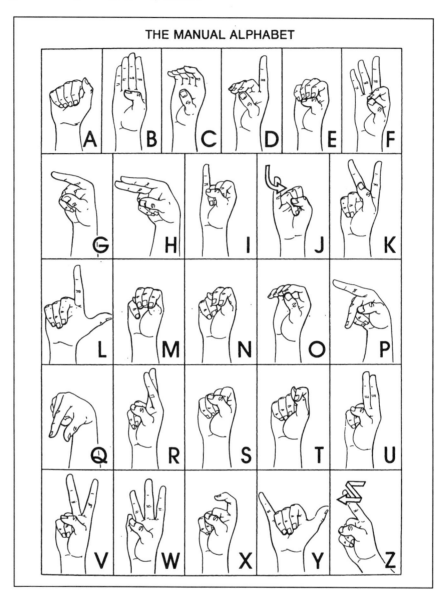

**Figure 4.2.** The American Manual Alphabet

SOURCE: From *The Joy of Signing,* second edition, 1987, p. 16, Dr. Lottie L. Riekhof. Copyrighted by Gospel Publishing House, 1445 Boonville Avenue, Springfield MO 65802. Used by permission.

NOTE: Drawings show a side view. In actual practice, the letters should face the persons with whom you are communicating.

Depending on the backgrounds of the signers, fingerspelling serves several functions in sign. If one of the signers is fluent in English and not in ASL, conversation may consist entirely of spelled words. Usually, though, fingerspelling is reserved for English words for which there is no corresponding ASL sign or for which one or the other of the signers may not know a sign. This occurs most often when one of the signers is nonnative; native language users usually find a way to express a concept that has no sign using phrases as descriptors. Finally, as with the borrowing of foreign words into English, words may be borrowed from English into ASL, and then they are fingerspelled.

It is in borrowing from English that we see incorporation of fingerspelling into pure ASL, in two ways. In fingerspelling *formulae* (Akamatsu, 1985; Battison, 1978; Padden, 1991), the spelling pattern for words becomes conventionalized. The words are usually short, although some long words are fingerspelling formulae. *Conventionalization* refers to changes in the fingerspelling pattern, making it look less like discrete letters and more like a sign of the language. For example, fingerspelled J-0-B is produced with three almost separate motions, which you can see by making the three letters with the help of Figure 4.2. In contrast, JOB is *signed* with a fluid motion going from "j" to "b" (the "o" is never fully realized), and the "b" produced with the back of the hand facing the observer. The result is *one sign,* a sequence of two holds each with a different handshape and the movement between them: the "j"-hand in initial position and a modified "b"-hand in final position. *Fluidity* of motion or *flow* refers to motion in a single direction, with blending of separate hand configurations in a smooth movement (Frishberg, 1975).

In *initialization,* the second use of fingerspelling within true ASL, a sign is created by using the handshape corresponding to the fingerspelled first letter of an equivalent English word. For example, one sign for computer is made by a "c" handshape of the dominant hand moving along the forearm of the nondominant hand. Initialized signs are usually words borrowed from English and may be avoided by signers wishing to dissociate themselves from influences of the hearing community (Battison, 1978). This is a social influence on "dialect" as we also see in spoken language (see Chapter 1 in this volume; in the companion volume, note particularly the Martha's Vineyard faithful [Chapter 8] and bilinguals' social use of code-switching [Chapter 10]).

It is interesting to note that British Sign Language uses a completely different system of fingerspelling, one way of demonstrating the independence of the two languages. In BSL, fingerspelling is two-handed, with one hand pointing to locations (fingers or different places on the palm) on the other hand. Each location corresponds to a different letter.

### Constraints on Sign Formation

I find studying signed language fascinating because it tempts me to ask "dumb" questions that would never occur to me to ask about English but that are just as applicable. For instance, the preceding discussion prompts questions like these: "Why is that the sign for computer?" or "Why does BSL use two-handed finger-spelling?" Recognizing the question for sign, I turn it around and apply it to any language, raising for myself age-old philosophical issues. Why are computers called computers? Why does the word for computers begin with a /k/ sound rather than a /g/? Or, even, why do we use our voices alone to indicate words, only rarely supplementing our vocal articulatory repertoire with hand gestures? At times the answer to such questions may be a simple "Why not?" but at other times the answer may tell us something very important about why language is the way it is.

Take, for example, the difference between one-handed and two-handed finger-spelling. An efficient one-handed speller might argue that two-handed finger-spelling is inefficient: It ties up both hands, involves coordination of the two hands, and requires more movement. A two-handed fingerspeller could rebut with the observation that movements are more visible on two hands than on one, or that the flexible index finger is used more than the clumsier fourth and pinky fingers. Both arguments use production and perception *constraints* on the form of the language: If a gesture is too hard to see or to make, it will not or does not exist. Obviously, both one-handed and two-handed fingerspelling (because both exist) must fall within the bounds of reasonably perceptible and producible, although in different ways.

What constraints can we observe in sign production? No sign would occur that had to be signed behind the back or the head because it would not be visible. Similarly, no sign would occur that had to be produced by bending down or stretching because those require too much production effort. In fact, the window in which signs are produced is exactly the area in which it is easiest to move the arms, and that is, at the same time, the most visible area to an observer looking at the face of the transmitter. (Notice that for speech there are probably similar constraints: Information most critical for speech—the first three formants—lies in the frequency range to which the ear is most sensitive, and all articulatory gestures are producible without great effort.)

It is in "looking at the face" that we see a second interesting set of constraints on sign production. In natural face-to-face conversation, people make eye contact and use it to signal turn-taking, social interest, and so forth. Eye contact is also something that develops very early in infants and presumably is a universal aspect of human contact. Is eye contact also made in a gestural language, where the temptation might be to watch the moving objects, the hands? The answer is yes; fluent signers watch each other's faces, and probably for that reason we see an interesting pattern in sign production (Siple, 1978): Signs with location on the face or neck are more finely differentiated in handshape and location than signs pro-duced in the lower part of the signing window. Note, for example, that fingerspelling (which entails fine handshape discriminations) is done at a location near the side of the face. If one is gazing at the face, one's central vision encompasses this area. As we have seen, central or foveal vision is more acute than peripheral vision (except for certain dyslexics) and is thus more capable of making fine differentia-tions: Try reading out of the corner of your eye! Signs that fall in the periphery tend to be much grosser, usually using two hands (thereby increasing redundancy where there is more likely to be a perceptual error) and involving larger movements than signs made at or near the face. Moreover, on the face very small differences in location, such as between the forehead and the nose, may be "phonemic," that is, signal different signs. On the body, much larger distances—like the shoulder versus the heart—distinguish "phonemes." So here we see an apparent match between the perceptual capacity of the visual system and the demands made on the system by the language.

The third constraint on signing has to do with manual coordination. Try to make your two hands do separate things simultaneously (such as drumming *different* rhythms with the fingers of each hand). Then coordinate them so they are doing the same thing. As you can see, it is much easier to move both hands if they are doing the same thing, or to move one hand while the other is doing nothing, than to have them act independently. These are the bases of the *dominance* and *symmetry* constraints in ASL (Battison, 1978; Liddell & Johnson, 1989): If both hands are used in making a sign, either one is passive and the other acts on it (dominance), or the two hands move together with the same handshape (symmetry).

One way of proving that these constraints serve as "phonological" *rules* is to look at what happens to signs introduced into the language that violate the constraints. Historically, there were signs that were made on the face with two hands that were made asymmetrically, or that were made on the body with one hand. Signs are also regularly introduced by educators of the deaf that may violate the constraints, having been invented by nonnative speakers. Frishberg (1975) and Battison (1978) looked at the course of change of signs in the language and noted general principles of historical change in ASL (there are films of signing from the early 1900s that were consulted for this purpose):

1. Signs made in contact with the face
   (a) tend to become one-handed and
   (b) tend to displace from the center of the face away from direct contact with the sense organs, to the periphery of the face.
2. Signs made without contact on the face
   (a) tend to become two-handed and
   (b) tend to centralize about the line of bilateral symmetry and move up toward the hollow of the throat.
3. Two-handed asymmetric signs become symmetric in handshape and movement (an assimilation of handshape as it were; Liddell & Johnson, 1989).
4. One-handed signs that become two-handed also become symmetric.

Examination of these rules should show clearly, in most cases, their relation to the constraints just outlined (see also Liddell & Johnson, 1989). We see also historically a tendency to minimize the productive effort in signing, *Zipf's Law* (the length of spoken words is inversely related to their frequency—see Chapter 3 of the companion volume) for sign. BIRD, for example, was originally signed by making the thumb and forefinger form a beak at the lips and then spreading the arms to flap wings. Over time the second movement was deleted—the two-handed sign with facial contact became one-handed—saving productive effort (Frishberg, 1975). Signs involving two separate locations tend to reduce the distance between their locations over time, as do sign sequences in conversation, an assimilation of place of articulation differences (Liddell & Johnson, 1989).

---

**Box 4.1. Perceiving and Producing Sign**

— Signed languages use handshape, location of the hand relative to the body, movement of the hand and arm, and orientation of the hand to distinguish signs.

— Accompanying hand and arm movements are facial gestures and head movements, some for nonlinguistic, communicative purposes as in spoken languages, and some for linguistic purposes. Linguistically, the face and head may redundantly convey the sign or may provide a semantic or grammatical marker not conveyed by the hands.

— Sign language phonology reflects perceptual and production constraints on form:

    — Sign is produced in the most visible window, given that people communicate looking at each other's faces.

    — Signs are more finely differentiated on the face than on the body, conforming to visual acuity given the eyes as social focus.

    — Signs are produced with either one hand/arm active and the other passive, or the two moving together, conforming to ease of coordinating the hands.

    — More frequently used signs become shorter, produced with minimal effort.

    — Introduced signs violating these constraints change historically to conform to them.

— Such constraints governed by the capabilities of the auditory and oral systems apply as well to spoken languages.

---

In sign the effects of perceptual and production limitations are easily seen. They exist also for spoken languages, as I have indicated. Try to think of examples in your native language.

### Face and Body Movements in Sign Production

In addition to moving the hands and arms, signers move their faces, heads, and bodies to communicate. Nonmanual gestures serve linguistic functions in sign, sometimes redundantly with manual gestures. As in oral languages, they also serve nonlinguistic functions (Baker & Padden, 1978). Examples of linguistic functions are making searching movements with the eyes while signing SEARCH (Baker & Padden, 1978), blinking at constituent boundaries (Baker & Padden, 1978), raising the eyebrows while making subordinate clauses (Liddell, 1980), flapping the tongue to intensify a point (Davies, 1985), or raising the head for a sign produced on the neck to expose the neck. Nonlinguistic functions of face and body movements in sign fall into the same general categories as in spoken language: eye gaze used to indicate turn-taking in conversation, blinking or eye narrowing to indicate emotional distress, and so on (Baker & Padden, 1978).

It should be noted that there are many signs produced by some combination of facial or head movement with the hand movement. The sign for MENSTRUAL PERIOD, for example, has a manual gesture accompanied by the puffing of one cheek. To WHISPER the sign in mixed company, the hand movement may not appear at all, with the meaning conveyed only by puffing the cheek (Baker & Padden, 1978). The old sign for WONDER had the head moving in small circles while the index finger pointed to the forehead. As the sign changed, the movement of the head was transferred to the hand, the usual direction of change in sign (Frishberg, 1975). This is seen also in the sign for YES, which is made with a closed fist bobbing at the wrist, imitating a head nodding. Although the head can nod too, either alone or with the hand, the meaning can be conveyed by the hand alone.

## Signs and Meaning

We cannot really equate a particular aspect of a signed language with one of spoken language, but, as a beginning, let us say that a sign roughly corresponds to a word. As we discuss sign and meaning, you will see that this is a gross simplification and generalization, but we need to begin somewhere. We start with the word level partly because as English speakers we think easily about language with respect to words, and partly because the sign dictionary makers also think this way. If you thumb through a dictionary of sign, you will note signs corresponding to many English content words. If the dictionary is a real ASL dictionary (as opposed to signed English—we will discuss this and the difference between signed English and ASL later), you may also note a strange absence of function words or inflectional affixes. That there are no independent "function signs" led early investigators to consider sign "primitive." We will see that instead it indicates that a sign is not equivalent to a word; inflecting occurs not by adding morpheme signs to a word beginning or end but by changing the whole sign movement in a regular way, *modulating* it.

### Functors and ASL

A few observations may be made concerning the lack of function signs. First, as we saw earlier, some have argued that sign is a creole and that creoles as a class have few words serving only grammatical function. Creoles tend to employ content words as function words, as in the example in Chapter 8 of *Language and Its Normal Processing* from Hawaiian Creole (Bickerton, 1982): /dei wen go ap dea erli in da mawning go plaen/; they went-go up there early in the morning go-to plant. Here the second "go" is redeployed as a function word. If sign is a creole, we should find a similar pattern. Indeed, FINISH may be used as a time marker in ASL (Fischer, 1978): An English translation for TOUCH+FINISH EUROPE, YOU? is "Have you been to Europe?" (Word-for-word translation from *any* language can produce strange-looking language. TOUCH here means "visit." *Glossing,* writing the signs literally in English, is not translation.)

The second and third explanations for the failure to find function signs derive from where one looks in the sign signal. Recall the discussion of "simultaneity and smear" from Chapters 1 and 2 (see also Chapter 7 of the companion volume). Any one segment of the speech signal can convey a number of things—consonant, vowel, who the speaker is *(speaker identity),* whether the speaker is happy or stressed (emotion), whether the segment is being asked or stated (syntax)—and the cues for any one of these appear across many segments of the signal. If you have been picturing sign production, you probably have already observed a similar situation, at least for simultaneity. We can move our faces and hands at the same time, and both hands at the same time. Hearing people who look at the language have a tendency to dismiss what happens on the face as paralinguistic because facial movements accompanying oral language are not considered real language. For this reason, it was assumed for many years that there were no function words in sign at all. However, in discussing facial markers in sign, I observed that the eyebrows are raised during subordinate clauses and that the tongue is flapped as an intensifier. Is it reasonable to exclude these as function words, or would it be wiser to note the eyebrow raise and translate it as *that* or *which*? (It is possible that these facial expressions may someday be conveyed on the hands, following the historical trend of lexical information shifting from the face to the hands.)

So we might give as the second explanation for the missing function words that the sign lexicographers omitted the function words carried on the face. The third explanation also rests on a failure to notice critical aspects of sign that differ from (many) spoken languages but, in this case, that do occur on the hands (Klima & Bellugi, 1979/1988). Because of the bias toward the English way of doing things, linguists studying sign looked for separate signs to convey each word of English, without noticing *parts* of signs that could have consistent morphological function, like inflections used in English and other languages. For example, GIRL is produced with closed fingers, thumb extended and touching the cheek; BOY is produced with a similar, though not identical, handshape at the forehead. MOTHER, GRANDMOTHER, and LADY share location with GIRL while FATHER, GRANDFATHER, and GENTLEMAN share location with BOY. MOTHER and FATHER share all parameters but location, as do GRAND-MOTHER and GRANDFATHER, and GENTLEMAN and LADY. One way to analyze this is to argue that *location here is a morpheme for gender* (as we have, say, in the Latin languages, among others). Indeed, signs introduced into the language that refer to things with obvious gender, historically, migrate to conform to these gender markings (Frishberg, 1975). (I wonder whether the gender marking is arbitrary. Note that the male marking is higher than the female, perhaps iconically suggesting dominance or greater height. The male marker is also made in the "THINK" location, perhaps giving it a connotation of intelligence the female marker lacks.)

A second example concerns ASL's treatment of pronouns (Bellugi & Klima, 1982); again, most are not marked by separate signs. *I* and *you* have specific signs, a point to the appropriate body. *He* and *her* are "variable" signs, created during conversation in what is called *indexing.* When a person is first mentioned, she or he is named with a sign, and if the signer expects to continue to talk about her or him, the signer will either gaze at a particular horizontal position at about waist level when the person is named and point to that approximate position, or terminate the name with the hand coming to rest in that position. The (fluent) observer now records the position on the invisible "stage" as representing that named individual. From then on in the narrative, the signer can sign any verb in that position and convey that it is the previously named person performing it without rementioning the person specifically. (We do something like this in speech when we look to where we last saw a person when we talk about him or her.) So *the location could be considered as indicating (indexing) pronominal reference.*

Note the subtlety for translation, though! The dictionary form of GIVE is one-handed, open, palm up, moving away from the signer, occurring between the chest and the waist. In conversation, that form is best translated as I GIVE YOU. In "you give me," the sign is performed almost identically; the difference is that the direction of movement is reversed. If the signer has previously been talking about Jane (stage right) and Dick (stage left), "she gives him" is signed by making GIVE move from right to left, and "he gives her" by making it moving from left to right. Technically, though, the different propositions "I give you," "you give me," "he gives her," "she gives him" are each produced with only one sign—an inflected variant of GIVE.

We have just seen that previously established positions in space can identify a person and that place of articulation on the face can mark gender. Position in space from the back of the signer to the front can mark tense. Signs produced immediately in front of the signer represent events of the near present; those extended in front are of the future; and those near the shoulder (as back as can be comfortably produced) and behind the eyes are of the past. Gestures pointing over the shoulder signify distant past. Verbs are marked for tense by producing them in any of these locations. A tense marker may be appended to the sentence as with YESTERDAY (at the shoulder), which would indicate a past tense for the whole sentence (Frishberg, 1975).

In the examples given so far, I have shown how movement or location functions as function "words" and I have restricted examples to morphological markings that have equivalents in English. In the next example, handshape conveys the grammatical function, and the equivalent part of speech cannot be found in English but is found in some oral languages such as Navajo (Newport & Bellugi, 1978). These are *classifiers,* markers for a single abstract dimension of a group of possible referents. ASL uses classifiers for, among others, person, regardless of age or sex (index finger raised); vehicle regardless of type, that is, car, boat, sled (hand horizontal, thumb, middle, and index fingers extended and spread); and small, thin objects (little finger alone extended). Classifiers are used as pronouns are used.

As a last example of ASL morphology, we will look at aspect markings in sign, which use differences in movement. As you may recall, like tense, aspect makes a temporal modification of the sentence but, instead of locating it at a specific time, aspect marks how an action occurs over time: Is the action a one-time occurrence? Is it habitual? Is it discrete but repetitive? In English, aspect and tense share the same suffix except in the progressive (-ing) aspect, so aspect is relatively invisible but still colors meaning. Consider, for example: I gave at the office [and will never give again]; I am [a] giving person (this is a continual quality); I gave to each of the charities (each is one-time but they happen serially).

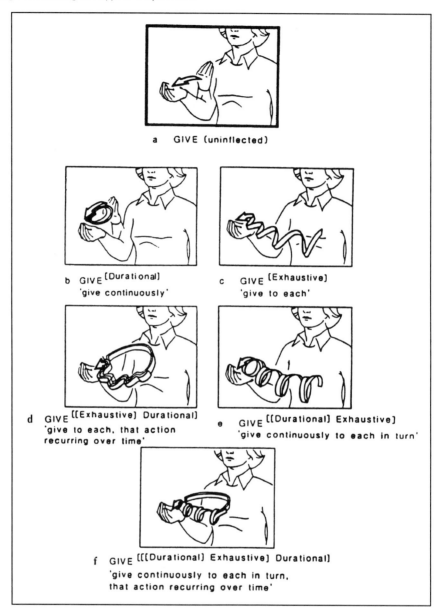

a    GIVE (uninflected)

b    GIVE [Durational]
     'give continuously'

c    GIVE [Exhaustive]
     'give to each'

d    GIVE [[Exhaustive] Durational]
     'give to each, that action
     recurring over time'

e    GIVE [[Durational] Exhaustive]
     'give continuously to each in turn'

f    GIVE [[[Durational] Exhaustive] Durational]
     'give continuously to each in turn,
     that action recurring over time'

**Figure 4.3.**  Some Inflected Forms of GIVE

SOURCE: From H. Poizner, E. S. Klima, & U. Bellugi (1987), *What the Hands Reveal About the Brain.* Cambridge, MA: Bradford Books of MIT Press. © 1987 Massachusetts Institute of Technology. Reprinted by permission.

   ASL directly marks verbs for aspect, independently of tense (Klima & Bellugi, 1979/1988; Poizner, Klima, & Bellugi, 1987), through modulation of the motion of the hands in space (see Figure 4.3, which displays some of the inflections discussed here). To mark durational aspect (continuous quality), the verb movement is repeated (note the reduplication). To mark iterative (repetitive) aspect (not shown in Figure 4.3), the verb movement is also reduplicated, but each repetition is an abrupt movement out, a halt, and then a slow movement back. To indicate giving to each (exhaustive aspect), the verb is repeated quickly in multiple locations in the space directly in front of the signer. (This is not a complete list of inflections of ASL but is illustrative; see Klima & Bellugi, 1979/1988, for others.)

ASL packs inflections, one on top of the other, recursively, so that we have different productions of the sense "give-to-each over and over again" (an exhaustively marked verb then marked for durational aspect) and "giving continuously, to each in turn" (a continuously marked verb then marked for exhaustive aspect), as displayed in Figure 4.3. The figure also shows how duration can be reapplied to mark an exhaustive-durational verb, conveying the sense of "over and over again giving continuously to each." As Poizner et al. (1987) point out:

> This creation of complex expressions through the recursive application of hierarchically organized rules is also characteristic of the structure of spoken languages. The form such complex expressions take in this visual-gestural language, however, is certainly unique: the sign stem [base sign] embedded in the pattern created by a morphological process with the pattern itself nested spatially in a pattern created by the same or a different morphological process. The proliferation of co-occurring components throughout language makes it obvious that ASL tends toward conflation, toward the systematic packaging of a great deal of information in co-occurring layers of structure. (p. 16)

### Discussion of Function Words

Initial observation (by English speakers) of ASL produces the impression that it is devoid of function words and that signs map rather directly to content words. This impression and a strong pro-English bias led many educators to consider sign an impoverished language, incapable of expressing the abstractions of normal, oral language. However, as we have seen, ASL does make use of functors, but not at the word or discrete sign level. With classifiers, gender, and aspect markings, ASL displays a morphology richer than that of English. The differences between English and ASL in terms of the grammatical categories marked morphologically is further evidence that they are separate languages.

At the beginning of the section on meaning, I said that signs only roughly correspond to words. The reason for this should be clear now. Depending on the inflections, one sign can represent an entire sentence, complete with agent (I), verb (give), adverb (repeatedly), recipient (to you). Combining that with facial expression, we can make this single sign a subordinate clause (= addition in English of the relative pronoun *that*). And if we add another adverb (tongue waggle—*really*), while it will appear to a naive observer that we are making only *give* and repeating it, the fluent signer will understand something equivalent to "That I really keep giving to you . . ."—a rather complex clause. Note how much can be transmitted simultaneously in one gesture!

It is interesting to observe the extensive duality of patterning in sign. The four dimensions used to produce sign were presented as articulatory descriptions without meaning. In some cases, that is a reasonable way of viewing them. In others, as we have seen here, it is not: Handshape, movement, or location can be meaningful. Classifiers are distinguished in handshape as free morphemes. Pronouns, gender markers, and the roots of some words (consider THINK, WONDER, and IDEA, for example) are distinguished by location as bound morphemes. Aspect is distinguished by movement, also a bound morpheme. Thus the parameters have an articulatory (meaningless) role as well as a morphemic (meaningful) role. Therefore, sign exhibits duality of patterning. And as we have just seen, sign exhibits recursiveness, simultaneity, and smear, with a single gesture incorporating and conveying layers of meaning, recursively applied.

### Iconicity in Sign Language

Examination of a sign dictionary or consideration of some signs mentioned here (e.g., THINK, BIRD) shows another apparent important difference between sign and spoken language in addition to the absence of function words. Signs frequently look like what they are supposed to represent: THINK points to the head; BIRD forms a beak. This property is called *iconicity,* and signs that look like their referents are called iconic. The existence of iconicity, if it is prevalent in sign, could be an important distinction between sign and spoken language: (a) It would indicate that sign is not arbitrary (arbitrariness is a high-level feature of language!), and (b) it could suggest a major *processing* difference between sign and spoken language because sign would be more transparent. We will return to the issue of processing differences as a result of iconicity in the section on psycholinguistics and sign. For now, I note only that there is very little evidence that it is used in *processing* the language.

With respect to arbitrariness, it is important to note that words in spoken language are seldom totally arbitrary if we look to their origins (discussed in Chapter 2 of *Language and Its Normal Processing*). Invention of a word usually takes place by making novel combinations of morphemes (which we know or think we know a meaning for, so might be *amoeboid* or *polyblob*), or extending the use of some other word (which also had a well-defined meaning, so new color names are often the word for an object with that characteristic color, as in *turquoise, amber,* and *jade*). The difference between spoken language and sign language arises because people more often describe how things look than how they sound. A visual language can mimic the appearance, iconicity. When we name sounds, we get the same effect in spoken language (onomatopoeia): *roar, growl, snarl, chirp, grunt, hiss, gong, tinkle,* and so on.

Also, by analogy to spoken language, we see that iconicity plays a small role in the maintenance of sign structure. Although all spoken languages have onomatopoeia, no two use exactly the same sounds. English roosters say cockadoodledoo; French, cokoriko—the sounds the language uses to mimic will follow its phonological constraints, and these override the attempt to mimic. Moreover, the onomatopoetic words must be learned through traditional transmission; they are not so obvious as to be reinvented by each generation or instantly understood.

These properties hold true in sign language also, which is why there is no universal sign (or universal speech). Each language has its own set of formational rules and modifies its depiction of the outside world with respect to them. Historically, the sign STEAL was made with the hand opening and closing in a grasp, clearly iconic and nonarbitrary. As it developed in the language, the handshape changed to bent index and middle fingers, less iconic but more in keeping with the "phonological" structure of the language. Indeed, Frishberg (1975) noted a historical trend in ASL away from iconicity. The result is that stories signed in one sign language are not comprehensible to users of another (Jordan & Battison, 1976).

It is worthwhile to consider previously iconic signs and to note how the iconicity changes either as the sign changes (as above) or as times change, making the origin unclear. I earlier mentioned the sign for COMPUTER, a c-hand moving along the arm. This sign likely stylized an old computer light panel, with the forearm representing the panel, and the moving hand, the changing light display. The sign has lost its iconicity because PCs do not have light panels. But the loss of transparency of meaning provides no impetus to replace the now-arbitrary sign.

Another example is GIRL, which I described as produced with a fist, thumb extended, brushing the side of the cheek. In a classroom demonstration, giving no hints, I asked naive observers what they thought the sign meant. Someone tentatively suggested "shaving" and was happy to accept "boy" as the meaning, extending from that concept. The class was quite confounded by the real meaning. Supposedly, the sign derives from an Old French Sign Language sign for girl, which may have indicated the strings of the bonnets worn by women at the time (Klima & Bellugi, 1979/1988). Now, in our culture, it has lost its iconic reference but not its power as a symbol. Moreover, GIRL's association with location, as I pointed out, has been incorporated into the morphological structure of sign, as a gender marker. Formal tests of transparency of iconic signs with nonsigners corroborate that the meanings are usually difficult to fathom, although, once told the meaning, people are quick to make up probable sources (Hoemann, 1975; Klima & Bellugi, 1979/1988).

*Poetry and Word Play*

One place where iconicity plays an important part in the language is in signed poems. The "literature" in sign is much smaller than the literature of English: Sign is relatively new as a language; it is newer still as an accepted language of the educated classes; and it has no written form with which to preserve literary creations. (Ironically, that means that sign literature must be preserved by an "oral tradition.") Our National Theatre for the Deaf renders literature in English into sign and creates its own signed plays. There are also individuals who write ASL poetry (Klima & Bellugi, 1976, 1979/1988). Because poetry is more image-evocative than prose and uses the evocativeness of sound (in alliteration, rhyme, rhythm, and sound symbolism) more than prose, it is not surprising that sign poetry uses the potential image evocativeness of iconic signs.

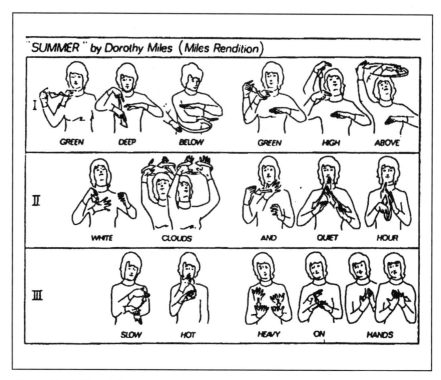

**Figure 4.4.** A Signed Poem

SOURCE: Reprinted from *Cognition, 4*(1), E. S. Klima and U. Bellugi, "Poetry and Song in a Language Without Sound," pp. 45-97 (figure p. 72), 1976 with kind permission of Elsevier Science—NL, Sara Burgerhartstraat 25, 1055 KV Amsterdam, The Netherlands.

Before seeing an example, it will help to understand something about the structure of the poetry so that the exaggerated iconicity may be understood in context. As we have noted, some signs are one-handed and some are two-handed. In normal signing, a signer tends to use the dominant hand for one-handed signs, although there are grammatical reasons that the hands might switch (an aside or parenthetical comment is often made with the other hand, while the dominant hand holds a marked position in space). In the signed poem quoted below, the hands are used symmetrically, with signs flowing between them, creating a rhythm in the alternation. A second rhythmic feature derives from shortening or lengthening individual signs to provide a beat or stress pattern. These two patterns structure the poetry. Then, within the poem, there are devices like repetition of a handshape (alliteration?) or exaggeration of the iconic qualities.

Figure 4.4 displays the signed version of a verse of a poem written in both English and ASL by Dorothy Miles (Klima & Bellugi, 1976), a person fluent in both. Miles structured the English version as a Haiku:

> Green depths, green heights, clouds
> And quiet hours, slow, hot
> Heavy on the hands.

Remember, as we discuss the sign version, that it is not a translation of the English but a poem in sign. First, note that in the first line the left hand is maintained as a base throughout the line. This is a distortion of the citation forms of some of the signs; the *base hand* (the passive hand that the other hand produces the sign on) would normally occur only in DEEP, BELOW, and ABOVE; its maintenance creates a balance and cohesion of the elements on the first line. Next, observe how few handshapes are used: the index finger alone, two fingers alone, and five fingers spread—only 3 of the 45 or so estimated possible. A third point, which cannot be observed in the sketch, is that when the poem is recited, signs are lengthened and shortened relative to normal production to yield lines of poetry of the same length. And this brings me to the last point—one of these lengthenings is a hold on SLOW, increasing its temporal length iconically.

Of the kinds of word play, poetry is probably the most interesting for us because it is formal and has its own structural properties. There are, of course, other kinds of word play in sign, and, to reinforce the concept that sign language has the creative power of spoken language, these are worth a brief mention. Examples are found in Klima and Bellugi (1979/1988). (a) The sign for THIRTEEN is very close in form to the sign for EJACULATE. Knowing this, one signer articulated EJACULATE in the sentence, "You know he's a man when he's ejaculate years old," an obvious pun. (b) A student at a school for the deaf was asked why he and his fellow students were so happy. He began his response with the sign TC, the sign for Total Communication, a method of deaf education where signing is done simultaneously with speaking to increase the available language channels. TC is made with a fingerspelled "t" on the left hand, while the right hand makes a fingerspelled "c" (see Figure 4.2)—this is a relatively recent and nonnative introduction into the language, and is asymmetric. The sign SMOKE is made with a t-handshape touching the lips, and DRINK with a c-handshape also in the mouth area. TC is made at chest level, but this student transformed TC into SMOKING (marijuana) and DRINKING, by moving his hands between the TC location and his mouth.

Ritualized word games also occur in sign. One such game, an alphabet game, is to produce the letters of the alphabet in turn but, in doing so, use the handshapes to pantomime a coherent story. For example, one might begin with the a-hand (closed fist, thumb up) representing a bottle, then take the spread, flat b-hand to wipe the mouth as a napkin, and so on. Another game involves producing all signs with a *single* handshape, distorting most of the signs, for a game of comprehension, which, surprisingly, is possible (except of course in fingerspelling).

Asking deaf informants for other such games, I found that no one remembered playing any as children, but all were happy to try to invent some. The two games they came up with were, first, to use one hand, forefinger only extended, as a representation for the body, and make all signs on locations on that finger rather than the body, and, second, to sign reversing all movements.

Whether their inability to recall language games played as children means that none were played is questionable. It may be that these particular individuals had not used any, or that they do not remember what they did. Alternatively, deaf children born into hearing homes very quickly become involved in the "game" of

---

**Box 4.2. Meaning and Morphology in ASL**

- Single signs or stems are produced with a relatively arbitrary value on one of four dimensions: handshape, hand movement, location in signing space, and hand orientation.
- Each of the first three features also exhibits a duality of patterning, sometimes marking a function morpheme as well.
  - Location marks gender (forehead = male, cheek = female).
  - Handshape marks a pronoun-type unit, called classifier, referring abstractly to a class of objects that share form or superordinate class (e.g., long-thin, vehicle).
  - Location in front of the signer is assigned as a pronoun.
  - Location from back to front of the signer indicates tense.
  - Movements applied recursively to verb stems mark aspect.
- Function "words" are also indicated on the face: An eyebrow raise marks relative clauses.
- ASL simultaneously layers "morphemes"; English sequentially affixes them. This makes sign's complex syntax and morphology opaque to naive observers.
- Signs initially may be iconic. As they incorporate into the language, they conform to the phonological properties, and the iconicity disappears. Also, as the world changes, what was iconic may no longer appear so.
- Apart from sign poetry and word play, iconicity does not seem to play a role in the language's structure or processing.
- Like spoken languages, ASL is creative, with poetry, literary devices, and word games.

---

inventing a language, and deaf children of deaf parents are, by the age of 6, involved in the very difficult "game" of trying to learn English through lipreading. These "games" may allow them little interest in more frivolous language games!

## The Syntax of ASL

Because English is relatively uninflected, with syntax and syntactic categories determined mostly by word order, the search for syntax by English speakers usually starts with a search for order restrictions. Early examination of sign suggested that it was relatively unstructured; that is, it had no syntax. In the last section, we saw that this cannot be true: Markers of subject and object may be incorporated into the verb, with their referents having been previously established either by convention (I, you) or by indexing (John-stage left); subordinate clauses are marked with a special facial expression; verbs are inflected for tense and aspect; and so on. Clearly, ASL has syntax capable of conveying pronominal reference, subject and object, embeddings, and tense. This has been revealed slowly in only the last two decades, during and after much of the debate on whether ASL has syntax.

*Order*

Initial observations of ASL suggested that word order was relatively free, but it appears that the basic structure of ASL is subject-verb-object (SVO), with other orders permitted only under special conditions (Fischer, 1975; Liddell, 1980). To some extent, this reflects a change in the language because it seems to have been order-free at the turn of the century. This change may have occurred through the continued influence of English on ASL. The apparent change may be in part in the observer as sign linguists have become increasingly aware of inflections articulated on the face, which mark pauses and sentence structure nonmanually.

Native signers presented with NNV (noun-noun-verb) and VNN sequences interpret them, provided there are well-defined pauses: NNV is interpreted with object as topic, subject-verb; VNN as verb-object, subject, with the verb phrase as topic. The topic is marked by a break between it and the rest of the sentence. The language reflects the SVO basic order in that "a very simple rule predicts the location of the subject and the object on either side of the 'Intonation break,' if the subject or object accompanies [is adjacent to] the verb, the subject precedes the verb and the object follows the verb" (Liddell, 1980, p. 70).

Aside from intonation altering the SVO word order, the basic order may be altered to accommodate "phonological" or semantic constraints. For example, Liddell (1980) cited the sentence "The woman put the pie in the oven," which is preferentially signed WOMAN PIE PUT-IN-OVEN (SOV). In this case, PIE is made with one hand flat, as a base, and this iconically may be "put in the oven" if it is signed first. In other examples, with verbs that move between subject and object already indexed in space, there is a similar semantic constraint (establishing reference for the pronoun first): The S and the O loci are established first, and then the verb moves between them. Finally, locations are usually signed first in sentences, especially if they are the grammatical focus: In "The accident happened on the bridge," "bridge" would be signed first. Thus we can see that although basically SVO, ASL permits OSV or SOV orders more frequently than English but still under rule-governed conditions.

*Argument Structures*

The verbs that we have discussed thus far are all capable of free movement in space and all capable of having subjects and objects. Not all verbs in ASL can move freely in space and, interestingly, those that cannot do so take different arguments from those that can. We have already encountered the verbs THINK and WONDER, which require contact with or near the forehead. LOVE is produced by crossing the arms at the chest, a modified self-hug; SURPRISE, by flicking the forefinger off the thumb near the eye. These verbs cannot take objects in ASL and, in fact, express a particular relationship between the subject and the verb, not an action the subject makes but an experience the subject feels. (In case grammar, this subject is called an *experiencer.*) To mark the experiencer in ASL, once the "stage" has been set, the signer produces the verb with a body tilt indicating the position of the experiencer: If John (stage left) is supposed to be surprised, the signer will make SURPRISE with the head inclined left, looking right, from John's perspective.

## Setting the Stage

We have already seen how characters are placed on a "stage" in ASL, with a look or a point to a position after an individual is named. The "stage is set" in other ways too, which provide the basic structure of ASL stories and sentences. Edge and Hermann (1977) note that telling a story or describing an event usually begins with a description of the setting, the location. After that is established, the topic is given and then possibly the time. Finally, the predicate or comment on the action is made. Descriptions of both settings and characters are conveyed by *listing,* mentioning the noun and then piling adjective descriptors on, painting in the details. This structure carries over from discourse to sentences: To sign "The bird flew out of the tree," the signer would begin with TREE (location), mark BIRD, locating it on the tree, thus establishing the setting and the topic, and then provide the predicate, FLEW, directionally moving the verb from the tree. For a sentence constructed by a deaf native signer that translates into "The cat knocked over the spaghetti," the signer made an evocative list of descriptive verbs: "ONE CAT CARELESS WALK-WRONG PUSH POUR-OUT SPREAD SPAGHETTI CHAOS" (from Tartter & Fischer, 1982).

## Other Signing Systems

I have been discussing ASL almost exclusively here, and it is important at least to mention that other signing systems exist in the United States. These were constructed to facilitate learning of English. Earlier, as part of a sign joke, TC was mentioned. TC, or Total Communication, is a method where speaking and signing are produced simultaneously. It is designed so that deaf people may learn to lipread with the backup of sign, and so that hearing-impaired people may hear speech along with lipreading and the backup of sign. It is also intended to facilitate the learning of English, as English and its signed translation are practiced.

You may well wonder how ASL may be signed while English is spoken! If order does not conform to English, if aspect is marked in ASL but not in English, if pronouns *(he, she)* are used in English and not in ASL, and so on, signing and speaking English simultaneously means producing two languages at once! Can you speak your second language while writing English?

The fact is that TC does not employ ASL but signed English or manually coded English. In signed English, structure is determined by English (strict SVO), inflections are omitted, and their senses conveyed instead by separate signs created for that purpose. In strict versions of signed English (e.g., Signing Exact English), signs are used for English inflections like -ing, -ed, or -s and then appended to the verb. Clearly, in these systems there are function signs. These systems were designed not for communicability among the deaf but to facilitate their interaction with hearing people and to develop their English skills, needed, of course, for reading and writing.

There is some evidence that signed English systems may be effective for teaching English (Stewart, 1993), but there also clearly are problems with them (Stewart, 1993; S. Supalla, 1991; see Siple & Fischer, 1991, for discussion of the issue). First, as designed, artificial languages do not get shaped by the constraints of a natural language, so we see difficult-to-make, asymmetric signs like TC in the language. Second, most often signed English is used only within the school in formal settings when someone is watching; as soon as the children are out of sight, they will use the more comfortable, naturally evolved ASL (S. Supalla, 1991). S. Supalla (1991) and Gee and Mounty (1991) find that children exposed to both ASL and manually coded English invariably choose ASL when communicating among themselves. And Goldin-Meadow and Mylander (1994) have studied how deaf children taught manually coded English modify the system in using it: developing a classifier morphology, and the stage for pronominal reference, without ever seeing that input. This creolization of a *full* language, making it conform to constraints for communication, indicates its inadequacy as a language to its users.

Another potential difficulty with signed English is that it is usually used by native English teachers who do not know ASL but may not be aware that they are not using it (Walworth, Moores, & O'Rourke, 1992, pp. 148-153). So the teachers are not communicating in the same language as the students.

Finally (in my view), there would be a natural but incorrect tendency on the part of less skilled teachers to interpret a sign as its gloss and a sign sequence as its gloss in English (because this is the way the teachers learn sign). Because the citation form of the sign and the dictionary definition do not convey use, there would be continual misunderstandings.

This is not the place to discuss or criticize such systems. They are mentioned in part because sign dictionaries frequently show signs for signed English, which are not in common use in ASL, and in part to underscore the difference in structure between ASL and English as it is conveyed on the hands. It is worth thinking about the validity of trying to literally translate a language shaped by the oral-aural modality into a visual-gestural modality. Do written sentences (visual and not rapid fading) have identical structure to spoken sentences of English? Aren't they longer and more convoluted, with more distant references, reflecting the absence of constraints produced by rapid fading? Should a modality with as many spatial channels as the visual modality—eyes, head, two hands, body—be constrained to use a strict temporal order expressed only by the hands, as spoken languages are constrained by the single channel vocal articulators (see S. Supalla, 1991)? Consider this on your own now; in sign processing we will see how cognitive and linguistic needs are fit to the visual-gestural systems.

---

**Box 4.3. Syntax of Sign**

— If an NP is adjacent to the verb, it is the subject if it precedes the verb, and the object if it follows the verb.
— Although ASL appears to have become more of an SVO language, perhaps influenced by English, its order is freer.
— In discourse and in sentences, location is at the front.
— SVO order may be subverted for phonological simplicity (alliteration?) or sense (to paint the sentence more iconically).
— *Listing:* A grammatical and discourse feature in which descriptors are piled together to evoke an image-rich sense in the sentence and to paint in details in narrative.
— *Inflections/setting stage:* Sign morphology involves modulation of the verb stem to mark pronominal reference, tense, and aspect.
— *Facial expression:* Marks pauses, abnormal sentence structure indicating the topic, and relative "pronoun."
— *Signed English systems:* Artificial languages incorporating dictionary definitions of sign either with spoken English (TC) or with signs contrived for English function words and inflectional morphemes (SEE) to facilitate the learning of English and to take advantage of any residual hearing the individual may have. Signed in English order and omitting grammatical and morphological features of ASL (and for TC, those of English), these may constitute only skeleton language, with the richness of neither of the forebears.

---

## Summary

We have reviewed some salient aspects of the structure of ASL, showing it to be a rich language capable of expressing what spoken language expresses, although differently. With respect to sign production, there are four formational parameters: location, handshape, movement, and orientation, values of which specify every sign. At one level, these parameters are meaningless; at another, they may serve as morphemes, marking gender, tense, aspect, or pronouns. Combinations of parameters are constrained phonologically and also, in part, by ease of production and perception. Signing also uses facial expression and body movements productively, as supplements to signing, as conveyors of paralanguage, and as syntactic markers.

Meaning seems to be conveyed in sign as it is in spoken language. There are signs corresponding to content words that occasionally appear to be nonarbitrary and iconic but nevertheless must be learned. Moreover, there is a historic tendency away from iconicity. There is a noticeable lack of specific separate function word signs as free morphemes, but this seems to be because those meanings are conveyed by bound morphemes, inflections incorporated into the sign or made on the face. Sign is capable of expressing abstract, arbitrary, and figurative meanings (as are all known languages).

The syntax of sign is markedly different from English. Word order may vary depending on facial expression and inflection. Reference must be established before the verb; location, setting, and topic seem to be established before the predicate also. Adjectives usually follow nouns. Descriptors may be in vivid succession, called listing. Embeddings are marked by a facial expression. Tense, aspect, and, for many verbs, subject and object are not marked independently of the verb but incorporated into it. Sign displays recursiveness, in sentence embedding and in iterated application of the inflection process.

Given the difference in structure between ASL and English, and the difference in modalities, which may impose different perceptual and production constraints, it seems that ASL might be processed differently from English or, more generally, that signed languages may be processed differently from spoken languages. We turn next to consider the evidence on this issue.

## PROCESSING OF SIGN LANGUAGE BY NORMAL ADULTS

In the last sections, I discussed the structure of ASL. I noted that, in terms of articulation, ASL can be described as a hierarchical combination of values on four formational parameters together with movements of the head and body. If ASL is processed like speech, we might expect to see some indication of perception of ASL in terms of these formational dimensions. We might also expect that all of the information from the visual signal is not extracted but that recognition of sign can be triggered by some set of cues abstracted from the sign signal. And we might expect to find context sensitivity in perception and production of sign, rather than invariance. Finally, with respect to perception, we might ask to what extent the face and body movements contribute to normal sign processing and to what extent they are redundant and perhaps not attended to, as "body language" is frequently ignored in speech.

With regard to the organization of meaning in ASL and of signs within sentences and discourse, we noted that frequently each sign contains information *simultaneously* about a number of elements of meaning that would be conveyed *successively* in English, in sequentially spoken words or morphemes. Given this difference, we might ask whether processing ease causes sign to employ simultaneity and speech sequentiality. We might also ask whether what we English speakers consider separate elements are extracted separately from a sign, or whether all that a sign conveys is processed as a whole. Another difference that we noted between the depiction of meaning in ASL and in English is an apparent iconicity or nonarbitrariness in sign. Will this affect the processing of meaning in ASL, or is it just an additional dimension of sign that has no particular psychological effect?

In this section, we will look at the existing research on these issues for normal native-signing adults. In the next section, we will examine child acquisition of sign. We will begin with perception and production of sign because it seems that sign processing is likely to differ most from spoken language processing at the level where modality has the greatest effects.

*Production of ASL*

We have evidence on the production processes of ASL from three sources: studies that have measured signing rate (Akamatsu, 1985; Bellugi & Fischer, 1972; Grosjean, 1977; Mayberry & Waters, 1991), studies that have been performed on motor movements in normal signing (Poizner, Newkirk, & Bellugi, 1983), and studies that have looked at the equivalent of slips of the tongue for sign, that is, *slips of the hand* (Klima & Bellugi, 1979/1988; Newkirk, Klima, Pederson, & Bellugi, 1980). The evidence suggests that signing is subject to articulatory constraints different from those of speech, but that in signing, the main ideas are transmitted at the same rate as speech, and that signs are not produced as undifferentiated wholes but, instead, have formational components. Like speech, some aspects of sign production are linguistically meaningful and some irrelevant, allowing for individual variation in production.

*Rate of Signing and Speech*

Bellugi and Fischer (1972) asked subjects who were bilingual in sign and English to tell a story under three conditions: in ASL, in English, and simultaneously signing and speaking. Subjects were not given a script, so stories differed somewhat in form and content. The overall duration of the stories minus the pauses was measured and then the number of words or signs, irrespective of inflections, in each story was counted. Signing rate (exclusive of pauses) was *half* (i.e., sign is much slower) the speaking rate! When the story was simultaneously signed and spoken, signs still took twice as long as uttered words, and pause duration was greater, perhaps reflecting the greater cognitive load.

Bellugi and Fischer proposed that this difference might result from the fact that the arms cannot move as fast as the vocal articulators. They also noted that in counting a sign as a word without considering the meanings of its inflections, sign is at a disadvantage. So in a second analysis, they counted the *number of propositions* rather than the number of signs/words in their stories. Propositions were determined by totaling the number of predicates. Under this analysis, sign and speech were produced at nearly the same rate! Moreover, when instructed to speed up or slow down, signers and speakers use the same range of rates (Grosjean, 1977). Thus both sign and speech may be under the control of some general language process with fixed output rates. Sign may use simultaneity to compensate for the slowness of the articulators, to conform to the constraint of this language process. In other words, *a cognitive constraint of optimal rate of proposition transmission may affect the structure of language*. (It is interesting to note in this regard that the proposition rate for manually coded English is twice that of either ASL or oral English—much slower. This deviance from a cognitive optimum may cause children to adapt it, to exploit the spatial properties of the visual modality [S. Supalla, 1991].)

We may also consider signing rate with respect to fingerspelling (Akamatsu, 1985; Mayberry & Waters, 1991; Padden, 1991). In Chapter 2, in discussing language transmission rate, I suggested that spelling (orally) was too slow to communicate effectively. Is that true also for fingerspelling? Recall that in ASL, fingerspelling is used in formulae, modifying both handshapes and movements to increase fluidity (real fingerspelling is used only to sign English and so is a derivative language). Akamatsu measured the rate to sign fingerspelled formulae, comparing it with the rate to spell the words named in the formulae. She reasoned that if each letter was made individually, the more letters there were, the longer it would take to spell a word. This was true for real fingerspelling, but producing the formulae showed no change in duration with increase in the number of letters and was faster for all lengths than the fingerspelled words. This result obtains for children older than 12 years; younger children take longer to spell more letters but develop fluidity, synthesizing the letters into a whole (Mayberry & Waters, 1991).

Akamatsu argued that in producing formulae, the hand configurations and movements outline a shape in the air; this whole shape is both the target (so letters are not produced as individuals) and the percept (so letters are not seen as individuals). Indeed, an anecdote supports the point. A deaf informant reported that in his childhood his mother used to shop at Safeway, which she spelled at him. He used the formula too, beginning at a very young age, and only at the age of 9 did he realize it looked like S-A-F-E + W-A-Y. When he tried spelling it to himself, he recognized that his mother's formula had in fact been a sequence of letters all the time. She never noticed a change in his production; the approximation he made by tracing the shape in space when he was young was equivalent to the sequential spelling he used after his realization.

The production and perception of spelled words as whole patterns can account generally for the otherwise remarkable ability of young deaf children to spell. It also indicates how a system can modify an awkward code around perceptual and cognitive constraints. Although vocally spelling English is impossibly slow, we too have formulae, *e.g., S.A.T., AAEV,* which we produce and perceive as "words," not a sequence like t-h-e.

### Motor Movements

To measure motor movements, Poizner et al. (1983) filmed signers wearing small incandescent lights at the major joints of the arm. By using a computer system that reconstructed the three-dimensional coordinates of each light, they independently manipulated movement characteristics like amplitude (size), final position, and pauses to see which were important in cuing inflection. They found that final position and overall tension were the most invariant articulatory characteristics, and these happen to be the ones most easily controlled motorically. Thus inflection production reflects a general articulatory constraint.

### Slips of the Hand

The last line of evidence on the nature of production of sign comes from unintentional errors made in the course of signing. Klima and Bellugi (1979/1988) and Newkirk et al. (1980) assembled a small corpus (131 items) of sign slips of the hand to determine the units of production. Few signs were substituted entirely for other signs (only 9 of the 131), indicating that signs are not produced as undifferentiated wholes. Few errors yielded combinations of formational values not permitted in ASL; instead, most errors preserved phonological constraints such as symmetry of two-handed movement. The vast majority of errors involved substitutions of one value of a formational dimension for the correct one while maintaining the target values on the other dimensions, for example, substituting one handshape for another.

As Klima and Bellugi (1979/1988) concluded, the pattern of slips of the hand mirrors the pattern in slips of the tongue: Sign errors reveal an arbitrary, sublexical structure, indicating a duality of patterning (meaningless elements combining to form meaningful units). The errors also show that sign, like speech, has productive "phonological" rules, allowing some combinations and arbitrarily disallowing others, and these rules govern the errors. Finally, note that both sign and speech productively use a small number of articulatory features to form a large vocabulary. The productive use of a limited number of elements may reflect the operation of a constraint on human information processing: *Employ only enough features to keep words from being confused and not so many as to create a burden for learning.*

## Perception of ASL

The study of low-level ASL perception has employed three methods borrowed from studies of speech (see Chapter 7 of the companion volume): confusions in noise, judgments of similarity between signs and identification, and discrimination of signs produced by minimal cuing. These studies indicate further that formational dimensions have a psychological reality, that the dimensions may be analyzed into smaller, perceptually valid features, and that a much-reduced signal for sign is intelligible—all findings comparable to those for speech perception. Studies of higher-level perception in sign duplicate the methods and effects found in study of short-term memory for speech and shadowing of well-formed utterances.

### Confusions in ASL

The studies of confusions in ASL are based rather directly on the classic study of confusions in speech performed by Miller and Nicely (1955). In that study, nonsense syllables were presented in various noise conditions for identification, and it was found that speech sounds tended to be confused with other sounds with which they shared distinctive features (e.g., the voiced stop consonants [b, d, g] tend to be confused with one another but not with the voiceless stops [p, t, k] or consonants of other manners of articulation such as [m, s]). With this as a model, researchers searched for distinctive features in sign. They used "nonsense" signs, varying in one dimension, handshape (Lane, Boyes-Braem, & Bellugi, 1976; Stungis, 1981), or location (Poizner & Lane, 1978), with values on the other dimensions constrained to very few of those possible. "Noise" was created by superimposing *video snow,* the kind of signal one sees when the television is disconnected from the cable or aerial.

Results showed that confusions increased with the noise level but were not random. Multidimensional scaling (for review, see *Language and Its Normal Processing,* Chapter 3, on factor analysis in the semantic differential) showed that handshape confusions divided into three principal clusters: closed or partly closed fist versus extended fingers and, within the extended fingers group, prominent thumb and index finger versus other finger extensions. These confusion patterns predicted performance on discrimination tasks (Stungis, 1981): The more confusable the two handshapes, the less discriminable they were. Unlike what researchers have found with stop consonants, small changes between features were discriminable.

Clusters were also found for location. The most important division was between signs made on the upper face versus anywhere else on the body. A second dimension separated areas of central body, palm-wrist-forearm, and neck and lower face.

Together the studies suggest what some of the salient features for sign perception are. They indicate that signers do not treat all variations in production equally (e.g., the difference between full and partial closure of the hand is less relevant than that between partial closure and extension) but divide both handshape and location into salient areas. This is an additional similarity with speech, although it seems that handshape, at least, does not produce as marked a division into perceptual categories as do the consonants in spoken language.

### Judgments of Similarity of Signs

In studying the perception of movement only, Poizner (1981) asked subjects to judge which two of three presented signs seemed most similar. As with confusion data, similarity data may be used for multidimensional scaling to obtain clusters of similarity (or confusability). What was particularly interesting about this study was that Poizner used both subjects naive to sign and native signers to see if knowledge of the language structure changed perception. For both groups of subjects, the most important bases for judging similarity were (a) whether or not the movement was repeated, (b) whether the sign was made in the vertical or transverse plane with respect to the signer's body, (c) how curved the movement was, and (d) whether the sign was to the left or right of midline. However, in making these judgments, the deaf subjects relied much more heavily on the movement dimensions (a and c) than on the location dimensions (b and d), whereas the hearing subjects did the opposite. The results suggest therefore that movement may also be analyzed into discriminable features and, more important, that which features are discriminable depends on experience with the language. This is similar to categorical perception in that language categories affect low-level perception (for an example for ASL of language affecting thought—or *linguistic relativity*—see Chapters 2 and 3 of the companion volume).

*Sufficient Information for Perceiving ASL*

Since the invention of the telephone, it has been known that it is possible to transmit speech using a small percentage of the normal frequencies present in the voice. The visual signal on a television set is much richer than the audio signal we hear on the telephone (although fiber-optic cables are changing that); it takes about 1,000 telephone lines to transmit the information that was carried on a *black-and-white* TV screen (see Tartter & Knowlton, 1980). We may ask whether the extra information is necessary to perceive ASL; if so, this result would suggest processes fundamentally different from those used in speech.

To study the cues to sign, as is done for speech, the signal is degraded, removing or masking information, so that people are more likely to make errors. If impoverishing the signal does not produce errors, we may conclude that the information that had been discarded was not necessary for perception.

Aside from superimposing snow, the most popular technique for degrading the sign signal has employed a method used in vision research to study motion perception. Johansson (1973) attached small lightbulbs or special reflective tape (bicycle tape) to the major joints of subjects and filmed them under lighting conditions such that only those points were visible. As long as the people were in motion, observers spontaneously organized the illuminated points (like fill-in-the-dots) as groups, and the movements of the subjects were identified easily as walking, running, dancing, and so on. (Cutting & Kozlowski, 1977, have in fact demonstrated that placement of only two lights, on the hip bones, is sufficient to allow judgments of the sex of the subject, if he or she is walking.)

Applying this technique to sign, Tartter and Knowlton (1980, 1981) found that sustained, comfortable conversation was possible in sign when the participants were viewing each other only as light configurations. In this case, as shown in Figure 4.5, the lights were placed on gloves, with a protruding light on top of each finger and lights on the back knuckles and around the wrists. One spot was also placed on the nose for reference. In all, no more than 23 spots were visible at any one time; nevertheless, conversation was possible, without training!

This study has several important implications for the perception of ASL. As you may have already realized, the face is not visible under these conditions. Signers continued to make facial expressions, but they were not received. Clearly the face is not necessary for comprehension, then, although under normal conditions, information conveyed on the face may be used. It is likely that the facial information was conveyed redundantly, in head movement, transmitted through the movement of the spot on the nose. For example, in questioning, we furrow our brows and usually also move our heads forward and to the side. Some facial movements may also be conveyed on the hands: One of the pairs of subjects became involved in an argument, during which one of the participants repeated herself three times, with increasing anger. Of course, her face reflected the increasing emotion, but so did her sign: The movements became exaggerated and tense to the point of almost shaking, and the final movement, a touch of the index finger on the wrist of the passive arm, changed from a touch to a slap with her increasing anger.

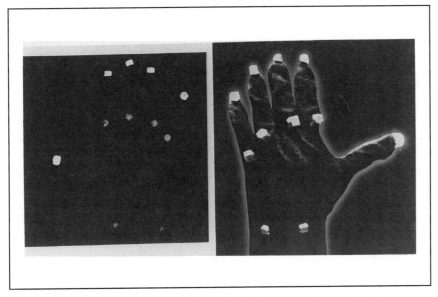

**Figure 4.5.** A View of the Back of the Hands Under Normal and Reduced Lighting Conditions

NOTE: Movement is necessary for the hand configuration and sequences to come to life.

A second important implication of the study is that perception of sign does not seem to need more information than speech. Tartter and Knowlton (1980) estimated that the moving light displays required about half a telephone line to be transmitted. Most of the distinctions of speech may also be minimally perceived (the first two formant frequencies) in about half a telephone line.

As Bellugi's and Fischer's (1972) study showed that sign does not transmit information more slowly than speech at the proposition level, Tartter and Knowlton's study shows that at low perceptual levels, sign does not transmit information faster than speech. Given that sign and speech use such different modalities, *the fact that their transmission rates are similar suggests that the rate may be a basic human constraint on language.*

### Minimal Cues to ASL

Using the illumination technique just described, Poizner, Bellugi, and Lutes-Driscoll (1981) and Tartter and Fischer (1982) tried to determine specifically which linguistic information was conveyed in moving light displays. Poizner et al. were interested in the recognition of movements of lexical items and those signaling inflections. They placed lights on each signer's head, shoulders, elbows, wrists, and index fingertips. The signers were then filmed for stereoscopic projection (like a 3-D movie) to ensure perception of depth. Subjects were asked to label the light configurations and to match them to normal videotaped signs. Subjects were good at the task, but better for inflections than for lexical movements. Poizner et al. systematically removed lights to determine their importance for recognition: Only removal of the fingertip light severely impaired performance. As long as it was present with reference lights on the head, shoulder, or arm, movement identification was possible.

Tartter and Fischer (1982) asked subjects to identify signs filmed using the configurations of Tartter and Knowlton (1981). Pairs of signs were selected that differed in only one of the formational dimensions and then were embedded in identical ASL sentence frames. Subjects had to select from two cartoons, each of which represented one of these two sentences, the cartoon that depicted the sentence they had viewed. For example, the ASL translations of "he had a bad headache" and "he had a bad toothache" contrast only in the location used for the "ache," the head or the mouth. The question was, with no redundancy available from the context: Would such minimal differentiations be possible, and, if not, which were less discriminable? Subjects again were given little practice, and for location and orientation differences performed only slightly worse than they did using normal videotape displays. Movement distinctions were seen somewhat more poorly, and handshape distinctions only slightly better than chance. In a follow-up, Fischer and Tartter (1985) modified the configuration by adding a line on the thumb, and this improved handshape discriminations to the level of the other dimensions. Note that differentiation of the thumb was found to be a salient feature preventing confusion in situations where signing was viewed through video snow.

Together the results suggest that the fingertips plus some anchor are sufficient to convey movement (Poizner, Bellugi, & Lutes-Driscoll, 1981), that an anchor on the nose (separating upper face and the rest of signing space) and spots on the hands are sufficient to convey location, and that marking the fingertips, back knuckles, and thumb specifically is sufficient to convey handshape (and orientation). The results also suggest that other information carried on the face or in a full video signal may supplement communication but is not necessary for sign perception.

*Top-Down Perception of Sign*

We have considered so far only the lowest levels of sign perception: formational features and meaningless "cues" in the visual signal. In speech, the perceptual process is also "top-down," with words, meaning, and syntax shaping perception (and production) of the signal (again, see Chapter 7 of the companion volume for review). Some of the procedures used to study top-down processing in speech have also been used to study top-down processes in sign.

Grosjean (1980) applied a *gating* procedure to determine when a sign was recognized. In this procedure, a clock is started at the onset of the sign and stopped at intervals during its production. After each interval, subjects are asked to guess the sign. As Grosjean reported finding in speech, subjects have a good idea of what the item is long before production is complete. Subjects first can guess location and orientation; a little later, handshape; and they need the most time (but not the entire duration of the sign) to guess movement and recognize the sign. The fact that recognition is possible before production of the entire sign indicates that the signal is redundant, and that subjects use their knowledge of possible forms in the language to guide their perception. The selection seems to take place through a process of narrowing down the sign, dimension by dimension, another indication that sign is in fact *sequential,* only *apparently* simultaneous.

Grosjean also reported two studies performed by using a shadowing task. (*Shadowing* is a procedure in which the subject repeats as closely in time as possible the speaker's utterance.) McIntyre and Yamada (1976) asked fluent signers to shadow videotaped signed narratives. The lag behind the model was 200 to 800 milliseconds, comparable to that found for speech (Marslen-Wilson, 1975). The errors also were comparable, being appropriate semantic or syntactic substitutions. This type of error would be unlikely if copying were done only at a perceptual level, without processing the sense and form of the narrative. Mayberry (1979) reported similar shadowing results, even when the model's face was blacked out, again pointing to redundancy of facial information with information conveyed by head movement or the hands.

## Is Speech Special?

In Chapter 1, arguments were reviewed that there may be something special about speech processing. Classic arguments included the categorical perception of speech sounds (at least consonants) and their right-ear advantage in dichotic listening (perhaps because of special processing by a left-hemisphere language center). If these effects occur for speech particularly, they suggest special processing that may give auditorily presented material an advantage or that may have evolved for vocal communication in particular. Where would that leave sign?

### Categorical Perception

The *categorical perception of speech* refers to superior discrimination of acoustic differences that span the boundary between two phonemes, relative to equivalent differences that are identified by speakers as instantiating the same phoneme. Only some speech sounds—notably, rapidly changing consonants [b, d, g, p, t, k]—are truly categorically perceived.

We have already seen that handshape is not categorically perceived. Stungis (1981), in his confusion study, found that subjects could discriminate handshape gradations between identifiable features "within-category." Further evidence supporting the noncategorical perception of handshape has been provided by Newport (1982). She showed that naturally produced signs varying in small increments between two signs differing only in handshape were assigned to distinct categories with an abrupt shift at the category boundary. Discrimination did not look categorical but was good throughout. Reduction of visibility through brief presentation impaired discriminability but no more so within than between categories.

While signs may not be discriminated categorically, like speech their linguistic import changes their visual processing, a weak categoricalness. We saw that once a feature of sign is perceived linguistically, it is perceived in terms of linguistic features, and differently by signers than by nonsigners (Poizner, 1981). And it is important to recall that not all speech is perceived categorically either; vowels are continuously perceived. So it is an open issue whether sign and speech differ critically with respect to categorical perception. There is a tendency to perceive both sign and speech differently once we perceive it linguistically. So, the conservative conclusion is that it is not a special *speech* processor but a *special language mode,* perhaps resulting from the vast experience with linguistically relevant distinctions.

## Laterality and Sign

In Chapter 1, I reviewed how simultaneous presentation of different speech sounds (consonants) to both ears (dichotic listening) yields a right-ear advantage, presumably recruiting a special left-hemisphere language processor. In Chapter 5, I will present evidence from brain-damaged native signers and speakers. For now, I note that speech and signing show very similar patterns in brain damage (Poizner et al., 1987). In the visual equivalent of dichotic listening, though, the similarity is not as striking (Poizner & Battison, 1980), but this may result from difficulties in the stimulus presentation.

The visual system is organized so that each eye projects to both brain hemispheres. If a line is drawn down the middle of each eye, the information to the right of the lines (the *right visual field*) goes to the left hemisphere, and the information to the left of the lines (the *left visual field*) goes to the right hemisphere. So, to create the visual equivalent of dichotic competition, one must present two stimuli simultaneously to the same eye. Obviously, this is easiest to do if the stimuli are stationary and brief because they will not cross the visual fields. However, stationary stimuli are not very "signlike" and so may not be processed in the same manner as natural sign.

Results with such stationary presentations to competing visual fields indicate a small right field advantage (left hemisphere) for moving signs and left field advantage for stationary stimuli (see Poizner & Battison, 1980). Because the moving stimuli have more signlike properties, it is reasonable to assume that they reflect natural sign processing. And they are consistent with the brain-damage evidence supporting left-hemisphere sign processing. If sign is processed by the left hemisphere, laterality effects do not indicate a special *speech* processor but a special language processor.

## Short-Term Memory for Sign

Crowder (1978, for example) proposed a special acoustic memory underlying short-term memory effects for speech. Short-term memory for lists of English words typically fits a bow-shaped curve, with recall of the initial (*primacy*) and final *(recency)* items better than recall of the middle items. This is true particularly for auditory presentation; if the lists are written, the recency effect is smaller and sometimes nonexistent. This difference is called the *modality effect.* The auditory recency effect may be eliminated by presenting an additional, not-to-be-remembered word at the end *(suffix effect)*. These results have been interpreted as indicating a special memory of short duration capable of holding a limited amount of speech.

Once again we may ask whether speech, because it is speech, has a special processing advantage, in this case a memory, that sign does not have. Shand (1982; Shand & Klima, 1981) tested short-term recall for sign by native signers. As with speech, recall was in writing and lists were presented in two conditions: signed or written. Across experiments, both recency and suffix effects were measured. Shand found that signed lists showed typical "auditory" effects—pronounced primacy and recency advantages—with the recency effects eliminated by a signed suffix. Written tests, although also visual, showed the usual absence of recency effects. Because both written and signed lists were visual, Shand concluded that the recency and suffix effects do not derive from a modality-specific memory that is responsible for the effect but from a memory specific to the subject's native language. In essence, there is a processing advantage for material presented in the language form one thinks in, and this advantage is reflected in the recency effect. Thus, here too, sign, although visual, appears to work not like visual writing but like speech to give rise to a special advantage in short-term memory.

### Other Short-Term Recall Effects for Sign

Researchers in memory have demonstrated that for both auditory and written English lists, recall is better if the lists are phonologically distinct than if they are not (Wickelgren, 1965, for example). For instance, a list of rhyming letters (v, g, d) is harder to recall than a list of unrelated letters (f, c, h), and the errors in the recall of rhyming lists are intrusions of other similar-sounding letters. Written lists are also confused if phonologically similar, and not if visually similar.

Short-term recall studies of sign have shown sign-based coding analogous to the phonetic coding indicated by the preceding results. Lists of formationally similar signs (all sharing the same handshape, for instance) are harder to recall than formationally distinct lists (Bellugi, Klima, & Siple, 1975; Hanson, 1982; Poizner, Bellugi, & Tweney, 1981; Shand, 1982). Moreover, written lists show the same effect for deaf subjects as do signed lists, suggesting that, in reading, signers sign silently as we might silently say the words to ourselves.

Some signers are also able to use a phonological code (Hanson, 1982; Shand, 1982), given their intensive training in English and lipreading, and this group also shows phonological confusions. Hanson (1982) found that the more signers relied on a phonological code, the better their *ordered* recall—perhaps because speech and English syntax are relatively order-dependent. Free recall, remembering words in any order, was as good whether the deaf person was using a sign-based or a phonological code. Shand (personal communication, July 1980) found that one deaf signer also fluent in English strategically switched codes in reading so as to avoid confusing similar words: He mentally signed lists of similar-sounding words and mentally spoke lists of formationally similar words to avoid confusion!

We have just seen short-term memory advantages when material is presented in speech or sign and confusions in short-term memory when the language coding the material is too similar. Speaking people can improve their retention of writing by *rehearsal,* saying it over and over to themselves. Bonvillian, Rea, Orlansky, and Slade (1987) demonstrated that instructing deaf subjects to explicitly rehearse written word lists improved their recall as well. Thus speech and sign are both effective short-term memory codes.

A final study showing memory similarities between speech and sign was performed by Hanson and Bellugi (1982). They studied signers' abilities to recognize sentences immediately or after a delay, when the recognition item differed from the target in meaning, in form, or not at all. Meaning differences were created by changing inflection or changing word order, which changed the sense, as in switching MATH and MUSIC in the sentence MY WIFE TEACH[continuative] MATH ALL-MORNING; AFTERNOONS TEACH[habitual] MUSIC. Form changes changed word order without changing meaning. As I reviewed in Chapter 1, English syntactic structure is not recalled for long; rather, the sense seems to be rapidly encoded and the particular structures giving rise to it rapidly fade in working memory. Hanson and Bellugi found that the same was true for sign: Immediate testing produced accurate detection of all the foils; delayed testing produced accurate detection only of inflection and meaning-changing foils. Thus sign and speech both form a short-lived working memory code, which underlies abstraction of meaning, encoded in longer-term memory.

*Summary*

A phonological code or special speech processing has been implicated in studies of categorical perception, right-ear advantage in dichotic listening, recency advantage for auditory presentation, and phonological confusions in both spoken and written memory lists and in working memory. For the most part, equivalent, but not *phono*logical, effects occur for sign in native speakers of that visual language: experience with sign language affects perception of its features; there is a right-field, left-hemisphere processing of sign; recency effects occur for signed but not written lists; short-term memory for signed or written lists is in terms of articulatory features of ASL; and rehearsal in ASL preserves a working memory representation, which otherwise fades to a meaning-based semantic code as with speech. There is some evidence of difference in that phonological codes (or English practice) may better preserve order information, and sign is not categorically discriminated. However, the results for speech and sign are largely comparable, suggesting that it is not speech that makes spoken language special but language that makes speech special. As Whorf (1956) said, "Language is the great symbolism from which other symbolisms take their cue" (p. 42), and once we think in a language, whatever its form, we use that language code to interpret the incoming signals.

## Semantic Processing in ASL

In reviewing semantic processing of English, we looked at four models of meaning organization within an abstract verbal system (prototype, network, PDP, and feature) and two models of less abstract systems (imagery and emotion). Research on meaning processing in sign has been limited and has chiefly addressed the question of the role of nonarbitrariness or iconicity in extracting meanings from sign. The evidence indicates that although sign is obviously amenable to image and motor codes, it is nevertheless processed in terms of abstract meanings and abstract characteristics of the language.

We have already seen indications of this in the just-mentioned studies of short-term memory: Sign lists are recalled in terms of abstract formational dimensions, just as spoken words are recalled through phonetic features. Looking at semantic similarity (items from the same category) and imageability as well as formational similarity, Poizner, Bellugi, and Tweney (1981) found that, compared with a random control list, formational similarity (like rhyming in spoken language) severely depressed recall, but semantic similarity only slightly affected recall, as is found in spoken lists for hearing subjects. Highly imageable lists were better recalled than the others, again as is found for English. But iconicity of the sign had no effect on recall regardless of the imageability of the referents.

Thus memory studies indicate that signs are encoded in terms of abstract formational parameters, as are spoken words, and stored in terms of semantic factors such as imageability and category membership, again as are spoken words. Iconicity has no measurable effect on encoding or storage or the word.

Another finding from short-term recall studies of sign shows that the uninflected form of the sign (called the *base*) and its inflections are separately encoded and stored, despite their simultaneous production (Poizner, Newkirk, Bellugi, & Klima, 1981). Errors that subjects produced revealed that the inflections were transposed to different base forms within a list more often than whole signs (base + inflections) were transposed; you can think of this like a slip-of-the-tongue transferring a suffix to another word. As with the previously mentioned studies, the results indicate a coding of sign in terms of abstract linguistic, formational properties rather than in terms of iconic or holistic properties of the sign itself.

One study of semantic organization within sign looked at the structure of the language from the prototype/basic-level view described by Rosch, Mervis, Gray, Johnson, and Boyes-Braem (1976), reviewed in Chapter 1 (see also Chapter 3 of *Language and Its Normal Processing*). In their study, Rosch et al. (1976) claimed that signs show a different taxonomy than English words, almost exclusively representing words at the basic level. The basic level, as you may recall, is the level that captures the most stimulus similarity, while transmitting the most information: Compared with the basic-level *screwdriver, tool* is too general and *Phillips screwdriver* too specific. *Screwdriver* captures critical differentiations among tools and similarities among screwdrivers.

Newport and Bellugi (1978) reinvestigated the structure of sign to verify this claim. They noted that most single signs are at the basic level but that syntactic processes in sign allow for combinations of elements to represent superordinates and subordinates. The properties of these combinations are interesting both for what they say about category perception generally and for what they indicate about sign specifically. To form superordinate categories, such as "fruit" or "jewelry," signs for category members are strung together, as in

APPLE BANANA ORANGE or RING BRACELET NECKLACE

Not all category members may be used to form such compounds; those that can be so used are invariably prototypical items. The compound is formed differently from a list: Movement and handshape are smoothed between the individual signs, the compound has a special rhythm or stress pattern, and the members are listed in an invariant order. Similar constraints on articulation apply to forming compounds for subordinates, but here the prototype name is combined with a modifier as in SCHOOL TRUCK for school bus (the English translation is also a compound with a stress pattern different from a list, like school, bus . . . ).

The study of compounding in sign is interesting for what it tells us generally about prototypicality and basic level. First, what is prototypical in sign is prototypical in English, as it should be given that prototypicality in theory arises not from use in the language but from differences and redundancies among category members. Second, it is interesting that the basic level is so directly reflected in the semantic structure of sign.

Thus the studies of semantic processing of ASL indicate that there are more similarities than differences to processing of spoken language. Although signs of ASL themselves are iconic, this property of sign does not appear to affect encoding or retrieval. Rather, signs are stored and recalled in terms of abstract formational properties and "abstract" linguistic properties like semantic similarity, morphological structure, and concreteness or abstractness (imageability) of the referent. Sign categories begin with prototypes at the basic level but are hierarchically organized, as are categories of spoken language.

## Syntactic Processing in ASL

There have been few studies of syntactic processing in ASL. In the sections on perception and semantic processing, I have already discussed processing of inflections and root verbs—they seem to be separately extracted—and will not review it further. We also saw that as with spoken or written language, signers do not recall syntactic structure long, retaining the meaning but not the form of the input sentence. I also mentioned that studies of shadowing of sign have shown attentiveness to the syntactic structure of the narrative, with errors usually consistent with that structure.

Further evidence for syntactic processing in ASL was provided by Tweney, Heiman, and Hoemann (1977), who showed that good ASL sentences could be more easily recognized, despite disruption by frequent interruption, than syntactically correct but semantically anomalous sentences, which in turn were more resistant to disruption than random sign strings. As with English, this result confirms that syntax is used in the processing and recall of incoming sentences, although it does not say how.

Grosjean and Lane (1977) attempted to specify the syntactic processing units of ASL by examining pauses between and within sentences produced at normal and slowed rates. In normal signing (of an assigned story), there is a marked pause between sentences, suggesting the sentence is a production unit (at least for production of nonspontaneous narratives). When signing is slowed, pauses also appear between constituents, suggesting a psychological reality to constituent structure in ASL. For example, the first sentence of the story was

LONG-TIME-AGO GIRL SMALL DECIDE WALK IN WOODS

40    0      60      30    0  0

Below the sentence are the pause durations in milliseconds. LONG-TIME-AGO is a manner adverb and one sign. It is separated from the NP GIRL SMALL by a break, but there is no break between the constituents of the NP, GIRL and SMALL. The largest pause occurs between the NP and the rest of the sentence, the usual major constituent boundary between subject and predicate. There is also a pause between DECIDE and WALK, the main sentence and the embedded sentence, but not between WALK, IN, and WOODS, a unitary embedded clause. Except for the lack of an expected break between WALK and IN WOODS, the pause structure does reflect the constituent structure we would have assigned the sentence. Thus constituent structure affects production of ASL.

## Summary

Processing of sign generally manifests more similarities to processing of speech than differences. We have seen that perception of sign is affected by linguistic experience, and that the sign signal may be greatly reduced without severely impairing intelligibility. Effective communication presumably requires the same rate of idea transmission in sign as in speech, and this has apparently modified ASL to facilitate efficient communication. ASL, like spoken language, is perceived and coded in working memory with respect to abstract formational properties but demonstrates effects of imageability, semantic similarity, and prototypicality, like spoken language. Like spoken language, rehearsal refreshes working memory, and without it formation details fade, with meaning coded in long-term memory. In sign

---

**Box 4.4. Sign Processing**

— In general, sign is processed like spoken language.
— The complex visual signal of sign may be reduced to the same information capacity needed for transmitting speech.
— Critical "features" of sign may be minimally signaled by a point on each fingertip, differentiation of front from back of the hand, and an indicator of head position. Position of fingers relative to the thumb may be especially critical.
— Fingerspelling is fluid, probably perceived in terms of the motion pattern "cut out" in space, not as individual letters.
— Inflections in sign are critically perceived in terms of the final position in space and overall tension, which are also easiest to control in production.
— Propositions in sign are transmitted at the same rate as propositions in speech, although individual signs take longer than individual words. Morphemes are layered in sign, so that a single gesture entails several morphemes.
— Signs are confused in production and perception in terms of formational parameters, with some values within the formational parameters more confusable than others, which is different for native signers than naive viewers.
— It is harder to demonstrate categorical perception or laterality effects for sign than speech, perhaps reflecting the differential abilities of the visual (spatial, with features and morphemes signaled simultaneously) and auditory (temporal, with features and morphemes signaled sequentially) modalities.
— Like speech, sign shows recency and suffix effects in short-term memory.
— Signs are remembered in terms of formational parameters and component morphemes, like speech.
— Working memory uses either a sign-based code or a speech-based code, holding precise information ephemerally. Working memory can be refreshed in either code with rehearsal. Meaning is abstracted from working memory and passed to a longer-term memory with loss of the form details in both oral and signed languages.
— Memory for sign is not facilitated by iconicity. There appears to be a hierarchical organization and organization by semantic similarity in semantic memory in sign like speech.
— Sign categories reflect a prototype and basic-level organization, even overtly in the names applied. Individual signs most often name basic-level instances, and superordinate names are often compounds of prototypical instances.
— Sign is produced with pauses at sentence boundaries. If slowed, pauses also materialize at constituent boundaries, showing that phrase structure constraints apply in sign processing as they do in speech.
— Shadowing studies for sign mirror speech: Shadowing latency is the same, and errors reflect both semantic and syntactic structure.

---

as in spoken language, syntactic structure governs production of sentences and is used in perception, at least under difficult viewing conditions, perhaps for top-down processing. Finally, some processing differences obtained between speech and nonspeech, which have been used to argue that speech was special, seem to obtain also between sign and other visual signals, suggesting the specialness is in the language, not the modality.

## CHILD ACQUISITION OF SIGN

It might seem that ASL is an easy language to acquire. There is considerable use of pointing, iconicity, and "pantomime" of motion, which might make it less abstract and thus easier for a child than spoken language. In fact, at least initially, this is the strategy adults acquiring ASL as a second language use—recalling vocabulary items by using (often-incorrect) iconic mnemonic strategies, such as GIRL referring to the "softness of the cheek." Our discussion of the structure of sign and its processing by adults suggests, alternatively, that there might be little difference between the acquisition of sign by children of signers and the acquisition of spoken language by hearing children. Commonalities between acquisition of sign and speech would support either modality-independent general cognitive heuristics or an innate modality-independent language guide (UG).

### Earliest Stages of Sign Production

Hearing infants enter a canonical babbling stage (discussed in Chapter 9 of *Language and Its Normal Processing*), producing many of the phonemes of their language in a controlled way, not simply playing with vocalizing but experimenting with their developing phonology. Petitto and Marentette (1991) demonstrated that a *manual* babbling occurs in sign language as vocal babbling does in speech. Both deaf and hearing infants gesture, as in raising their arms to be picked up. Both also play-babble, like rubbing a finger with the thumb or changing handshape. However, deaf infants also show canonical manual babbling, very different from hearing infants raised without exposure to sign. For example, the deaf infants produced more than half of the typical movements of ASL, appropriately within the signing window. Each of the infants studied also had a preferred set of handshapes and locations. Finally, like hearing infants' babbling, their manual babbles were repeated, reduplicated. Thus it is not sounds per se that are innate, but the imitation, abstraction, and resynthesis of regularized production features, a step to the "phonology" of speech or sign.

The first real signs are reported to appear earlier than the first words (e.g., Bonvillian, Orlansky, & Novack, 1983; Meier, 1991). Bonvillian et al. found that the majority of their subjects produced their first sign by the age of 9 months (11-14 months for the first word), with 10 signs acquired by the age of 1 year. Earlier production appears unrelated to iconicity, because early signs are often not iconic, and those that are—like MILK, produced by opening and closing the hand, resembling milking a cow—reflect real-world properties that young children are likely to be ignorant of. (How many modern, urban 1-year-olds know how to milk a cow?)

The precocious development of sign as compared with speech is attributed to motor differences between hand and tongue. We are likely to acquire control over our hands earlier. Moreover, we can see our hands move and correct their movement pattern, which is not true for vocal articulation. Finally, parents can mold the children's hands and arms into the right shapes, which we cannot do with the tongue. The earlier acquisition of sign has not been universally accepted, however. Volterra (1983; Volterra & Caselli, 1985) agrees that gestures are made earlier than words, but argues that it is necessary to distinguish between gestures and signs-as-symbols. She noted that signs and spoken words seem to be used at about the same time as symbolic or generalized reference.

As might be expected, there is a regular developmental sequence in the ability to form signs. The earliest handshapes make use of the opposition of the thumb, then the extension of one or more fingers, and finally finger contact with the thumb (McIntyre, cited in Hoffmeister & Wilbur, 1980). Presumably this sequence is shaped by motor development, and such sequences exist similarly for other formational dimensions.

At a young age, children internalize the phonological rules governing sign, as we can see in their acquisition of proper names, *name signs* (S. Supalla, 1980). Young children who are not yet able to make a particular name sign will change it to one they can make but always also one that conforms to the restrictions of the name-sign system (S. Supalla, personal communication, July 1980). This suggests that they infer the rules of ASL and that what limits their performance is motor coordination.

Recall that in development of speech, some productions are not controlled until late, 8 or 9 years of age. We see similar late acquisition of fluent fingerspelling, as mentioned earlier: Mayberry and Waters (1991) found that not before 12 years of age were words fingerspelled as a unit, with words with more letters modulated to the same duration as shorter words.

## Acquisition of Meaning in ASL

Meaning acquisition in ASL has been studied with respect to the order in which specific semantic relations appear in sign as compared with speech, and with respect to the effect that iconicity in particular has on acquiring ASL. In the few studies that compare semantic stages in English and ASL, no difference has been found: Deaf children express possessor-possessed, object-attribute, agent-object, action-object, and so on as do hearing children and at the same ages (see, for example, Hoffmeister & Wilbur, 1980; Newport & Meier, 1985). This likely reflects the universal *conceptual* importance these relations have.

For the iconicity issue, several specific features have been addressed: whether verbs that look like the actions they symbolize are acquired more easily than arbitrary verbs (Meier, 1982), how pointing is incorporated into the linguistic system (Hoffmeister & Wilbur, 1980), whether pronouns with reference conveyed by pointing are acquired differently from noniconic pronouns (Petitto, 1987), and whether inflecting verbs that move between subject and object are learned earlier than noniconic inflections, like aspect markings (Fischer, 1973; Meier, 1982, 1991). Generally, as with adults, iconicity has been found to play a surprisingly small role in the processing of sign by children.

Some signs for verbs look very much like their actions. DRINK, for example, is made by cupping the hand and touching it to the mouth. Other verbs are more abstract; LOOK-AT is made with the index and middle fingers extended to form a "v." Examining productions of three deaf children, Meier (1982) found no difference in age of acquisition of the base forms of iconic and noniconic verbs, or in the acquisition of inflections for them.

Hoffmeister (Hoffmeister & Wilbur, 1980) found that deaf children tend to use pointing for expression (they also use nonpointing signs), but use it symbolically and show the same constraints on length of utterance as hearing children. In the first stage, utterances use two points, such as to a toy and the child, perhaps indicating "my toy," or to the toy and a toy chest, perhaps indicating the usual location for the toy (the deaf children raised without sign developed pointing systems like this, as we discussed in Chapter 3). At the next stage, three-point gestures are used, indicating additional case relations, as hearing children develop from two-word to three-word utterances. Sometimes the three-point utterances use a sign and two points.

As children learn sign, they will change from using just an index finger point to pointing with the whole hand or the thumb and little finger only, handshapes common in ASL. There is no indication that being able to point to the object directly rather than using an abstract word for it speeds acquisition of the underlying concepts or case relations, suggesting that the emergence of the points reflects the growing conceptual structure of the child rather than the obvious relation to the environment.

Another linguistic structure that might be expected to be acquired early in ASL is pronominalization, given that the pronouns for *I* and *you* are made by pointing at the individual. Of interest, once again this does not seem to facilitate acquisition. Petitto (1987) found that children of less than a year freely pointed to objects and people but stopped pointing to people just before the age at which hearing children begin to use *me*. The deaf children at this time used proper names for people and, over the next few months, reintroduced points to people into their repertoires. First, the sign for *you* was used—but in situations where the meaning *me* was clearly intended. Note that if the parent is indicating the child with a pronoun, she or he will be pointing at the child; if children *imitate* this gesture to indicate themselves, they will be pointing back at the parent, incorrectly making YOU. Once the child realizes that pronouns are variable and not names—that is, once the child has the concept of deixis—the child ceases imitating and correctly points at the appropriate referent. This happens in deaf children, as in hearing children, at about 2 years of age.

What is particularly interesting about this result is that it indicates that pointing is not transparent. Gestures underspecify, as do words; as Wittgenstein (1973) said, a gesture at two nuts could indicate nut, two, or the group. A gesture at the child could mean you, the child's name (in which case it *should* be imitated), or some aspect of the child. Initially children seem to use points to indicate objects; as they learn that signs stand for objects, their concept of pointing changes, and they stop pointing. Once it is clear what a point means, it is reintroduced as the correct pronoun.

## Morphology and Syntax Acquisition

In ASL, as we observed, much of the grammar is conveyed through morphological markings rather than word order. Study of syntax acquisition has concentrated on acquisition of morphological inflections. Although word order is relatively free in ASL as compared with English, most children begin signing SVO word order and may continue to do so after they have learned the verb agreement rules that permit freer order (Meier, 1991).

Acquisition of negation in ASL resembles acquisition of negation in English: The first use of negation is the sign NOT or NO or a headshake preceding the utterance; subsequently, the negation sign moves into the sentence, perhaps accompanied by the headshake. Acquisition of other complex syntactic structures like relative clauses has not been studied (Newport & Meier, 1985).

Acquisition of morphological markers has been studied with respect to inflectional morphemes, marking sentence relations such as subject or object; deictic reference in discourse; and derivational morphemes, changing nouns to verbs. Meier (1982, 1991) looked at the acquisition of verbs for which the movement changed to indicate subject, object, indirect object, and so on. He specifically examined only the contexts in which the referents were present in the environment so that there was no need for the children to remember or set up reference; rather, they could just make the verb with respect to the objects. The youngest children did not attempt to inflect the verb at all. When slightly older, they inflected some verbs but not others, suggesting that these inflected verbs had been learned as unanalyzed rote forms. Still later, inflections appeared slowly, across verbs, indicative of the learning of inflections as part of the linguistic system. By the age of 3½, all the children correctly used the inflections. Meier's results are consistent with an early finding of Fischer's (1973) that, at 2 years of age, verbs are used without inflection, and subject or object is indicated by a separate point, and at 3 years, the inflections are used but generalized to verbs that are not inflected in the adult language. (Overgeneralization is interpreted as indicating abstraction of a pattern or rule, as in hearing children's acquiring the add "-ed" rule, then making "she teached.") Meier (1982) showed, in addition, that the first inflections used are those required for grammaticality; optional inflections are acquired later. This, too, suggests that children are acquiring a linguistic system—responding to regularity, frequency, and salience of a production—not memorizing individual items.

Together the results indicate a similarity in the acquisition process of deaf and hearing children. Iconicity is unimportant; frequency, regularity, and salience are; form follows function. The similarity in acquisition, despite the apparent differences in representation of speech and sign, suggests that *the limiting factors for language acquisition are basic cognitive abilities in symbolizing.* Moreover, it appears that the *process of symbolizing is arbitrary, regardless of whether the symbol, the word, or the sign is itself arbitrary.*

Meier had looked at use of space for deictic reference at a sentence level. Loew (1981) looked at children's acquisition of deixis at a discourse level in storytelling. Recall that to enable subsequent pronominal reference in ASL, the narrator, on first mentioning someone, indicates a position on an imaginary stage by moving the hand, head, or eye toward that point. This position then can be used to indicate that person, or body movements from that position can be used to indicate the person's perspective. To establish consistent use of position requires not just recognition of this rule but also memory for where an individual had been assigned and recognition of whether the "listener" is likely to remember that assignment. Loew found that beginning at about 3½ years, the stage was used, but not systematically; all characters were piled up in the same location. At this time, facial expression was used appropriately to indicate what a character was feeling but spatial position did not indicate who the character was. At 4½, the use of space was better in that characters were distributed across locations, not just piled in one place, but a given location was not maintained throughout the story for a particular character. Proper attention to who was assigned where was given by the age of 4 years and 9 months.

One study has looked at the acquisition of derivational inflections. Launer (1982) examined children's knowledge of a morphological rule that can convert nouns to verbs in ASL as the English stress rule could "convért" a "cónvert." In ASL, verbs and nouns derived from them share handshape, location, orientation, and many aspects of movement. However, the movement for the verb is more stressed, and for the noun, more restrained and invariably repeated (T. Supalla & Newport, 1978). Launer found that, initially, children do not differentiate nouns and verbs at all; they seem to be simply acquiring vocabulary items. Between ages 2 and 3, nouns and verbs are occasionally marked appropriately but not with any regularity. Between 3 and 5, the rule seems to be internalized to the extent that children now extend it to new items, "verbing their nouns" creatively. The productive application of the movement difference between verbs and nouns suggests a knowledge of nouns and verbs as syntactic categories.

*Summary*

From the small amount of work done on syntax acquisition in ASL, there appears to be a developmental sequence consistent with that obtained for hearing children with spoken language. At first, vocabulary items are acquired as unanalyzed wholes, independent of function or inflection. Inflections are initially used only if they are rote-learned; subsequently, they may be used productively, but not in all the instances they should be; and, finally, they are used correctly, as the adult uses them. In sign, as in speech, form follows function, even though in sign form often indicates sense, the iconicity. Obligatory inflections, those that occur reliably, are acquired earlier than optional, less regular inflections. Processes that are demanding cognitively, requiring memory of multiple locations, are acquired later than processes that require a smaller cognitive load.

## Parent-Child Interaction

The two principal differences between signing parents' and speaking parents' interactions with their children involve the greater manipulability of sign: Signing parents frequently sign directly on their infants' bodies rather than on their own, and signing parents frequently "correct" a production by molding the child's hands into the proper position (Newport & Meier, 1985). This additional sensory stimulation may account in part for the earlier acquisition of the first word. In other respects, signing parents play the same "teaching" role as speaking parents: signing grammatically but simply (showing few inflections), enlarging sign movements, and exaggerating "intonation" markers and, on occasion, iconicity (Newport & Meier, 1985).

As far as corrections, expansions, or tailoring utterances to the child's level are concerned, indications are that there is no difference between signing parents and speaking parents, and no difference in the effects that these alterations have on the children. Launer (1982) found that parents did not make the noun-verb morphological distinction to the youngest children in the study; they intentionally simplified. They also sometimes exaggerated iconicity, and repeated and elaborated for the youngest children, but stopped this as the children became older. Parents of older children used more complex and morphologically marked sentences. Moreover, as is seen in oral language acquisition, when parents repeatedly correct their children—here, molding their hands—it has no apparent effect (Petitto, 1987).

Thus it seems that parents are sensitive to the emergent linguistic abilities of their children and tailor their language accordingly. Whether this speeds language acquisition is not clear, any more than it is clear in spoken language.

## Late Acquisition of Sign Language

As we saw in Chapter 3, deaf children often are not exposed to sign language until they "fail" to learn a spoken language and thus may be acquiring their first, formal, socially shared language anywhere from childhood through adulthood. What is the effect of learning sign language late? Rachel Mayberry and collaborators (Mayberry, 1993; Mayberry & Eichen, 1991; Mayberry & Waters, 1991) have assessed the relative competence of signers who acquired sign at different ages on performing difficult language tasks, such as verbatim sentence recall or shadowing. As we have noted, shadowing requires a subject to mimic as closely in time as possible the productions of a fluent user of a language. The mimicry appears to entail both semantic and syntactic processing because shadowers automatically correct—that is, they do not mimic—errors in the model.

Mayberry has shown that the later sign is learned, the poorer the ability is to shadow, recall, and answer questions afterward on the shadowed material. The decrement in performance is *not* in surface fluency: Late-learners sign as quickly, recall the same number of words, and mimic the "intonation" of the target sentence. However, late-learners appear to attend more to production than sense dimensions. They are more likely to make strictly "phonological" errors (e.g., signing AND instead of SLEEP, both made with the same handshape, movement, and orientation of the palm toward the producer but never produced in the same context!). At the same time, they are less likely to make plausible lexical or syntactic substitutions than native signers, if those substitutions involve different production parameters. Late-learners are also slower to recognize signs and less likely to acquire the complex morphology (Newport, 1990).

Mayberry suggests that late acquisition at least occasionally strands the learner at a surface level of language, preventing him or her from automatically and quickly reaching deeper meaning. Thus comprehension is poorer, and intrusion errors reflect surface but not deep similarities.

Of interest, Mayberry (1993) found that the critical variable was the age of *first* language acquisition, not the age at which the *language being tested* was acquired. She studied subjects who learned sign late but had already learned English; these were people who were born hearing and became deaf in childhood usually due to a disease like meningitis. They recalled signs nearly as well as native signers and better than signers who had acquired sign as their first language at the same age that these subjects had acquired it as their second language!

Why should early language experience help sentence recall in a different language? It may be because basic universal language structures are in place, or because the first, early language can be tapped to code cognitive events, even another language.

## Summary

Acquisition of a signed language does not appear very different from acquisition of a spoken language. The first sign seems to precede the first word, but, subsequently, articulation, vocabulary acquisition, and acquisition of inflections and syntax follow similar patterns, with age of acquisition dependent on processing difficulty. Somewhat surprising, transparency of sign in both semantics and syntax (the case relations marked by iconic, deictic inflections are transparent) does not aid acquisition, suggesting that observation and internalization of the rules are abstract linguistic processes. It may be important to acquire a full language in childhood so as to automatically and easily analyze productions to their deep meaning.

---

**Box 4.5. Acquisition of Sign**

---

— Infants raised by signing parents babble manually at about the same time as hearing infants babble vocally. Babbling may reflect the extraction of the emerging formational system.

— First signs are formed before first words, probably because of earlier hand than mouth coordination. Symbolic use may occur at the same time for both signed and spoken words.

— Children's reformations of hard-to-make name signs reflect understanding of the phonological constraints of name signs.

— Children's earliest sign combinations reflect the same case relations as are produced in the earliest speech.

— Iconicity does not provide any acquisition advantage in, for example, learning pronoun reference or inflections.

— The rule-governed nature of signed language is learned as an abstraction, with form following function and acquisition dependent on frequency and regularity in the language. Signing and speaking children go through similar stages in producing both sentence constituents and forms. For forms, the sequence is holistic, analytic and overgeneralized, and, finally, correct.

— The later sign language is acquired, the more likely the individual will attend preferentially to surface forms (more phonological errors), unable to access deep meaning efficiently (less syntactic/semantic fill-in).

— Early acquisition of any language facilitates cognitive processing of that or another language in terms of deep processing and semantic/syntactic versus phonological confusions.

---

## SUMMARY AND CONCLUSIONS

In this chapter, we looked at structure and processing of a system with very different surface characteristics from spoken language. Like spoken language, sign appears to be formed through a combination of a small number of distinctive features, which mediate its perception and memory. Like some spoken languages, ASL marks cases using a system of inflections, and these seem to be acquired, produced, perceived, and remembered somewhat independently of the base sign. Like spoken language, sign can express complex linguistic relations like anaphoric reference, embedding, and figurative language. Sign appears to show laterality, short-term memory, and top-down language-mediated perception effects similar to spoken language, and appears to be perceived through redundant minimal features, as is spoken language.

Although sign is visual and not auditory, it seems to contain most of the features we consider defining characteristics of language. Hockett's features of vocal-auditory channel, broadcast transmission and reception, and specialization of the channel are not met by sign. However, sign, like speech, is rapid fading and allows interchangeability and total feedback. More important, sign shows semanticity, arbitrariness and discreteness (at least in processing), displacement, productivity, duality of patterning, traditional transmission, learnability, metalanguage, medium transferability, simultaneity and smear, recursiveness, and the human information transmission rate.

Thus comparing ASL and spoken language not only reveals that ASL is a language, because it meets our most important criteria, but also, *because ASL has the potential for being so different and is nonetheless similar, suggests that there are real cognitive/linguistic and social pressures affecting the shape of language.* In Chapters 5 and 6, we will look at the shape of language when some of these pressures are removed or altered—by brain damage or psychological disease.

## REFERENCES

Akamatsu, C. T. (1985). Fingerspelling formulae: A word is more or less the sum of its letters. In W. Stokoe & V. Volterra (Eds.), *SLR '83* (pp. 126-132). Silver Spring, MD: Linstok.

Baker, C., & Padden, C. A. (1978). Focussing on the nonmanual components of American Sign Language. In P. Siple (Ed.), *Understanding sign language through sign language research* (pp. 27-57). New York: Academic Press.

Battison, R. (1978). *Lexical borrowings in American Sign Language.* Silver Spring, MD: Linstok.

Bellugi, U., & Fischer, S. D. (1972). A comparison of sign language and spoken language. *Cognition, 1,* 173-200.

Bellugi, U., & Klima, E. S. (1982). From gesture to sign: Deixis in a visual-gestural language. In R. J. Jarvella & W. Klein (Eds.), *Speech, place and action: Studies of language in context* (pp. 297-313). Sussex: Wiley.

Bellugi, U., Klima, E. S., & Siple, P. (1975). Remembering in signs. *Cognition, 3,* 93-125.

Bickerton, D. (1982). Learning without experience the creole way. In L. Obler & L. Menn (Eds.), *Exceptional language and linguistics* (pp. 15-29). New York: Academic Press.

Bonvillian, J. D., Orlansky, M. D., & Novack, L. L. (1983). Early sign language acquisition and its relations to cognitive and motor development. In J. Kyle & B. Woll (Eds.), *Language in sign* (pp. 116-125). London: Croom Helm.

Bonvillian, J. D., Rea, C. A., Orlansky, M. D., & Slade, L. A. (1987). The effect of sign language rehearsal on deaf subjects' immediate and delayed recall of English word lists. *Applied Psycholinguistics, 8,* 33-54.

Crowder, R. G. (1978). Mechanisms of auditory backward masking in the stimulus suffix effect. *Psychological Review, 85,* 502-524.

Cutting, J. E., & Kozlowski, L. T. (1977). Recognizing friends by their walk: Gait perception without familiarity cues. *Bulletin of the Psychonomic Society, 9,* 353-356.

Davies, S. (1985). "The tongue is quicker than the eye": Nonmanual behaviors in American Sign Language. In W. Stokoe & V. Volterra (Eds.), *SLR '83* (pp. 185-194). Silver Spring, MD: Linstok.

Edge, V. L., & Hermann, L. (1977). Verbs and the determination of subject and object in American Sign Language. In L. Friedman (Ed.), *On the other hand* (pp. 137-179). New York: Academic Press.

Fischer, S. D. (1973). *Verb inflections in American Sign Language and their acquisition by the deaf child.* Paper presented at the Winter Meetings, Linguistic Society of America.

Fischer, S. D. (1975). Influences on word order change in American Sign Language. In C. N. Li (Ed.), *Word order and word order change* (pp. 3-25). Austin: University of Texas Press.

Fischer, S. D. (1978). Sign language and creoles. In P. Siple (Ed.), *Understanding language through sign language research* (pp. 309-331). New York: Academic Press.

Fischer, S. D., & Tartter, V. C. (1985). The dot and the line: Perception of ASL under reduced conditions. In W. Stokoe & V. Volterra (Eds.), *SLR '83* (pp. 101-108). Silver Spring, MD: Linstok.

Frishberg, N. (1975). Arbitrariness and iconicity: Historical change in American Sign Language. *Language, 51,* 696-719.

Gee, J. P., & Mounty, J. L. (1991). Nativization, variability, and style-shifting in the sign language development of deaf children of hearing parents. In P. Siple & S. Fischer (Eds.), *Theoretical issues in sign language research: Vol. 2. Psychology* (pp. 65-83). Chicago: University of Chicago Press.

Goldin-Meadow, S., & Mylander, C. (1994). Beyond the input given: The child's role in the acquisition of language. In P. Bloom (Ed.), *Language acquisition: Core readings* (pp. 507-542). Cambridge: Bradford Books of MIT Press.

Grosjean, F. (1977). The perception of rate in spoken and sign languages. *Perception & Psychophysics, 22,* 408-413.

Grosjean, F. (1980). Psycholinguistics: Psycholinguistics of sign language. In H. Lane & F. Grosjean (Eds.), *Recent perspectives on American Sign Language* (pp. 33-59). Hillsdale, NJ: Lawrence Erlbaum.

Grosjean, F., & Lane, H. (1977). Pauses and syntax in American Sign Language. *Cognition, 5,* 101-117.

Hanson, V. L. (1982). Short-term recall by deaf signers of American Sign Language: Implications for encoding strategy for order recall. *Journal of Experimental Psychology: Learning, Memory, and Cognition, 8,* 572-583.

Hanson, V., & Bellugi, U. (1982). On the role of sign order and morphological structure in memory for American Sign Language. *Journal of Verbal Learning and Verbal Behavior, 21,* 621-633.

Hockett, C. F. (1960). The origin of speech. *Scientific American, 203,* 88-96.

Hoemann, H. (1975). The transparency of meaning of sign language gestures. *Sign Language Studies, 7,* 151-161.

Hoffmeister, R., & Wilbur, R. (1980). Developmental: The acquisition of sign language. In H. Lane & F. Grosjean (Eds.), *Recent perspectives on American Sign Language* (pp. 61-78). Hillsdale, NJ: Lawrence Erlbaum.

Johansson, G. (1973). Visual perception of biological motion and a model for its analysis. *Perception and Psychophysics, 14,* 201-211.

Jordan, K., & Battison, R. (1976). A referential communication experiment with foreign sign languages. *Sign Language Studies, 10,* 69-80.

Klima, E. S., & Bellugi, U. (1976). Poetry and song in a language without sound. *Cognition, 4,* 45-97.

Klima, E., & Bellugi, U. (1988). *The signs of language.* Cambridge, MA: Harvard University Press. (Original work published 1979)

Lane, H. (1979). *The wild boy of Aveyron.* London: Granada.

Lane, H., Boyes-Braem, P., & Bellugi, U. (1976). Preliminaries to a distinctive feature analysis of American Sign Language. *Cognitive Psychology, 8,* 263-289.

Launer, P. (1982). *"A plane is not to fly": Acquiring the distinction between related nouns and verbs in American Sign Language.* Unpublished doctoral dissertation, City University, New York.

Liddell, S. (1980). *American Sign Language syntax.* The Hague,The Netherlands: Mouton.

Liddell, S., & Johnson, R. (1989). American Sign Language: The phonological base. *Sign Language Studies, 64,* 195-278.

Loew, R. C. (1981). Learning American Sign Language as a first language: Roles and reference. In F. Caccamise, M. Garretson, & U. Bellugi (Eds.), *Teaching American Sign Language as a second/foreign language* (pp. 40-58). Silver Spring, MD: National Association of the Deaf.

Marslen-Wilson, W. (1975). Sentence perception as an interactive parallel process. *Science, 189,* 226-228.

Mayberry, R. (1979). *Facial expression and redundancy in American Sign Language.* Unpublished doctoral dissertation, McGill University.

Mayberry, R. I. (1993). First-language acquisition after childhood differs from second-language acquisition: The case of American Sign Language. *Journal of Speech and Hearing Research, 36,* 1258-1270.

Mayberry, R. I., & Eichen, E. B. (1991). The long-lasting advantage of learning sign language in childhood: Another look at the critical period for language acquisition. *Journal of Memory and Language, 30,* 486-512.

Mayberry, R. I., & Waters, G. S. (1991). Children's memory for sign and fingerspelling in relation to production rate and sign language input. In P. Siple & S. Fischer (Eds.), *Theoretical issues in sign language research: Vol. 2. Psychology* (pp. 211-229). Chicago: University of Chicago Press.

McIntyre, M., & Yamada, T. (1976). *Visual shadowing: An experiment in American Sign Language.* Paper presented to the Linguistics Society of America, Philadelphia.

Meier, R. P. (1982). *Icons, analogues and morphemes: The acquisition of verb agreement in American Sign Language.* Unpublished doctoral dissertation, University of California, San Diego.

Meier, R. P. (1991). Language acquisition by deaf children. *American Scientist, 79,* 60-70.

Miller, G. A., & Nicely, P. (1955). An analysis of perceptual confusions among English consonants. *Journal of the Acoustical Society of America, 27,* 338-352. (Reprinted in J. L. Miller, R. D. Kent, & R. S. Atal (Eds.), 1991, *Papers in speech communication: Speech perception,* pp. 623-637. Woodbury, NY: Acoustical Society of America)

Newkirk, D., Klima, E. S., Pederson, C. C., & Bellugi, U. (1980). Linguistic evidence from slips of the hand. In V. A. Fromkin (Ed.), *Errors in linguistic performance: Slips of the tongue, ear, pen, and hand* (pp. 165-197). New York: Academic Press.

Newport, E. L. (1982). Task specificity in language learning? Evidence from speech perception and American Sign Language. In E. Wanner & L. R. Gleitman (Eds.), *Language acquisition: The state of the art* (pp. 450-486). Cambridge: Cambridge University Press.

Newport, E. L. (1990). Maturational constraints on language learning. *Cognitive Science, 14,* 11-28.

Newport, E. L., & Bellugi, U. (1978). Linguistic expression of category levels in a visual-gestural language: A flower is a flower is a flower. In E. Rosch & B. B. Lloyd (Eds.), *Cognition and categorization* (pp. 49-71). Hillsdale, NJ: Lawrence Erlbaum.

Newport, E. L., & Meier, R. P. (1985). Acquisition of American Sign Language. In D. L. Slobin (Ed.), *The cross-linguistic study of language acquisition* (pp. 881-938). Hillsdale, NJ: Lawrence Erlbaum.

Padden, C. A. (1991). The acquisition of fingerspelling by deaf children. In P. Siple & S. Fischer (Eds.), *Theoretical issues in sign language research: Vol. 2. Psychology* (pp. 191-210). Chicago: University of Chicago Press.

Petitto, L. A. (1987). On the autonomy of language and gesture: Evidence from the acquisition of personal pronouns in American Sign Language. *Cognition, 27,* 1-52.

Petitto, L. A., & Marentette, P. F. (1991). Babbling in the manual mode: Evidence for the ontogeny of language. *Science, 251,* 1493-1496.

Poizner, H. (1981). Visual and "phonetic" coding of movement: Evidence from American Sign Language. *Science, 212,* 691-693.

Poizner, H., & Battison, R. (1980). Neurolinguistic: Cerebral asymmetry for sign language: Clinical and experimental evidence. In H. Lane & F. Grosjean (Eds.), *Recent perspectives in American Sign Language* (pp. 79-101). Hillsdale, NJ: Lawrence Erlbaum.

Poizner, H., Bellugi, U., & Lutes-Driscoll, V. (1981). Perception of American Sign Language in dynamic point-light displays. *Journal of Experimental Psychology: Human Perception and Performance, 7,* 430-440.

Poizner, H., Bellugi, U., & Tweney, R. D. (1981). Processing of formational, semantic, and iconic information in American Sign Language. *Journal of Experimental Psychology: Human Perception and Performance, 7,* 1146-1159.

Poizner, H., Klima, E. S., & Bellugi, U. (1987). *What the hands reveal about the brain.* Cambridge: Bradford Books of MIT Press.

Poizner, H., & Lane, H. (1978). Discrimination of location in American Sign Language. In P. Siple (Ed.), *Understanding language through sign language research* (pp. 271-287). New York: Academic Press.

Poizner, H., Newkirk, D., & Bellugi, U. (1983). Processes controlling human movement: Neuromotor constraints in American Sign Language. *Journal of Motor Behavior, 15,* 2-18.

Poizner, H., Newkirk, D., Bellugi, U., & Klima, E. S. (1981). Representation of inflected signs from American Sign Language in short-term memory. *Memory & Cognition, 9,* 121-131.

Riekhof, L. L. (1987). *The joy of signing* (2nd ed.). Springfield, MO: Gospel Publishing.

Rosch, E., Mervis, C. B., Gray, W., Johnson, D., & Boyes-Braem, P. (1976). Basic objects in natural categories. *Cognitive Psychology, 8,* 382-439.

Sandler, W. (1990). Temporal aspects and ASL phonology. In S. D. Fischer & P. Siple (Eds.), *Theoretical issues in sign language research: Vol. 1. Linguistics* (pp. 7-35). Chicago: University of Chicago Press.

Shand, M. A. (1982). Sign-based short-term coding of American Sign Language of signs and printed English words by congenitally deaf signers. *Cognitive Psychology, 14,* 1-12.

Shand, M. A., & Klima, E. S. (1981). Nonauditory suffix effects in congenitally deaf signers of American Sign Language. *Journal of Experimental Psychology: Human Learning and Memory, 7,* 464-474.

Siple, P. (1978). Visual constraints for sign language communication. *Sign Language Studies, 19,* 95-110.

Siple, P., & Fischer, S. (Eds.). (1991). *Theoretical issues in sign language research: Vol. 2. Psychology.* Chicago: University of Chicago Press.

Stewart, D. A. (1993). Bi-Bi to MCE? *American Annals of the Deaf, 138,* 331-337.

Stokoe, W. C., Casterline, D., & Croneburg, C. (1965). *A dictionary of American Sign Language on linguistic principles.* Washington, DC: Gallaudet University Press.

Stungis, J. (1981). Identification and discrimination of handshape in American Sign Language. *Perception & Psychophysics, 29,* 261-276.

Supalla, S. (1980). *ASL name signs do not have to be iconic* (Working paper). La Jolla, CA: Salk Institute.

Supalla, S. (1991). Manually coded English: The modality question in signed language development. In P. Siple & S. Fischer (Eds.), *Theoretical issues in sign language research: Vol. 2. Psychology* (pp. 85-109). Chicago: University of Chicago Press.

Supalla, T., & Newport, E. (1978). How many seats in a chair? The derivation of nouns and verbs in American Sign Language. In P. Siple (Ed.), *Understanding language through sign language research* (pp. 91-132). New York: Academic Press.

Tartter, V. C., & Fischer, S. D. (1982). Perceiving minimal distinctions in ASL under normal and point-light display conditions. *Perception & Psychophysics, 32,* 327-334.

Tartter, V. C., & Knowlton, K. C. (1980). Sign language communication over telephone bandwidth channels: A proposal. In B. Frokjaer-Jensen (Ed.), *The sciences of deaf signing* (pp. 141-147). Copenhagen: University of Copenhagen.

Tartter, V. C., & Knowlton, K. C. (1981). Perception of sign language from an array of 27 moving spots. *Nature, 289,* 676-678.

Tweney, R. D., Heiman, G. W., & Hoemann, H. W. (1977). Psychological processing of sign language: Effects of visual disruption on sign intelligibility. *Journal of Experimental Psychology: General, 106,* 255-268.

Volterra, V. (1983). Gestures, signs and words at two years, or when does communication become language? In J. Kyle & B. Woll (Eds.), *Language in sign* (pp. 109-115). London: Croom Helm.

Volterra, V., & Caselli, C. (1985). From gestures and vocalizations to signs and words. In W. Stokoe & V. Volterra (Eds.), *SLR '83* (pp. 1-9). Silver Spring, MD: Linstok.

Walworth, M., Moores, D. F., & O'Rourke, T. J. (1992). *A free hand.* Silver Spring, MD: T. J. Publishers.

Whorf, B. L. (1956). *Language, thought, and reality* (J. B. Carroll, Ed.). Cambridge: MIT Press.

Wickelgren, W. A. (1965). Acoustic similarity and intrusion errors in short-term memory. *Journal of Experimental Psychology, 70,* 102-108.

Wittgenstein, L. (1973). *Philosophical investigations* (3rd ed.; G. E. M. Anscombe, Trans.). New York: Macmillan.

Woodward, J. (1978). Historical bases of American Sign Language. In P. Siple (Ed.), *Understanding language through sign language research* (pp. 333-348). New York: Academic Press.

---

## STUDY QUESTIONS

---

1. Discuss the role of iconicity in the structure of sign language and in its processing. Why is this issue interesting?

2. Compare ASL sentence structure with that of English. Consider differences and similarities in the use of content and function words, order and inflection as syntax markers, and indexing and explicit reference. Is there any reason to consider one device better or more advanced than its counterpart in the other language? Discuss.

3. There is a long history of considering speech special, both in terms of its processing and in terms of its effect on language. Given what you know about sign, discuss whether speech is special. Consider issues such as categorical perception and auditory memory (among others of like ilk), as well as issues such as information rate, simultaneity and smear, and broadcast transmission (and others of like ilk), as special characteristics of language as derived from speech.

4. Comparing sign and English processing and acquisition leads to hypotheses of specific perceptual, cognitive, and social constraints on language. List at least five examples of such possible constraints. Do you think language is shaped by such general constraints or by a language-specific bioprogram? Explain your position.

# 5

## The Dissolution of Language: Brain Damage

Our discussion of language has assumed that language is structured, and structured on many levels. Children must acquire that structure either by modifying an innate scheme for it, inferring it from what they experience, or both. The inferred structure is presumably filed permanently in the brain for productive generation and comprehension of language.

What happens if the brain is damaged either in development or in adulthood, disrupting the language knowledge? Is language totally lost? Or is only a part of the language "machine" broken, with the other parts functioning—maybe producing words without sentence structure, or producing speech sounds but not words? What can the language skills that remain after disruption tell us about the normal mental organization of language? Is it possible, for example, to lose only the "a" section of the mental dictionary, or all associations of *canary,* or the ability to process embedded sentences, or the ability to understand but not to speak? "Damage" to a single such language skill would indicate that it was independent of other language processes, perhaps its own module of language processing.

Now if only one of these things was lost, what would the remaining language seem like? Would it still appear organized? Would it still appear sensible? Would loss of a category mean loss of the underlying thought or of the most direct way of expressing it? Would language bereft of inflections or constituent structure still satisfy our criteria for language?

Finally, after such damage, is it possible to relearn the lost functions or knowledge, to teach the individual language again? Does this occur like first or like late (like Idelfonso's) language acquisition? Or is it very different because some of the necessary underlying brain structures are destroyed and the remaining structures are not equipped for language learning?

This chapter explores these issues. We examine some aspects of language after disruption arising from obvious brain damage caused by trauma, stroke, or tumor. We look at this in two respects: briefly, what the language impairments reveal about brain organization, and then, more substantively, what the impairments together with the location and severity of the damage imply about language organization in the normal brain. In Chapter 6, we compare with language dissolution from brain damage the very different language dissolution caused by personality disorders.

## INTRODUCTORY REMARKS ON BRAIN ORGANIZATION

The search for a pattern in language dissolution from brain damage has been conducted with respect to what it says about underlying *brain* organization, and also what it says about underlying *language* organization. It is the second of these that we are most interested in, but it is worth mentioning the conceptual frameworks and methods of the first, given that we will encounter them from time to time.

### Anatomy of the Brain

Looking at a human brain from above as in Figure 5.1 (top), we see two large sections, the left hemisphere and the right hemisphere. If the brain is turned so we are looking at one ear, as in Figure 5.1 (middle), we can see other anatomical structures: the cerebellum, at the back, and the brain stem. We will be interested here in the rest of the brain, the *cerebrum,* which is also divided into sections according to major grooves: the *central sulcus* (also called the *Rolandic fissure*), which divides the *frontal lobe* from the *parietal lobe;* and the *lateral cerebral sulcus* (also called the *Sylvian fissure*), which separates the *temporal lobe* from the frontal and parietal lobes. One other region is marked in the figure, a bump at the back, above the cerebellum, the *occipital lobe.*

The top and middle drawings of Figure 5.1 depict the *surface* of the brain. If the brain is sliced from the middle of the top of the head to the chin, we see layers of anatomical structure as in the bottom part of the figure. We will be primarily discussing the effects of damage to the surface layers of the structure, the "curly" part, called the *cortex* (for the cerebrum, the cortex is called the *cerebral cortex*), and the region just below it in the bottom drawing, the *corpus callosum.*

The brain may be divided into regions exclusively on the basis of anatomy, that is, which cells are connected to which. The corpus callosum, for example, stretches between the left and right hemispheres, and each nerve cell (or neuron) has a

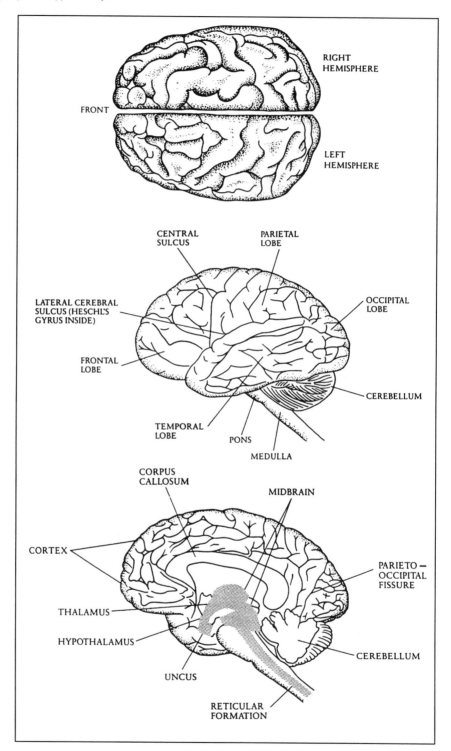

**Figure 5.1.** Three Views of the Brain

NOTE: View (top) shows the brain from above; (middle) shows the surface of the brain from the side; and (bottom) shows a slice through one hemisphere, from the side. Major structures are marked in the lower two.

*terminus,* or end point, in each hemisphere. The neurons of the occipital lobe connect to those of the midbrain, in a region of the *thalamus,* which in turn connect to, among other regions, the visual *receptors* (neurons stimulated by other than neural energy, for vision, light), the rods and cones. A different region of the thalamus receives connections from the auditory receptors and makes connections with a different region of the cortex, near *Heschl's gyrus* (a language "center"). The region of the cortex that first receives sensory input is called *primary;* the regions it *projects,* or passes information, to are *association areas.*

In addition to gross anatomical connections, the brain structures' relation to brain functions may be mapped through *positron emission tomography (PET scan), computerized tomography (CT scan), magnetic resonance imagery (MRI),* changes in cerebral blood flow, or *electrical brain stimulation (EBS)* (Ojemann, 1983, 1991). MRI, PET, and CT (pronounced "CAT") scans image the brain, like X-rays, but X-rays penetrate soft tissue to picture hard tissue, like bones underneath. To "X-ray" the brain, one must do the opposite, penetrate the hard tissue of the skull, to picture the soft tissue of the brain underneath. MRI and CT scans do this, picturing anatomical structures of the brain and differentiating live from dead or cancerous brain cells, that is, regions of healthy and unhealthy brain tissue. Abnormalities in the brain may then be related to abnormalities in behavior.

Cerebral blood flow, PET scans, and EBS studies indicate brain activity during cognitive processing. In cerebral blood flow studies, a subject performs a task while the brain areas involved in doing so are mapped: The blood increases in certain areas, presumably those needing extra oxygen and nutrients to perform the task. (PET scans likewise measure changes in metabolic activity in different regions of the brain as they are engaged in tasks.) In EBS, patients undergoing brain surgery are tested. An alternating current is applied to localized regions of the cortex while the patient is awake and performing some cognitive task. The electrical stimulation neither hurts nor causes any permanent damage (Ojemann, 1983) but, while on, disrupts performance of those tasks on which the region presumably works. Together the techniques permit mapping of brain regions to behavior and demonstrate the interconnectivity or, sometimes, the independence of brain regions.

## Functional Architecture and Localization Versus Distributed Models

Functions of the regions of the brain often relate obviously to their connections. For example, the corpus callosum, which stretches between the right and left hemispheres, transfers information between them. The occipital cortex connects with the rods and cones, and the *auditory cortex* connects with auditory receptors; they are involved with, respectively, seeing and hearing. This assignment presumes that different locations of the brain have different functions: the *localization hypothesis.*

Most people subscribe to the idea of localization to some extent. Localization applies easily to specific perceptions like vision and hearing, which seem to be separate experiences. It may be more of a leap to localize general mental functions like memory and attention: Are these the domain of a specific region of the brain, or are they general processes, reflecting patterns of neural activity across the brain? Historically, and again recently, distributed processing, or mental function as a consequence of a general activity pattern rather than a localized group of cells, has been a plausible alternative to localization. (Distributed processing in computer [PDP] models was discussed extensively in *Language and Its Normal Processing;* it was born in models of neural organization.)

Consider, for example, your memory of an event, like your getting up this morning. You should be able to recall many disparate details about it: the sound of the alarm, the warmth of the covers, the smell of breakfast, the glare of the sunlight, and so on. These memories come from different modalities of experience. Are they stored in separate modality-specific locations? If so, how do you evoke them as a unitary memory of the event?

The connections among sections of the brain could enable information distributed in different modality-specific locations to be simultaneously or successively activated as the event is imagined. Alternatively, the memory trace of each event could be located in one place, independent of the modality of the component experiences, with successive events in time stored in successive locations. (Our abilities to sequence things in time would then arise from activating successive spatial locations.)

Models assigning brain regions to event memory with successive events stored in successive locations within the region, or to particular processes like visual memory or short-term memory, are localization models. They simply differ with respect to what is being localized. Brain organization by location suggests that damage to a specific area of the brain will have a specific and constant effect. Localization of events suggests that it would be possible to destroy memory for the events of perhaps a month of one's life, while localization by cognitive function suggests it would be possible to destroy, say, recognition of visual patterns independently of other functions.

There is a logical difficulty with localization models. Language skills involve memory: memory for events, memory for order, memory of perceptual commonalities. Events must be recalled to language when they are to be discussed, and they also are needed to construct *scripts,* a mental organization of extralinguistic knowledge needed to fill in typical details in discourse comprehension (see Chapter 5 of the companion volume). Order must be recalled to determine syntactic (case) relations in English and in many other languages. Perceptual similarities must be recognized to form and organize categories or to develop prototypes. At the same time, memory involves language: We recall word strings better if they are grammatical and sensible than if they are random or anomalous; we are more likely to confuse items in short-term recall if they share phonetic (or, in sign, formational) features; language categories guide perception and memory (categorical perception and linguistic relativity). So, in this case, we see memory dependent on language and language dependent on memory, a *mutual dependence of cognitive functions.* Mutual dependence suggests that destroying a neural language "center" will affect memory, and destroying the seat of memory will affect language. This in turn implies that functions are smeared together, or distributed.

An alternative to localization is to assume that most portions of the brain, indeed most cells, have some, but not all, information about all skills and memories, that they are smeared together, and partially, but simultaneously, activated as a particular location is activated. This is *distributed memory,* where activation of any one cell or region activates connected memories and skills, and complete information about any one memory or skill derives only from activation of a large "network" of the brain. (The distributed approach to modeling the brain has also been called *mass action* or *holographic memory.*) The advantage of a distributed system as a neural code is the same as the advantage of distributing or smearing information across the speech signal: built-in redundancy so that destruction of a portion of the brain, like destruction of a portion of the acoustic signal, does not result in loss of all "cues" to a particular pattern, memory, or skill.

Distributed memories may also be more flexible than localized memories because they do not depend on permanent structures but on the flow of activation between the connections. In PDP systems, this was modeled by changing weights; in real neural networks, it may be accomplished by the amount of *neurotransmitter* (a chemical messenger) released at the *synapse,* the junction between neurons. Modifying activity in this way is more flexible than building new neurons or new interconnections.

There is strong evidence that there is at least some localization of function, nevertheless. For example, destruction of a particular portion of the left hemisphere always results in right-sided paralysis, whereas destruction of the same portion of the right hemisphere always results in left-sided paralysis. (It may be a weakening rather than a complete paralysis, called then left or right *hemiparesis.*) This suggests that the control for each half of the body is located on a different side of the brain, or localization of body image. The question is whether we can similarly localize general or specific cognitive functions, whether the actions controlled by a region of the brain will correspond to "meaningful" structures or processes like the mental dictionary, short-term memory, or a year in one's life.

## On Interpreting Loss of Function From Brain Damage

Distributed models suggest that minor brain damage should cause loss of the most abstract, complex skills (those for which complete representation occurs only when most cells are activated), while greater damage will cause loss of additional, less abstract skills. They predict that the same pattern of language loss should occur regardless of the location of damage, determined only by the number of cells destroyed. Rather, as we will see, specific language syndromes arise from specific sites of damage, supporting localization of function.

Is it reasonable to conclude that a region in the intact brain is responsible for a function that is lost when that region is damaged? At first glance, it may seem reasonable but consider that if we damage the heart, thinking stops: Does that mean that the heart is responsible for thinking? The relation between destruction of a particular region of the brain and loss of a particular skill is subject to several

---

### Box 5.1. Brain Structures and Brain Models

— There are two cerebral hemispheres, which are connected by a fiber tract, the corpus callosum.

— The left cerebral hemisphere controls tactile sensation and movement on the right side of the body, and the right hemisphere, on the left side of the body.

— The brain is divided into "lobes," tissue masses separated by grooves: the frontal, temporal, parietal, and occipital lobes. The important "groove" for language is the lateral cerebral sulcus or "Sylvian fissure," separating the temporal from parietal and frontal lobes. Deep within it is Heschl's gyrus.

— Localization of function is a brain model that suggests that specific brain regions are responsible for specific cognitive, sensory, or motor functions.

— Distributed models of the brain suggest that a particular cognitive function arises from a pattern of neural activity, and that no one neuron or neural group stores all the information needed for a specific skill.

— Distributed models suggest that minor damage will differentially affect skills dependent on most neurons, the most abstract skills, with increasing damage increasingly affecting more concrete functions.

— Localization models suggest that damage to a particular region will affect the skills that region directly encodes or the skills dependent on communication through that region.

---

interpretations within a localization approach: the lost skill may have been represented in the damaged portion of the brain; the damaged portion of the brain may have bridged the representation; and the execution of the lost skill or the damaged portion of the brain may have been responsible for a skill that underlies the lost skill. Thus we must be cautious in assigning a single explanation to a pattern of loss from brain damage.

---

## BRAIN DAMAGE AND LANGUAGE

It has been known since antiquity that brain damage can cause language impairments, although, as I said in Chapters 1 and 4, these were at first misconceived as sensory disorders (affecting hearing). In the nineteenth century, Paul Broca and Carl Wernicke each described the language symptoms of patients who had an autopsy and whose region of brain damage was therefore known. Figure 5.2 shows the side view of the brain marked with the areas that Broca and Wernicke discovered, and other areas that we now know also result in language impairments if damaged. As you can see, Broca's and Wernicke's areas surround the lateral cerebral sulcus (or Sylvian fissure), within which is Heschl's gyrus, an auditory association area. Electrical brain stimulation of areas around the Sylvian fissure confirms their importance in language processing: The current produces temporary disturbances

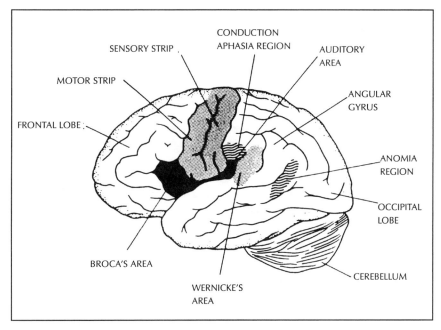

**Figure 5.2.** A Side View of the Left Hemisphere With Regions Marked That, When Damaged, Result in Characteristic Aphasias

in naming, reading, speech discrimination, and muscle movements of the mouth and face (Ojemann, 1983, 1991).

To provide an idea of what damage to these areas does to language, some passages of conversation with patients suffering a lesion in Broca's or Wernicke's area follow. They are presented without regard to where the damage is. Try to sort the passages into two categories. See if you can characterize the qualities of the language that are guiding your sorting.

1. But I figured that if I defective my my talking see my talking itself I I get my tongue back again to where I can talk from what they say why then it's liable to that will straighten me out again and bring me back to where I can hear something see and until I talk I under talk I got to do the interfering has got to act with me for a while see because it doesn't it won't interfere with me properly now now I hear them talking you know. (de Villiers, 1978, p. 131)

2. Well I had trouble with . . . oh, almost everything that happened from the . . . eh, eh . . . Golly, the word I can remember, you know, is ah . . . when I had the . . . ah biggest . . . ah . . . that I had the trouble with, you know . . . that I had the trouble with, and I still have a . . . the ah . . . different . . . The things I want to say . . . ah . . . The way I say things, but I understand mostly things, most of them and what the things are. (Goodglass, 1973, p. 186)

3. [Describing a picture of a boy standing on a stool stealing cookies from a cookie jar, with a girl helping him on the left, and a woman on the right, washing dishes, distracted by water overflowing in the sink]

a. Cookie jar . . . fall over . . . chair . . . water . . . empty . . . ov . . . ov . . . [examiner: "overflow"?]

Yeah.

b. Well, this is . . . mother is away here working out o'here to get her better, but when she's working, the two boys looking in the other part. One their small tile into her time here. She's working another time because she's getting, too. (Blumstein, 1982, pp. 204-205)

4. [Patient Peter Hogan explaining what brought him to the hospital] Yes . . . ah . . . Monday . . . ah . . . Dad and Peter Hogan, and Dad . . . ah . . . Hospital . . . and ah . . . Wednesday . . . Wednesday nine o'clock and ah Thursday . . . ten o'clock ah doctors . . . two . . . two . . . an doctors and . . . ah . . . teeth . . . yah . . . And a doctor an girl . . . and gums, and I.

[Answering about his former work in a paper mill]

Lower Falls . . . Maine . . . Paper. Four hundred tons a day! And ah . . . sulphur machines, and ah . . . wood . . . Two weeks and eight hours. Eight hours . . . no! Twelve hours, fifteen hours . . . workin . . . workin . . . workin! Yes, and ah . . . sulphur. Sulphur and . . . Ah wood. Ah . . . handlin! And ah sick, four years ago. (Goodglass, 1973, p. 185)

5. Boy, I'm sweating, I'm awful nervous, you know, once in a while I get caught up, I can't mention the tarripoi, a month ago, quite a little, I've done a lot well, I impose a lot, while, on the other hand, you know what I mean, I have to run around, look it over, trebbin and all that sort of stuff. (Gardner, 1975, p. 68)

6. (E) Were you in the Coast Guard?

(P) No, er, yes, yes . . . ship . . . Massachu . . . chusetts . . . Coastguard . . . years. [Raises hands twice indicating "19"]

(E) Oh, you were in the Coast Guard for nineteen years.

(P) Oh . . . boy . . . right . . . right.

(E) Why are you in the hospital?

(P) [Points to paralyzed arm] Arm no good. [Points to mouth] Speech . . . can't say . . . talk, you see.

(E) What happened to make you lose your speech?

(P) Head, fall, Jesus Christ, me no good, str, str . . . oh Jesus . . . stroke.

(E) Could you tell me what you've been doing in the hospital?

(P) Yes sure. Me go, er, uh, P. T. nine o'cot, speech . . . two times . . . read . . . wr . . . ripe, er, rike, er, write . . . practice . . . getting better. (from Gardner, 1975, p. 61)

## Types of Aphasia

*Aphasia* refers to brain damage that causes a language disturbance, and traditionally applies only to left-hemisphere damage in the regions shown in Figure 5.2.

Left-hemisphere damage in these areas produces aphasia in nearly all right-handed and in many left-handed individuals. Some left-handers may become aphasic only after damage to the right hemisphere, some only after damage to the left hemisphere, and others after damage to either hemisphere, indicating a more distributed language representation than that found among most right-handers.

### Broca's Aphasia

Quotations 3a, 4, and 6 are from patients diagnosed with *Broca's aphasia* (called *aphemia* by Broca), which is produced by damage to the back of the frontal lobe, near the motor regions. It is characterized by dysfluent speech: many pauses, hesitations, word-finding difficulties, and a telegraphic style—characteristics that you may have noted as you sorted the passages. Because of the telegraphic style, that is, the noticeable absence of function words, Broca's aphasics are sometimes called *agrammatic*. Broca's aphasics give the impression in conversation of understanding the speech of others and also of awareness of their own dysfluencies. They seem frustrated at talking in a perpetual tip-of-the-tongue state and usually report knowing what they want to say although they are unable to express it. Broca's aphasia is therefore characterized as an *expressive disorder* or *nonfluent aphasia*. Because Broca's aphasia results from a lesion toward the front of the brain, it may be called an *anterior* (front) aphasia.

In addition to word-finding difficulties and the absence of function words, the speech of Broca's aphasics is abnormal, containing many errors or slips of the tongue as well as phonetic distortions affecting both sound segments and speech melody. These are known as *paraphasias*. As we have seen in normal speech errors, a slip may involve a single phoneme or feature, called a *literal* (one letter, if you will) *paraphasia,* or may involve an entire word substitution, called *verbal* or *semantic paraphasia*.

Because Broca's area borders on the left motor cortex, Broca's aphasia is frequently accompanied by right-sided paralysis. It is important to recognize that articulatory difficulties found in speech production do not result directly from this paralysis. Broca's aphasics usually can perform nonverbal tasks using the articulatory apparatus without difficulty. They can, on command, pantomime blowing out a match or brushing their teeth. (Difficulty with such tasks, when it occurs, is called *apraxia*.) Moreover, they often show the same problems in writing, indicating that it is not exclusively a motor-articulatory deficit producing the speech errors.

### Wernicke's Aphasia

Conversation with a Wernicke's aphasic is very different from conversation with a Broca's aphasic. Wernicke's aphasics speak fluently, without obvious effort and without particular distress at what they are saying. The difficulty in talking to Wernicke's aphasics comes in trying to interpret what they have said: The speech, although fluent-sounding, does not go anywhere; there are few substantive content words (there are empty words like *thing,* however) and no obvious development of ideas. It may be difficult to stop a Wernicke's aphasic from speaking, to ask a question, and it is frequently not clear that the response is, in fact, an attempt to answer the question. Because it is difficult to elicit appropriate responses from Wernicke's aphasics, their problem is seen as reflecting an inability to understand the question. Therefore, Wernicke's aphasia is considered a *receptive* or comprehension disorder. Because their output is fluent, they are also called *fluent aphasics.*

Wernicke's area is located in the temporal lobe, as can be seen in Figure 5.2, behind (*posterior* to) Broca's area. Because Wernicke's area does not border on the motor areas, Wernicke's aphasics rarely show a paralysis. However, if the damage is extensive, it may extend into the occipital lobe, creating visual disturbances. At the cortical level, a visual disruption does not necessarily produce blindness (although it may): The individual can still detect light and, for example, be able to walk around a room, appropriately avoiding articles of furniture. Cortical disturbances cause individuals to be unable to identify the visual input; the light pattern has lost meaning. Recognition failure is called *agnosia;* if the failure is in visual recognition (it can occur in other modalities), it is *visual agnosia.*

Characterizing Wernicke's aphasia as a comprehension disorder can be misleading with respect to the quality of the productions. Wernicke's patients were represented in passages 1, 2, 3b, and 5. As you can see, they also had problems in speech output. First, substantive content words are missing, as I have already indicated. Second, although the flow is smooth with few hesitations, there are still slips of the tongue, that is, paraphasias. Again, these may be either phoneme or whole-word slips. In phoneme substitutions, in Wernicke's aphasics, the error may be so extreme as to render the word unrecognizable, particularly if there are several phoneme substitutions in one word. The word then looks like nonsense and is called a *neologism,* like "tarripoi" in the fifth quotation. Patients who produce frequent neologisms are called *jargon aphasics;* their speech is syntactically interpretable but nonsense because of the inclusion of meaningless lexical items.

Word substitutions by Wernicke's aphasics are characterized by *perseveration* (the tendency to repeat a word once it has been used), as the passages demonstrate. They also may result in ungrammatical sentences, by substitution, for example, of a conjunction for a noun or verb as in "to that," in quotation 1. So we see in the productions of Wernicke's aphasics problems on the phonological, semantic, and syntactic levels.

*Other Types of Aphasia*

I have described classical, stereotypical Broca's and Wernicke's aphasias. It is important to realize that the descriptions are idealized and that, in fact, no two patients are ever exactly alike, although patterns are observable in the disruption. The individual differences observed may be due to individual differences in organization before the damage and/or to differences in severity and location of the damage.

In addition to the "classical" Broca's and Wernicke's aphasias, there are other regions of brain damage that have been categorized according to their effects on language. Patients with damage principally in Broca's area, but with greater comprehension deficits than usual for Broca's aphasia (perhaps because there is a wider area of damage), are known as *mixed anteriors.* If there is great damage to both anterior and posterior portions, the patient is a *global aphasic,* who may have no apparent comprehension, and production reduced to only a single word (like *hello* or an obscenity) or phrase, produced repetitively. Patients with large lesions surrounding Broca's and Wernicke's areas, but not directly affecting them, have *isolation of the speech areas* and may be unable to produce *(transcortical motor aphasia)* or understand *(transcortical sensory aphasia)* spontaneous, meaningful speech because the language area is effectively detached from other areas of meaning association. These patients, however, are good at repetition and often display *echolalia,* repeating or echoing whatever is said to them.

Damage to the brain may also spare large regions of Broca's and Wernicke's areas, leaving more language functions intact. If the damage occurs between Broca's and Wernicke's areas (severing the neural pathway connecting the regions), the patient is a *conduction aphasic.* Comprehension and production are both likely to be good, but the patient will have great difficulties with repetition because, presumably, to repeat a sentence comprehended in Wernicke's area, Broca's area must be activated for production, and the activation spread is blocked. A small *lesion* (area of damage) in an area adjacent to Wernicke's area, the *angular gyrus* (see Figure 5.2), can result in difficulty naming objects in isolation. This is known as a *pure naming deficit* and in its purest form is very rare. These patients often can come up with word names in fluent speech but not in isolation. After being prompted to say the word "no," the patient may exclaim in frustration, "No, no, I told you I can't say no!" and still not be able to produce the word in isolation (Gardner, 1975, p. 78).

A lesion behind Wernicke's area, marked in Figure 5.2, produces naming problems both in spontaneous speech and in isolated naming tasks. This deficit is known as *anomia,* and patients with it are sometimes called *amnestic aphasics.* The speech of such patients is described as *circumlocutory* because, to communicate a concept for which they cannot recall a word, the patients frequently detour around that word, substituting vague words such as *that thing* for specific concepts, or using ingenious but nonverbal ways of communicating. For example, one patient discussing his daughter's wedding did not have the word, and said, " 'And then, she, you know . . . dum-dum-dedum' to the tune of the melody of the wedding march" (Goodglass, 1980, p. 647).

*Summary*

In this section, I presented classic aphasias. Broca's aphasia, produced by a lesion in the frontal lobe, is characterized by slow, hesitant, errorful speech, a telegraphic style, and seemingly good comprehension. Wernicke's aphasia, pro-

---

**Box 5.2. Types of Aphasia**

---

— Aphasia is brain damage resulting in language disturbance.
— For most people, damage to the left hemisphere produces aphasia.
— Broca's aphasia results from damage anterior to the left temporal lobe, at the back of the frontal lobe.
  — It is often accompanied by right-sided paralysis or weakness, that is, hemiparesis.
  — It is characterized by apparently good comprehension, labored speech output with many errors (paraphasias), and omissions of function words and morphemes.
  — It is also called agrammatic aphasia, nonfluent aphasia, and anterior aphasia.
— Wernicke's aphasia results from damage to the posterior left temporal lobe.
  — It is often accompanied by deficits in visual pattern recognition.
  — It is characterized by poor comprehension and fluent-sounding, but empty, speech devoid of content words. Speech may contain many speech errors at all levels of language, including creation of nonsense words, or neologisms. Frequent neologisms may classify a Wernicke's aphasic as a jargon aphasic.
  — It is a fluent and posterior aphasia.
— Massive damage creates both comprehension and production problems: global aphasia. Lesser damage creates comprehension problems together with Broca-like symptoms, or mixed anterior aphasia.
— Damage surrounding, near to, between, or to only a part of Broca's or Wernicke's areas can preserve (transcortical motor or sensory) or damage (conduction) repetition separately from comprehension and production, or affect only naming functions (anomia).

---

duced by a lesion in the temporal lobe, is characterized by fluent speech, full of function words and complex structure but devoid of content words and sense, and with poor comprehension. Patients with scattered lesions in Broca's and Wernicke's areas show a variety of comprehension and production deficits depending on the nature and extent of the lesions.

## Effects on Language of Other Brain Damage

In the last section, we discussed the effects of damage to the "language hemisphere" in adults who had normal language before the damage. For most of this century, it was thought that damage to the right hemisphere had no effect on language. However, the right hemisphere is not completely "silent": There are observable language deficits as a result of right-hemisphere damage. In this section, we discuss effects of right-hemisphere damage on language as well as effects on language of damage to the corpus callosum, disconnecting the two hemispheres.

Finally, we briefly consider the results of damage to any portion of the brain on acquisition of language in the child.

## Right-Hemisphere Lesions

For people with language-dominant left hemispheres, lesions in the right hemisphere do not dramatically disturb either production or comprehension of language: Patients are able to construct sentences, repeat, find words, and respond to sentences on the basis of semantic and syntactic content. However, right-hemisphere damage can produce a variety of cognitive impairments, some of which, at least indirectly, affect language skills. Particular agnosias are associated with right-hemisphere damage, such as the inability to recognize faces, which of course means that a patient cannot produce a person's name from the sight of the face alone. The right hemisphere may generally be responsible for person recognition because right parietal lobe damage also impairs the ability to recognize familiar voices (Van Lancker, Kreiman, & Cummings, 1989), a paralinguistic function of speech. Both right and left temporal lobe damage impairs the discrimination of new voices (Van Lancker et al., 1989).

Right-hemisphere damage also produces severe disorientation: inability to locate oneself in space, read maps, and so forth. It can result in loss of musical skills, called *amusia*. Finally, right-hemisphere damage can produce an odd attentional disturbance, known misleadingly as *left visual neglect*, in which a patient thoroughly ignores the left side of space, copying only the right sides of pictures, dressing or shaving only the right side of the body, and so on. Although called "visual," the attentional disturbance clearly involves a tactile neglect as well.

Aside from difficulties in naming or describing experiences to which they no longer attend, right brain-damaged patients (RBDs) do exhibit abnormalities of language. In particular, prosody and emotional content in language are disturbed. Intonation contours may be flat, failing to differentiate emotional qualities (Ross, 1982; Ross & Mesulam, 1979) or sentences in which tone of voice is needed to signal questions versus statements (Behrens, 1989).

RBDs also evidence a number of subtle language disturbances, all of which relate to language as communication, or pragmatics. As I said, they have difficulty expressing emotion by intonation. They also seem to have difficulty categorizing newly experienced emotions and identifying emotion vocabulary. Thus, for example, Ross reported a patient who spoke of being "brokenhearted" at the arrest of her brother some years before her stroke but who used no emotional vocabulary to describe her own brain-damaged condition. Ross describes other patients who clearly showed symptoms of depression but did not label themselves as depressed or report any change after receiving antidepressants that clearly changed their moods.

Because they cannot express their emotions either in content words or in intonation changes in sentences, RBDs may have difficulty in making others respond to them appropriately. Patients with difficulties expressing emotion through intonation also show impairment in other noncontent communication behavior: facial expressions are flat, gestures do not indicate emotional content, and patients may be unable to pantomime effectively (Borod, 1992; Ross & Mesulam, 1979). Together the results suggest a right-hemisphere control of emotional expression in communication, regardless of modality.

There is some evidence that emotion production and perception may be differentially affected by anterior and posterior damage to the right hemisphere, equivalent to the production/comprehension dissociation seen with language in Broca's and Wernicke's aphasia. (A *dissociation* is independent impairment suggesting separation of function.) Ross (1981) found this for intonation, and others, for facial expression (Borod, 1992), but these failed to replicate Ross with intonation (Borod, 1992; Cancelliere & Kertesz, 1990, for review).

The emotional impairment of right-hemisphere patients not only affects paralinguistic behavior, as just described, but may also affect higher-level linguistic behavior in interesting ways. In controlled tests where patients must label an emotion expressed in a sentence like "I was furious at what he said" (label = *angry*) or identify whether two words are from the same emotion category (e.g., *terror-dread* are both instances of *fear*), RBDs performed significantly more poorly than left brain-damaged patients or normals (Borod, Andelman, Obler, Tweedy, & Welkowitz, 1992). Similar tests using words representing characteristics of people, like *beauty* or *stupidity,* showed no poorer performance for RBDs than left brain-damaged patients.

RBDs also show "semantic" deficits when the situation demands response to nuances of meaning, if you will, to the emotional coloring the situation gives the word. Winner and Gardner (1977) found that patients asked to paraphrase figurative sentences like "He had a heavy heart" did so normally, but when asked to match the sentence meanings to cartoons, selected one representing the concrete meaning of the sentence (someone carrying a heavy heart on his back) as often as the less bizarre picture of the metaphorical meaning. Presumably, when presented with options equally reasonable in terms of the sense of the individual words, they were unable to rule out the bizarre in terms of the whole context, affecting metaphor comprehension.

This inability to relate word sense to context has been formally studied with respect to jokes. Asked to select an appropriate ending for either a verbal or a cartoon joke, RBDs preferentially choose a non sequitur, recognizing that jokes end with a surprise but failing to select a surprise consistent with the framing of the joke (Bihrle, Brownell, Powelson, & Gardner, 1986). So, for example, given the story:

> A woman is taking a shower. All of a sudden the doorbell rings. She yells, "Who's there?," and a man answers "Blind man." Well, she's a charitable lady so she runs out of the shower naked and opens the door. (p. 404)

The punch line is "The man says, 'Where should I put these blinds, lady?' " which is both plausible and surprising, and is the choice selected by normal subjects. "The man says, 'Can you spare a little change for a blind man?' " is coherent (and not funny) and is the preferred choice of left-hemisphere-damaged patients. "Then the blind man throws a pie in the woman's face" retains the element of surprise but does not cohere to the framework set up by the joke; this is the preferred selection of the RBDs.

RBDs also appear to be unable to rule out the bizarre in interpreting *indirect requests,* requests for an action framed as a request for information, as in "Can you pass the butter?" So, given a living room setting and asked, "Can you play tennis?" RBDs will swing a tennis racket (Hirst, LeDoux, & Stein, 1984). And they judge as appropriate conversations that violate the cooperative principles (see Chapter 1) of relevance and minimal redundancy, that is, those that include statements that are redundant or beside the point (Rehak, Kaplan, & Gardner, 1992).

Abnormalities in judging nuances of meaning are also reflected in RBDs' interpretations of denotative and connotative meaning. Brownell, Potter, Michelow, and Gardner (1984) presented patients with trials consisting of three words from which they had to pick the two that went together best. Trials differed in whether the pairs were denotatively similar, like *deep* and *shallow,* metaphorically similar, like *deep* and *wise,* or connotatively similar like *shallow* and *hateful,* both of which are negative characteristics. RBDs were relatively insensitive to metaphorical or connotative similarity, focusing on the denotative connection (unlike left brain-damaged or non-brain-damaged control subjects). Sensitivity to connotation, of course, is important pragmatically, for example, in selecting the polite rather than the slang word for a body part or bodily function.

Examination of the patterns of behavior of patients with unilateral right- or left-hemisphere damage has led to overly simplistic conclusions that the two hemispheres have different specialties in cognitive processing and to a popular, but incorrect, idea that our society favors the cognitive style of the left hemisphere (Borod, 1992; Springer & Deutsch, 1989). It is important to recognize that they reflect different impairments in brain damage but that both hemispheres contribute in most tasks in normal people. As we have seen, damage to the left hemisphere shows severe language impairment. So does damage to the right hemisphere, but of a different kind.

The left hemisphere seems specialized for detailed linguistic analysis of segments and their combinations. This underlies production and perception of sequential phonetic elements and also production and perception of sequential morphemes for syntactic processing. The left hemisphere also appears to be the seat of semantic memory, so that damage to the left side may disrupt both semantic processing and word finding. The right hemisphere is specialized for spatial processing and global characteristics, the overall effect of the sequential combinations. Thus damage to the right hemisphere disturbs map reading, visual pattern recognition, production or perception of intonation contours, and relation of meaning to context.

It is important to note, however, that this characterization of the skills and function of the regions of the brain is somewhat misleading. As we have seen, phonetic and grammatical elements are arranged not just sequentially but also hierarchically and are "smeared" in production and perception; we must perceive the whole to derive the structure. Even at the lowest levels of language, speech perception and production, segments are context-sensitive and must be derived from the whole, and so must rely on specializations assigned to *each* hemisphere in the characterization above. While semantic and syntactic processing are differentially affected by damage to the two hemispheres, it would be incorrect to say that the right hemisphere had no role in language. We have seen that right-hemisphere damage impairs interpretation of denotation of emotion words and sentences, connotation generally, figurative and indirect language, and coherence and cooperative principles in discourse. And the melody of language is not the exclusive domain of the right hemisphere: Broca's aphasics cannot produce cohesive melodic word strings. So the division of labor commonly assigned to the hemispheres is clearly somewhat simplified.

## Split-Brain Patients

As I pointed out earlier, it is somewhat suspect to draw conclusions about normal brain functions from the skills that are deficient following brain damage. When looking at a right brain-damaged patient's performance, for example, we see the results of damage to the right hemisphere as well as the effects of communication breakdown between the two hemispheres. We cannot therefore assume that a change in performance reflects normal right-hemisphere control of that skill. For that reason, an important converging line of evidence about brain functions is provided by patients who have a lesion of the corpus callosum, so that communication between the hemispheres is disrupted without damage to the hemispheres themselves. These patients are called *split-brain* patients. To determine the cognitive functions of each of the cerebral hemispheres of such patients, stimuli must be designed very carefully.

As with other types of brain damage, a lesion of the corpus callosum may arise spontaneously. In addition, as treatment for severe cases of epilepsy, the corpus callosum has been deliberately severed surgically (Sperry, 1982). In all cases, the effects of the lesion are not immediately obvious because usually stimuli are processed automatically by both hemispheres, each of which still has control over behavior.

As we have seen in dichotic listening, the right ear seems to have more direct access to the left hemisphere, and the left ear to the right hemisphere. Each ear does connect, however, to both hemispheres, and unless earphones are worn, any sound stimulus affects both ears anyway. When both ears are stimulated simultaneously through earphones, however, there is evidence that the information traveling from one ear to the hemisphere on the same side is suppressed en route by information traveling to that hemisphere from the opposite ear (see Milner, Taylor, & Sperry, 1968; Rosenzweig, 1951, and for somewhat conflicting results, Bryden & Zurif, 1970; Sparks & Geschwind, 1968). Thus, in split-brain patients, dichotic presentation probably ensures that stimulation from each ear is reaching only one hemisphere.

As we discussed for sign language, eye movements usually cause a visual stimulus to stimulate both halves of the retina, and therefore both hemispheres.

Information may be restricted to one half of the retina by causing the scene to move with the eye (by projecting an image onto a contact lens, for example; Zaidel, 1978, 1983) or by presenting a stimulus that is too brief to allow an eye movement. In such cases, in split-brain patients, only one hemisphere will be able to process the stimulus.

Finally, tactile information automatically divides between the hemispheres according to the side of the body receiving it: The left hemisphere receives information from the right hand, and the right hemisphere, from the left hand. In split-brain patients, contributions of each hemisphere may be independently assessed by allowing only one side of the body to touch an object.

Because, normally, ears, hands, and visual fields are stimulated by the same object, a split-brain patient can use the processing capacities of both hemispheres. Differences between them emerge only in subtle tests.

Testing of split-brain patients has confirmed the pattern of cerebral specialization observed with unilateral brain damage. When objects are presented to the right hand, right ear, or right visual field (left hemisphere), the patient is able to name or describe the object. When presentation is to the left side of the body, the patient *reports* sensing nothing but is able to match what was presented by pointing and may give an appropriate emotional response, as in surprised laughter to a presentation of a picture of a nude woman (Gazzaniga, 1967). In other words, the patient is able to sense and recognize the object but not describe it verbally (Gazzaniga, 1967). With experience, patients may become adept at cuing the verbal hemisphere: Gazzaniga (1967) reports one person who, when receiving stimulation only to the right hemisphere, would frown when he heard his left hemisphere giving the wrong answer, and the frown's feel would cue the left hemisphere to correct the response.

Support for cerebral specialization for particular functions has been obtained in split-brain patients by using stimuli that convey a different impression on the left and the right sides, called *chimeric stimuli.* Focusing on the "*," "LA*LL" will send "LA" to the right hemisphere and "LL" to the left. (Information on the *left* side of the *visual world* or *left visual field* goes to the *right* half of the retina and from there to the right hemisphere, with some stops along the way; conversely, the right visual field maps to the left half of the retina.) Instructions to match the stimulus with "LADY" or "BALL" should set up competitive responses, with the right hemisphere wanting to match "LADY" and the left hemisphere wanting to match "BALL." Which response is made will indicate which hemisphere dominates in the decision. Chimeric stimuli may use verbal material, as in the example, or emotional material, as in ⊛ , which should send a smile to the left hemisphere and a frown to the right.

Using such stimuli, Levy and colleagues (Levy, 1983; Levy & Trevarthen, 1977) have shown that the right hemisphere dominates in recognizing complex visual patterns such as faces or line drawings. This includes recognition of written words, provided recognition is measured by matching the visual chimeric pattern to a normally written word. If recognition requires comprehension as in pointing to the object named by the word, or saying the word, the left-hemisphere view of the stimulus dominates. This suggests that the left hemisphere does not efficiently use visual pattern recognition except for linguistic purposes. The right hemisphere's dominance in visual and spatial perception is also supported.

Although in most cases the capabilities of the right hemisphere reflected by callosal severing are the same as those suggested by hemispheric damage, the area of linguistic ability is a notable exception, still rife with controversy (see, for example, Gazzaniga, 1983; Levy, 1983; Sperry, 1982; Zaidel, 1983). Initial tests showed that if only the right hemisphere is presented with pictures, it can match them to spoken words. However, if presented with simple written commands such as "smile" or "frown," it is not able to respond; perhaps the right hemisphere is limited to a vocabulary of concrete nouns. Of course, these particular examples use emotion words, which may be a particular domain of the right hemisphere.

Subsequent tests of split-brain patients and one patient who had had her left hemisphere removed at a young age indicated additional right-hemisphere linguistic skills. Zaidel (1978, 1983) has shown that the right hemispheres of select patients are capable of making semantic associations to words (such as selecting the *superordinate,* the category name to which the word belongs), understanding who is the actor and who is acted upon in short simple sentences, and recognizing words in noise—about as well as can a child between the ages of 2 and 6 years. He also found the right hemispheres to have the skill of *young adults* in recognizing and understanding frequently used words from various grammatical classes. The advanced skills of these patients, he suggests, argues that the right hemisphere learns language with the left up to adulthood.

Gazzaniga (1983) pointed out, however, that the good linguistic performance of the right hemisphere is found for only a small subset of split-brain patients. These particular patients, he suggested, may have unusual right-hemisphere capabilities because of early onset of brain damage (see the next section) leading to development of linguistic skills in the right hemisphere. He cautioned that insufficient care may have been taken to prevent cuing of the left hemisphere in these tests.

Whether Zaidel's claims are warranted or not, there is evidence that the right hemisphere plays some role in language understanding and production. It seems to have some vocabulary, either of concrete nouns or high-frequency words (which, of course, are often one and the same) and emotion words, some ability to recognize words as visual patterns, and some ability to recognize spoken words in simple sentences. When noise is added or the sentences are long, the right hemisphere experiences difficulties, suggesting that the right hemisphere may not be able to perform either phonetic or syntactic processing or have extended memory for temporal order. The right hemisphere also seems to be specialized for paralinguistic functions. And as the studies of RBDs suggest, an intact right hemisphere is necessary for interpreting language in context, for connotation as well as denotation, and for pragmatic appropriateness.

### Brain Damage in Children

As we have seen, the brains of adults show distinct patterns of specialization of function. Damage to a region of an adult brain is permanent given that brain cells do not grow back; the patient can recover the function of a damaged portion only by recruiting the undamaged portions, which often have little (or different) linguistic skill at the time of the damage. Attempts to reteach language, to establish linguistic skills in regions where there had been none before the damage, have for the most part been unsuccessful in adults, although small improvement may be made (Lenneberg, 1967; Schuell, in Sies, 1974). Usually function recovers some during the first few months after the injury, but this is from a reduction in the swelling after the damage, with recovery of *prior* physiological and psychological function rather than from *(new)* learning in an undamaged site.

Because some distributed processing theories might hold that the different aphasic syndromes arise due to the size and not the location of the lesions, it is important to note that the recovery process does not reflect a transition from Broca's to Wernicke's aphasias (or conversely) but an improvement in skills *within the domain* of the initial lesion. A patient with severe Broca's aphasia initially may develop less hesitation and greater ease of production as the swelling recedes but will not change from a telegraphic style to a fluent style lacking content words. This suggests that aphasic symptoms are tied to location of the lesion, not to the extent of the damage (Goodglass, 1978).

The pattern of recovery is markedly different if brain damage occurs in childhood: Even in cases of total removal of the left hemisphere, recovery of language is excellent. There is some question regarding the age at which the excellent recovery chances diminish: Krashen (1973) argued that all cases in the literature that showed good recovery involved children no older than 5 years. Recently, a case of a mute (epileptic) 8-year-old whose left hemisphere was removed was reported to be speaking in sentences within one and a half years of the operation and to be extremely fluent at 16 years of age (Zuger, 1997). Similar recovery patterns were noted for epileptics operated on at 13 years of age. It is of course possible that a child suffering from severe epilepsy may exhibit different brain organization and adaptabilities than a child with normal brain electrical activity. And, thus far, there is no question that after puberty the prognosis for language recovering from left-hemisphere damage is poor (Searleman, 1977).

If brain damage is sustained just after the child has begun to acquire language, there is usually a period of silence and then a reacquisition of language, which proceeds through all the usual stages (babbling, single word, two words . . . ). If the injury occurs after the child has acquired language, the child exhibits aphasic symptoms, which diminish gradually if the child is prepubescent (Lenneberg, 1967). The aphasic symptoms in children are not as differentiated with respect to location as in the adult (Goodglass, 1980).

The two hemispheres do not begin as equals at birth. Witelson and Pallie (1973) have shown that even in newborns, there is a region in the left hemisphere that is usually larger than the corresponding region in the right. In adults, this region is associated with language. According to current theory, however, the two hemispheres are each *potentially* capable of learning language at birth but, under normal conditions, the left hemisphere assumes this function, perhaps suppressing the right hemisphere's capability (Lenneberg, 1967; Searleman, 1977). Damage to the left hemisphere during this period will allow the right hemisphere to assert its linguistic capacity, and this may allow the child to recover language function. It may be that for a period, both hemispheres learn language, with the result of this early right-hemisphere language acquisition seen in the language capabilities of adult right hemispheres.

## Summary and Conclusions

Studies of right-handed adults and right-handed children who have sustained left-hemisphere damage, right-hemisphere damage, or callosal severing suggest an innately determined separation of cognitive functions. At birth, the hemispheres may be considered equally capable. If development is normal, the left hemisphere becomes dominant for many language functions, perhaps suppressing language learning in the right hemisphere. There may be a period when both hemispheres acquire language, providing a redundant store for high-frequency, concrete content words (those learned early). While the left hemisphere dominates for most language skills, the right hemisphere dominates in other domains such as spatial reasoning, person recognition, and emotion, and appears influential in paralinguistic and pragmatic language processes. If there is brain damage before completion of cerebral specialization, the intact hemisphere takes over; if the lesion occurs after specialization, recovery of function is unlikely. The critical period for cerebral specialization is in dispute (see Snow, 1987) but is not likely to extend past puberty.

In addition to providing information on brain maturation, the studies discussed thus far suggest some division of language processes. Because the right hemisphere appears to dominate in paralinguistic (emotion, intonation, and so on) processing, and the left hemisphere in linguistic processing, we have evidence for separation of these two communication components. The different semantic capacities of the right and left hemispheres suggest a separation of connotation from denotation, and of selecting (or interpreting) words for a sentence frame from selecting (or inter-preting) words or sentences pragmatically to fit a discourse context. There also is evidence for separation between comprehension (posterior) and production (ante-rior) in both right- and left-sided language processes. Finally, our discussion of the different aphasic syndromes suggests separation of content from function words: Broca's aphasics retain the content words and lose the function words; Wernicke's aphasics retain function words and empty content words like *thing* but lose meaningful content words. In the next section, we examine aphasics' language comprehension and production more precisely, in studies aimed at determining the independence and interactions of language processes as reflected in brain damage.

## LANGUAGE PROCESSING AND APHASIA

As I have described language after brain damage, there are several general types: right-hemisphere damage, with preserved syntax, phonology, and semantics but disturbed communication of emotion, paralanguage, and pragmatic use of lan-

---

**Box 5.3. Right-Hemisphere Processes Relevant to Language**

— The right hemisphere handles emotion as produced or comprehended by facial expression, gesture, intonation, and emotion words. The anterior brain regions may be responsible for production, and the posterior, for perception/comprehension.
— The right hemisphere handles recognition of familiar voices.
— The right hemisphere assists in interpretation of language in context.
　— RBDs have difficulty recognizing and establishing coherence, relevance, and redundancy.
　— The right hemisphere appears to process affective meaning of words, connotation, and figurative meanings. RBDs have difficulty with indirect requests and judgments of bizarreness of language.
— Perhaps redundantly with the left hemisphere, the right hemisphere has some vocabulary and syntax, perhaps very frequent, early-learned items.
— The right hemisphere is responsible for visual pattern recognition, including written words.
— The right hemisphere uses, roughly, holistic, rather than sequential/analytic, processes.
— The right hemisphere may learn language with the left, up to a critical period, when they specialize. Damage to the left hemisphere in childhood will produce a temporary aphasia, and then acquisition of language in the right hemisphere. Damage through seizure activity may prolong or alter the pattern of specialization.

---

guage; Broca's aphasia, an expressive disorder, preserving comprehension and content words but otherwise producing agrammatic speech; Wernicke's aphasia, a receptive disorder, preserving production of fluent sentences but omitting all but empty content words and lacking comprehension; conduction aphasia, with relatively preserved language skills except in repetition; and anomia, with preserved comprehension and fluent production but disturbed naming. Our discussion of the left-hemisphere patients characterizes the language deficit principally from clinical observation, not from careful analysis of the structure of the patients' speech or from careful experiments in production or comprehension. In this section, we will look more closely at how language is processed after different kinds of brain damage.

## Semantic Processing in Aphasia

In discussing normal semantic processing, we can consider four types of processes: basic concept organization (semantic memory), figurative and literal uses of word names, integration and interaction of concepts in sentence (and discourse) processing, and interfacing of concepts with word names. Each of these areas has been studied with aphasics. The processes indicated in brain damage provide support for some of our conclusions concerning normal semantic processes.

## Conceptual Structure

The basic question to ask with respect to brain damage and conceptual structure is whether specific semantic knowledge is lost. Given models of normal semantic processing, we might expect loss of semantic knowledge to manifest as an inability to name or answer questions about a particular category. It could also show up as loss of a particular kind of associative link, such as superordinate-subordinate relations (a canary is a bird is an animal . . . ). Or it could manifest as loss of infrequent concepts, abstract ones, or peripheral rather than prototypical ones.

With respect to loss of conceptual structure, the simplest pattern appears in *category-specific anomia* in which processing is normal for all semantic classes except, for example, fruits and vegetables, or colors or animals; alternatively, one of these categories may be preserved better than other semantic knowledge (Farah & Wallace, 1992; Hillis & Caramazza, 1991; Spreen, 1973; Warrington & McCarthy, 1983). Some patients have problems exclusively with generating an item name (e.g., Farah & Wallace, 1992), but there are patients who seem to have comprehension problems, mistakenly verifying as the name of a picture a related item (e.g., orange for apple). These patients may also be unable to define terms from the category (e.g., Hillis & Caramaza, 1991).

Category-specific impairments support a localized storage (and destruction or sparing) of the category. They could also arise if a specific type of information, a marker (see Chapter 1) or general feature for, say "food" or "animal," was selectively affected (Hillis & Caramazza, 1991). Farah and Wallace (1992) argue that the syndrome is also consistent with a distributed (PDP) model, with the damage selectively affecting *hidden units,* ones reflecting neither input nor output directly but intermediate correlations of category members (see Chapter 3 of the companion volume for more detail).

Category-specific anomias are rare and may reflect the idiosyncratic semantic organization of the particular patients in whom they occur. More generalizable findings concerning the associative structure of semantic memory after brain damage have been obtained by looking at patterns in many patients in their verbal paraphasias and in experimental studies of word association, picture selection in response to words, and similarity clustering.

The first thing to note is that when aphasics make a slip of the tongue, a verbal paraphasia, it is usually a close associate of the target word, such as *man* for *boy, table* for *chair,* or *June* for *July;* never, *table* for *July* (Schuell, in Sies, 1974). In fact, nearly all verbal paraphasias are normal word associations, suggesting that the *organization of semantic memory is spared.*

This is supported also by word-association studies, at least for Broca's aphasics, who show essentially the same association pattern as normals. Wernicke's and other patients with posterior lesions make radically different associations not readily amenable to classification (Howes, 1973). Goodglass and Baker (1976) modified the association task to examine whether different kinds of associative links were preserved. To measure the different kinds of associations, a concrete object—say, an orange—was pictured and then words were presented with it relating identically *(orange)*, not at all *(shoe)*, as a superordinate *(fruit)*, an attribute *(juicy)*, another member of the same category *(apple)*, an associated action *(eat)*, a situation in which the item was likely to be found *(breakfast)*, or a sound-alike *(arrange)*. If the word related to the picture, subjects squeezed a bulb, thus not needing to respond verbally.

All subjects responded equally quickly to the identity condition. So, they understood the task and recognized the name. For the other conditions, the anterior patients responded like normal subjects, indicating for them that the different kinds of associative links were preserved. Posterior patients responded abnormally, most notably failing to recognize actions or contexts, although recognition of all associations was slower than normal. Thus, for posterior patients, semantic memory organization appeared generally disturbed.

Zurif, Caramazza, Myerson, and Galvin (1974) had aphasics judge the similarity of 12 high-frequency stimulus words—*shark, trout, dog, tiger, turtle, crocodile, mother, wife, cook, partner, knight, husband*—which could be categorized into a semantic hierarchy with the highest-level feature human-animal, and then these subdivided, respectively, into the features male-female, fish-mammal-reptile. Subjects were presented three words at a time and asked to select the two that seemed most similar. Patients with anterior lesions, like normals, structured their answers with respect to the human-nonhuman dimension (although they put *dog* with the humans), clustered the humans normally (*husband* or *mother* was the closest to *wife*), and categorized the animals logically. Unlike normals, the logic was based not on biological categories but on relations to people (which may be why *dog* was with the humans, as a household member), so *shark, crocodile,* and *tiger* were together (all ferocious and wild) apart from the other tamed, perhaps edible, animals. These (including the *dog* one) may be normal associations, which we suppress to produce "scientific" answers. In contrast, posterior patients showed *no* hierarchical organization in their associations, not even breaking down human and nonhuman systematically. All patients abnormally organized the terms, but posterior patients again were more severely impaired.

We have seen that fluent (posterior) aphasics do not respond to contextual and action associations, respond more slowly to all associations, and show no apparent recognition of semantic similarity in their clustering: Patients with posterior lesions seem to have little residual semantic structure. More recent data suggest moderating this conclusion. These derive from visual (Milberg & Blumstein, 1981) and auditory (Blumstein, Milberg, & Shrier, 1982) lexical decision tests. In a lexical decision task, subjects indicate only whether a group of letters is a word; they do not have to respond explicitly with respect to meaning. Meaning associations are measured as a change in reaction time when a related (primes or speeds) or unrelated (inhibits or slows) word precedes the target.

The researchers found, unsurprisingly, that normal subjects were faster for all decisions, primed or not, than brain-damaged subjects. Wernicke's aphasics were much slower than other brain-damaged patients. However, all patients showed the same priming effects: Semantically related primes speeded decisions. Thus *Wernicke's aphasics, as well as anteriors, know that items are semantically related.* They cannot access the relations in *explicit* recall or recognition tasks, that is, those requiring naming, naming of associates, or matching of items to associates. Wernicke's aphasia may produce an increase in the threshold needed to fully activate an item in semantic memory.

Recall that the pattern of verbal paraphasias also suggests that fluent aphasics have residual semantic structure. And studies in which subjects indicate whether a pictured item belongs to a category show that fluent aphasics, like nonfluents, do better with prototypical instances than peripheral ones. This also indicates residual "normal" structure (Brownell, Bihrle, & Michelow, 1986; Koemada-Lutz, Cohen, & Meier, 1987; Kudo, 1987; McCleary, 1988; McCleary & Hirst, 1986). Anterior and posterior aphasics differ in their use of the basic level in naming: The posterior aphasics sometimes avoid the basic-level name in naming subordinate category members (e.g., the *drill* in *power drill*) but describe the item; anterior aphasics avoid the *preposed* modifier (*power* in *power drill),* adding it to a descriptor list following the basic item. Thus, while both seem to recognize objects and have some residual structured separation between the prototype, basic level, and periphery, they do not access this information similarly.

Initial examination of semantic processes suggested that Wernicke's aphasics' semantic memories were differentially impaired relative to Broca's aphasics. But the bulk of recent evidence suggests that Wernicke's aphasics, while more impaired, still have *implicit* access to a relatively normally structured semantic hierarchy. They have difficulty with explicitly using it in naming and associating. This suggests that semantic memory as such is located neither in Broca's nor in Wernicke's areas, and that perhaps it is distributed through them.

As you may recall, the information available in semantic memory of left brain-damaged patients is not limited to the most common denotative meaning. In discussing right brain-damaged patients, I presented a study by Brownell et al. (1984) in which subjects selected from three words sharing denotative, affective, or metaphoric meaning the two that were most similar. Aphasic (Broca's, and mildly impaired posterior) patients did not pair the denotatively similar words as often as normals but did select the affectively and metaphorically related words as similar, like normals and unlike RBDs.

So far we have looked at studies of the state of preexisting semantic knowledge and access to it after brain damage as though comprehension were a relatively passive retrieval process. It is interesting to consider the fate of active semantic construction processes after brain damage, as in determining the likely meaning of a newly introduced word (Grossman & Carey, 1987) or of a homonym (Grossman, Carey, Zurif, & Diller, 1986). In these studies, a stimulus is presented in context with other words and with objects or pictures in the environment. For example, a subject might see pictures of a person and a flower and be asked to select "Rose" (a proper name), "the rose," or "a rose" (or the same task with a newly introduced word, "Pitta" or "a pitta"). Or the person might have an array of pens of different colors and be told that the experimenter is selecting "the bice pen" as the experimenter selects a dark green one, which, in some trial later, the subject must also do to the stimulus "bice." These studies are modeled on studies done with children acquiring language (see Chapter 9 of *Language and Its Normal Processing*) to see how aphasics attend to language properties to construct meaning and form categories.

Like the retrieval studies with aphasics, the construction studies show that semantic processing is impaired, but not destroyed, after brain damage. In the proper-common noun study, only Broca's aphasics were tested, and while they made more errors than normals, they were significantly better than chance, indicating that they do attend to the *determiners* (*a, the,* or no determiner) in classifying items as common or proper nouns.

In the new-adjective study, both Broca's and fluent aphasics were tested, and as you should now expect, fluent aphasics were poorer than the Broca's, who in turn were poorer than normal. Unlike the normals, the Broca's aphasics did not assume that *bice* referred only to color but categorized it as describing a color and shape combination, still selecting bice-colored objects more often than chance but also selecting non-bice-colored long thin objects. They saw as ungrammatical sentences that used the new word *bice* either grammatically or not. Fluent aphasics were also better than chance (after more trials) at selecting bice-colored objects, but they established broader categories of bice-coloredness than did normals or Broca's aphasics and did not integrate shape with the color dimension. Fluent aphasics judged correctly the grammaticality of sentences containing the new word.

The studies suggest that concept acquisition is slowed, but not devastated, by brain damage. Fluent aphasics are more impaired but, importantly, are *differently* impaired than the Broca's aphasics: They are more attentive to syntactic properties of the word and less attentive to its conceptual/perceptual properties. Both anterior and posterior aphasics, however, can make use of syntactic and conceptual information in processing both old and new items. We will look more at constructive language processes in aphasia in the syntax section.

### Naming in Aphasia

Our discussion of semantic memory has examined principally comprehension and associative processes, measuring "production" when necessary, by nonverbal means like squeezing a bulb or pressing a button if a word is a label or an associate (or for lexical decision, a word) or selecting associated or similar representatives from among provided choices. These studies indicate a greater impairment among posterior than anterior patients but also, for both, evidence that much of the organization of semantic memory is intact. In the "basic-level" study in which subjects produced as well as comprehended names (Brownell et al., 1986), different retrieval strategies seemed to operate between Broca's and Wernicke's aphasics. This suggests that access to semantic memory for naming and comprehending is different, and affected differently in brain damage, and thus that there may be *localized processing operations,* if not localized memories. Indeed, Ojemann (1991) reports for subjects undergoing electrical brain stimulation that only about one third of the neurons stimulated in the language areas are implicated in a variety of different language tasks; different tasks like naming and verbal memory use a majority of different neurons. There is also considerable evidence from aphasia that naming and comprehending are indeed separate processes (Caramazza & Berndt, 1978), supplementing such evidence in normal language acquisition and in attempts to teach animals language.

Nearly all brain-damaged patients experience word-finding difficulties analogous to those normal people experience from time to time but increased in severity. The increased severity manifests not just in a quantitative increase in word-finding problems but also in qualitative changes. In brain damage, the word-finding difficulty may be restricted to a particular semantic class (fruits and vegetables, as we have discussed) or grammatical class (e.g., verbs and action names; Ardila & Rosselli, 1994), or may cut across more classes than normal as in loss of prepositions or other function words. (Verbs and function words seem to be particularly affected in Broca's aphasia, which we will return to in the section on syntactic processes.) In brain damage, a word just provided may be lost while, for normals, a tip-of-the-tongue state rarely occurs for a recently heard word. In brain damage, words may be lost from speech but not in writing, or conversely (Goodglass, 1980), and there are even cases where a particular word class (e.g., verbs) is lost only in speech *or* writing, but not both (Caramazza & Hillis, 1991).

Goodglass, Klein, Carey, and Jones (1973) performed one of the earliest systematic studies of word-finding problems in aphasia. Patients were asked either to name a picture or to point to the picture when the name was provided. The pictures represented objects, actions, letters, numbers, or colors. The most interesting finding was that for each patient, classes easy to name were not the same as those easily comprehended, indicating a dissociation between the naming ability and the ability to recognize an object from the name. For example, objects were among the best comprehended words but were most poorly produced, while letter names were poorly comprehended but well produced. Because the ability to comprehend the name was not predictive of the ability to produce it, we can conclude that the two skills are separate. In addition to the dissociation between name production and comprehension, the study also showed that naming skills varied with location of the lesion: All aphasics were equally poor at object naming, Broca's aphasics were relatively poorer at number and letter naming, and Wernicke's aphasics were relatively better at letter naming.

There have been various attempts to relate the accessibility of names to properties of the *lexicon* (semantic memory, the mental dictionary) or of the referents. We already have evidence that concrete words may be lost as well as abstract ones: Letters and numbers are both concrete and imageable; category-specific anomias have been noted for color names (Spreen, 1973) and highly imageable categories like fruits and vegetables or animals (Hillis & Caramazza, 1991; Warrington & McCarthy, 1983).

Nevertheless, *across* studies it appears that the less frequent, concrete, picturable, or manipulable a referent is, the less likely its name will be retrieved (Caramazza & Berndt, 1978). Generally one can conclude that the richer the associations to the name (object or action), the more sensory modalities over which the referent may be experienced, the more frequent the experience, and so on, the more likely it is that the name will be accessible. Perhaps this is because damage to one link between the concept and the name can be offset by the other links. None of these factors, however, is exclusively responsible for loss or preservation of naming.

Using the pattern of naming results from aphasia, Goodglass (1980) hypothesized that naming is a two-stage process. The first stage is quick and involves access of a direct link between the concept of an object (or whatever) and its name. If for some reason that link is disturbed, as in the normal tip-of-the-tongue state, a slower associative process takes over in which the individual attempts to self-prompt, using associated concepts or sounds. In brain damage, it is assumed that some of the direct links between concepts and names are broken, forcing patients into Stage 2 more often and accounting for the across-the-board word-finding difficulties. (We have seen two-stage—automatic and labored—semantic models before. In Chapter 1, we reviewed one for sentence verification: A first step quickly assessed degree of feature overlap between instance and supposed superordinate; a second stage engaged only when overlap was intermediate, laboriously comparing—"self-prompting"—defining features.)

Goodglass suggests that the ability to activate the associative links for Stage 2 naming is differently impaired in anterior and posterior aphasias. For anterior aphasics, they are largely accessible, so items like object or action names that are associatively rich are well retrieved. Letter and number names, which will not have rich semantic associations, cannot use Stage 2 prompting (and Stage 1 is impaired for these patients). For posterior aphasics, the associative network—or getting explicit information from it, to account for the results of Milberg and Blumstein discussed earlier—is disturbed, so the second stage process cannot help when Stage 1 fails. Note that reliance on the slower second stage process could account for the slow, tortured speech of Broca's aphasics. And raised thresholds to uniquely activate an item using the Stage 2 process would produce several equally, but weakly, activated associates, resulting in the verbal paraphasias and confusions within category that have been observed.

We may add the results of the category-specific modality-specific patients to this model: There may be separate direct links to the name for the *orthographic* (writing) and speech systems. Differential impairment of one of these direct links for a category will result in the patient's forced reliance on the slow Stage 2 process in that modality for that category alone.

### Grammatical Morphemes in Aphasia

In discussing semantic processing with brain damage thus far, we have considered words as the unit of processing. It is reasonable to ask whether brain-damaged language reflects morphological processes: Are only word roots preserved in brain damage? Are words used together with their inflections? Are all grammatical morphemes equally available?

Examination of the aphasic quotations should indicate that grammatical morphemes are preserved in fluent aphasics but are lost at least in part in anterior aphasia. Broca's aphasics do use the plural and progressive (-ing) morphemes. They have difficulty with pronouns: In quotation 4, the patient called himself by name, Peter Hogan, avoiding the pronoun; in quotation 6, the patient improperly used "me" as the subject form.

Formal studies of use of 14 common English grammatical morphemes (Brown, 1973, began extensive study of these in language acquisition; see Chapters 9 and 10 in the companion volume) in nonfluent aphasia have shown the order of difficulty to be (from easiest to hardest): progressive, plural, contractible *be* form (e.g., *isn't*), noncontractible *be* form, determiners (articles), negative past, irregular past, and third person singular -s (de Villiers, 1978). Broca's aphasics are more likely to omit the possessive "s" than the plural "s" and less likely to notice the omission of the possessive than the plural in the speech of others (Goodglass, 1973).

We should note, however, that Broca's aphasic speakers of highly inflected languages (Italian and German, for example) are much more likely to produce inflections than are speakers of less inflected languages, like English (Bates, Friederici, & Wulfeck, 1987). In inflected languages, the morphemes are produced more regularly (in English, for example, verb agreement in the present tense is marked only on the he/she form) and carry more meaning. Aphasic speakers of these languages do not omit morphemes as frequently as English aphasics but produce them paraphasically; that is, they substitute a related, but incorrect morpheme. They often then correct themselves. The difference between English and inflected-language aphasics suggests that the salient, reliable, and frequent language properties are likely to be preserved. The self-correction suggests that knowledge of the form is not lost but, as with content words, access to it is impaired.

There are reports of patients who have retained productive use of rules of morpheme combination, inventing words by combining morphemes, while showing the typical word-finding difficulties (Semenza, Butterworth, Panzeri, & Ferreri, 1990). This suggests that morphemes and morphological rules may be processed independently of the rest of the lexicon. There are also reports of patients who have specific morphological impairments. Kehoe and Whitaker (1973) described aphasics who avoided verbs, using in their stead nouns derived from them, such as "decision" for "decide." They also reported one patient who was able to produce derived words correctly but paused between the root and the derivational morpheme, decomposing "bandaged" to "bandage + ed" and "bacteriological" to "bacteriology + ical," for example. However, in general, patients seem to access derivationally complex words as a unit, as do normals: Lexical decisions on words that are morphologically complex due to addition of derivational morphemes (like "excitement") are made more slowly than normal by both Wernicke's and Broca's aphasics, but, for both, decision time correlates with the frequency of the derived word (the more common, the faster), not the stem, suggesting it is processed as a unit (Eling, 1986).

The pattern of breakdown in grammatical morphemes in aphasia has interesting implications for normal processing. First, the fact that Broca's aphasics lose some inflectional and derivational morphemes while preserving content morphemes suggests that inflecting and deriving may be active processes, that words are not always stored in all possible forms. This is supported also by the case study in which the root and derivational morpheme seemed to be independently produced. Second, the fact that at times a patient may have access to one form of a word (like *me* or the noun) but not others and that patients recognize derived forms as a unit suggests that not all morphological changes are actively produced; some are directly stored. And that some patients can productively use morphology to create new words indicates that morphological processes may be preserved independently of other semantic processes.

As with naming, normals appear to have two routes available to inflect words: direct retrieval or slow process. Either can be impaired after brain damage, with the other route taking over, in production. In comprehension, as is true for free content words, bound morpheme meaning, function, and associations seem to be retained in memory but access to them is impaired, perhaps again a raising of the threshold for complete activation.

Finally, it is interesting to observe that at least in some cases the grammatical morphemes better preserved in aphasia are not the ones earliest acquired. In particular, the past-tense markers usually precede use of the *copula* (the verb *be* in identity relations, such as "I am happy") in acquisition but are more likely to be affected by brain damage than the copula (de Villiers, 1978). Because the acquisition order has been attributed to semantic or phonetic salience, the pattern in breakdown is clearly not just a result of low salience, given that it is not identical to the pattern in acquisition.

### Summary and Conclusions

Analysis of semantic processing at the word and morpheme levels in aphasia suggests a separation between naming and the concept network, with breakdown possible in either one or in the link between the two. Access to the conceptual network appears to be particularly affected by posterior lesions, resulting in a diminished ability to make normal associations or to use associative cues to word retrieval. In addition, it appears that individual semantic categories such as colors, letters, or fruit or animal concepts may be specifically and exclusively affected, perhaps indicating localized and organized storage.

Generally, it seems that the richer the associations for particular words are—as in words or morphemes used often and obligatorily in the language, and those with imageable, concrete, manipulable referents—the more likely they are to be retrieved in Broca's aphasia, perhaps because there are more connections that can be activated in a slow, deliberate process. Finally, both free and bound forms seem to be produced normally by a two-stage process: (a) fast access of names or of unanalyzed whole forms directly and (b) slow, deliberate association or derivation. Fast naming seems impaired in Broca's aphasia; either morphological process may be spared in brain damage.

---

### Box 5.4. Semantic Processes in Aphasia

— Broca's aphasics seem to preserve content words, and Wernicke's aphasics, function words, in their spontaneous speech, suggesting, for English, that there may be different stores and processes for these word classes.

— All aphasics are slower and less accurate at associating, naming, classifying, identifying, or making lexical decisions than are normals, perhaps indicating a raised threshold for full activation from semantic memory. Wernicke's aphasics do not explicitly recognize semantic associations or organize semantic features hierarchically. They do not use context but are sensitive to typicality. Broca's aphasics are more normal.

— All aphasics show normal priming effects in lexical decision, suggesting that the semantic associative network is largely intact. Similarity and association measures suggest it is less accessible to Wernicke's than Broca's aphasics.

— In naming, posterior aphasics avoid the basic-level content word (circumlocutory description, e.g., no *drill* in *power drill*); anterior aphasics, modifiers (no *power* in *power drill*).

— Both Broca's and Wernicke's aphasics appear able to use some phrase structure cues (like determiners to differentiate proper from common nouns) to disambiguate homonyms and/or determine the meaning of a new word. Wernicke's aphasics rely more on syntactic information than do Broca's.

— Both Broca's and Wernicke's aphasics can acquire new words from context. It takes longer than normal, and there is more overgeneralization, which is different in quality for the two types of brain damage, suggesting differential locus of process.

— The more frequent, reliable, salient, concrete, and multimodal a stimulus (the more access routes it has to consciousness), the more likely it is preserved, indicating perhaps a distributed memory.

— Words that are comprehended well may not be those whose names are most accessible, suggesting that naming and comprehension are dissociable processes.

— Naming (of whole words and morphologically composed words) is a two-stage process normally: (a) fast, direct access to the unit and (b) slow, productive activation of associates or components. The processes appear to be damaged more than the stored information after brain damage.

— Case studies suggest, at least for some individuals, localized storage of categories (colors or animal names), of a word class (verbs), or of derivationally complex words.

— Inflectional morphemes are not lost in the order they are acquired. It is not just semantic or perceptual salience that accounts for either acquisition or breakdown processes. Languages dependent on inflection preserve inflection to a greater extent than English in brain damage.

— Sometimes words are preserved with their inflections; sometimes, not. Derived words may be stored as such, or they may be "computed."

In the next section, in discussing syntactic processes, we will consider possible differences between content and function words, and meaning, both figurative and literal, at sentence and discourse levels, because they require integration and interpretation of meanings from syntactic combinations.

## Syntactic Processes in Aphasia

Examination of the productions of Broca's and Wernicke's aphasics gives the impression of distinct syndromes, with content words and their meanings preserved in Broca's aphasia, and structure without meaning in Wernicke's aphasia. Our exploration of semantic processes in aphasia belies this simple picture. Both aphasias involve naming problems, slowed access to semantic memory, and some disturbance of semantic structures and processing. Both appear to have much of the associative structure intact, although not necessarily readily accessible. The differences between the aphasias are subtle ones of access and use of the associations.

Perhaps the seeming difference between aphasias arises not in semantic processing but in syntax. The quotations indicate that Broca's aphasics do not produce syntactically integrated sentences, while Wernicke's aphasics do use complex sentence structure, complete with embedding in almost every instance. Goodglass, Christianson, and Gallagher (1994) in fact found that Broca's aphasics disproportionately use single-constituent utterances focused on nouns, not verbs, relative to conduction aphasics, whose utterances were elaborated with prepositional phrases and adverbs. To what extent are syntactic processes preserved in aphasia? Do aphasia data indicate that syntactic processing can be divorced from semantic processing?

There have been several different characterizations of the nature of syntactic deficits after brain damage, particularly in Broca's ("agrammatic") aphasia: failure to process function words and closed-class morphology, failure to create hierarchical structures, failure to create hierarchical structures using syntax per se, and a specific impairment in tracking movement transformations. We examine the evidence for each, in turn.

### Closed-Class Processes

With respect to the closed-class hypothesis, we can see in the quotations from the Broca's aphasics that few function words appear. Their perception of function words also is often impaired. First, note that normal readers show "a missing letter effect"; they are worse at targeting a particular letter in grammatical text if it appears in a function word than in a content word. Normally, function words seem to be read as structure cues and fade rapidly into the background (Koriat & Greenberg, 1991; see Chapter 11 of *Language and Its Normal Processing* for elaboration).

Now, let us look for a missing letter effect in aphasics. For Broca's aphasics, there is none: They detect letters as easily in function words. Fluent aphasics show the normal advantage for letter detection in content words. However, unlike normals, that advantage persists for scrambled, ungrammatical prose (Rosenberg, Zurif, Brownell, Garrett, & Bradley, 1985).

Rosenberg et al. suggest that normal "automatic" identification of function words is syntactic, to form the parse. This is damaged in Broca's aphasia, so that they activate the slow, controlled associative process we saw for content words. It is intact for Wernicke's aphasics, so the automatic syntactic recognition takes place, but then, unable to construct meaning, they are not hampered by anomalies in the scrambled sentences.

In another indication that function words are ineffective structure signalers for Broca's aphasics, Zurif and Blumstein (1978) found that patients who were asked to "select (a, the) black one" from an array of one or several black ones were not impeded by the determiner's being inappropriate to the situation (*the* fits for one; *a* when there are many). In contrast, mild aphasics and normal adults took longer and showed confusion.

However, Linebarger, Schwartz, and Saffran (1983) pointed out that Broca's aphasics understand the difference between "in" and "on," so they are not simply failing to attend to function words, and they can recognize the ungrammaticality of sentences with inappropriate function words (see also Shankweiler, Crain, Gorrell, & Tuller, 1989). For example, their subjects recognized that "the policeman was talking a woman" is wrong (a *subcategorization* violation; "talking" cannot take a direct object, the function word "to" is omitted), whereas the similar "the policeman was lecturing a woman" is acceptable. Indeed, we have seen that they used the presence of a determiner to differentiate proper and common noun meanings of the homonymous "rose." The researchers contend that Broca's aphasics have not lost grammatical knowledge but its facile use for parsing sentences.

Finally, Bates et al. (1987; Bates, Wulfeck, & MacWhinney, 1991) showed some preservation of comprehension of inflectional morphology in both Broca's and Wernicke's aphasics. They tested aphasics who spoke languages with different dependencies on inflectional morphology and function words versus word order to signal sentential relations, asking the patients to use objects placed before them to enact the sentences. Both Broca's and Wernicke's aphasics (and non-brain-damaged controls) were better able to comprehend morphological function the more necessary it was syntactically in their language. Both Broca's and Wernicke's aphasics preferentially used the canonical word order of their language (SVO in English) to determine sentence relations, but both were able to override this interpretation using morphology, *if morphology was salient in their language.* In a task of grammatical judgment, English-speaking Broca's aphasics were better able to detect word-order violations, and Italian-speaking Broca's aphasics, morphological violations, suggesting that grammatical features are preserved in relation to their importance and frequency of use in the language. Finally, as we might expect, Broca's aphasics were always better able than Wernicke's aphasics to use semantic information (like animacy of the noun or gender and number markings) to determine probable sentential relations.

Bates et al. suggest that it is neither that Broca's aphasics are literally *a*gram-matic, nor that closed-class items (function words and inflectional morphology) are differentially impaired in Broca's aphasia. Rather, these items are perceptually, attentionally, and linguistically less salient (less important in cue competition, MacWhinney, 1987; see Chapter 1 and, in the companion volume, Chapters 9 and 10) than other cues to meaning, and so are more vulnerable—in brain damage, in acquisition, in aging, and in normal perception. The more salient the cue in a language, the less likely it will be lost. And because cue vulnerability arises for multiple reasons, its selective impairment may arise from different causes in different patients or brain-damage types. Therefore, different patients may employ different compensatory strategies, such as attention to order or semantic information.

### Creating and Understanding Hierarchical Relations

If Broca's aphasics have sufficient grammatical competence to recognize ungrammaticality in some instances, it seems clear, nevertheless, that they do not use it to derive a syntactic representation of the sentence. Using a clustering procedure, Zurif, Caramazza, and Myerson (1972) directly measured the ability of aphasics to comprehend the hierarchical organization of sentences. Given that the subjects were brain damaged, they could not simply be asked to diagram the sentence. Instead, each patient was shown a sentence, such as "He hit the ball," which was kept in view throughout the task. Then the subject was given three words from the sentence like "ball, he, the" and asked to select the two that went together best. Normal subjects usually select words that are part of the same constituent, so, in this case, would pick "the ball." With many trials for a single sentence, the selections reveal constituent structure; words that belong to the same constituents will go together often, while words that belong only to the sentence constituent (one from the subject and another from the predicate) will be grouped together seldom.

In this task, posterior aphasics grouped the words randomly. Anterior aphasics' groupings reflected constituent structure for the content words. However, depending on the patient, either the function words were grouped together or they were ignored. Based on such results, some have tried to write a grammar for Broca's aphasics' productions, arguing that syntactic categories and relationships are retained, but each is represented only by a single word or word part (such as the uninflected noun in a noun or prepositional phrase; Kean, 1980; Lapointe, 1983).

However, on-line syntactic processing studies indicate that Broca's aphasics do, at least temporarily, create some hierarchical grammatical structures. In an *on-line* study, a sentence is interrupted as it is being understood (see Chapter 5 of *Language and Its Normal Processing*) for the subject to perform another task (like lexical decision). Normal people perform the task more slowly if the sentence appears agrammatical or ambiguous. Using an on-line task, Baum (1989) found that, like normal subjects, Broca's aphasics were slowed by grammatical violations within a constituent, as in subcategorization, auxiliary verb agreement, or *reflexivizing* (him versus him*self*) pronouns. However, unlike normals, Broca's aphasics were unaffected by global syntactic structure violations, such as when a filler subject for an embedded clause is mismatched (as in "the businessman knew which article the secretary called this morning"; a sentence from Garnsey, Tanenhaus, & Chapman, 1989). Creation of local structures appears within a Broca's aphasic's ability; maintaining them to create a complete parse appears beyond it.

A difference in creating and remembering structure by Broca's aphasics was also found by Haarmann and Kolk (1994) for subject-verb violations in conjoined sentences. The patients noted the violations, but only if the second clause was presented within 750 milliseconds of the first. So, syntactic knowledge (competence) may not be gone, but there are severe performance limitations impairing its use in Broca's aphasia.

Shapiro and Levine (1990) compared processing of sentences with potentially ambiguous argument structures to those with only one structure. For example, the verb *suspect* can take either a direct object ("he suspected the butler") or a *complement* (a that-clause as in "he suspected that the butler did it"). In contrast, *insist* has an unambiguous argument structure; it must take a complement. Normals are slower at processing sentences with potential ambiguities, until the ambiguity is resolved—say, when the *that* appears (see Chapter 5 of the companion volume for more detail). Like normals, Broca's and, to a lesser extent, Wernicke's aphasics were slowed in responding to sentences with verbs that could take different argument structures. However, for the aphasics but not the normals, the effects of the potential ambiguities disappeared *immediately* after the verb; they did not retain the structure possibilities through their resolution.

Thus the aphasics do activate, and therefore have retained, needed syntactic information, but *cannot maintain the activation to create a structure.* Here, for the Broca's aphasics, is a pattern like we saw in semantic memory for the Wernicke's aphasics. Linguistically relevant information still appears to exist but cannot be activated and maintained in the deliberate fashion necessary for language processing.

### Semantic Heuristics in Processing Sentential Relations

The difference between the use of syntactic information (relatively preserved in Wernicke's aphasia) and lexical information (relatively preserved in Broca's aphasia) suggests an independence of lexical and syntactic processes in language (Caramazza & Berndt, 1978). This is further indicated by a number of studies that have teased apart semantic and syntactic cues to sentential relations.

Broca's aphasics have difficulty when usually redundant lexical-semantic cues are absent. Blumstein, Goodglass, Statlender, and Biber (1983) tested assignment of the correct antecedent to pronouns when gender and number (singular-plural) markings were absent. Normally, pronouns and their antecedents are linked both through "lexical" markings (e.g., the word *her* must refer to the female or *they* to the plural noun) and through syntax (*binding* and *indexing* principles, as described in the most recent versions of generative grammar; see Chapter 4 of the companion volume). Broca's aphasics had little difficulty with sentences like "The woman watching the man bandaged herself," where "herself," though distant from "woman," clearly refers to it by gender alone. Wernicke's aphasics, in contrast, did not use the lexical information, consistently selecting as antecedent the nearest preceding noun, a simple, and often (as here) incorrect, syntactic heuristic. When the lexical cues were absent, as in "The boy watched the man bandage him," like the Wernicke's, Broca's aphasics selected the nearest noun.

Caramazza and Zurif (1976) contrasted sentences that were clear both through the semantics and the syntax, such as "The apple the boy is eating is red," with those interpretable only through syntax, such as "The cat that the dog is chasing is brown." Patients matched the sentence to a picture chosen from several containing the same objects in different relations. Posterior aphasics performed more poorly than anterior aphasics on such tasks but, critically, showed no difference between the semantically transparent sentences and those that required attention to syntax. In contrast, the anterior patients performed almost perfectly on semantically unambiguous sentences but near chance on the syntax-only sentences, indicating a clear syntactic impairment together with semantic preservation. Because language is normally redundant both extralinguistically with real world events and intralinguistically with semantics, these patients may appear to have good comprehension—without processing syntax.

Sherman and Schweickert (1989) replicated this finding and examined Broca's aphasics' abilities to comprehend reversible and irreversible active and passive sentences. The patients were better able to process active than passive sentences, which in turn were easier to comprehend than center-embedded sentences. The easier the sentence was grammatically, the less the patient relied on semantic plausibility; that is, patients correctly comprehended *implausible* active sentences like "The plant waters the boy" but not implausible center-embedded sentences like "The boy the plant watered wore a red hat." This again suggests that Broca's ("agrammatic") aphasics have available some syntactic processes. These can overrule semantic plausibility.

I should note that other studies of Broca's aphasics' comprehension of reversible passive and active sentences (Schwartz, Saffran, & Marin, 1980) have shown significant syntactic impairment. For such sentences, invariably, Broca's aphasics' comprehension was still better than Wernicke's aphasics' comprehension but was impaired compared with normal. These Broca's aphasics failed to make use of most syntactic structure for comprehension, even the basic "SVO" interpretation of active sentences. (On the basis of such individual differences in processing capabilities of patients, all classified as "agrammatic," Badecker and Caramazza, 1985, have questioned the experimental efficacy of studying aphasics as though they represented a "homogeneous" population as we study a group of normals as representatives of "homogeneous" normal language processors. They argue forcefully that we should consider patients on a case-by-case basis, as we did with the category-specific anomias and the feral children.)

The discussion of syntax thus far has concentrated primarily on comprehension processes in Broca's aphasics and has demonstrated severe impairment, at least when there are no semantic anchors. Of course, Broca's aphasics also are impaired syntactically in production. This is obvious from the quotations: They omit function words and inflections, leaving the speech telegraphic, for example. But more serious grammatical problems have also been noted. Saffran, Schwartz, and Marin

(1980) asked patients to describe pictures designed to be describable in a single sentence like "The girl runs to the man." Broca's aphasics could not order the noun phrases in the sentences appropriately if both were animate or both were inanimate. The results suggest that the most salient feature of a lexical item for a Broca's aphasic is whether or not it is likely to serve as an actor, and that underlies ordering all lexical items. In sentences where there is one animate and one inanimate noun, the animate one is usually the actor, normally resulting in good production and comprehension. On other sentences, the strategy provides no information. Thus the syntactic deficit in Broca's aphasics' productions is not limited to "the little words" but extends to the most fundamental sentence relationships.

In both production and comprehension, across studies, we see patients who have impaired ability to create syntactic structure without semantic cues but who have semantics relatively well preserved. This suggests that syntax and semantics are independently affected (and localized) in brain damage. For patients with residual syntactic processes, the studies also point to the greater difficulty of center embeddings over passives in brain damage—true also for the non-brain damaged.

## Damage to Particular Syntactic Operations

Grodzinsky (e.g., 1989) has argued that for those patients with an impairment in processing center-embedded sentences, the problem is specifically in keeping track of relations after a movement transformation, connecting the gap (where the trace is; see Chapter 1) to the filler. He proposed that aphasics have lost the ability to represent the trace. They do retain some rudimentary heuristics, but not a real syntactic analysis, for assigning *thematic* relations (caselike sentence relations as described in government and binding theory: Chomsky's 1986 version of generative grammar). The following is an example of such heuristics: The agent is the first NP or is marked by the preposition *by*.

For active sentences, the heuristics appropriately assign the agent role to the first NP. For passive sentences, the competing possibilities leave aphasics with chance performance, because they have two candidates for the agent. Similarly, in object-gap constructions, like "The *cat* that the *dog* is chasing [*t*] is brown," patients fail to recognize the movement of "cat" from object position in the relative clause and are left with two potential agents and chance performance. In subject-gap constructions like "The dog who is chasing the cat is brown," the heuristic unambiguously assigns the agent role to the first NP. Thus patients are correct on these, although not for the right reason of a full syntactic analysis.

Grodzinsky found consistently poorer performance for object-gap than subject-gap sentences regardless of whether the relative clause was center embedded or right branching (as are the ones in "The house that Jack built"). Right-branching structures are easier for normals but, in themselves, did not advantage the patients. Thus the patients were not simply affected by general cognitive complexity but by a particular grammatical construction, which they could no longer process.

Grodzinsky's hypothesis has stimulated considerable research, much of it not confirming the strong claim. Druks and Marshall (1991), for example, found patients with equal difficulty with passive sentences involving movement and a trace as with those not involving one. Lukatela, Shankweiler, and Crain (1995) confirmed that object-gap sentences were harder for Broca's aphasics, but they were also harder for normal controls and fluent aphasics. They concluded that the object-gap sentences are simply harder and the relatively poorer performance for Broca's aphasics reflects the processing difficulty, not the loss of a syntactic process per se. The trace-loss hypothesis is intriguing, but in aphasics, as is true for normal syntactic processing, it is often difficult to differentiate between general operating principles and specific syntactic parsing operations (see Chapter 5 of *Language and Its Normal Processing*).

The ability to link traces to either subjects or objects in embedded relative clauses seems to be preserved in Wernicke's aphasics in on-line comprehension, even when they do not understand the sentence (Zurif, Swinney, Prather, & Love, 1994). The link was measured by lexical decision just after the trace (gap) to words related to the filler, the moved NP. Wernicke's aphasics showed a priming effect indicating that they had activated the filler. In these studies, like Grodzinsky's, Broca's aphasics did not construct the syntactic relations; they had no priming effect.

## *Summary*

Our discussion of syntactic processes in aphasia leads to the following general observations. First, there appears to be evidence for the *lexicalist* hypothesis, that argument structures are specified with words themselves and used to construct the parse. Both Broca's and Wernicke's aphasics seem to have relatively intact semantic memories, which include not just hierarchical and prototypical semantic relationships but also the subcategorization rules and argument structures of the items.

Access to semantic memory information and automatic use of it appears differentially impaired with different kinds of brain damage. Broca's aphasics seem less able to retain or use the argument structures to construct a parse than they are to use the semantic information to construct a plausibility representation. For Wernicke's aphasics, the converse is true: The argument structure is used and not overridden by anomaly. For no patient is either syntactic or semantic processing unimpaired: In all cases, access is slow, strained, and errorful, but the relative dominance of syntactic or semantic process dissociates the two.

Finally, as Bates et al. (1991) point out, there are processing differences between Broca's and Wernicke's aphasics. For Broca's aphasics, activation is slow, does not spread, and cannot be maintained, leading to word-finding difficulties, labored associations, and disappearance of hypothesized structures before the necessary disambiguating information. For Wernicke's aphasics, a higher threshold is needed to attain unique activation of an item and there may be a problem inhibiting associations that are partially activated, leading to substitutions of syntactically or semantically related but incorrect words: "loose" associations. For both, the more salient, frequent, and important an item is, the more likely that it is attempted or preserved.

Given that both Broca's and Wernicke's aphasics show some syntactic and some semantic impairments, and that both seem to be affected by the frequency of occurrence of an item or structure in the language, it is perhaps not surprising to learn that both Broca's and Wernicke's areas are implicated in sentence processing in non-brain-damaged subjects, as revealed by magnetic resonance imaging. Moreover, and more important, the more complex a sentence is (conjoined actives versus subject-relative clauses versus object-relative clauses, from least to most complex), the greater the area of both regions involved in the processing. And, in fact, the right-hemisphere equivalents of Broca's and Wernicke's areas are also increasingly involved in processing as sentences become more complex, although always considerably less involved than the left-hemisphere regions (Just, Carpenter, Keller, Eddy, & Thulborn, 1996). It is clear from studies of both brain-damaged and normal individuals that structurally complex sentences require more "brain power," and that their understanding depends on syntactic and semantic and perhaps paralinguistic operations in both Broca's and Wernicke's areas.

### Figurative Language and Discourse Processes

It is important to recognize that even if Broca's aphasics have limited ability to use their syntactic competence in sentence processing, they are not restricted to deriving sentence meanings only by "adding" likely meanings of individual words. I noted in the semantics section that aphasic patients have access to affective and metaphoric meanings of individual words. They also appear to be able to process figurative sentences. Winner and Gardner (1977) tested brain-damaged patients' comprehension of figurative speech—sentences such as "A heavy heart can make a difference." (We have already looked at their results for right-brain-damaged patients.) Each sentence was given along with pictures; for this sentence, the pictures showed someone depressed, someone carrying a heavy heart (the sentence meaning, but literal and strange), a heart alone, or a weight alone. If the patient used only individual word meanings, either of the last two pictures would be as likely to be selected as the first. Wernicke's aphasics performed generally very poorly. Broca's aphasics, like normals, chose the figurative pictures, indicating comprehension of the entire sentence *and* of figurative speech.

Studies of discourse processes in aphasia reveal findings similar to those of studies of sentence processing in aphasia. Much of text understanding depends on the ability to access scripts of likely sequences of events with their attendant objects and characters: A restaurant contains waitresses, tables, dinner plates; menus arrive before placing an order; and so on (see Chapter 5 of *Language and Its Normal Processing*). Specific tests of Broca's and fluent aphasics' abilities to access scripts, sequence their events, and recognize typical versus atypical events showed this information to be largely intact and available for both types of patients; only sequencing was performed (slightly) more poorly than by non-brain-damaged controls (Armus, Brookshire, & Nicholas, 1989).

This script information facilitates discourse processing in both groups of aphasics as well: Chapman and Ulatowska (1989) found that moderately impaired

Broca's and Wernicke's aphasics were nearly normal in linking pronouns to antecedents across sentence boundaries as long as the paragraph told a plausible story. When the story was not plausible, the aphasics were significantly impaired in tying the pronouns to their referents—a "semantic" strategy for syntactic processing in discourse, as we saw in sentences. In fact, it appears often that *aphasics comprehend better the more context given,* when they can use extralinguistic "script" knowledge along with lexical-semantic knowledge and syntactic structure.

On the production side, aphasics appear able to carry on conversation, selectively recounting essential but not peripheral information in retelling a story (Li, Williams, & Della-Volpe, 1995). Turn-taking is appropriate, as is use of script knowledge, speech acts, and other language features, although they produce less language with less complexity than do normals (Ulatowska, Allard, Reyes, Ford, & Chapman, 1992).

## Summary and Conclusions

In this section, we looked at syntactic processing in brain-damaged patients. In anterior patients for whom comprehension is good and concept structure is preserved, there are comprehension problems when sentence meaning may be obtained only through syntax. Usually this does not create a problem because of the redundancy of the language: Broca's aphasics are able to use semantic processing strategies to recover basic sentence relations, or to use general processing strategies like the minimum distance principle without performing a complete syntactic analysis. They recognize some subtleties of grammar, judging ungrammaticality, even if they cannot use these subtleties to recover structure. And they can create some simple syntactic structures temporarily, suggesting preservation of some grammatical competence but inability to use it for processing.

Assessment of syntax in Wernicke's aphasics is difficult in comparison with Broca's aphasics because the semantic abilities of Wernicke's aphasics are significantly impaired. Therefore, naturally, they have difficulty with picture verification tasks or word clusterings apart from any syntactic impairments. However, we saw some lines of evidence that their abilities to create constituent structures and map traces to their NPs were preserved, even in the absence of understanding the sentence.

It is important not to lose sight of the fact that Wernicke's aphasics' productions are grammatically abnormal: They violate both subcategorization rules (e.g., using a noun rather than a prepositional phrase as the object of an intransitive verb) and *selection restrictions* (e.g., using an inanimate word like *thing* when an animate one is required; Caramazza & Berndt, 1978). Coupled with repetitions of items, these give a strange syntactic appearance to their speech.

Bates et al. (1991) suggest that one way to consider the language of Wernicke's (as well as Broca's) aphasics is with respect to new and old information. Aphasics tend to omit the redundant, known, already indicated information: pronouns, the article *the* more often than *a,* and redundant subject nouns. Each of these signals

**Table 5.1**  Approximations to English

10-Word "Sentences"

| | |
|---|---|
| 1st order: | abilities with that beside I for waltz you the sewing |
| 2nd order: | was he went to the newspaper is in deep and |
| 3rd order: | tall and thin boy is a biped is the beat |
| 4th order: | saw the football game will end at midnight on January |
| 5th order: | they saw the play Saturday and sat down beside him |

20-Word "Sentences"

| | |
|---|---|
| 1st order: | tea realizing most so the together home and for were wanted to concert I posted he her it the walked |
| 2nd order: | sun was nice dormitory is I like chocolate cake but I think that book is the wants to school there |
| 3rd order: | family was large dark animal came roaring down the middle of my friends love books passionately every kiss is time |
| 4th order: | went to the movies with a man I used to go toward Harvard Square in Cambridge is made fun for |
| 5th order: | road in the country was insane especially in dreary rooms where they have some books to buy for studying Greek |

SOURCE: From Miller and Selfridge (1953).

NOTE: The second-order approximations are derived by giving a speaker one word and asking for a next word and stringing those pairs together; third order, by giving two words and asking for the next word and stringing the triples; and so on. First-order approximations are a random scramble of higher orders.

old information: *the,* a definite, known referent or only one alternative; a pronoun, an already mentioned noun, which is linked to the pronoun clearly by context; and the subject, the already mentioned topic of the conversation. When all cannot be uttered, they concentrate on items providing new information. In this context, it is interesting to recall that aphasic discourse processes are relatively intact and that they can successfully screen essential from peripheral details in storytelling: They seem to know what needs to be said and where to put their energies.

A final way to look at the syntactic impairment of Wernicke's aphasics' productions is to compare the productions cited at the beginning of this chapter with approximations of English produced by randomizing sentence chunks, shown in Table 5.1. The examples in 5.1 are generated by limiting speakers' knowledge of preceding words and asking them to generate a next word, and then gluing these together. You might note a strange similarity to the Wernicke's aphasic sentences. The scrambled sentences of course still have substantive content words but fail to hang together even at the higher orders because there is random association between chunks of the string. Likewise, Wernicke's aphasics seem to be randomly splicing large chunks of words like "I figured that," "it's liable to," "I had trouble with," and so on, which have internal consistency and structure perhaps because they are stored as a unit. When they are combined, there is an apparent superficial structure, as in the English approximations, not necessarily because they have been productively and hierarchically generated but perhaps because the phrasal units have been chained together. If Wernicke's aphasics do not productively generate syntax, they do evidence a syntax impairment. That the phrasal units are spared may indicate that in normals too some are accessed as a unit.

---

### Box 5.5. Syntax in Aphasia

— Across languages, there are distinct syndromes for anterior and posterior aphasics.

— Relative to posteriors, anteriors lose skills in comprehending and producing the syntactic role of function words and/or morphological inflection; they may understand their meaning.

— Inflections salient to the language and canonical word order are relatively preserved even for anterior patients.

— Anterior patients have not entirely lost competence for function words and other grammatical markers: On-line studies indicate that they are immediately activated as in normals, but the activation dissipates before the structures are completed. Anterior patients can also make grammaticality judgments for structures they may not be able to produce or use correctly.

— Anterior patients retain part-of-speech and subcategorization rules along with semantic information in the lexicon. They can construct simple phrase structures but cannot combine them into larger constituents.

— Anterior patients rely preferentially on semantic and extralinguistic information to determine sentence relations.

— There may be a fast process of the syntactic function of function words that anteriors have lost, and posteriors retain, allowing posteriors to generate structures for sentences that they do not understand, while anteriors may laboriously access function word meaning through residual lexical processes.

— Posterior aphasics are harder to test than anteriors because their comprehension overall is poor. Some tests have shown that they are unable to create grammatical hierarchical relationships altogether, and other tests show that these are relatively intact in the absence of understanding.

— Theories of the loss of syntactic function in anteriors include failure to create complex hierarchies beyond linear ordering, loss of function elements, and loss of traces.

— Despite the recognizability of an anterior and posterior aphasic syndrome cross-linguistically, there is sufficient individual difference among patients that it may be best to consider case studies rather than considering each patient as a representative of an aphasic group.

— Across cases and studies, there is good evidence for (i.e., relative preservation or damage to) a separation of semantic heuristics to sentential relations (relatively preserved in anterior patients) from syntactic heuristics, such as the syntactic role of function words and the retention of filler-gap (trace) links (which are relatively preserved in posterior patients). There is also evidence for separation of derivational and inflectional morphological processes from semantic and syntactic functions.

— In aphasia, as in acquisition, there is good evidence that frequency and perceptual salience of an element or a "rule" make it easier: learned earlier, more likely to be preserved, and more likely to be used to override semantic or other syntactic cues.

*(Continued)*

---

**Box 5.5 Continued**

— MRI studies show that both Broca's and Wernicke's areas (and less so their homologues in the right brain) are involved in sentence understanding. The more complex the sentences, the greater the brain areas involved.

— In posterior aphasics, the relatively "fluent" speech may derive from the stringing together of overlearned phrases, not necessarily hierarchical generation of the sentence structure.

— Aphasics may focus effort on the new information and err on the unimportant or redundant.

— Anterior aphasics can construct both connotative and metaphorical interpretations of sentences, so they are not limited to a strategy of adding most frequent meanings.

— Difficulties in discourse mirror difficulties in sentence processing: linking references across sentences and so on. As in sentence processing, plausibility helps all aphasics construct the links, which indicates that script knowledge is intact.

— Aphasics seem to have retained the essentials of discourse, able to recount essential information selectively and take turns, maintain script essentials, and interpret and produce speech acts correctly, although with less grammatical complexity than normal.

---

## Phonological Processing in Aphasia

At various times, it has been proposed that the problem in aphasia is at the level of speech: inability to recognize the incoming sounds or to generate a sound representation in response to a picture or written word (e.g., Luria, 1973). We might explain Broca's aphasia, for example, as arising not in *representation* of function words but in production and perception of unstressed syllables (most inflections and function words are not stressed). In fact, Wernicke argued that Broca's aphasia was a disturbance of the "motor image" of words (Sies, 1974). Certainly a breakdown at these low levels of processing would have ramifications at the higher levels.

### Speech Production in Aphasia

We have already noted that all aphasics are likely to make "slips of the tongue," and these include literal paraphasias, single phoneme slips, as well as verbal paraphasias. Intonation also is deviant: Broca's aphasics' speech is labored and hesitant with long silences between words, which may burst out individually. However, for phonemic purposes, as in distinguishing words differing only in contrastive stress (con'trast versus contrast'), like normals (and right brain-damaged patients), Broca's aphasics raise their fundamental frequency and amplitude for the stressed syllable (Ouellette & Baum, 1994).

Intonation changes may result in aphasics not sounding like native speakers; there are even anecdotes of patients suffering embarrassment when their speech acquired a foreign accent—from an enemy country (Critchley, 1973). Such occurrences are rare but arise from intonation rather than segmental changes.

Although aphasic speech contains many speech errors and dysfluencies, it preserves the phonemes and phonological rules of the native language. I stress this because it indicates that even in the extreme cases of the neologisms of Wernicke's aphasics, phonological competence is intact; neologisms are not the product of random groupings of articulatory features.

The maintenance of the phonological structure of the parent language is also reflected in finer-grained analyses of the phonemes produced as well as in the error pattern reflected in aphasic "slips of the tongue," the paraphasias. To discover such patterns, Blumstein (1973a, 1973b) analyzed tape recordings of free conversations of English-speaking Broca's, Wernicke's, and conduction aphasics. Not surprising, Broca's aphasics produced fewer phonemes per unit time than other subjects. However, for all patients, phoneme inventories reflected the frequency of occurrence of phonemes in the language: The most common English phonemes remained the most common in the aphasics' speech. In addition, for all aphasics, the more common a phoneme was, the more likely it was to be produced correctly.

Analysis of the literal paraphasias showed that, like normal slips of the tongue, they most often were substitutions of one phoneme for another (e.g., *book* → /gök/). Next most common were paraphasias arising from deletion of a phoneme (e.g., *prince* → /plns/) or accommodation of a phoneme to the phonemic environment (as in assimilation, such as *Crete* → /trit/). Least common were phoneme additions (e.g., *boot* → /blut/). The relative frequency of each type of error was the same for all aphasic groups. As we see in normal speech errors, more single-feature changes were made than multiple-feature changes, and the feature most likely to be altered was place of articulation. As I noted earlier, the main difference in production between groups of patients was in "fluency": Broca's aphasics needed more time to make a set number of phonemes than did Wernicke's aphasics, and Broca's aphasics had flatter intonation contours.

Given that the pattern for Broca's and Wernicke's aphasics is similar at the phoneme level, we cannot argue that the production deficit for Broca's aphasics, who appear to be particularly impaired in production, lies in loss of skills for producing particular phonemes. However, one might argue that the deficit in Broca's aphasia comes in organizing these individual motor programs into hierarchies of motor commands—into syllables, words, or phrases. Indeed, Goodglass (1973) noted that Broca's aphasics usually emit speech in bursts of less than four words, which he attributed to "an increased threshold for initiating and maintaining the flow of speech—either after a silence or as a combination of sequences already in progress" (p. 204).

He suggested that the patient compensates by focusing on the most salient point of the utterance (the real information), usually the noun or verb, and utters it and one or two surrounding words, rarely including more than one unstressed sound. If so, the pattern of speech production in Broca's aphasia reflects disturbance at the highest level of organization of the motor production hierarchy (see Chapter 7 of the companion volume for discussion), in concatenating individual phoneme motor programs into phrasal units. It also suggests that a basis for each unit of organization, wherever in the hierarchy, might be the syllable that receives the main stress.

The studies discussed thus far use listener transcriptions of aphasic speech as data. There have been some studies that have analyzed speech acoustically, and these have demonstrated interesting differences between Broca's and Wernicke's aphasics. Blumstein, Cooper, Goodglass, Statlender, and Gottlieb (1980) asked aphasics to identify pictures differing in the voicing value of the initial consonant, as in *pin* versus *bin.* They acoustically measured the onset of voicing for each production, comparing the variability and modal value to the normal range of production (see Chapters 6 and 7 of *Language and Its Normal Processing* for discussion of voicing measurement—*voice onset time* or *VOT*). Wernicke's aphasics clearly divided their productions into two "normal" voicing categories, occasionally erring by a clear production of the wrong member of the voicing pair. Such errors were considered "phonemic" in origin, as though the patient had accessed the wrong category. Broca's aphasics' productions, in contrast, were highly abnormal: Voiced and voiceless targets could have *any* VOT, showing a *unimodal* (single peak frequency) rather than *bimodal* (two-category) distribution. This was considered a "phonetic" error, an inability to control or produce voicing appropriate to the category.

Tuller (1984) replicated these findings for different Broca's and Wernicke's patients. She also looked at another voicing cue (in addition to VOT), vowel length before voiced or voiceless consonants. In normal speech, the /i/ in *heed* is longer than it is in *heat,* and that added vowel duration signals the voiced phoneme. Tuller found no relation of the vowel duration results to the VOT results of the same patient; some who were unimodal for one acoustic feature were bimodal for the other, and conversely. If an error is "phonemic" in origin, one would expect all the acoustic correlates to be equally affected, so it is not clear that this is a productive classification of production characteristics of different aphasic groups. And Ryalls (1986) found greater than normal variability but no difference between aphasic groups in vowel formant frequencies, showing no phonemic-phonetic distinction for vowel production.

The last result to consider in speech production in aphasia is the aphasics' monitoring ability. Normal speakers vigilantly attend to their output and correct many of their mistakes, or rephrase productions that may lead to a misunderstanding (again, see Chapter 7 of the companion volume). Do aphasics, who make so many speech errors, also monitor their output? Schlenck, Huber, and Willmes (1987) had both Broca's and Wernicke's aphasics describe line drawings with instructions to attempt to convey the description in a single sentence. They coded the output for *prepairs*—evidence of planning, like hesitation pauses or a comment like "How do you say . . ."—and for *repairs,* backtracking corrections of their speech. Prepairs occurred equally frequently in both aphasic groups, indicating planning and monitoring of the speech before it was output. Despite the large number of errors in the speech, repairs occurred very seldom for either group. Perhaps the task of monitoring and correcting an effortful and now complete production is too much after brain damage—as we may feel when asked to reread and revise a paper once the thing is finally done. That the aphasics can prepair indicates that they do plan and monitor their output.

### Speech Perception in Aphasia

Although the VOT production results differentiate Broca's and Wernicke's aphasics, speech perception testing indicates more commonality than difference and supports the general hierarchy of difficulty also seen for normal subjects. On minimally contrasting pairs of words (e.g., *pin* versus *bin*), aphasics can better discriminate sounds that are two features rather than a single feature apart and phonemes that differ in voicing rather than in place of articulation (Blumstein, Baker, & Goodglass, 1977). Not a surprise, brain-damaged patients also better identify and discriminate place of articulation when it is redundantly and naturally cued (both burst and transitions) than when it is impoverished (Blumstein, Tartter, Nigro, & Statlender, 1984). As we might expect from our study of language-learning disabilities, attention to phoneme order—distinguishing, for example, *main* from *name*—is difficult after brain damage (Blumstein, Baker, & Goodglass, 1977). And, as we might expect from our study of aphasia thus far, brain-damaged patients perform more poorly than normals, and Wernicke's aphasics are impaired relative to Broca's aphasics, having difficulty even categorizing vowels (Lund, Splud, Anderson, & Bojsen-Moller, 1986).

Blumstein, Cooper, Zurif, and Caramazza (1977) looked at VOT perception, relating it to the production findings I presented in the last section. Here, Broca's aphasics were more normal than Wernicke's, who were better in production, suggesting that production and perception are separable processes. Some patients could both identify and discriminate the stimuli normally, and some could do neither, but no patient performed well on identification without also performing well on discrimination. Blumstein et al. (1984) found similar results for place of articulation.

Tallal and Newcombe (1978) explored the possibility that slowing speech might help aphasics process language, as Tallal has proposed for language-learning disabilities and dyslexia (see Chapter 3). They synthetically lengthened stop consonant transitions, so that the rate of information change was slower, and claimed that perceptibility of place of articulation was enhanced. However, Blumstein et al. (1984) found an improvement only for a slightly slowed transition rate, and a degradation in performance at a very slow rate. And Blumstein, Katz, Goodglass, Shrier, and Dworetsky (1985), looking at the effect of slowing speech, found that it helped little at the phonetic and word levels. They lengthened the vowel in the word (a low-level change like the transitions), paused between words, or lengthened the pause between constituents in a sentence. Wernicke's aphasics were tested and were helped only by the lengthening of natural pauses, at constituent boundaries. Thus the evidence does not strongly support a deficit in processing rapidly changing information as an underlying cause of aphasia.

Results on low-level speech perception, as I said, basically support the hierarchy of difficulty in speech perception that we found in normals. Apart from this support, they address two important issues: (a) Unlike syntax and semantic processing, phonological processing seems to be distributed through Broca's and Wernicke's areas, because they are similarly affected, and (b) perception and production of speech are relatively independent. This latter conclusion derives both from the dependence of identification on discrimination and not the reverse (contradicting the motor theory explanation of categorical perception; see Chapter 7 of the companion volume) and from the relatively normal perception of VOT in Broca's aphasics who produce it abnormally.

I note, though, that brain stimulation results implicate motor movement production in speech perception: Those regions that, when stimulated, produced disturbances in phoneme identification and discrimination also produced disturbances in making *orofacial* (the mouth part of the face) gestures (Ojemann, 1983, 1991). So, while perception and production of speech may be partly independent, they may also share some processes.

It is important to note that aphasics generally have difficulty perceiving *nonsense* syllables; in fact, most of the studies discussed above use real words (*pin-bin* rather than /pɪ/-/bɪ/) for just that reason (Blumstein, Cooper, et al., 1977). This suggests that, as do normals, brain-damaged patients perceive speech using lexical information (as reviewed in Chapter 1).

Conversely, sound cues facilitate semantic access for all aphasics. Broca's and conduction aphasics' naming is greatly facilitated when phonemic cues like the first letter of a rhyming word are provided (Li & Williams, 1990). Likewise, lexical decisions are primed for normal and nonfluent aphasics by phonologically related words: rhymes (Gordon & Baum, 1994) or phonetically intact semantic associates (Milberg, Blumstein, & Dworetzky, 1988). Wernicke's aphasics are less affected by sound composition: For them, rhymes were ineffective primes, and phonologically distorted semantic associates (like *gat* instead of *cat*) primed as well as the nondistorted word. These results support our observations that speech perception is preserved in Broca's aphasia relative to Wernicke's.

*Summary*

Studies of speech production and perception in aphasia have shown impairments in both these low-level language abilities across aphasic groups, for the most part consistent with speech processing results in normals: The sounds normals have difficulty with when mixed with noise, for instance, are the ones aphasics most likely confuse. Thus single-feature differences, particularly in place of articulation, particularly if it is minimally rather than redundantly cued, are poorly perceived. And perception is best the more different stimuli are at the acoustic and phonetic levels, when they constitute real words and in sentences with structural cues enhanced—in short, when there is a multiplicity of redundant information.

Generally Broca's and Wernicke's aphasics seem to be similarly impaired in speech. For Broca's, which is perhaps not surprising, there is more likely to be a

---

**Box 5.6. Speech Processes in Brain Damage**

---

— Broca's aphasics produce less speech per unit time than Wernicke's, but both show the same distribution of phonemes, reflecting the distribution in English.

— While Broca's aphasics' speech is hesitating and has broken intonation, fundamental frequency and amplitude are controlled appropriately at the segmental level to indicate linguistic stress.

— All aphasics' literal paraphasias are more likely to represent substitutions of one phonetic feature than two (and two, than three), and are least likely to be correct in place of articulation. Substitution errors are more common than deletion or addition of a phoneme.

— Broca's aphasics' speech problem may reflect a deficit in hierarchically organizing motor commands, resulting in the patient focusing on the main stressed syllable of each phrasal unit, bursting out with it and two or three adjacent syllables.

— VOT analyses indicate Broca's aphasics may have a problem at the phonetic level: All voicing onset values are equally likely to be produced. Wernicke's aphasics produce two categories of VOT, like normals, sometimes producing a token from the wrong category—possibly a phonemic confusion. This distinction has not been replicated with vowels and final voicing measures.

— Neither Broca's nor Wernicke's aphasics spontaneously repair their utterances to a noticeable degree, although their speech reflects evidence of planning and monitoring the "internal sound" of the plan before outputting it.

— All aphasics show some impaired speech perception, especially if lexical and/or contextual cues are omitted.

— All aphasics have an easier time discriminating sounds that are two features than one feature apart, and have the greatest difficulty with place of articulation.

— All aphasics discriminate and identify speech better the richer it is: Both burst and transition or longer transitions help over less redundant stimuli. Discriminating words rather than nonsense syllables, and longer pauses at constituent boundaries, also help.

— Speech results with aphasics suggest that discrimination is more dependent on identification than conversely, and that speech may be produced well without being perceived well (Wernicke's aphasics), and conversely (Broca's aphasics). Both of these results are not supportive of the motor theory, although brain stimulation studies do suggest that the same region mediates production and perception.

— Broca's aphasics appear more sensitive to the sound properties of words than Wernicke's aphasics in retrieving names or priming related words.

---

production impairment, perhaps at a phonetic/motor level with little perceptual impairment, and for Wernicke's, the opposite. Both patient types, though, are impaired in both perception and production, although differently. Wernicke's aphasics, as we have seen, have a more disabling disorder: they are relatively oblivious to the actual sound structure of a word in higher-level language tasks, producing, and not correcting, the wrong voicing feature; are not assisted in name-finding by a rhyme; and are untroubled by phonological distortions of a word for lexical access.

## Aphasia and Exceptional Language Skills

Thus far we have discussed the patterns of breakdown of language when a single spoken language was the native language. It should be noted that although in most cases here the discussion was of English, these patterns are not exclusive to English: Broca's patient was French and Wernicke's German, and research in aphasia has been conducted across the world (see Bates et al., 1987; Bates et al., 1991, for example and review), with comparable results to those reported for English. (Indeed, without specifically noting it, the research I have reported includes Hebrew, French, Scandinavian languages, Italian, and Dutch aphasias.) In this section, we will not discuss any other spoken language specifically but briefly discuss the pattern of breakdown in multilingual speakers and with sign language.

### Aphasia and Multilingualism

There are problems in calibrating an individual's experience with multiple languages, as you may be able to imagine from our discussion of the acquisition of sign language by deaf children raised in hearing cultures: For example, when were they exposed to the languages? In what contexts was each language used? Did they continue to use more than one language relatively interchangeably through their lives? These issues are presented in detail in Chapter 10 of the companion volume; note here that the answers, for each individual, *must* have implications for the representation of the languages in the brain.

It is interesting to consider whether two languages known by the same individual share a conceptual structure and thus show equivalent deficits in Wernicke's aphasia, share syntactic operations and thus show equivalent syntactic deficits, and so on. While many different patterns are reported, the most usual pattern is that both languages are similarly affected by brain damage particularly if predamage experience with them was similar. (However, Ojemann, 1991, observed that electrical brain stimulation of multilinguals implicated different neurons in naming objects or reading their names in the different languages.) If one language was used preferentially, it is likely to be better spared and recover first after brain damage. Finally, there are also "exceptional" patterns—people who lose one, presumably native language completely and retain mastery of another (Kinsbourne, 1981; Vaid & Lambert, 1979).

### Aphasia and Sign Language

Sign language presents an interesting contrast for spoken language with respect to brain damage. Sign is a *spatial language*—and spatial processing is considered primarily right-hemisphere based. So a question immediately presents itself as to whether native signers will show aphasic symptoms with left-hemisphere damage or with right-hemisphere damage. (For people who acquire sign later in life, the age of acquisition could affect cerebral specialization; recall that Genie showed right-hemisphere language, perhaps because she learned language after the critical period for left-hemisphere language.) As with people fluent in several spoken languages, we might also want to ask whether a deaf person schooled in speech and sign shows similar impairments in both. Finally, because sign has a more simultaneous than sequential organization in comparison to speech, it is interesting to ask whether the pattern of deficits for Broca's and Wernicke's aphasias occurs for sign also.

Poizner and colleagues (Poizner, Bellugi, & Iraqui, 1984; Poizner, Kaplan, Bellugi, & Padden, 1984; Poizner, Klima, & Bellugi, 1987) have investigated linguistic and nonlinguistic processing in six brain-damaged deaf individuals. All had hearing parents but learned sign at a young age. Three were born deaf, two became deaf at 5 years, and one became deaf at 6 months. Three of the patients suffered left-hemisphere brain damage, and three, right-hemisphere damage. Of the left-hemisphere patients, one was described as a Broca's aphasic, one as a mixed anterior, and one as a Wernicke's aphasic.

The first point of interest is that the left-hemisphere-damaged patients had no difficulties arranging blocks, copying or producing drawings, or recognizing faces, while the right-hemisphere patients showed marked impairment in these tasks. The right-hemisphere patients also exhibited left visual neglect in copying drawings, which the left-hemisphere patients did not. Therefore, lateralization of nonlinguistic function appears the same in these patients as in hearing patients.

Organization of language also seems comparable in these patients to organization in hearing patients. The right-hemisphere patients remained fluent in sign. The left visual neglect, however, affected some signing, although it usually does not affect speech. Specifically, for one patient, for signs that required movements in both sides of space, such as SQUARE, which is made by tracing a square with the index finger, the left side was omitted. All the right-hemisphere patients also exhibited difficulties using the left side of space in "setting the stage" for pronoun reference (see Chapter 4), and thus had disturbances in verb agreement. None of the right-hemisphere patients could describe the layouts of their bedrooms, essentially by "drawing" the bedroom spatially before them in sign. Thus, here, general language processing appeared intact but a specifically spatial component of it was impaired by the spatial neglect. Because sign employs space in its grammar, the spatial neglect also resulted in impairment in pronominalization and agreement of subject and object with the verb. (This is like the deficit we saw in hearing right-hemisphere patients, who could not describe or convey emotion. Emotion, like space, is a right-hemisphere function. It reveals a language problem when it must be used linguistically.)

The left-hemisphere patients demonstrated severe aphasic symptoms. As with speaking aphasics, they made many production errors, had word-finding (that is,

---

**Box 5.7. Sign Language and Multilingualism and Aphasia**

— Most cases of people equally fluent in more than one language show equivalent aphasic symptoms in both languages, although there are reported cases of only one language being affected.
— When a patient is more fluent in one language, that one tends to be better preserved.
— This is true as well for sign and for English, for those patients fluent in both.
— Sign appears to be organized in the brain as is speech: Left-hemisphere lesions produce sign aphasia; right-hemisphere lesions produce spatial problems relatively independent of language.
— A lesion in Broca's area produces halting sign, deletion of inflection and other grammatical markers, overreliance on content words, and so on.
— Posterior lesions produce fluent aphasias with sign-finding difficulties, poor comprehension, and sometimes confusion of inflectional markers—paragrammatism rather than agrammatism as with frontal lesions.
— Right-hemisphere damage, in causing visual neglect, can affect those aspects of sign that require constructing and maintaining spatial relations, such as setting the stage for pronominal reference, inflecting verbs so they move between subject and object, and creating spatial descriptions. We do not see such a loss in spoken languages, which do not similarly use space.

---

*sign*-finding) difficulties, and were limited in comprehension of complex constructions. For those who wrote English as well as signed, their writing looked like their signing, with similar deficiencies. The Broca's aphasic was nonfluent, unable to produce more than one sign at a time. She also had difficulties with inflections but not uninflected base forms, indicating the same general pattern of breakdown with function elements as is seen in spoken language. Thus grammatical morphemes disappear, not because of their form (e.g., unstressed in spoken but not signed language) but because of their function, as syntax markers rather than meaning carriers.

The posterior aphasic's output resembled that of posterior speaking patients, with fluent but uninterpretable signing. The mixed anterior was relatively fluent, with little aphasic impairment aside from word-finding problems, paraphasias, and failure to make index references clear.

The other cases reported in the literature (see Poizner & Battison, 1980; Schuell, in Sies, 1974, for review) also point to the comparability of aphasic symptoms in sign and speech. Given the basic differences in modality and organization of the two languages, the similarity in breakdown is particularly striking, supporting similar underlying brain organization and processing operations. Because the languages seem so different, it is tempting to conclude that the similar brain organization derives from an innate predisposition for so organizing and processing language.

## Alexia or Acquired Dyslexia

Aphasia is usually, but not always, accompanied by at least as severe reading and writing problems. There may also be reading and writing problems in the absence of aphasia. Researchers distinguish among three principal forms of alexia or acquired dyslexia: surface dyslexia, deep dyslexia, and phonological dyslexia (Coltheart, Curtis, Atkins, & Haller, 1993).

It was the separate syndromes of surface and deep dyslexia that gave rise to the dual-route model of reading (Coltheart, Patterson, & Marshall, 1980; Patterson, Marshall, & Coltheart, 1985; described in Chapter 11 of *Language and Its Normal Processing* and reviewed in Chapter 1 of this volume). Basically, this holds that in reading an English letter sequence, we can relate the visual pattern to the word's meaning and recognize its name afterward, recognize the sound of the word's name from a direct map of the visual pattern to its "address" in the name portion of the mental dictionary, or compute how the word should be pronounced given known letter-to-sound (grapheme-to-phoneme, or GPC) correspondences.

*Surface dyslexia* disturbs the visual routes, the retrieval of an item's lexical address, or its semantic representation from its orthography. This allows patients to access words only by assembling GPCs. This indirect route may also be partially damaged or it may be completely spared (Coltheart et al., 1993).

*Deep dyslexia* seems to disturb the phonological route, the ability to assemble GPCs, with direct access from orthography to semantics intact and phonology activated after the word is recognized from the semantics. The two dyslexias may be interestingly dissociated in Japanese, which has two writing systems, if patients can read both scripts. *Kana* is a phonologically based script, but *Kanji* roughly is not, with graphemes corresponding more to meaning directly (see Chapter 11 of the companion volume). Japanese aphasics may become dyslexic only in Kana (deep dyslexic) or in Kanji (surface dyslexic; Sasanuma, 1980; Tzeng & Wang, 1983).

Like deep dyslexia, *phonological dyslexia* affects the ability to sound out and assemble words (Coltheart, 1996). It produces a lesser impairment than deep dyslexia because it still allows the patient to access whole-word names directly from the writing as well as indirectly from the semantics.

Phonological dyslexics are particularly impaired in reading nonwords, which must be assembled, but can read regular and irregular words through the intact whole-word (addressed phonology) and semantic routes. Surface dyslexics are particularly impaired in reading irregular words, which cannot be assembled. Deep dyslexics are strikingly impaired in reading regular words, which, like irregular words, they cannot address directly but they can also not assemble.

However, all this is a caricature more than a characterization of the dyslexias; each has a set of symptoms, not a single diagnostic feature. In diagnosing acquired dyslexia, researchers typically ask patients to read words in isolation or in a short context. Deep dyslexics' errors are characterized by semantic confusions, as in *act* → *play* or *close* → *shut*. They may make visual errors, reading *gallant* as *gallon,* but are unlikely to make phonological confusions, like reading *phrase* as *freeze* (Coltheart, 1980). Apart from a preponderance of visual and semantic reading errors, the deep dyslexic syndrome (Coltheart, 1980) includes inability to read nonwords and special problems reading function words or derivationally related words, substituting, for example, *wisdom* for *wise*.

Each of these symptoms can be explained if the only access to the word's pronunciation is from semantics. Semantics arouses a number of associates (a *cohort*), which are not filtered appropriately by the letter-to-phoneme information. An associate is therefore as likely to be mistakenly retrieved as the target. The cohort seems to contain any kind of semantic associate: Errors reflect both paradigmatic and syntagmatic intrusions; that is, deep dyslexics might misread *bride* as *girl* or *income* as *tax*. Nonwords cannot be read because they have no lexical representation and therefore cannot be directly addressed. Henderson (1985) points out that deep dyslexics employ semantic access in reading to a degree absent in normal reading, perhaps as compensation for their inability to use GPC rules.

The difficulty with function words is consistent with lexical access from semantics. As we reviewed in aphasia, function words are read largely to establish structure, after which they fade into the background. The deep dyslexic, who may be retrieving phonology postlexically from semantics, would not have a strong semantic representation for function words and so makes more errors on these. Of interest, deep dyslexics make substitutions within the function word class— misreading *where* as *because* or *his* as *theirs*—indicating that they are accessing them as a "semantic" class. And they do have some semantic information relevant to function words, able to decide, for example, person and number information for pronouns (Morton & Patterson, 1980).

The final deep dyslexic symptom is erratic reading of inflections. As we saw in aphasia, some words are stored with their inflections as a whole, and, for some, the inflections are computed separately. The deep dyslexic may be retrieving whichever word form is directly addressable, unable to compute the derivational difference.

Apart from these differences clearly attributable to an absent grapheme-to-phoneme system, deep dyslexics are better able to read nouns than verbs or adjectives and are better with highly imageable, concrete words than low-imageable abstract words (Coltheart, 1980). These properties reflect a richer semantic representation and thus, perhaps, easier direct accessability.

Surface dyslexia is often described as an impairment of direct access, with both regular words and nonwords read via GPCs (but see Marcel, 1980). Errors are less likely to be semantic substitutions but are overregularizations even of common words, so *glove,* for example, may be misread as though it rhymed with *cove,* or *flood* as though it rhymed with *mood.* Unlike deep dyslexics, surface dyslexics can read nonwords—which have no lexical representation—provided they follow the regular rules of GPC. Surface dyslexics have a problem with irregular words, which, it is argued, they cannot pronounce through direct addressing and, instead, incorrectly assemble.

Marcel (1980) argues that direct access to the lexicon must still be involved in surface dyslexics' reading because they are more likely to be correct on words that

---

**Box 5.8. Acquired Dyslexias**

---

*Alexia or acquired dyslexia:* Loss of acquired reading skill secondary to brain damage. Usually accompanies aphasia. Three principal types reflect the dual-route model:

— *Deep dyslexia:* Damages assembly of grapheme-to-phoneme correspondences, leaving patients with access to a word name directly and through semantics. Reading displays many semantic and visual substitutions, with better performance on high-imagery, content nouns than on other types of words. They perform poorly on nonwords.

— *Surface dyslexia:* Impairs access to direct route. There are few semantic errors; regular words and nonwords are read well; irregular words are regularized erroneously. They read better high-imagery, high-frequency content words.

— *Phonological dyslexia:* Like deep dyslexia, it impairs assembly of GPCs but with better preservation of direct addressing, so common words, both regular and irregular, are usually correct. Nonwords and rare words are selectively impaired.

---

are high frequency, concrete, and highly imageable and on nouns than adjectives or verbs (see Patterson, Marshall, & Coltheart, 1985, for supporting data). Surface dyslexic errors resemble those of beginning readers, with less attention to context and sense, and a great reliance on guesses suggested by some, but not necessarily the critical, letters in the word. This, Marcel argues, reflects problems segmenting the letters or even misapplication of GPC rules. Thus we see errors such as reading *niece* as *nice, bike* as /bɪk/, or *reapply* as *reply.* Like beginning readers, surface dyslexics seem to assume that the input is a recognizable word and make a guess that accounts for many of the letters. Because they incorrectly segment the orthographic input, they may ignore a critical regularity, like the final "e" changing the pronunciation of the "i" in *bike.* Indeed, one suggestion is that at least some surface dyslexics see only single letters as graphemes, segmenting, for example, "ph" into p + h with schwa between rather than seeing it as a unit itself (Newcombe & Marshall, 1985). This accounts also for the fact that surface dyslexics, like unskilled readers, take longer to name longer letter strings, either word or nonword, whereas normal readers show only a small effect of letter length (Henderson, 1985).

Low-frequency words produce more errors because they have a weaker representation in the lexicon, with direct and postsemantic addresses less accessible. Surface dyslexics are not necessarily unable to make orthographic-to-semantic connections; the stronger the ties between orthography and semantics or the more possible connections (for highly imageable, concrete words), the more likely the direct connection is preserved.

Marcel argues that surface dyslexics are impaired in segmenting the visual input, and they thus mismatch it with regard to relevant phonological rules *and* semantics. Deep dyslexics are impaired in applying the phonology to the analyzed segments obtained either from the visual input directly or from its semantic associations.

Phonological dyslexia impairs the reading of nonwords and rare words only. It never, or at least rarely, occurs without a phonological, perceptual impairment as well (Coltheart, 1996). Like the deep dyslexic, the phonological dyslexic has an intact direct route, but rather than accessing semantics from orthography and phonology from semantics, the phonological dyslexic can use orthography to narrow the word choice. Unlike a deep dyslexic, a phonological dyslexic may be able to read abstract, infrequent, and derivationally complex words like *satirical* or *preliminary.* And Coltheart et al. (1993) cite compelling evidence that some phonological dyslexics read words well even when their abilities to define them or match their semantic characteristics are impaired. Thus the good reading arises either from direct accessing of the addressed word or from some residual ability from the indirect GPC system.

*Summary*

While there are individuals who display a problem only with print, the majority of cases show both oral- and written-language problems; rarely is there an oral-language problem without a reading/writing one as well. This is unsurprising, given that literacy is dependent on primary language acquisition.

The dyslexic syndromes support much of what we learned about the nature of primary language processing as well as the processing of print from the study of normals. First, for all subjects there appears to be relative preservation of frequent, regular, salient words—where by "salient" I mean highly imageable, concrete, early-learned contentful words. These words may have privileged access because of the strength of their connections to both the basic sensory experience of their underlying concept and to their language representation, the visual and auditory instantiations of their names, and the associated semantic connections. It is the relative strength of the language connections that helps frequent and regular words: These reflect habitually experienced letter-sound patterns, and their strength is augmented with each experience.

Second, the pattern of loss and preservation of different subgroups of dyslexics supports the notions of word retrieval from direct visual access to the semantically based lexicon and to an addressed word name, as well as of an assembly process of GPC "rules."

Finally, examination of the errors made by dyslexics supports the notion that the fluent reader, like the fluent speaker, chunks language segments into productive units of variable size as needed. We see some dyslexic errors reflecting storage of multimorphemic, derivationally complex words, and some indicating that these words are analyzed and accessed by components. Print, like speech and sign, is complex and redundantly determined, and fluent readers make use of many routes to decode it. Any of these routes may be damaged, leaving the reader slower and less accurate than normal but with some routes intact, so not completely illiterate.

## SUMMARY AND CONCLUSIONS

The studies of language processing in brain damage have important implications for the development, organization, and processing of language normally. First, they suggest that there is a special left-hemisphere mechanism for processing *language,* regardless of modality or form. This left-hemisphere capability appears to be specified at birth, and if development is normal, will take over phonetic, semantic, and syntactic processing of language by the age of puberty, while the right hemisphere specializes in paralinguistic processes. If development is abnormal, if there is brain damage early, the right hemisphere appears capable of assuming language processing. The critical period for lateralization of language function appears to be before puberty, and lateralization does not depend on spoken language input.

A second important conclusion that may be drawn from studies of brain damage concerns "modules" of language processing:

1. Because right-hemisphere impairments produce paralinguistic deficits while left-hemisphere impairments produce linguistic deficits, there is evidence supporting the separation of paralinguistic and linguistic processing.

2. The impairment of naming as opposed to comprehending words in Broca's aphasia supports the notion of separating a word-meaning memory from one with word names and pronunciation rules: Either can be selectively impaired.

3. The differential effects of brain damage on content and function words, on syntactic processes generally relative to semantic processes, suggest a psychological reality to separating these language processing components: Some function words (or some inflections in sign) may have a dual role as meaning items and as syntax guides, and the latter function only is destroyed in Broca's aphasia. This accounts for the inability of the patients to organize function words with respect to the sentence, the abnormally good recognition of target letters in function words, and the loss of inflection in the speech or sign of Broca's aphasics. Moreover, the ability of Broca's aphasics to comprehend semantically unambiguous sentences but to fail to comprehend sentences rendered unambiguous only through syntax indicates a selective impairment of syntax and separation of syntactic and semantic processing.

4. Studies of the speech of aphasics indicate an independence of phonological processing difficulties from semantic and syntactic difficulties. For all patients, more frequently used phonemes are less disrupted than less frequently used phonemes; place of articulation differences are harder than differences in other features to perceive or produce; and deleting phonemes is easier than adding them. All patients benefit from redundancy: Synthetic speech is more reliably processed when there are multiple cues to a feature than when there is one; multiple-feature differences are easier to distinguish than single-feature differences; and feature differences are easier to distinguish in real words than in nonsense syllables. This

last result may indicate an increased reliance on top-down processing.

5. Speech results support a separation of production and perception. Wernicke's aphasics show greater impairment in perceiving speech, and Broca's in producing it, particularly in combining low-level motor programs into higher ones and in timing voicing.

6. Print processing is asymmetrically dependent on primary language processing, with aphasias rarely occurring without dyslexia but dyslexia sometimes occurring without observable speech problems. The patterns of preservation and disruption in reading suggest that there are several ways to recognize a printed word: directly getting its whole name, directly recognizing its meaning and indirectly accessing its name from there, and laboriously assembling its name from GPC rules.

A third important conclusion derives from the aphasic symptoms in signers: They look remarkably like speaking aphasics despite the vast differences in the languages, suggesting that the underlying commonality of brain organization is biologically determined, not a result of specific language experience.

Aphasic data do support the importance of experience, however. In many cases, we see the best preservation of skill or the best recovery for the most practiced language arena: The more used language of a multilingual will show less impairment, the more common phonemes will show fewer paraphasias, frequent words will be better recalled and more likely directly recognized from print, and the obligatory inflection will be preserved over the less reliable one.

As a last conclusion, it is worthwhile to raise the philosophically interesting issue, given our criteria, of *when* after brain damage we can say that an individual no longer "has language." Obviously, some global aphasics, who are reduced to uttering a single word, no longer have language; they have lost productivity, recursiveness, metalinguistics, hierarchical organization, and duality of patterning at least, and perhaps also semanticity in the sense that the relation between word and referent is no longer clear.

To some extent, the same argument may be made for less severe types of aphasia. We noted in Wernicke's aphasia, for example, that there may be a limited use of hierarchical organization in syntax; rather large chunks of language seem to be simply chained together. Broca's aphasics, too, lack normal hierarchical language abilities, breaking down in speech production in the organization of speech into large units and faltering in syntactic analysis in the comprehension of hierarchical constituent structure. There are also difficulties in some symbolic aspects of language at least in Wernicke's aphasia. And, finally, learnability is damaged if the aphasia strikes in adulthood because learning alternative systems or relearning the original system is impaired. Thus, we might have to conclude, if we use our criteria consistently, that most adult aphasics no longer "have language."

In this chapter, we examined dissolution of language as a result of observable brain damage. We have seen how language "tests" may be used to diagnose clinical pathology, and, further, how clinical pathology may be used to support theories about normal and aphasic language processing. In the next chapter, we examine language breakdown in the absence of obvious physical damage—in the language of individuals with personality disorders. Again, we will see that language tests may be used for diagnosis, and that diagnostic groups may show different patterns of dissolution, which are informative about normal language processing.

## REFERENCES

Ardila, A., & Rosselli, M. (1994). Averbia as a selective naming disorder: A single case report. *Journal of Psycholinguistic Research, 23,* 139-148.

Armus, S. R., Brookshire, R. H., & Nicholas, L. E. (1989). Aphasic and non-brain-damaged adults' knowledge of scripts for common situations. *Brain and Language, 36,* 518-528.

Badecker, W., & Caramazza, A. (1985). On considerations of method and theory governing the use of clinical categories in neurolinguistics and cognitive neuropsychology: The case against agrammatism. *Cognition, 20,* 97-125.

Bates, E., Friederici, A., & Wulfeck, B. (1987). Grammatical morphology in aphasia: Evidence from three languages. *Cortex, 23,* 545-574.

Bates, E., Wulfeck, B., & MacWhinney, B. (1991). Cross-linguistic research in aphasia: An overview. *Brain and Language, 41,* 123-148.

Baum, S. R. (1989). On-line sensitivity to local and long-distance syntactic dependencies in Broca's aphasia. *Brain and Language, 37,* 327-338.

Behrens, S. J. (1989). Characterizing sentence intonation in a right hemisphere-damaged population. *Brain and Language, 37,* 181-200.

Bihrle, A. M., Brownell, H. H., Powelson, J. A., & Gardner, H. (1986). Comprehension of humorous and nonhumorous materials by left and right brain-damaged patients. *Brain and Cognition, 5,* 399-411.

Blumstein, S. E. (1973a). *A phonological investigation of aphasic speech.* The Hague, the Netherlands: Mouton.

Blumstein, S. E. (1973b). Some phonological implications of aphasic speech. In H. Goodglass & S. Blumstein (Eds.), *Psycholinguistics and aphasia* (pp. 124-137). Baltimore: Johns Hopkins University Press.

Blumstein, S. E. (1982). Language dissolution in aphasia: Evidence from linguistic theory. In L. Obler & L. Menn (Eds.), *Exceptional language and linguistics* (pp. 203-215). New York: Academic Press.

Blumstein, S. E., Baker, E., & Goodglass, H. (1977). Phonological factors in auditory comprehension. *Neuropsychologia, 15,* 19-29.

Blumstein, S. E., Cooper, W. E., Goodglass, H., Statlender, S., & Gottlieb, J. (1980). Production deficits in aphasia: A voice-onset time analysis. *Brain and Language, 9,* 153-170.

Blumstein, S., Cooper, W., Zurif, E., & Caramazza, A. (1977). The perception and production of voice-onset time in aphasia. *Neuropsychologia, 15,* 371-383.

Blumstein, S. E., Goodglass, H., Statlender, S., & Biber, C. (1983). Comprehension strategies determining reference in aphasia: A study of reflexivization. *Brain and Language, 18,* 115-127.

Blumstein, S. E., Katz, B., Goodglass, H., Shrier, R., & Dworetsky, B. (1985). The effects of slowed speech on auditory comprehension in aphasia. *Brain and Language, 24,* 246-285.

Blumstein, S. E., Milberg, W., & Shrier, R. (1982). Semantic processing in aphasia: Evidence from an auditory lexical decision task. *Brain and Language, 17,* 301-315.

Blumstein, S. E., Tartter, V. C., Nigro, G., & Statlender, S. (1984). Acoustic cues for the perception of place of articulation in aphasia. *Brain and Language, 22,* 128-149.

Borod, J. C. (1992). Interhemispheric and intrahemispheric control of emotion: A focus on unilateral brain damage. *Journal of Consulting and Clinical Psychology, 60,* 339-348.

Borod, J. C., Andelman, F., Obler, L. K., Tweedy, J. R., & Welkowitz, J. (1992). Right hemisphere specialization for the identification of emotional words and sentences: Evidence from stroke patients. *Neuropsychologia, 30,* 827-844.

Brown, R. (1973). *A first language.* Cambridge, MA: Harvard University Press.

Brownell, H. H., Bihrle, A. M., & Michelow, D. (1986). Basic and subordinate level naming by agrammatic and fluent aphasic patients. *Brain and Language, 28,* 42-52.

Brownell, H. H., Potter, H. H., Michelow, D., & Gardner, H. (1984). Sensitivity to lexical denotation and connotation in brain-damaged patients: A double dissociation. *Brain and Language, 22,* 253-265.

Bryden, M. P., & Zurif, E. B. (1970). Dichotic listening performance in a case of agenesis of the corpus callosum. *Neuropsychologia, 8,* 371-377.

Cancelliere, A. E. B., & Kertesz, A. (1990). Lesion localization in acquired deficits of emotional expression and comprehension. *Brain and Cognition, 13,* 133-147.

Caramazza, A., & Berndt, R. S. (1978). Semantic and syntactic processes in aphasia: A review of the literature. *Psychological Bulletin, 85,* 898-918.

Caramazza, A., & Hillis, A. E. (1991). Lexical organization of nouns and verbs in the brain. *Nature, 349,* 788-790.

Caramazza, A., & Zurif, E. B. (1976). Dissociation of algorithmic and heuristic processes in language comprehension: Evidence from aphasia. *Brain and Language, 3,* 572-582.

Chapman, S. B., & Ulatowska, H. K. (1989). Discourse in aphasia: Integration deficits in processing reference. *Brain and Language, 36,* 651-668.

Chomsky, N. (1986). *Knowledge of language: Its nature, origin, and use.* New York: Praeger.

Coltheart, M. (1980). Deep dyslexia: A review of the syndrome. In M. Coltheart, K. Patterson, & J. C. Marshall (Eds.), *Deep dyslexia* (pp. 22-47). London: Routledge & Kegan Paul.

Coltheart, M. (1996). Phonological dyslexia: Past and future issues. *Cognitive Neuropsychology, 13,* 749-762.

Coltheart, M., Curtis, B., Atkins, P., & Haller, M. (1993). Models of reading aloud: Dual-route and parallel-distributed processing approaches. *Psychological Review, 100,* 589-608.

Coltheart, M., Patterson, K., & Marshall, J. C. (Eds.). (1980). *Deep dyslexia.* London: Routledge & Kegan Paul.

Critchley, M. (1973). Articulatory defects in aphasia: The problem of Broca's aphemia. In H. Goodglass & S. E. Blumstein (Eds.), *Psycholinguistics and aphasia* (pp. 51-68). Baltimore: Johns Hopkins University Press.

de Villiers, J. G. (1978). Fourteen grammatical morphemes in acquisition and aphasia. In A. Caramazza & E. B. Zurif (Eds.), *Language acquisition and language breakdown* (pp. 121-144). Baltimore: Johns Hopkins University Press.

Druks, J., & Marshall, J. C. (1991). Agrammatism: An analysis and critique, with new evidence from four Hebrew-speaking aphasic patients. *Cognitive Neuropsychology, 8,* 415-433.

Eling, P. (1986). Recognition of derivations in Broca's aphasics. *Brain and Language, 28,* 346-356.

Farah, M. J., & Wallace, M. A. (1992). Semantically-bounded anomia: Implications for the neural implementation of naming. *Neuropsychologia, 30,* 609-621.

Gardner, H. (1975). *The shattered mind.* New York: Knopf.

Garnsey, S. M., Tanenhaus, M. K., & Chapman, R. M. (1989). Evoked potentials and the study of sentence comprehension. *Journal of Psycholinguistic Research, 18,* 51-60.

Gazzaniga, M. S. (1967). The split brain in man. *Scientific American, 217,* 24-29.

Gazzaniga, M. S. (1983). Right hemisphere language following brain bisection. *American Psychologist, 38,* 525-537.

Goodglass, H. (1973). Studies on the grammar of aphasics. In H. Goodglass & S. E. Blumstein (Eds.), *Psycholinguistics and aphasia* (pp. 183-215). Baltimore: Johns Hopkins University Press.

Goodglass, H. (1978). Acquisition and dissolution of language. In A. Caramazza & E. B. Zurif (Eds.), *Language acquisition and language breakdown* (pp. 101-108). Baltimore: Johns Hopkins University Press.

Goodglass, H. (1980). Disorders of naming following brain injury. *American Scientist, 68,* 647-655.

Goodglass, H., & Baker, E. (1976). Semantic field, naming, and auditory comprehension in aphasia. *Brain and Language, 3,* 359-374.

Goodglass, H., Christianson, J. A., & Gallagher, R. E. (1994). Syntactic constructions used by agrammatic speakers: Comparison with conduction aphasics and normals. *Neuropsychology, 8,* 598-613.

Goodglass, H., Klein, B., Carey, P., & Jones, K. J. (1973). Specific semantic word categories in aphasia. In H. Goodglass & S. E. Blumstein (Eds.), *Psycholinguistics and aphasia* (pp. 251-266). Baltimore: Johns Hopkins University Press.

Gordon, J. K., & Baum, S. R. (1994). Rhyme priming in aphasia: The role of phonology in lexical access. *Brain and Language, 47,* 661-683.

Grodzinsky, Y. (1989). Agrammatic comprehension of relative clauses. *Brain and Language, 37,* 480-499.

Grossman, M., & Carey, S. (1987). Selective word-learning deficits in aphasia. *Brain and Language, 32,* 306-324.

Grossman, M., Carey, S., Zurif, E., & Diller, L. (1986). Proper and common nouns: Form class judgments in Broca's aphasia. *Brain and Language, 28,* 114-125.

Haarmann, H. J., & Kolk, H. H. (1994). On-line sensitivity to subject-verb agreement violations in Broca's aphasics: The role of syntactic complexity and time. *Brain and Language, 46,* 493-516.

Henderson, L. (1985). Issues in the modelling of pronunciation assembly in normal reading. In K. E. Patterson, J. C. Marshall, & M. Coltheart (Eds.), *Surface dyslexia: Neuropsychological and cognitive studies of phonological reading* (pp. 459-508). Hillsdale, NJ: Lawrence Erlbaum.

Hillis, A. E., & Caramazza, A. (1991). Category-specific naming and comprehension impairment: A double dissociation. *Brain, 114,* 2081-2094.

Hirst, W., LeDoux, J., & Stein, S. (1984). Constraints on the processing of indirect speech acts: Evidence from aphasiology. *Brain and Language, 23,* 26-33.

Howes, D. (1973). Some experimental investigations of language in aphasia. In H. Goodglass & S. E. Blumstein (Eds.), *Psycholinguistics and aphasia* (pp. 231-249). Baltimore: Johns Hopkins University Press.

Just, M. A., Carpenter, P. A., Keller, T. A., Eddy, W. F., & Thulborn, K. R. (1996). Brain activation modulated by sentence comprehension. *Science, 274,* 114-116.

Kean, M. (1980). Grammatical representations and the description of language processing. In D. Kaplan (Ed.), *Biological studies of mental processing* (pp. 239-268). Cambridge: MIT Press.

Kehoe, W. J., & Whitaker, H. A. (1973). Lexical disruption in aphasia: A case study. In H. Goodglass & S. E. Blumstein (Eds.), *Psycholinguistics and aphasia* (pp. 267-279). Baltimore: Johns Hopkins University Press.

Kinsbourne, M. (1981). Neuropsychological aspects of bilingualism. In H. Winitz (Ed.), *Annals of the New York Academy of Sciences: Vol. 379. Native language and foreign language acquisition* (pp. 50-58). New York: New York Academy of Sciences.

Koemada-Lutz, M., Cohen, R., & Meier, E. (1987). Organization of and access to semantic memory in aphasia. *Brain and Language, 30,* 321-337.

Koriat, A., & Greenberg, S. N. (1991). Syntactic control of letter detection: Evidence from English and Hebrew nonwords. *Journal of Experimental Psychology: Learning, Memory, and Cognition, 17,* 1035-1050.

Krashen, S. D. (1973). Lateralization, language learning, and the critical period: Some new evidence. *Language Learning, 23,* 63-74.

Kudo, T. (1987). Aphasics' appreciation of hierarchical semantic categories. *Brain and Language, 30,* 33-51.

Lapointe, S. G. (1983). Some issues in the linguistic study of agrammatism. *Cognition, 14,* 1-39.

Lenneberg, E. (1967). *Biological foundations of language.* New York: John Wiley.

Levy, J. (1983). Language, cognition, and the right hemisphere: A response to Gazzaniga. *American Psychologist, 38,* 538-541.

Levy, J. R., & Trevarthen, C. (1977). Perceptual, semantic, and phonetic aspects of elementary language processes in split-brain patients. *Brain, 100,* 105-118.

Li, E. C., & Williams, S. E. (1990). The effects of grammatical class and cue type on cueing responsiveness in aphasia. *Brain and Language, 38,* 48-60.

Li, E. C., Williams, S. E., & Della-Volpe, A. (1995). The effects of topic and listener familiarity on discourse variables in procedural and narrative discourse tasks. *Journal of Communication Disorders, 28,* 39-55.

Linebarger, M. C., Schwartz, M. K., & Saffran, E. M. (1983). Sensitivity to grammatical structure in so-called agrammatic aphasics. *Cognition, 13,* 361-392.

Lukatela, K., Shankweiler, D., & Crain, S. (1995). Syntactic processing in agrammatic aphasia by speakers of a Slavic language. *Brain and Language, 49,* 50-76.

Lund, E., Splud, P. E., Anderson, E., & Bojsen-Moller, M. (1986). Vowel perception: A neuroradiological localization of the perception of vowels in the human cortex. *Brain and Language, 29,* 191-211.

Luria, A. R. (1973). *The working brain.* Harmondsworth, Middlesex: Penguin.

MacWhinney, B. (1987). The competition model. In B. MacWhinney (Ed.), *Mechanisms of language acquisition* (pp. 249-308). Hillsdale, NJ: Lawrence Erlbaum.

Marcel, T. (1980). Surface dyslexia and beginning reading: A revised hypothesis of the pronunciation of print and its impairments. In M. Coltheart, K. Patterson, & J. C. Marshall (Eds.), *Deep dyslexia* (pp. 227-258). London: Routledge & Kegan Paul.

McCleary, C. (1988). The semantic organization and classification of fourteen words by aphasic patients. *Brain and Language, 34,* 183-202.

McCleary, C., & Hirst, W. (1986). Semantic classification in aphasia: A study of basic, superordinate, and function relations. *Brain and Language, 27,* 199-209.

Milberg, W., & Blumstein, S. E. (1981). Lexical decisions and aphasia. *Brain and Language, 14,* 371-385.

Milberg, W., Blumstein, S. E., & Dworetzky, B. (1988). Phonological processing and lexical access in aphasia. *Brain and Language, 34,* 279-293.

Miller, G. A., & Selfridge, J. A. (1953). Verbal context and the recall of meaningful material. *American Journal of Psychology, 63,* 176-185.

Milner, B., Taylor, L., & Sperry, R. W. (1968). Lateralized suppression of dichotically presented digits after commisural section in man. *Science, 161,* 184-185.

Morton, J., & Patterson, K. (1980). "Little words—No!" In M. Coltheart, K. Patterson, & J. C. Marshall (Eds.), *Deep dyslexia* (pp. 270-285). London: Routledge & Kegan Paul.

Newcombe, F., & Marshall, J. C. (1985). Reading and writing by letter sounds. In K. E. Patterson, J. C. Marshall, & M. Coltheart (Eds.), *Surface dyslexia: Neuropsychological and cognitive studies of phonological reading* (pp. 53-71). Hillsdale, NJ: Lawrence Erlbaum.

Ojemann, G. A. (1983). Brain organization for language from the perspective of electrical stimulation mapping. *Behavioral and Brain Sciences, 6,* 189-230.

Ojemann, G. A. (1991). Cortical organization of language. *Journal of Neuroscience, 11,* 2281-2287.

Ouellette, G. P., & Baum, S. R. (1994). Acoustic analysis of prosodic cues in left- and right-hemisphere-damaged patients. *Aphasiology, 8,* 257-283.

Patterson, K. E., Marshall, J. C., & Coltheart, M. (Eds.). (1985). *Surface dyslexia: Neuropsychological and cognitive studies of phonological reading.* Hillsdale, NJ: Lawrence Erlbaum.

Poizner, H., & Battison, R. (1980). Neurolinguistic: Cerebral asymmetry for sign language: Clinical and experimental evidence. In H. Lane & F. Grosjean (Eds.), *Recent perspectives on American Sign Language* (pp. 79-101). Hillsdale, NJ: Lawrence Erlbaum.

Poizner, H., Bellugi, U., & Iraqui, V. (1984). Apraxia and aphasia in a visual-gestural language. *American Journal of Physiology: Regulatory, Integrative, and Comparative Physiology, 246,* R866-R883.

Poizner, H., Kaplan, E., Bellugi, U., & Padden, C. A. (1984). Visual-spatial processing in deaf brain-damaged signers. *Brain and Cognition, 3,* 281-306.

Poizner, H., Klima, E. S., & Bellugi, U. (1987). *What the hands reveal about the brain.* Cambridge: MIT Press.

Rehak, A., Kaplan, J. A., & Gardner, H. (1992). Sensitivity to conversational deviance in right-hemisphere damaged patients. *Brain and Language, 42,* 203-217.

Rosenberg, B., Zurif, E., Brownell, H., Garrett, M., & Bradley, D. (1985). Grammatical class effects in relation to normal and aphasic sentence processing. *Brain and Language, 26,* 287-303.

Rosenzweig, M. R. (1951). Representation of the two ears at the auditory cortex. *American Journal of Physiology, 167,* 147-158.

Ross, E. D. (1981). The aprosodias. *Archives of Neurology, 38,* 561-569.

Ross, E. D. (1982). The divided self. *Sciences, 22,* 8-12.

Ross, E. D., & Mesulam, M. M. (1979). Dominant functions of the right hemisphere? *Archives of Neurology, 36,* 144-148.

Ryalls, J. H. (1986). An acoustic study of vowel production in aphasia. *Brain and Language, 29,* 48-67.

Saffran, E. M., Schwartz, M. F., & Marin, O. S. M. (1980). The word order problem in agrammatism: II. Production. *Brain and Language, 10,* 263-280.

Sasanuma, S. (1980). Acquired dyslexia in Japanese: Clinical features and underlying mechanisms. In M. Coltheart, K. Patterson, & J. C. Marshall (Eds.), *Deep dyslexia* (pp. 48-90). London: Routledge & Kegan Paul.

Schlenck, K.-J., Huber, W., & Willmes, K. (1987). "Prepairs" and repairs: Different monitoring functions in aphasic language production. *Brain and Language, 30,* 226-244.

Schwartz, M. F., Saffran, E. M., & Marin, O. S. M. (1980). The word order problem in agrammatism: I. Comprehension. *Brain and Language, 10,* 249-262.

Searleman, A. (1977). A review of right hemisphere linguistic capabilities. *Psychological Bulletin, 84,* 503-528.

Semenza, C., Butterworth, B., Panzeri, M., & Ferreri, T. (1990). Word formation: New evidence from aphasia. *Neuropsychologia, 28,* 499-502.

Shankweiler, D., Crain, S., Gorrell, P., & Tuller, B. (1989). Reception of language in Broca's aphasia. *Language and Cognitive Processes, 4,* 1-33.

Shapiro, L. P., & Levine, B. A. (1990). Verb processing during sentence comprehension in aphasia. *Brain and Language, 38,* 21-47.

Sherman, J. C., & Schweickert, J. (1989). Syntactic and semantic contributions to sentence comprehension in agrammatism. *Brain and Language, 37,* 419-439.

Sies, L. F. (Ed.). (1974). *Aphasia theory and therapy: Selected lectures and papers of Hildred Schuell.* Baltimore: University Park Press.

Snow, C. (1987). Relevance of the notion of critical period to language acquisition. In M. H. Bornstein (Ed.), *Sensitive periods in development: Interdisciplinary perspectives* (pp. 183-209). Hillsdale, NJ: Lawrence Erlbaum.

Sparks, R., & Geschwind, N. (1968). Dichotic listening in man after section of neocortical commisures. *Cortex, 4,* 3-16.

Sperry, R. (1982). Some effects of disconnecting the cerebral hemispheres. *Science, 217,* 1223-1226.

Spreen, O. (1973). Psycholinguistics and aphasia: The contributions of Arnold Pick. In H. Goodglass & S. Blumstein (Eds.), *Psycholinguistics and aphasia* (pp. 141-170). Baltimore: Johns Hopkins University Press.

Springer, S. P., & Deutsch, G. (1989). *Left brain, right brain* (3rd ed.). New York: Freeman.

Tallal, P., & Newcombe, F. (1978). Impairment of auditory perception and language comprehension in dysphasia. *Brain and Language, 5,* 13-24.

Tuller, B. (1984). On categorizing aphasic speech errors. *Neuropsychologia, 22,* 547-557.

Tzeng, O. J. L., & Wang, W. S.-Y. (1983). The first two R's. *American Scientist, 71,* 238-243 [The following letters to the editor and replies are on correspondence pages: D. Besner, pp. 452-456, and N. A. Hall, pp. 566-570].

Ulatowska, H. K., Allard, L., Reyes, B. A., Ford, J., & Chapman, S. (1992). Conversational discourse in aphasia. *Aphasiology, 6,* 325-331.

Vaid, J., & Lambert, W. E. (1979). Differential cerebral involvement in the cognitive functioning of bilinguals. *Brain and Language, 8,* 92-110.

Van Lancker, D. R., Kreiman, J., & Cummings, J. (1989). Voice perception deficits: Neuroanatomical correlates of phonagnosia. *Journal of Clinical and Experimental Neuropsychology, 11,* 665-674.

Warrington, E. K., & McCarthy, R. (1983). Category specific access dysphasia. *Brain, 106,* 859-878.

Winner, E., & Gardner, H. (1977). The comprehension of metaphor in brain-damaged patients. *Brain, 100,* 717-729.

Witelson, S. F., & Pallie, W. (1973). Left hemisphere specialization for language in the newborn: Neuroanatomical evidence of asymmetry. *Brain, 96,* 641-646.

Zaidel, E. (1978, September-October). The elusive right hemisphere of the brain. *Engineering and Science,* pp. 10-32.

Zaidel, E. (1983). A response to Gazzaniga: Language in the right hemisphere, convergent perspectives. *American Psychologist, 38,* 542-546.

Zuger, A. (1997, August 19). Removing half of brain improves young epileptics' lives. *New York Times,* p. C4.

Zurif, E. B., & Blumstein, S. E. (1978). Language in the brain. In M. Halle, J. Bresnan, & G. A. Miller (Eds.), *Linguistic theory and psychological reality* (pp. 229-245). Cambridge: MIT Press.

Zurif, E. B., Caramazza, A., & Myerson, R. (1972). Grammatical judgments for agrammatic aphasics. *Neuropsychologia, 10,* 405-417.

Zurif, E. B., Caramazza, A., Myerson, R., & Galvin, J. (1974). Semantic feature representations for normal and aphasic language. *Brain and Language, 1,* 167-187.

Zurif, E., Swinney, D., Prather, P., & Love, T. (1994). Functional localization in the brain with respect to syntactic processing [Special issue: Sentence Processing: III]. *Journal of Psycholinguistic Research, 23,* 487-497.

---

## STUDY QUESTIONS

---

1. Discuss the differences between Broca's and Wernicke's aphasias with respect to syntactic, semantic, and speech processing. Which aspects of language seem to be affected by anterior lesions and which aspects by posterior? Given these data, is it reasonable to say that the normal brain's parser, for example, is in Broca's area? Why or why not?

2. To what extent is it reasonable to argue that the left hemisphere has a tunable blueprint for language? In discussing this question, consider evidence from childhood brain-damaged and deaf aphasics as well as evidence from earlier chapters. Make clear why each piece of evidence is relevant to the question.

3. Given the pattern of breakdown in Broca's and Wernicke's aphasias, discuss how language processes are normally performed. Consider which aspects of language processing seem relatively independent of one another (because of independent effects in brain damage) and which of our earlier proposals about syntactic, semantic, speech, and print processing seem to be psychologically real from the studies in brain damage.

4. In Chapter 1, we briefly reviewed PDP models, and in this chapter, the neural equivalent—distributed models of brain organization—and its antithesis, the localization hypothesis. Consider which is better supported by the data in this chapter. List instances where researchers first believed there might be a loss of skill but where later it was shown that the skill was intact, and the difficulty was in reaching

an activation threshold, maintaining the activation, or failing to inhibit associated, but incorrect, activations. How would this be accounted for by a localization model? A distributed model? The PDP model in particular? Consider also whether it is possible to order semantic and syntactic tasks from easy to hard, given data on normal language processing and on language acquisition. Is this order followed in all types of aphasia as well? Why is this relevant to the distributed versus localization question?

5. This chapter presents evidence of independence of production and perception/comprehension processes in language. Summarize that evidence. Discuss other such evidence in the animal studies, in acquisition of language, and from normal language processing.

6. Compare the acquired dyslexias (discussed in this chapter) with developmental dyslexias (discussed in Chapter 3). Do they seem to reflect damage of similar processes? What do the dyslexias tell us about normal reading and its relation to primary language?

# Language in Personality Disorders

Much discussion of normal language has focused on the relation between language and thought. Consider how language would be affected by the thought changes of deep depression, a "personality split," or schizophrenia? Do such psychological states affect our cognition generally, our communication abilities specifically, or our physical state (e.g., our hormones) with broad effects including language? If personality changes affect communication, do they affect pragmatics, altering perceived social and communication needs, or our language competence as happens in aphasia? Are individual differences in topic, vocabulary, or grammar merely individual differences in "style," or can they derive from distinct language processes, as we suggested might be the case in acquisition between "analytic/referential" and "social/expressive" children?

For the final introductory question, I must point out that schizophrenics and Wernicke's aphasics have occasionally been mistaken for each other (with unfortunate therapeutic consequences, as you might imagine), as the title "Schizophrenic and Aphasic Language: Discriminable or Not?" (Rausch, Prescott, & DeWolfe, 1980) suggests. Are their language and language processing that alike? If we could specify differences, they could be used diagnostically to prevent such mistakes in the future.

In this chapter, we investigate individual differences in language as a result of personality disorders. As in Chapter 5, we approach this from two standpoints: (a) how language reflects, or may be used to diagnose, personality characteristics and (b) how language changes indicate organization and processing of language normally. The former is analogous to using language impairments to diagnose regions of brain involvement; the latter, to using language breakdown to ascertain relative independence of the parts of the language "machine." We will discuss the first briefly and then concentrate on the second.

## PERSONALITY DISORDERS

Brain damage is a well-defined physical abnormality. There are many objective ways to measure the existence, location, and extent of the damage, which may then be associated with clinical impressions of behavior and with tests of language abilities, as we saw. In contrast, personality disorders are not clearly defined physically, and therefore there is no conclusive way to assign patients to diagnostic categories independent of their behavior. Categorization is accomplished through a combination of clinical judgment and behavior tests, both of which are less reliable than the physical tests diagnosing many other diseases. Physical correlates of personality disorders such as brain abnormality or imbalance of hormones or *neurotransmitters* (the chemicals brain cells use to communicate with one another) have been found (see Seidman, 1983, for review of such findings in schizophrenia), but these are not consistent in all patients with the same diagnosis. Because the assignment of individuals to clinical categories is more variable in personality disorders than in brain damage, we may expect to find less consistent patterns of language breakdown here than in aphasia.

The search for reliable behavior patterns in personality disorder is confounded further by the fact that there is no generally accepted classification system. In this chapter, we will be looking primarily at schizophrenia, a form of psychosis. *Psychoses* are characterized by a loss of touch with reality. A psychotic may experience hallucinations (in any modality, that is, may see things, hear voices, feel things crawling on the skin). A psychotic may also experience delusions, a thought system removed from reality. For example, one might believe himself to be Jesus Christ or believe that there are enemy agents plotting against him. The first is a *delusion of grandeur;* the second, *paranoia.* A psychotic may also display emotions independent of obvious external cause, such as wild fits of laughter.

The other major division of personality disorder is *neurosis,* believed to be caused by anxiety or the defenses against it. Neurotics are not out of touch with reality to the same degree as psychotics, although there may be a similarity of symptoms. A neurotic might have an unrealistic fear of heights, for example, while a psychotic fears a delusional enemy. The neurotic is aware usually that the fear is unfounded in reality but is still unable to control it. The psychotic is unaware that there is a discrepancy between the experience and reality.

Schizophrenia is one form of psychosis, and there appear to be many forms of schizophrenia. Bleuler (1911/1950) identified four based on behavior patterns. There is *simple schizophrenia,* characterized by withdrawal from society and no particularly dramatic symptoms. A second form is paranoid schizophrenia; as already discussed, its principal distinctive symptom is a delusion of persecution. A third form is *catatonia,* in which patients assume a rigid position—possibly resisting being moved—for extended periods. The last form is *hebephrenia* and corresponds most closely to the stereotypical portrayal of insanity: a loss of interest in personal appearance and cleanliness; wild, inappropriate mood swings; fits of talking or laughter; and so on. These descriptions show clearly that the term *schizophrenia* applies to a wide range of psychotic behavior.

The forms of schizophrenia described by Bleuler are not consistently accepted today. Andreasen, Hoffman, and Grove (1985) classified patients roughly according to Bleuler's categories and then examined them along with nonschizophrenic psychotics with respect to some carefully designed language, communication, and thought disorder measures. In some of these, schizophrenics resemble other psychotics, and in some, they differ, or differ from one another. Andreasen et al. classified psychotics further into those with negative and those with positive formal thought disorder. *Negative formal thought disorder* is reflected in little and slowed speech with vague content, a language pattern sometimes called *alogia*. *Positive formal thought disorder* is characterized by rapid pressured speech, with tangential, illogical, and incoherent comments.

Other investigators have separated schizophrenics into those who are "speech-disordered" and those who are not (see, for example, Chaika, 1990, or Landre, Taylor, & Kearns, 1992). Some diagnosticians classify schizophrenics with regard to the origin of their symptoms rather than their nature. Schizophrenics whose histories indicate a sudden onset of disease, perhaps from a traumatic incident, are *reactive* schizophrenics, and seem to have a better prognosis than *process* or *chronic* schizophrenics, who show a slow deterioration over a long period.

In studying schizophrenic language, researchers sometimes treat patients as a homogeneous group, sometimes consider patients with respect to any of the classification systems described, and sometimes select only a few individuals for intensive study without considering whether they are representative of any particular population. This inconsistency in patient selection limits the likelihood of finding definitive, consistent language patterns across studies of schizophrenic language. An analogous situation would be if language in brain damage were studied without regard to location or extent of the lesion, attempting to draw reliable conclusions by sometimes looking at the relatively unimpaired right brain-damaged patients and at other times looking at global aphasics as examples of the same disease! Thus, from the outset, we may expect to draw less compelling conclusions about both schizophrenic language and normal language processes as reflected in personality breakdown than we did from study of aphasia.

## PSYCHOLINGUISTICS IN CLINICAL PSYCHOLOGY

Much of psychiatry in this century has used language as a diagnostic tool and an integral part of therapy. For example, psychoanalysis effects a personality change through increasing one's self-awareness by the verbalizing of unconscious preverbal experiences (Forrester, 1980). Language, as an easily observable indicator of thought, has also been used in psychiatry to uncover underlying, perhaps disturbed, emotional and conceptual structure. Before proceeding with our main topic—language disturbance in schizophrenia—I will describe some clinical procedures and theories directly relevant to psycholinguistics.

## Freud's Analysis of Speech Errors

In psycholinguistics, slip- and tip-of-the-tongue phenomena usually are examined from a structural standpoint: The item actually uttered or the parts of it recalled are analyzed with respect to structural similarity to the target (see Chapters 3 and 7 of *Language and Its Normal Processing;* see also Chapter 5 in this volume on literal and verbal paraphasias). Freud (1901/1960, 1917/1961) analyzed these speech lapses from a different stance, as indicators of the presence of some unconscious wish.

### Slips of the Tongue

Freud argued that a slip of the tongue (*parapraxis,* using his term) reflects the existence and incomplete suppression of a message in competition with the target message. The slips in which he took the greatest interest (and that he claimed erroneously to be the most common) were slips in which the target word was replaced by its opposite—as in "Gentlemen, I take note that a full quorum of members is present and herewith declare the session *closed*" (Freud, 1917/1961, p. 33). The argument is that the wrong word appeared because the speaker wished to end the meeting but had to begin it. This created competing messages, one of which he attempted to suppress—unsuccessfully.

Freud's analysis comfortably fits within the framework for slips of the tongue developed on the basis of structural and psycholinguistic analyses, as reviewed in Chapter 1. Suppose that at any given time several thoughts are activated. Only one can be vocalized, the one most activated. The amount of activation of words will be great for those relating to a thought highly salient to the individual—the point Freud emphasized. A word's name is also activated by its relation to the context; the ideas being described stimulate meaning features and sounds associated with them; associations among commonly co-occurring sounds cause them to be activated. So, both sound associations (first letters and rhymes) and meaning associations (opposites) effectively prime a word, and conversely, a word activates sound and meaning associates. When we ultimately utter a sound, we have suppressed numerous less activated, but still competing, units. Sometimes the winning one is not the one we intended, a slip of the tongue.

All slips of the tongue thus reflect the incomplete suppression of another thought, sometimes one salient to the individual, often one associated in sound and meaning with the target. Suppression of competing words is most difficult when the person has a strong urge to speak the message, when attention lags through fatigue, for example, or when there is extra activation spread by structural or semantic associations. For the purposes of personality analysis, what is of interest is the competing message. (As an experimental psycholinguist, I support the

Freudian concept that a slip reflects a competing activation, but I do not believe that all competing activations are necessarily *interesting*. Some, in fact, may only reflect the competing activation of a common phoneme sequence that shares all but one phonetic feature with the target word.)

## Tip-of-the-Tongue (TOT) States

The TOT phenomenon is studied in normal language processing (see Chapter 3 of the companion volume) to determine how a name may fail to be activated when its semantic representation is activated as well as the kind of information still available when the name seems to have disappeared. Psychoanalytic interest in TOT phenomena focuses on *why* a particular word is forgotten, again pointing to unconscious feelings as the reason. Freud (1901/1960) distinguished between two types of TOT states: those in which the forgotten name touched directly on something unpleasant, and those in which the forgotten name was associated with another word, which in turn touched on something unpleasant. In either case, the task for the analyst is to discover the unpleasant association and bring it to the patient's awareness. In indicating potential trouble spots for the individual, TOTs take on clinical significance.

## Word Associations

Word associations constitute an important source of data on the organization of the semantic network in normal and brain-damaged individuals and in language acquisition. Among the first experimental studies of, and norms for, word association were those designed for clinical purposes (see Spitzer, 1992, for review; Jung, 1905/1973).

Jung measured the reaction time to make an association as well as which words were given as associations. Associations were elicited under normal conditions and also under conditions of "stress," where there was acoustic distraction (noise) or where the individual was fatigued. In addition to producing associations, subjects were asked to recall previously produced associations.

We have already noted Jung's primary results: Under normal conditions, adults usually make paradigmatic associations; that is, the words they produce match in grammatical class the stimulus word and usually differ from it semantically in only one feature (e.g., *mother → father, plant → animal*). Jung also noted that frequent responses included syntagmatic associations (which are common in children; see Chapter 9 of the companion volume), words that frequently follow the stimulus word in ordinary speech, such as *Christmas → tree*. He also noted intrusions in associations, where the word produced might be a carryover (a perseveration) from an earlier word in the list. Finally, under conditions of stress, when subjects are not fully attentive to the task, a tendency emerged to produce associations of sound only—called *clang* associations—either repeating the stimulus word or producing a rhyme. This Jung considered the lowest form of association, a carryover from childhood. (Spitzer, 1992, reports studies that show that clang associations are also more common under the influence of alcohol, as is the appreciation of jokes based on sound similarities.)

For clinical purposes, Jung's principal interests were in abnormal responses, either associations that took an unusually long time to produce or associations that were idiosyncratic, pointing to a salient event in the individual's experience. For example, one of his subjects made the unusual association *ring-garden*, which he explained with the story that he had found a ring in the garden of the place where he worked and the owner had still not claimed it. Another subject, who was in love with a woman from a different religion, produced a cluster of unusual associations to words dealing with love, such as *wedding* → *misfortune* and *to love* → *is useless* and *to kiss* → *never.*

When the stimulus word or its associations were emotionally troublesome, reaction times to produce the associations were longer than if the words were neutral. Thus a particularly long reaction time could be indicative of a clinically interesting area, even if the association ultimately produced was normal. Jung, for example, tested a crime suspect with stimulus words marginally related to the crime. The subject's associations to these words were abnormally slow, and when this was pointed out to him, together with the suspected reason, he confessed.

As one might expect from Freud's analysis of TOT phenomena, associations connected to emotionally troublesome areas are more poorly recalled than neutral ones, another emotional indicator in word association. And emotionally troublesome words tend to produce more sound (clang) associations than neutral words, indicative of their stressfulness. Finally, stress, such as fatigue or distracting noise, tends to accentuate the associative differences between neutral and emotionally charged words.

We can argue that the subject is inhibiting the meaning and meaning associations of the trouble spot, slowing reaction time, and resulting in greatest activation of a distant associate. The distant associate is associated enough to receive some activation, but distant enough not to be inhibited, perhaps only associated through the sound links of the name. As with slips and tips of the tongue, word-association analyses can reflect underlying personal factors of clinical interest, consistent with standard psycholinguistic models of semantic memory.

## The Semantic Differential

In the semantic differential (see Chapter 3 of *Language and Its Normal Processing* for a more complete description), an individual is presented with a word like *mother* and asked to rate it on polar adjective scales like *warm-cold, hard-soft,* and so forth. Responses to a number of target words are then analyzed to determine clusters, which almost universally fall along dimensions describable as evaluative (good versus bad), potency (strong versus weak), and activity (active versus passive). Based on these data, Osgood, Suci, and Tannenbaum (1957/1978) described semantic memory as organized in relation to these dimensions (I argue that only the connotative part is so organized), and that individuals' conceptual organizations could be measured by seeing where particular concepts were located relative to the norm.

It should be obvious that this could be used as a clinical measure. In fact, it has been used twice to describe the conceptual spaces of each personality of a split personality: once, the famous case known as "the three faces of Eve" (Osgood et al., 1957/1978), and later, another triple split personality, Evelyn (Osgood, Luria, Jeans, & Smith, 1976). (Split personality is a different clinical disorder from schizophrenia. They are often confused by the layperson because *schiz* is a prefix meaning "split," but in schizophrenia, it refers to a split from reality.) In both cases, the patient was asked in each of her three personalities to rate a number of concepts, such as love, child, my mother or my father, on a number of scales such as valuable-worthless, clean-dirty, or tasty-distasteful. In both cases, the psychiatrist administered the test and the results were analyzed by people with no familiarity with the patient or her history (a blind analysis). In addition to describing the organization of the conceptual space for each personality, Osgood et al. made clinical inferences such as which personality was more "real," under what conditions the split had occurred, how the patient was progressing in therapy, and so on. These were then compared with independent evaluations from the psychiatrists, which were surprisingly similar.

The results for each of the (two) individuals showed access of conceptual space differently for her three personalities. This was so distinct that Osgood et al. (1976) commented, "It is easy . . . to forget that we are dealing with a single human being with a single brain" (p. 286).

An alternative interpretation of the data is that each individual maintained three separate conceptual networks, one for each of her personalities. This seems unlikely, given that after therapy the personalities were integrated, and we would not want to assume that this resulted from a massive brain reorganization or loss of several conceptual networks. Moreover, it is clearly possible for different "personalities" to access a single semantic network but elect to access it differently. Each of us could, for example, follow instructions to rate words as we would if we were a "goody two-shoes" or a "playboy."

Osgood et al. note that when individuals assume a "role" (are not "real"), their use of semantic space as indicated by the differential is very rigid, showing little of the variability normally shown and sticking closely to the major dimensions. For some of the personalities assumed in the splits, the researchers observed this type of rigidity, indicative of role-playing rather than a different conceptual structure. Indeed, recognition of the pretense from the rigid use of semantic space formed the basis of the diagnosis of which of the personalities was "real."

How the patients responded in each of their personalities is also of interest. I will not present this in detail here. However, as an indication, consider two of Eve's faces: Eve White and Eve Black. Eve White was described by the clinician as retiring, demure, feminine, and industrious, a competent wife, mother, and housekeeper with some anxieties about her performance in these roles. It was Eve White who sought therapy. In one session, she complained of a headache and, reaching her hands to her head, became Eve Black, a "party girl," shrewd, vain, deceptive, and sexy. (Neither Eve White nor Eve Black remained after therapy.) On the differential, Eve White rated doctor, child, mother, father, love, job, and peace as very positive; with sex, me, spouse, and sickness as negative; and fraud and hatred as maximally negative. From this Osgood et al. concluded that Eve White looked "normal" except for low self-esteem and a wide discrepancy in her view of love and sex. Eve Black rated doctor, me, peace, father, hatred, and fraud very positively on the evaluation scales; mother and control negatively; and child, sex, love, job, spouse, confusion, and sickness as most negative. Osgood et al. called particular attention to the reversal in view of the mother in the two personalities, and Eve Black's obviously abnormal evaluation of fraud and hatred as positive and love as negative.

## Summary

Standard psycholinguistic techniques may be used to assess individual differences for clinical diagnosis and indicate that personality differences do not alter basic language processing: All individuals make slips and tips of the tongue, form similar kinds of word association, and organize their concept evaluations with respect to evaluativeness, activity, and potency. Moreover, all individuals seem to show similar effects of emotional stress: increasing reaction time, inhibiting highly weighted associations, and producing rigid, artificial, bizarre responses. In fact, it is the commonality of processing that permits clinical diagnosis through psycholinguistics; one can be assured, for example, in word association that no matter how idiosyncratic the response is, there is a memory linking the stimulus word and the response, and therefore that deviant responses are worth following up on. Conversely, clinical use of psycholinguistic techniques has added to our understanding of normal language processing by demonstrating reliable effects of stress on language. Thus, for example, we might be tempted to explore the mental processes contributing to the long reaction times for emotionally stressful word associations. Are the normal associations actually harder to access as a result of stress, causing a less salient and thus slower association to be aroused? Or is the slower response time a result of several processes, such as retrieval and rejection of the normal association, followed by retrieval of another?

## Vocal Indicators

Physical and physiological factors influence tone of voice. Some of these factors will also influence or be influenced by personality or mood. A person's size (and sex) affects formant frequencies and pitch. Emotions that affect breathing and fluids in the tissues affect the voice. Characteristic behaviors like smoking affect vocal tissue and the voice. Facial expressions that change with mood, like smiling, alter the vocal tract, affecting the voice in predictable and audible ways (see Chapter 7 of the companion volume). Vocal characteristics can therefore be used as indicators of behavioral traits, both short term (mood) and long term (size or habits).

Scherer (1979) reviewed findings from studies relating vocal characteristics to clinical personality diagnostic categories. He noted that categorization on the basis of tone of voice alone does not reliably predict diagnosis from other means, and that across studies of vocal indicators of psychopathology there are frequently conflicting results. However, reasonably consistently, studies have shown that, compared with normals, chronic depressives have abnormally low pitch with staccato, stepwise intonation contours rather than smooth ones, as well as reduced range in loudness contour, lack of emphatic stress, and slower, more halting speech. Schizophrenics are reported to have unusual vocal qualities, but, depending on the individual, these may manifest as either increased or decreased pitch range. For other vocal dimensions, similar variation has been reported, suggesting no specific vocal pattern for schizophrenia.

The results in general suggest that although the voice may be affected both by personality and by mood, individual variation is sufficiently great that vocal cues may not be used as reliable indicators of psychological state.

## Behavioral Techniques and Childhood Schizophrenia or Autism

Psychosis may begin at a very young age: Before 3 years of age, it is called *infantile autism,* and between 3 and 5 years of age, *childhood schizophrenia* (Bloom & Lehey, 1978), although sometimes the terms are used interchangeably (Wolff & Chess, 1965). The word *autism* has as a root *aut* or "self," and these children are characterized by a variety of self-stimulating behaviors (like thumb-sucking, hair-twirling, rocking, and even destructive ones, like hitting themselves or banging their heads against the wall). At the same time, the children do not exhibit normal "other-directed" behaviors, instead using people or their body parts as though they were inanimate objects and failing to make eye contact, smile, or acquire speech or language.

The language that they do acquire is noncommunicative: They confuse terms, reverse pronouns, and often stereotypically and rigidly repeat utterances that have just been said to them, which is *echolalia* (Bloom & Lehey, 1978; Shapiro, Roberts, & Fish, 1970; Wolff & Chase, 1965). Echolalia may be a form of self-stimulation, where the stimulation is in vocal "play," like the early babbling of normal infants. Unlike normal children, schizophrenic children do not expand or incorporate the imitated utterance or portions thereof into a new framework; it is identical to the original (Shapiro et al., 1970).

Schizophrenic and autistic children are a serious challenge because one has to explicitly train an interest in others, in getting social approval, before attempting to teach language and cognitive and motor skills (like toilet training). One method that has been successful with some schizophrenic and autistic children is behavior modification (Hewett, 1965; Lovaas, Berberich, Perloff, & Schaeffer, 1966), like that used in teaching the chimpanzees language (see Chapter 2). As a first step,

---

### Box 6.1. Psycholinguistics and Personality Disorders

— Slips of the tongue arise from arousal of a competing message that the speaker fails to suppress completely.

— Tips of the tongue arise from failure to arouse the word, either because it is inhibited because it is related to emotionally sensitive material, or because it is blocked, like a slip of the tongue, by a competing message.

— Both errors can indicate an area of emotional disturbance. Clinical explanations of both errors are consistent with PDP or competition-type models in which retrieval results from a combination of activations and inhibitions among associated sounds and concepts.

— Word associations that either take longer or are unusual can indicate an area of emotional disturbance and inhibition of the normal response. Clang (sound) associations are more common under conditions of stress than in normal conditions.

— The semantic differential has been used to analyze the personalities of two "split personalities." It shows different use of semantic memory, connotation, and association under the different guises. "Role-played" responses are more rigid than normal.

— Tone of voice indicates both temporary and stable personality characteristics, although less reliably for personality diagnostics than many other measures.

— Depressives have lower pitch, a staccato vocal quality, and flat intonation contours. These qualities also materialize in a temporary sad mood.

— Autistic and schizophrenic children fail to develop language probably because they are nonsocial and so feel no inherent need to communicate. Language can be developed through behavior modification techniques, which stress socialization, like cessation of self-stimulation and maintenance of eye contact. The language developed is still rigid and does not transfer to spontaneous communication; it is bound by the pragmatics of the learning situation (perhaps also a problem with training the apes using similar techniques).

---

self-destructive and self-stimulating behaviors (including echolalia) are eliminated (through punishment), and social behaviors like making eye contact are developed, by shaping them using food or another desirable primary reinforcement. (Of course, these steps are unnecessary with apes or normal children, for whom it seems that social reinforcement is part of the innate repertoire.) Then, vocalization is reinforced and painstakingly formed into speech using shaping, imitation, molding, reinforcement, and fading in the same manner that we saw for signs and tokens in the apes. Vocabulary and some sentence frames ("I want _") have been successfully taught but do not successfully "transfer" to spontaneous vocalization and communication (Colby, 1968), as we saw also with the animals.

Bonvillian and Blackburn (1991) have applied such techniques to sign language as well as speech. They too note that the techniques are effective *in the testing situation.* However, reaching the criterion in the training situation does not translate to spontaneous communication; researchers must concentrate also on training pragmatics, and recognize that there is a specific pragmatic set in the teaching situation. Bonvillian and Blackburn found better transfer for sign than speech, perhaps because speech is less visible and less moldable. Regardless, the disorder and the difficulty in training language for those who have it underscore the importance of language emerging from communicative/social needs with normal language relating to specific contexts. It also suggests that behavioral techniques can be effective in language teaching, but that this is not the normal route.

## Summary

The aspects of language that have been employed for clinical diagnosis index either conceptual processing or physical changes that are reflected in the voice; syntactic measures are notably absent. The language measures indicate common processing mechanisms between normal individuals and those suffering personality disorders. Chronic depressives show slower, more low-pitched speech than normal, but normal individuals experiencing a temporary sadness reflect the same direction of vocal change. Study of slips of the tongue, word forgetting, word association, and use of the semantic differential show similar conceptual processes in normal and disturbed individuals. For the most part, the ability to access the conceptual network is not impaired.

The only highly deviant effect of personality disorder on language is in childhood psychosis, where a child who is not naturally responsive to social stimulation fails to develop language. This underscores the importance of looking at language acquisition as a part of social communication in particular pragmatic contexts. As we will see with schizophrenic language, inability or lack of motivation to monitor the other's needs when framing a communication produces deviant language.

The studies of language processing in adults with either temporary mood shift or a more stable mood shift in personality "disorder" converge to show the effect of mood on language processing: Words associated with unpleasant experiences are more likely to be forgotten, are harder to make associations with, and may cause disruption of other messages; stereotyped personalities, assumed for role-playing or from trauma in personality splits, show less than normal flexibility and variability in concept access. These common patterns can be used by clinicians to diagnose conceptual trouble spots.

In the next section, we will look at language processing in one particular personality disorder, schizophrenia. From time to time, particular attention has been paid to the language of schizophrenics; indeed, language has been among the most studied psychological processes in schizophrenia (Rubin, Doneson, & Jentons, 1979). We will examine schizophrenics' language and their performance in language tasks to see if their language processing is disturbed, and what their language processing strategies can tell us about normal language processes.

## LANGUAGE BREAKDOWN IN SCHIZOPHRENIA

Given that language is intimately associated with thought, it is not surprising that a breakdown in thought in psychosis is associated with language deviancies. Schizophrenic language has been studied in some detail to assess the nature of the thought disturbance. In this section, we look at the structure and processing of language in schizophrenia to make inferences about normal processing, to determine the nature of the language dissolution, and to compare the dissolution with that in aphasia.

### Do Schizophrenics Have a Language Disturbance?

Before discussing schizophrenic language processing, I should note that there is some controversy over whether there is a linguistic deficit in schizophrenia (see Anand & Wales, 1994, for a recent review). On the one hand, the speech of some schizophrenics is described as *word salad,* "a senseless ungrammatical succession of words" (Brown, 1958, p. 293)—as in "the house burnt the cow horrendously always" (cited by Chaika, 1974, p. 266). In such cases, it would seem that language processing must be severely disturbed.

On the other hand, it has been frequently claimed, beginning with Bleuler (1911/1950), that the disturbance is not in language processing but in language content. Indeed, Brown (1973) concluded that reports of word salad were much exaggerated and that schizophrenic language was normal, except when discussing the delusional area. For example, one patient with whom Brown conversed appeared normal, until claiming that when he left the hospital he would be starring in the movie version of *Fiddler on the Roof,* to be filmed in Scotland. The language used to make this claim was all fine; in fact, Brown commented that if the patient had begun the claim with "I dreamt that . . . ," there would be no deviance at all. The difficulty was in real world knowledge: he was too young for that part, the film was not being made, and if the film were being made, Scotland would have been an unlikely location. Thus the content of the speech was disturbed, but there was no apparent disturbance of language specifically.

Brown suggested that schizophrenics have intact language and intact comprehension but for one delusional area. Others have suggested that schizophrenics have normal language processes but autistic or egocentric communication skills, a failure to recognize the need for making things clear to others. One patient (Whitehorn & Zipf, 1943), for example, referred continually and cryptically to *airplane messages* that she was receiving, causing the nurses to monitor her when airplanes passed overhead. Eventually her meaning was deciphered; she did not mean *airplane* but *air plain* (plain as air), and she failed to recognize (perhaps deliberately) that this was a private and ambiguous usage. Note that the derivational process she used was grammatical within English; we have compounds like *lily white* or *ice cold* that derive from the same structure as *air plain.*

With regard to communicability of schizophrenic messages, Whitehorn and Zipf (1943) compared the frequency and range of words used in the speech of schizophrenics with those of normals. In their view, optimal communication occurs within the bounds of sufficient repetition or redundancy for clarity and sufficient diversification for informativeness. If too many different kinds of words are used, the repetition boundary is broken and communication is poor, and if too few are used, the diversification criterion is violated and the message is not informative. They found that normals and schizophrenics use the same number of different words but that schizophrenics crowd "an inconveniently large number of meanings onto a relatively small number of words" (p. 844), overusing their most frequent words relative to normals, and thus rendering their speech less informative. Simultaneously, schizophrenics also tended to have a greater diversity of words that they used only once relative to normals: Schizophrenics, "inconsiderate of others, might indulge in a diversified polysyllabic discourse, using such a large and unfamiliar vocabulary as to be incomprehensible to most" (p. 844). This feature makes their language less redundant than normal and therefore more difficult to follow. Thus, with respect to both redundancy and informativeness, schizophrenic language deviates from normal language.

In this kind of analysis, the deviance in schizophrenia is attributed not so much to language processes as to communication processes, pragmatics, and cooperative principles. Patients do not take into account the needs of others in designing their speech, perhaps because of an inability or deficit in perceiving those needs, or perhaps because of a deliberate desire to be less well understood. In Brown's analysis, the disturbance is in neither language nor communication but in one delusional thought area.

Alternatively, the disturbance could be a linguistic one. Consider the following examples of schizophrenic speech from one patient of Herbert and Waltensperger (1982):

1a. I don't like the way I'm pupped today. (p. 226)

b. . . . with syndicates organized and subsicates in the way that look for a civil war. (p. 226)

c. I'm write letters in self defense and have been write for 25 years already. Russia and Israel is try to drive me to approve of war against Canada I'm not interested in become a socialist. (p. 230)

d. Hawaiians are very sick mental way people. (p. 231)

Or from several different patients cited by Maher (1972):

2a. I like coffee, cream, cows, Elizabeth Taylor. (p. 9)

b. [translated from German] It is from the Imperial House, they have it from ancestors, from the ancestral world, from the preworld. Frankfort-on-Main, there are the Franks, Frankfurter sausages, Frankenthal, Frankenstein. (p. 9)

c. [define "fable"]

Trade good sheep to hide in the beginning. (p. 13)

d. Kindly send it to me at the hospital. Send it to me Joseph Nemo, in care of Joseph Nemo and me who answers by the name of Joseph Nemo will care for it myself. Thanks everlasting and Merry New Year to Metholatum Company for my nose, for my nose, for my nose, for my nose, for my nose, for my nose. (p. 14)

e. The subterfuge and the mistaken planned substitutions for that demanded American action can produce nothing but the general results of negative contention and the impractical results of careless application, the natural results of misplacement of mistaken purpose and unrighteous position, the impractical serviceabilities of unnecessary contradictions. (p. 13)

Or from three other patients cited in the literature:

3. [Complete the sentence "I get warm when I run because . . . ]
Quickness of blood, heart of deer, length
Driven power, motorized cylinder, strength. (Cameron, 1951, p. 61)

4. In spite of the fact of that you insist on exercising your patriarchal influence, my mind (even if not my pocket-book) is emancipated from that feudal conception of parental domination. No doubt you can arouse a certain amount of public sympathy from such narrow-minded goops as the Dovers and the Clarks, but it only goes to prove the futility of the development of intelligence and makes me realize that this is an unredeemable civilization of grocery men and fishmongers. (Whitehorn & Zipf, 1943, p. 845)

5. Patient: I said I could remember when my mother's hair was down her back and she kept cutting it off.
Dr.: I don't know what that means.
Patient: That's what I mean. There's been a pass over me. I've been passed over.
Dr.: I still don't know what that means.
Patient: Well, look at the dark shadows. What do you see? Same old monkeys.
    (Garfield, 1989, p. 450)

As you can see, although the language is odd, it is not particularly disturbed syntactically, compared with Broca's aphasia, for example. Not only are the sentences well constructed but also both content words and function words are used, and used appropriately. The features to observe in the language, which make it deviant, are the neologisms, like "pupped" and "subsicates" (1), the repetitions of "frank" (2b), "Joseph Nemo" and "for my nose" in (2d), and the sentence anomalies in most of the passages. You may also note the inappropriate use of inflection in the first passage, but this is atypical and is rarely reported. Because there is little disturbance in phonology or syntax in schizophrenia, I will quickly review them and concentrate on semantic processing. As we examine studies of schizophrenic language processing, consider whether they are compelling in showing a language impairment. We will return to this question later. Whether or not they indicate deficiency in the language mechanisms, the deviations from normal can be informative about the components and functionings of the normal language mechanism.

## Speech Processing in Schizophrenia

### Paralanguage

The few reports of speaking disturbances in schizophrenia have been concerned primarily with paralanguage and show little consistent disturbance across patients. Bleuler (1911/1950), for example, described schizophrenic speaking patterns as

> abnormally loud, abnormally soft, too rapid or too slow. Thus one patient speaks in a falsetto voice, another mumbles, a third pants. A catatonic speaks in precisely the same fashion during inspiration as during expiration. . . . When the patients think of themselves as different persons, they utilize a correspondingly different tone of voice. (p. 148)

Although this description indicates a speech deviance, it does not suggest a loss of function, such as inability to control motor programs or to create melodic speech units, as we saw in aphasia. In fact, the ability to speak on the inhale or to create different voices for different characters suggests good control of speech skills. Moreover, we see similar "melodic" disturbances in deaf, signing schizophrenics: Thacker (1994) reported patients who either fingerspelled or signed consistently backward! Such deviancies in either speech or sign stem from the failure to follow conventional conversational practices, not from inability to organize the language.

Goldfarb, Goldfarb, and Scholl (1966) reported disturbances in the speech of schizophrenic children in pitch, loudness, and rate that hurt their intelligibility. For these aspects of the voice, the problems were that the modulations were inappropriate: Increased loudness did not correspond to syllable stress or emotional stress, and, similarly, pitch changes occurred independently of syntax and mood changes. Because syllabic stress was inappropriately marked, the speech took on a slurred quality. (This points to the importance of suprasegmental information in guiding normal speech interpretation.) In some patients, overall intonation was either excessively high pitched or monotonic.

Recent studies have examined schizophrenics with "flat affect" (*affect* is mood) or alogia apart from other schizophrenics. The flat affect, alogic patients speak less and pause more than patients without flat affect. Their pauses are distributed normally, with more occurring between clauses and before content words than within clauses or before function words (Alpert, Clark, & Pouget, 1994). These patients vary amplitude less than do normals or other schizophrenics (Alpert, Rosen, Welkowitz, Sobin, & Borod, 1989). After antipsychotic medication, the flatness of affect disappears, as does the relative monotony of the speech (Rieber & Vetter, 1994).

## Segmental Deficits

Pathology in production of speech segments likewise does not indicate difficulty in motor programming of speech. Two deficiencies have been described, however. First, like Wernicke's aphasics, schizophrenics may produce neologisms, such as "subsicates" (1b). Those produced, however, generally conform to the phonological structure of the native language, whether speech or sign (Chaika, 1974, 1990; Rieber & Vetter, 1994; Thacker, 1994), indicating normal phonological competence and appropriate use of it for production. The neologisms may occur because the patient was avoiding using an intelligible word or spontaneously outputting several equally activated words. Alternatively, as in aphasia, the neologism could occur because the patient has tried unsuccessfully to access the phonological representation of a particular word or has accessed it and implemented it unsuccessfully, producing multiple slips of the tongue.

Chaika (1974) points out that schizophrenics rarely try to correct these neologisms, as a normal individual would if the words were correctly accessed but mispronounced. Of course, the failure to correct may reflect a failure in monitoring, not access, or a disinterest in expending the effort to improve the production. Supporting deliberate word creation is a schizophrenic's self-report (Bleuler, 1911/1950):

> I used some words in order to express a concept entirely different from the usual one. Thus, I blithely employed the word *mangy* to mean *gallant*. If I could not immediately find an appropriate word to express the rapid flow of ideas, I would seek release in a self-invented one, as for example, *wuttas* for *doves*. (p. 150)

To me it seems likely that neologisms remain uncorrected because of failure to understand that people talk to *communicate* (implying awareness of the receiver), not just to *express* an idea. I think it less likely that they arise from deviant speech or word representation.

The second commonly noticed deficiency in the speech of schizophrenics is their perseveration on particular sounds, clang associations. Most frequently, these occur for the beginning syllables of a word, as in the "frank" example in the quotations or, more subtly, in 2e in "subterfuge" and "substitution" (there are others in that extract that you might try to find). It may occur at word ends, as in the repetition of "tion" (in 2e) or in the rhyme of "length" and "strength" in the next quotation. It clearly occurs also on the word and phrase levels, as in "Joseph Nemo" and "for my nose." Similar perseverations on, or associations to, formational features, rather than meaning, are made by signing schizophrenics (Thacker, 1994).

As our discussion of clang associations indicated, they occur in normal people as well, when fatigued, stressed, or under the influence of alcohol. Normally, clang associations are inhibited, which the schizophrenic may be less able to do. Alternatively, the schizophrenic may be using the normal process of avoiding emotionally laden meaning associations, which results in the clang associations. The deviance then lies in schizophrenics' having more emotional words to avoid than do normals.

### Speech Perception

Low-level speech perception has not been tested in schizophrenics, but there is no reason to expect it to be abnormal. Maher (1972) reported that schizophrenics were more likely to make slips of the ear than normals, to hear one word when another had been spoken. As we will see, there are reports that schizophrenic responses to word association tasks are abnormal, and Maher has contended that such findings result from misperceptions, not bizarre associations: When it is clear that the patient has correctly heard the word, the word associations are normal (see Moon, Mefferd, Wieland, Pokorny, & Falconer, 1968). The misperceptions could derive from a failure in top-down processing. If patients have trouble attending to the speech and deciphering the message, an incorrect expectation could lead them to encode the wrong words.

Top-down (lexical and syntactic) processes appear more influential in schizophrenics' speech perception than in normals'. Carpenter (1976) played sentences with clicks superimposed on them to schizophrenic and normal subjects with instructions to write the sentence and record the position of the click. In normal subjects, there is a bias to perceive or report the click as occurring at the major syntactic boundary of the sentence (see Chapters 5 and 7 of *Language and Its Normal Processing*). This could indicate an effect of syntactic structure on perception, if the click is perceived to migrate. However, in the click studies, subjects usually write the sentences and mark the click. Thus perception, memory, and response are confounded because it is not clear when in the task the click "migrated" to the constituent boundary. Carpenter found that schizophrenics showed a greater migration effect than normal, indicating possibly a strong top-down effect in their speech perception but also normal syntactic awareness of the major constituent boundary. Given that attention and memory may both be impaired in schizophrenia (Schwartz, 1978), it is especially unclear where in performing this difficult task the syntactic intrusion occurs.

## Syntactic Processing in Schizophrenia

### Syntax Reception

We have just seen that schizophrenics are able to detect the major constituent boundary within a sentence and, to that extent, to parse normally. We have also seen that schizophrenics with flat affect pause more and have longer pauses than normal, but their distribution of pauses reflects normal structural constraints of the sentence, with more pauses between clauses and before content words, where a speaker normally plans the next constituent. Carpenter (1976) also showed that for schizophrenics, like normals, clauses contained within a sentence better prompt each other than when they are expressed as separate sentences. This shows a normal sensitivity to sentence boundaries as a guide to parsing.

Like normals, schizophrenics better recall meaningful sentences than anomalous sentences, and anomalous sentences that are syntactically correct than random word strings, although, overall, their performance is worse than normals (Koh, 1978). Like normals too, they can recall more words following word strings composed of higher-order than lower-order approximations of English (see Table 5.1), although again their overall performance is poorer than normal (Rieber & Vetter, 1994). Thus they make use of the redundancy provided by syntax to aid recall, and therefore they parse appropriately.

A somewhat more sensitive test required schizophrenics and normals to unscramble sentences that had been scrambled to look like random word strings (Rausch et al., 1980). This task tests generative capacity while not making strong memory demands because the words are visible at all times. In this task, for almost all syntactic structures tested, schizophrenic and normal subjects performed equally well. The single exception may be semantic rather than syntactic: a confusion in placement of the last noun phrases in sentences like "The boy gave the girl the book," which normals would correctly arrange but schizophrenics would sometimes organize to "The boy gave the book the girl." (The examples are mine.) The grammatical distinction is between direct and indirect object or, in case grammar terms, between patient and recipient. The failure here may be recognizing that humans or animate objects are unlikely to be given, and that inanimate objects are unlikely to receive, that is, in applying *selectional restrictions* (see Chapter 2 of the companion volume). The general sentence structure and subcategorizations are not impaired; verbs are not used where nouns are called for. Alternatively, it may be that the patients did not notice the absence of the grammatical marker *to* and ordered the words of the sentence as if it were there.

Anand, Wales, Jackson, and Copolov (1994) asked normals and schizophrenics to make grammaticality judgments on a set of items designed to be abnormal either semantically or syntactically. The same subjects also performed a metaphor comprehension test as well as a test of their ability to determine the referent of a pronoun within the same well-constructed sentence. Anand et al. emphasize that on *all* measures, the normals performed significantly better than the schizophrenics, particularly when the latter's performance was measured close to a "florid" psychotic episode. The importance of this in their view is that it reflects a syntax impairment in the schizophrenics. However, they did not report a breakdown of their data to indicate which syntactic structures were difficult, nor did they present raw scores to show how much poorer the schizophrenics were; the analyzed data were in terms of ranks, and the schizophrenics ranked more poorly on their tests. Finally, by their own admission, a statistical analysis could differentiate schizophrenics from normals 80% of the time from their performance on the semantic and metaphor tests, with the syntax test performance providing little additional resolution. Therefore, their results do not implicate a problem in grammaticality judgment, apart from the usual finding that schizophrenics do not perform as well as normals on any test.

Thus, on tests measuring the use of syntax in comprehension, schizophrenics appear normal. The only possible exception is the test that showed misordering of direct and indirect objects, which could reflect a lesser sensitivity to grammatical markers such as prepositions. Usually their performance is poorer than that of normals, particularly if memory or attentional demands are great, but on tasks that normals find more difficult, schizophrenics have proportionally greater difficulty, so the pattern of results looks similar. This suggests that syntactic processing is not particularly impaired in schizophrenia. The confusion of direct and indirect object might be a semantic error, confusing what is likely to be given and who is likely to receive. As we will see, there is other evidence of semantic or conceptual deficits in schizophrenia. And it is not unreasonable to consider selectional restrictions part of the semantic system.

### Syntactic Deficits in Spontaneous Production

Whether schizophrenics' spontaneous sentence structures are impaired is controversial, in part perhaps because not all schizophrenics have impaired language, and those who do are impaired only intermittently (Chaika, 1990). The failure to screen patients for a language problem may underlie some authors' findings that schizophrenic language "rarely (if ever) includes hard instances of agrammatism or word-finding deficits" (Cohen, 1978, p. 1), while others do find consistent language deficits. For example, Thomas, Leudar, Newby, and Johnston (1993) cite recent studies that showed that schizophrenics' vocalized sentences were shorter, with fewer embeddings, than those of normal controls or of psychotic patients suffering from mania. The differences were sufficient that the *sentence structure alone* classified the psychosis of the speaker with 95% accuracy. Similar differences did not appear in writing. The social demands of the speech situation may particularly impair schizophrenics.

*Morphology and closed-class deficits?* Researchers who have selected patients for disordered language and studied them during psychotic episodes note that their sentences may confuse mass and count nouns *(a milk* or *milks),* or confuse or omit prepositions when needed. Hoffman (1992) cites the following:

That was a decent things to do.
  We could be wheelchairs (intended: we could be *in* wheelchairs). (p. 202)

There is also a report of a patient who evidenced morphological impairments (Herbert & Waltensperger, 1982). Some examples of his utterances were given in the first quotation in the samples of schizophrenic speech. According to the researchers, his language indicated confusions of tense and aspect (as in "organized and subsicates"), violations of subcategorization rules (as in his persistent substitution of "I'm" for "I"), and failure to use common inflections (as in substitution of the content word "way" for the adverb inflection "-ly"). Unfortunately, they did not describe his linguistic background. To me, while his speech does not look like normal English, with the exception of the neologisms, it does look like a normal language *process*—that is, creolization, discussed in Chapters 1 and 4 (see also Chapter 8 of the companion volume). Moreover, as the researchers point out themselves, these particular linguistic peculiarities are highly atypical of schizophrenic language and so cannot be used as descriptive of the breakdown as, for example, the function word omission is descriptive of Broca's aphasia.

In the signing of deaf schizophrenics, we see some syntactic deviancies, but these also indicate the operation of idiosyncratic rules, not loss of grammatical function. Thacker (1994), for example, reports a patient who reversed direction on directional verbs, transposing agent and object, and another patient who identified the left side of her body with her brother and the right side of her body with herself.

*Syntactic blends?* More consistently reported as syntax problems in schizophrenic speech are "fluent run-on sentences," which Chaika (1990) terms *syntactic gapping* and Hoffman (1992) attributes to *syntactic blending*. In these structures, the patient combines two sentences where they share words, without appropriately conjoining them or indicating that a new thought is being introduced. Chaika, for example, provides "She still is her destination is not known in a few minutes," which, she contends, would be normal if there were a hesitation or "er" after "is"; the patient began "she still is in the same place" and then changed to "her destination is not known." The deviance, Chaika points out, is that the combination is produced as a fluent whole, leaving an unfinished predicate for the first sentence.

Hoffman (1992) presents instances like this: "I'm very sad to see it in some of the patients aren't really that rotten you see." He interprets the sentence as the realization of two planned sentences—"I'm very sad to see it in some of the patients" and "Some of the patients aren't really that rotten you see." The deficit in his view is that both sentences compete for expression and the patient fails to select only one. The result is a blend of the two structures at the common words.

While these run-on sentences are certainly structurally deviant, it is not clear to me that they reflect a problem in syntactic competence, like the one we saw in aphasia. As Chaika suggests, patients may be backtracking and restarting, as we all do, but fail at the communication level to indicate to the listener that they are doing so. From Hoffman's point of view, two syntactically correct sentences are planned, and the deficit arises in translating them to phonetic form, when one must be suppressed. As we will see when we discuss semantics and schizophrenic speech, schizophrenics may have a problem inhibiting competing associations, here manifesting in the blend of the two planned sentences.

*Discourse incoherence?* Many investigators have been struck by an apparent abnormality in structure at the discourse level in schizophrenic speech, which some have attributed to a syntactic disruption. Consider, for example, the sentence "I like coffee, cream, cows, Elizabeth Taylor." Although the sentence is syntactically well formed, the items included in the list reflect no common membership in a higher-order category, as underlies the more normal sentence "I like coffee, tea, and cocoa." This suggests that there might be fewer constraints on word selection in the schizophrenic utterance than normal. In fact, this has been assessed directly using a technique called the cloze procedure.

In the *cloze procedure,* a passage of speech is obtained usually through a prompted interview, and then words are systematically deleted from it; for example, every fifth word is removed (Maher, 1972; Pavy, 1968; Salzinger, Portnoy, & Feldman, 1978). The butchered word strings are then given to other individuals (normal or schizophrenic) to see if they can fill in the gaps. The greater the contextual constraints are on the words' identity, the more easily the missing elements should be guessed. From the word count results cited earlier (Whitehorn & Zipf, 1943), we might expect it to be harder to guess the missing words from schizophrenic speech, because their word choice involves more repetition and more one-time use than normal.

The technique has yielded several interesting results. First, it *is* harder to guess elements missing from schizophrenic speech than it is from normal speech, providing empirical support for the observation that there are fewer constraints and less redundancy than normal in schizophrenic utterances. Second, the results showed that the speech of schizophrenics is less predictable at the ends of the passages than at the beginnings, perhaps because the prompt that triggered the response is farther away in time and therefore exerts less control. The difference in redundancy between beginnings and ends of passages is not found in normal speech, and this suggests that schizophrenics may be less limited by distant contextual constraints than normals. Finally, examination of the responses of schizophrenics to gaps produced by the cloze procedure indicates that their guesses are determined primarily by constraints from the immediately preceding word rather than the whole sentence or passage (Salzinger et al., 1978).

Discourse analysis also reveals an absence of long-distance constraints on structure (Hoffman, 1992). Hoffman analyzed normal paragraphs as a tree structure with a single central "trunk" (the theme) and each sentence branching from it, with lower-level statements presupposing higher-level ones. Structure trees of schizophrenic discourse were distinguished from normal by blind raters with 80% accuracy: The trees had more than one trunk with sentences shifting between them, and failed to show logical presupposition. For example, the following passage reflects the dual "trunks" of schools of fish and education, intertwined on the pun of "school" and "see/sea" but not elaborated:

> School? Well there are schools of play and schools of fish, mostly you see fish school, people edumacating [sic] themselves, you see, sea is one thing and education is another. Fish is school in their community, that's why the community of man stands in the way of the community of the sea, and once they see the light of sunny sunshine then they will let it be. (p. 205)

Chomsky (1957) discussed and rejected finite state grammars as models for human language (see Chapter 4 of the companion volume). In these models, word or constituent choice is governed only by the preceding word or constituent. Finite state grammars fail as models of human language because human grammar requires long-distance constraints. (Consider "the men who fought so bravely for our country were honored . . ."—"were" agrees with the plural "men," taking its form not from the immediately adjacent noun "country" but from a word that is eight words away.) It is precisely the absence of distant constraints that the cloze technique and discourse analyses reveal as characteristic of schizophrenic speech, as does the absence of hierarchical structure in the list "coffee, cream, cows, Elizabeth Taylor." The *contrast* between normal speech and schizophrenic speech, in this regard, underscores the observation that normal speech is not generated by a finite state grammar.

*Does schizophrenic speech reflect disturbed language competence?* The question is whether speech-disordered schizophrenia reduces the operation of the mental syntax processor to a more primitive finite state grammar level, or whether syntactic competence is normal in schizophrenia but performance processes, like failure to inhibit competing associations and sentence frames, result in an output describable by finite state grammar. Hoffman (1992) argues that each may operate sometimes: There may be a failure in the schizophrenic to plan a hierarchically structured sentence or paragraph, and there may be a failure to suppress competing plans that intrude on an otherwise "competent" discourse. In fact, he suggests that this latter alternative may underlie the schizophrenics' hallucinating of voices: They know what speech they have planned but then hear what comes out uncontrolled, and attribute this actual speech to an other within them. Note though that Leudar, Thomas, and Johnston (1992) found that schizophrenics do try to repair utterances that incorrectly describe what they mean, but that they both produce such utterances and fail to repair them *correctly* more frequently than do normals. Their repair attempts indicate, however, that they do monitor their own speech and recognize remediable discrepancies between it and their intentions.

Chaika (1974, 1990) argued for distinctive features of speech-disordered schizophrenic language, that is, a unique, disturbed language competence: the inability to match semantic features with word names (her interpretation of the existence of neologisms), inappropriate attention to the sound of the words (as in alliteration and clang associations), failure to correct mispronunciations, syntactic gapping, *glossomania* or irrelevant and irrepressible chained associations, perseverations and other repetitions, gibberish and opposite speech, failure to limit the meanings of a word through the context (as in "my mother's name was Bill . . . and coo"), the structuring of both sentences and discourse around individual word meanings or sounds rather than around a topic, and the failure to apply appropriately redundancy rules such as the replacement of the second occurrence of a noun by a pronoun.

Fromkin (1975) countered that the speech errors, including the blends and neologisms, are found in normals, albeit with less frequency. Therefore they do not constitute a distinct grammatical competence. And we have already seen that substitutions of opposites and clang associations likewise are in the normal repertoire. Finally, I see no profound *structural* deviance in schizophrenic speech, like subcategorization violations or the failure to flesh out obligatory argument structure. Rather, each of the production problems contributes to a problem of cohesiveness, a lesser-than-normal context sensitivity. This might reflect a more rudimentary finite state-like grammar, operating only intermittently, or be an extralinguistic problem of coordinating ideas (Fromkin, 1975) rather than a specifically syntactic disruption.

As a final comment on schizophrenic syntax, it is perhaps instructive to examine quotation 4, an excerpt from a letter written by a highly educated schizophrenic patient. There is no question that this passage employs well-formed, elegant, and complex syntactic structure, although the point of the passage is obscured by the abundance of words and convoluted style. It seems that if there were an impairment in syntax per se, such a passage could never have been penned by a schizophrenic: In the last sentence, for example, the "it" is appropriately a singular pronoun, referring to the entire last clause and controlling the third person singular marking on the verbs "goes" and "makes," despite their distance and the intrusion of some plural nouns. So, there clearly is context sensitivity in the syntax beyond the single word. The passage also illustrates use of sentence embedding, complex constituent structure, inflection, and so on—all instances of difficult, high-level syntactic operations.

Thus it appears that if schizophrenia results in language oddities, it is not because there is damage to a syntactic processor but because the patients intermittently do not use the normal syntactic strategies they have available to produce coherent discourse. This may be described possibly as a semantic failure, because meaning is not appropriately put into words; a communication failure, because meaning is not appropriately structured for transmission; or a thought failure, if meaning is not appropriately conceptualized. We turn next to studies of schizophrenics' processing of linguistic meaning to consider whether there is evidence of semantic disruption.

## Semantic Processes in Schizophrenia

Most investigators of schizophrenia agree that schizophrenics show disturbances in thought, in conceptual structure. The level of language most likely to reflect disruption in schizophrenia therefore is the semantic system. As we shall see, semantic deficits have been noted in schizophrenics in categorization, in word selection, in rating word pairs, and also in determining sentence meanings. However, there is no agreement on how best to describe these deficiencies, or whether they are deficiencies in underlying semantic organization, in semantic processing, or in a disguising operation overlaid on normal semantic organization and processes. We will investigate the results of experiments in semantic processing in schizophrenia within the context of some of the hypotheses proposed to explain or describe the deviance.

### Concreteness and Immediacy Hypotheses

I have already observed that schizophrenic productions seem to be organized more than normal as a chain, with links between immediately adjacent words only.

---

### Box 6.2. Speech and Syntax Findings in Schizophrenia

— Schizophrenics with flat affect have reduced pitch and amplitude variability. This improves with antipsychotic medication, as affect normalizes. Flat emotion is normally conveyed by less suprasegmental variation; the abnormality is in the affect, not the language process used to express it.

— Schizophrenic speech reflects normal segmental phonology, including that used in the creation of neologisms.

— Schizophrenics' word selection is overly influenced by the sound of the word (clang associations)—rhymes and first phonemes or syllables—indicating normal sound perception but overreliance on it relative to semantics.

— Like normals, schizophrenics are sensitive to constituent boundaries, grammaticality of sentences, and greater approximation to English structure.

— Schizophrenics often produce shorter, less complex sentences and perform more poorly with grammaticality judgments and error detection than normals.

— Some schizophrenics produce sentences with unusual structure, as though they had run two sentences together, reflecting either their failure to inhibit one of two planned sentences or their failure to cue listeners that they have restarted.

— Some schizophrenic productions omit prepositions or determiners, confusing count and mass nouns.

— There is no evidence that these reflect a syntax impairment per se; misproductions are intermittent for a given patient, and no particular structure is consistently misproduced across schizophrenics.

— The cloze procedure, where words are selectively omitted from a discourse, and subjects asked to guess them, reveals less long-distance coherence in schizophrenic than normal speech.

— Schizophrenic discourse is less coherent than normal, perhaps reflecting less context sensitivity than normal grammar or, probably, reflecting the less coherent underlying thought.

---

This characteristic of sentence construction also seems to be characteristic of schizophrenic thought, sometimes referred to as the *immediacy hypothesis* (Salzinger et al., 1978) or reflecting a *concrete attitude* rather than an abstract, logical one (Goldstein, 1951).

Presumably, the schizophrenic's attention is captured by some immediate feature of the environment, either of the nonverbal context or of the last word uttered. For example, Angyal (1951) reported a patient who, when asked where her husband was, responded that he was in the wedding picture present in the room. Because the controlling stimulus is some aspect of the immediate environment, this response reflects immediacy. Because the response is selected on the basis of some specific and concrete characteristic like visibility, rather than on the basis of the symbolic meaning, it reflects a concrete attitude.

Concreteness manifests in overgeneral categories (those that include more than is appropriate), using too few general category names, and using words as names rather than symbols. Goldstein (1951) cited one patient, for example, who described a group of green objects individually as "bright green, bell green, baby green," and so on, as if he did not see the similarity in color.

If the problem in schizophrenia is an underlying difficulty in abstract thinking or in using nonimmediate information, we should expect schizophrenics to have deficits in semantic categorization, and these might be reflected in tests of word association, perception of semantic similarity, recognition of semantic classes, and sentence comprehension, which would involve abstraction of relevant meanings from the individual words. These abilities have been measured in schizophrenics.

*Word association and immediacy.* Schizophrenics' word associations fall within the normal range, provided care is taken to ensure that the stimulus word is correctly perceived (Maher, 1972; Moon et al., 1968). However, there have been a number of reports of lack of continuity or "loosening" of association in schizophrenia (Bleuler, 1911/1950) caused by words losing their most salient meaning features and thus deviating in normal meaning. Moreover, schizophrenics are occasionally reported to emit rare associations (Pavy, 1968; Schwartz, 1978, for review), perhaps reflecting defects in, or in use of, the abstract associative network. Finally, as already noted, the associations in spontaneous speech of schizophrenics are indeed deviant. There are clang associations, in which the immediate sound of the word seems to capture attention, and chained associations based on a single concrete semantic feature, as in the "coffee, cream" example, rather than on membership in the same abstract category.

To account for the variety of results, it has been proposed that schizophrenics have available two types of association: a normal, logical, abstract association, and a personal idiosyncratic association, based on concrete, immediate experience. We should note that these types of association are not just found in schizophrenia: We have seen concrete, idiosyncratic association in normals in the "ring-garden" example, and we have also seen clang associations in normals. Schizophrenics may be less able or less willing than normals to suppress such associations in favor of abstract, conventionalized ones, but they do not appear unable to produce the abstract ones.

*Semantic similarity and concreteness.* Schizophrenics' recognition of semantic similarity has been measured in recall and direct ratings. Koh (1978) presented normal and schizophrenic subjects with lists of words to recall. The lists consisted of either semantically similar items (e.g., all dogs), which are better recalled by normals, or unrelated items. Note that there should be a difference in recall of the lists only if the subject is able to abstract the similar semantic feature from the different list items. The schizophrenics did not benefit by the organization in the list. In fact, their performance was poorer on semantically similar than random lists. That there was an observable effect of semantic similarity suggests that the schizophrenics were able to abstract it from the list items; however, it should have helped recall rather than hurt it.

One possible explanation for the poorer performance on semantically similar lists derives from the concreteness hypothesis. When asked to add items to a list like *trot, gallop,* ____ , normals respond *canter,* which shares both the horse and the movement aspects of the other words. The response of schizophrenics to this example is *horse,* which is a strong association to each of the other words but misses the movement feature they have in common (Pavy, 1968). Now, suppose that *trot, gallop,* and so on were words presented in a short-term memory list. We might expect an intrusion error from the schizophrenic subjects of *horse,* making their performance poorer than on random lists. That is, it is possible that their poorer performance on semantically similar lists derives from failure to inhibit intrusions from a related semantic category, one aroused perhaps by immediacy and con- creteness. Note that we are postulating an inhibition failure here, which we proposed also to account for schizophrenics' syntactic blends.

Chapman and Chapman (1965) directly measured the ability of schizophrenics to abstract semantic similarity by asking them to rate pairs of words with respect to the similarity between members of the pair, and later to choose from a pair of words the word most similar to a target word. Schizophrenics tended to overrate the similarity of all the word pairs relative to normal. However, words that were rated as less similar by normals were also rated less similar by schizophrenics. That the subjects recognized the similarity indicates that they can abstract. That the ratings decreased with decreasing similarity indicates appropriate sensitivity to abstract word meaning. And in the second task, the schizophrenics exhibited normal responses.

Finally, schizophrenics have been shown to exhibit stronger semantic priming effects than normal (Kwapil, Hegley, Chapman, & Chapman, 1990). In their task, a word either related or unrelated to a perceptually degraded target was presented in advance of the target, and speed and accuracy for target recognition were measured. Unrelated words slowed (inhibited) processing normally in schizophren- ics, but related words facilitated (primed) recognition abnormally strongly. The results indicate the presence of the appropriate associations but also abnormalities in the interplay of excitation and inhibition in producing a stable activation pattern. And Spitzer (1992) reported that for schizophrenics, context does not reduce the priming of irrelevant meanings of homonymous words as rapidly as it does for normals.

The semantic studies reviewed thus far, like the ones for syntax and speech processing, show poorer performance among schizophrenics than normals but also show the normal pattern of semantic associations—that is, no language-specific deficit.

*Categorization and concreteness.* To measure semantic categorization in schizo- phrenia, two tasks have been used: (a) giving subjects a criterion for generating or selecting instances and (b) giving subjects words to sort into categories. An example of the first is the feature "has a head," and correct responses include most animals and also inanimate objects like "hammer," "nail," or "beer." Normal people can generate or recognize atypical instances, but schizophrenics are more concrete in their definitions and typically generate only animate examples (study cited by Pavy, 1968).

Davis and Blaney (1976) presented subjects with a category name and then a set of related words. Subjects had to decide whether the related words helped define the category. For example, defining features of "bird" might be feathers, beak, two feet, egg-laying, while a merely related feature might be small size. Normal subjects consistently separated the features into two classes, while the schizophrenic subjects checked all related words. This was interpreted as overgeneralization, and thus as a deficit in categorization.

It should be noted that schizophrenics do not just overgeneralize; they also overdiscriminate. Chapman and Chapman (1965) reported patients who labeled some vegetables as fruits (overgeneralization), and others who could not say why a dog and lion were similar because one barked and the other roared (overdiscrimination). Overgeneralization seems to involve abstraction, an observation of similarity, while overdiscrimination reflects a concrete thought process. Deviance from normal in either reflects a problem with the abstraction process. Again, though, the deficit appears to be in applying intact semantic knowledge to the task—determining whether a stored feature is defining or characteristic—not in having the semantic knowledge itself.

Larsen and Fromholt (1976) gave subjects a list of words to sort into categories. The subjects were not told how many categories to make nor were they given any categorization rules. They were not permitted to examine their sortings, so at all times they could see only the top word in the category. After the sorting, the words were shuffled and the subjects were asked to duplicate their sorts: 92% of the normal subjects were able to reconstruct their work, whereas only 71% of the schizophrenic subjects could. The categories that the two groups made were not structured differently, but the schizophrenics changed the number of categories they were using while sorting, and the normals did not. This appears to be an attentional problem, not a problem forming categories or recognizing semantic similarity.

Generally the results suggest that schizophrenics and normals have the same conceptual bases for organizing the words but that schizophrenics are more variable in the criteria they apply at any given instant. This could be interpreted as support for the immediacy hypothesis in that schizophrenics may be distracted from applying a rule that they had used before by a minor change in the immediate conceptual environment (such as a new order that would put different words near one another).

*Metaphor interpretation and concreteness.* The last way I suggested looking at immediacy and concreteness as modes of thinking that affect language in schizophrenia was in deriving meaning from word combinations. An early test was proverb interpretation, which not only looked at sentence processing generally but also at figurative reasoning specifically. Benjamin (1951) reported that schizophrenics were impaired at this task. In mild instances, they would interpret literally, such as in the following: "while the cat's away the mice will play," "when nobody's around they do things they wouldn't do if the cat was there." Literal interpretation implies a concrete attitude, an inability to abstract meaning. In more severe cases, the interpretation bore little relation to either the literal or the figurative meaning as in "that means feline absence and rodential job which has its sources in the nature of the Savior, divine forgiveness, Heaven, Hell and inscrutability." (Note that both interpretations are syntactically fine!)

Others have also reported disturbances in figurative interpretation (Pavy, 1968), but inconsistently (Maher, 1972). Vigotsky (1934) proposed that schizophrenics could interpret proverbs they knew from childhood, presumably because the meaning of the proverb did not have to be generated but just recalled. He argued that their failure was in interpreting new proverbs, for which they would have had to construct the meaning.

### Summary

Generally speaking, there does not seem to be strong or exclusive support for either a concrete attitude or immediacy governing schizophrenic language disturbances. In controlled settings, often schizophrenics can sort words into categories, replicate their performance despite a reshuffling of the words with new possibilities for chained associations, recognize semantic similarities between words, and interpret figuratively.

Of course, there are also indications that semantic skills are impaired. Relative to normals, schizophrenics as a group

1. were less able to repeat their categorizations;
2. were less able to keep track of the number of categories they were using (both of these might suggest a memory deficiency rather than a semantic one);
3. were more influenced by characteristic features;
4. more often produced erratic word associations; and
5. had greater difficulty with figurative interpretations, perhaps especially when they had to be constructed.

However, in general, it seems that impairment on semantic tasks in schizophrenia does not result from deviant language *processing* or *structures,* as would be reflected by concrete rather than abstract thinking or loss of semantic features and categories. The difficulty may be pragmatic—metacognitive—understanding that features are defining rather than simply associated with a particular category. Alternatively, it may derive from deviant general cognitive processes like attention, which stimulates and mediates between excitation and inhibition of competing concepts.

*The Dominance Hypothesis*

Chapman and Chapman (1965; Chapman, Chapman, & Daut, 1976) suggested that schizophrenics' underlying semantic organization and general semantic processing may be normal, with their attention abnormally overwhelmed by the dominant meaning or dominant association of a word. Given our discussion of semantic organization, this could occur if the spread of activation was limited so that fewer associations than normal were aroused, or if the most highly weighted unit more completely suppressed activation from other units. (Both of these are the opposite of the failure-to-inhibit explanation of syntactic blends and semantic problems like intrusion errors and bizarre associations. They are consistent perhaps with the semantic priming results.)

To test the dominance hypothesis, Chapman et al. (1976) presented subjects with ambiguous words in a disambiguating sentence context. Subjects were instructed to select the best meaning for the word from three choices. One choice was the most common meaning of the word, which should be expected to be most strongly activated in the absence of context. A second was a less usual meaning, but one that the context preferentially activated. A third choice was irrelevant, simply a control for guessing. For example, for the sentence "when the farmer bought a herd of cattle he needed a new pen," the choices were as follows:

1. He needed a new writing implement (strong word meaning).
2. He needed a new fenced enclosure (weak word meaning but correct given context).
3. He needed a new pickup truck (irrelevant).

In this task, schizophrenics ignored the information provided by context and uniformly selected the dominant meaning. This result could arise if the patients did not know the weaker meanings or if those meanings did not receive activation also from the context. To differentiate these possibilities, Chapman et al. presented the patients with the words in isolation and asked them to select all the meanings for each. The schizophrenics could do this, indicating that they recognized the less common meanings. Thus their performance in the first task suggests an inability to weigh in the contextual information.

The dominance hypothesis can account for some of the results we have observed already. First, in schizophrenic sentence production, we may consider that chained associations ("coffee, cream, cows . . .") occur through arousal of dominant associations rather than through a synthesis and abstraction of meanings as a whole (Maher, 1972). Second, the difficulty with interpretation of unfamiliar proverbs could arise because each word in the proverb arouses a dominant association that cannot be integrated with those aroused by the other words. For familiar proverbs, the dominant association is the figurative meaning of the whole.

The dominance hypothesis fails to account for results that indicate that schizophrenics employ nondominant meanings, as they must to judge words of medium similarity as similar or to generate the phrase "airplane message" with the meaning "plain as air." It is also inconsistent with some results supporting the immediacy hypothesis, such as the patient's selection of a picture of her husband to answer a question about his whereabouts, given that the dominant association should be the individual, not his photograph. This example suggests that patients do indeed make use of immediate context to modify meanings, albeit strangely.

Because the results as a whole suggest that schizophrenics employ nondominant associations as well as dominant associations, the semantic system seems to be intact, and activation must spread from a concept to related, but nondominant, associations. That schizophrenics do not always use the better association suggests that their deficit lies in judging which is better, that is, which was more activated in a particular circumstance. The deviance in selection or comparison of a competing response has been discussed as a mechanism for schizophrenic language and is known as the *self-editing* hypothesis.

### Abnormalities in Self-Editing

As I observed, it is possible to explain schizophrenics' disregard of context in selecting the nondominant word meaning of a homonymous word as a problem in editing, in monitoring meaning activation and selecting the meaning that was best primed by all sources. There are other results that suggest an editing problem. For one, schizophrenics' performance on recall tasks, where they must generate the response, is poorer than that of normals, but on recognition tasks, where items are selected for them, they show no deficit in memory (Cohen, 1978). This difference suggests that memory is not impaired but that the ability to select a *given* memory spontaneously is. For another, in production tasks that require careful selection among alternatives, schizophrenics perform much worse than normals.

In one such task, two people are shown a pair of stimuli, and one is told which of the pair is the target. The task is to communicate the target to the other person. Cohen (1978) used colors as stimuli and varied the difference between them. Red and green would be easy to signal between, but two shades of pink would require finer verbal tuning, a careful selection from among irrelevant, noncommunicative responses. The close colors were more difficult for normal subjects, but with extra time they correctly signaled the target. With the pink example, for instance, a normal subject initially gave the clue "salmon," and then realized both choices were salmon-colored, and added "the pinker one," the addition reflecting a monitor and editing process. Schizophrenics elaborated less and less helpfully: Also beginning with "salmon," one subject continued, "from the can."

Smith (1970) used a similar task but with stimuli entirely from a verbal domain. Subjects were paired and then each was shown a word pair such as "robber-thief." One of the subjects, the transmitter, was also told which of the words in the pair was the target (for example, "robber") and the task, like a game of Password, was for the transmitter, without directly naming the target, to make the other subject say it. Abilities to select a good clue can be measured in this task for both the transmitter and the receiver. Note that for the example here, a clue like "one who steals" is ineffective because it prompts both words equally. A better clue for "robber" might be "baron," and for "thief," "jewel," because of the associations "robber baron" and "jewel thief." This task should be difficult for schizophrenics when the words share a dominant meaning, which the transmitter might not be able to ignore to provide an effective clue.

In selecting the target from the clues given, schizophrenics performed like normals in the receiver position, suggesting once again that their associative structures are intact. They were considerably worse as transmitters, at cuing the target, however, indicating an inability either to generate the clues spontaneously or to select among clues they had generated.

To differentiate these possibilities, Smith gave the same subjects a forced-choice task in which they were to select the better of two clues provided for a given word of a word pair. If they performed normally here, when the clues were given to them, then it could be concluded that their difficulty lay in generating possible clues. Difficulties in this task would focus the problem on selection of the better of the alternative clues.

The schizophrenics were able to select the better clue only when it related strongly to the target word, and were impaired if the better clue was a weak association of the target. As an example, consider the pair "below-beneath," with "below" as target and "under" and "belt" as possible prompts. "Under" is a stronger association of "below" than is "belt," but it is also a good prompt for "beneath." The association of "belt" to either "below" or "beneath" occurs only in the expression "below the belt" and therefore uniquely signals "below." Because "under" relates to both words, "belt"—although weakly related to "below"—is a better clue for it. Schizophrenics had trouble selecting this kind of clue, apparently unable to assess the *difference* in the association of the two clues to the potential targets. Thus their problem appears to lie in selecting among clues, if not also in generating the associations. It also appears to be limited to a particular kind of selection.

Description of the processes necessary to perform well on this task is similar to that of a process deemed necessary for normal metaphor appreciation (see Chapter 3 of *Language and Its Normal Processing*). In a good metaphor, a prominent feature of the vehicle (predicate) is applied to the topic (subject), highlighted by *the background of differences* between topic and vehicle. So in "billboards are the warts of the highway," the "ugly" feature of warts is thrown into prominence for "billboard" in view of its being the only similarity.

The forced-choice "Password"-like task I just described requires a similar kind of weighting, not a simple judgment but a complex comparison of the similarity of each clue to the possible targets, judged against a background of the difference. The difficulty in the editing task may also underlie schizophrenics' difficulties in proverb and metaphor interpretation.

Be that as it may, it is important to observe that schizophrenics are as able as normals to select the target from the clue given (to act as receiver) and so must be performing the comparisons properly. The failure they exhibit is a failure to communicate, which may be construed either as a failure to select among the clues, to recognize the perspective of the other, or as a failure in motivation to be clear.

---

**Box 6.3. Semantic Processes in Schizophrenia**

— *Immediacy hypothesis:* The schizophrenic's attention is overly drawn to some connection between the word and the present environment, what is immediately present.

— *Concrete attitude:* Schizophrenics are more likely to be struck by a concrete, perceptible feature of the word or context than they are to use an abstract categorizing principle.

— *Dominance hypothesis:* The schizophrenic has available all meanings and associations of a word, but the most highly weighted one captures attention exclusively.

— *Self-editing hypothesis:* Schizophrenics have available all meanings and associations of words but are unable to select the alternatives likely to arouse the desired associations in others, to weigh the appropriate associations against the inappropriate ones.

— Word-association studies show more clang associations and bizarre associations than normal, but also normal, abstract associations. And the deviancies, though more frequent, are within the corpus of normal word associations.

— Schizophrenics are less reliable, more variable, than normals in categorizing but seem to sort with the same rules.

— Schizophrenics recognize semantic similarity, but it does not help them in recalling word lists, nor can they differentiate reliably between defining and characteristic features or between words sharing a single strong association versus those sharing a conjunction of associations.

— Schizophrenics show stronger than normal semantic facilitation priming effects and less inhibition of irrelevant meanings by context.

— Schizophrenics' proverb interpretation is often literal or irrelevant, perhaps when they may have to construct the proverb meaning rather than recall it.

— Schizophrenics do not seem to be able to use sentence context to select nondominant meanings of a word, like *enclosure* for *pen,* given that it is a "pen for cattle."

— In tasks where schizophrenics must fine-tune language to cause another to select the best word from two close alternatives, they do not recognize or provide effective differentiating cues. They can select the better alternative given the cues but do not seem able to put themselves in the other's position, to select the better alternative for a desired response.

— If there is a "language" processing deficit, it is in the interplay of excitation and inhibition of competing word names, alternative meanings, or thoughts. More likely this is a general cognitive problem, one of attention and arousal, not a specifically psycholinguistic one.

---

As we have already seen, the speech of schizophrenics is egocentric—that could be from a desire to be cryptic as easily as it could be from idiosyncratic definitions (a problem in semantic structure) or semantic processes or from neglect of the other person's position (an attention problem). Most of the hypotheses that we examined consider breakdown in definitions or in semantic processes. But, as I pointed out earlier, many researchers consider schizophrenia a problem in communication generally, not language specifically (Brown, 1973; Cohen, 1978; Whitehorn & Zipf, 1943, to name a few).

## Summary and Conclusions

Our examination of schizophrenic communications reveals a number of abnormalities. I will review these here to consider whether there is reason to assume that they derive from a breakdown in language processing.

In schizophrenia, there may be an unrealistic set of concepts (a delusion), but this is often verbalized correctly, suggesting it is not a linguistic problem.

Schizophrenics may use words idiosyncratically and may structure their communications to be less informative than normal either by increasing or by decreasing the redundancy necessary for optimal communication. This does not appear to be a linguistic deficit but one in communication, arising either from an inability to take the other's perspective in selecting phrasing or from a deliberate desire to be cryptic.

Schizophrenics have an abnormal tendency to mishear words spoken to them and to perseverate on, or attend to, the sounds of the words rather than the meanings in constructing their speech. I am not arguing here that schizophrenics, like Wernicke's aphasics, have impaired access to the meaning features of the network from the sound features of the name. Recall that Jung found a tendency for sound-based associations in normals when the stimulus word was associated with psychological distress or when they were experiencing physical stress. Schizophrenia may cause stress as part of the disease, or it may be a psychological reaction to stress, and so the abnormalities in sound production and perception may be an outgrowth of normal linguistic processes together with the normal reaction to stress.

In aphasia (Chapter 5), we discussed a dissociation between access to the word name in production and the word meaning in both production and comprehension. Broca's aphasics seemed to use a slow system of semantic association to prompt a name, indicating intact associative processes with disturbance of the normal fast association between a name and its referent. Wernicke's aphasics seemed unable to generate names from meaning associations, indicating a higher threshold for naming or poorer inhibition of competing names. Anomics were unable to produce word names in isolation but could often generate them in the context of the speech stream. Landre et al. (1992) found that aphasia-diagnostic tests of repetition, object naming, communicativeness and fluency in picture description, and performance of short sequences of spoken commands *failed* to differentiate between a selected group of schizophrenics and fluent aphasics (anomic, Wernicke's, and conduction aphasics). However, the studies we have reviewed here indicate that the breakdown between naming and association appears far more tenuous in schizophrenia; schizophrenics can and do make normal associations, both with respect to producing the words and with respect to the meaning relation between them. The problem is that they fail to do this sometimes, but the fact that this is occasional suggests that the disturbance does not indicate damage, as in aphasia.

Schizophrenics seem to have normal abilities to parse sentences spoken by others, and their own sentences frequently use high-level syntactic operations like embedding and recursion. However, their spontaneous discourse uses shorter sentences with fewer constraints than normal, as we saw with the difficulty in guessing words deleted from schizophrenic utterances. In some instances, the speech of schizophrenics does not appear to be hierarchically structured but, instead, structured as a chain. I suggested something like this for Wernicke's aphasics, where phrasal chunks, with little meaning, were linked nonhierarchically—such as "I figured that," "it's liable to." In schizophrenia, the chaining is different and does not indicate a breakdown in the syntactic ability to form higher-order constituents because the looseness of association it suggests rarely produces ungrammatical or vacuous sentences as in aphasia but, at worst, semantically anomalous ones. Thus, at present, there is little evidence for syntactic processing disturbances in schizophrenia.

We might consider the unusual choice of words resulting in the anomalies to reflect a semantic problem. Other semantic deviations include an occasional failure to use selectional restrictions appropriately (e.g., selecting an inanimate noun as recipient), a less-than-normal ability to use extended, distant, or weaker meanings of words (e.g., difficulty with "pen" as enclosure), and a difficulty in dissociating from strong but irrelevant associations aroused either verbally (e.g., pen as writing instrument) or nonverbally (e.g., the picture in the immediate environment as husband).

However, none of this suggests damage to the *language* structures or processes per se, such as we saw in aphasia, where, for example, inaccessible names of concrete nouns are replaced by *appropriate* charades like the tune of the wedding march for the word "wedding" (see Chapter 5). Rather, the disruption lies in the use of language knowledge, perhaps resulting from deviant excitation, inhibition, or their interaction on associates. Like the "semantic" deficit in split personalities, this is not deviant language organization but deviant *use* of it, either consciously or unconsciously. Rieber and Vetter (1994) conclude in fact that "communication problems [are] not due to general impaired interactional skills, but rather to isolated attentional lapses, breakdowns in comprehension monitoring, and derailments involving memory intrusions from past experiences that they [are] unable to suppress" (p. 177).

They also wonder how the language of a poet like e. e. cummings,

> anyone lived in a little how town
> (with up so floating many bells down)
> spring summer autumn winter
> he sang his didn't he danced his did (p. 190),

would fare on "schizophrenic language" batteries. It seems clear that the lovely language violations in the poem share features with some of the schizophrenic samples and thus, perhaps, that the schizophrenic reveals language competence. They differ in that the poem *communicates;* it is *intended* (remember, intent is a critical feature of true communication) to surprise and to create a beautiful image.

The intentional control and poet's awareness of how to manipulate the reader's images through self-editing differs from the schizophrenic's inability to do so.

Our examination of schizophrenic language is informative about the nature of language normally. First, it dramatically demonstrates the effect of loosening the powerful constraints of context on word selection in sentences. Normal language does not look like a schizophrenic chain (nor does e. e. cummings's). Second, it demonstrates the importance of considering language as communication: When the audience is not taken into account by speakers, productions are measurably abnormal and may cease to look like language because of too high or too low an information rate. Finally, comparing schizophrenic language with aphasic language, we see dramatically the difference between an intact but oddly accessed language machine and a broken one. Aphasics, but not schizophrenics, have difficulty with language complexities like embedding, noncanonical word order, or morphology, retrieving names apart from meanings, producing recognizable classes of words like fruits (category-specific anomias), content words (Wernicke's aphasia), or function words (Broca's aphasia). Schizophrenics, but not aphasics, show intermittent language problems that defy categorization on a linguistic basis. There is a tendency to credit aphasics with intact language competence but a deficit in performance, to assume that there is an ideal speaker-hearer imprisoned by damage to the brain (see, for example, Gardner, 1975, for discussion). Such a description may be applicable to the schizophrenic or split personality but, by contrast, seems unlikely for the aphasic.

## SUMMARY AND CONCLUSIONS

In this chapter, we examined some effects of personality disorder on language processing. We began by noting the effects of emotional stress on normal language processing. Competing messages may produce intrusions in word selection (and nonsense words as a result). Stressful associations may cause temporary loss of memory for a word, or stress may cause a normal individual to produce idiosyncratic or sound-based associations to a word. Pretense may produce rigid use of the semantic differential. And emotion changes may affect vocal quality. Finally, we noted that language does not develop in the absence of social interests. We then discussed some personality disorders and how they affect language behaviors with respect to some of these measures and others discussed in earlier chapters.

Comparison of language skills in personality upset (schizophrenia, in particular) with language processing after brain damage indicates very different patterns of disruption. Schizophrenics may make idiosyncratic associations, may perseverate on the sound of a word or a semantic feature seemingly irrelevant to the current context, and may be less informative and less redundant than necessary for normal discourse. However, careful tests indicate that their semantic categories are normal, that their associations are normal provided that they correctly hear the stimulus words, and that even under the unusual conditions of psycholinguistic testing they "play word games" like the variant of Password correctly. The disturbance seems to be in which features of the language they select to attend to (sometimes idiosyncratic meanings, sometimes sound, sometimes a meaning suggested by immediate context, and so on), the kind of language "disturbance" seen in normal people when experiencing emotional stress.

The abnormalities reflected in schizophrenic discourse underscore the importance of language as communication. When there is a loss of the perspective of the other in constraining transmission, there is noticeable deviance. In childhood, if one has no awareness of the other because of disease (autism) or abuse (like the wild children of Chapter 3), language does not develop, and teaching it must be piggybacked onto socialization.

For the most part, unlike aphasic language, schizophrenic language meets our language criteria, showing recursiveness, metalanguage, arbitrariness, and so on, although perhaps less-than-normal hierarchical structuring. The deficit seems to be in communication, perhaps in aspects of interchangeability, because schizophrenics perform normally as receivers in many tasks we discussed, but not as transmitters. Moreover, they seem to show a reluctance to alter their own mental structures around what is being transmitted to them as well as an inattention to whether they are successful in altering others' structures when they transmit—both of which are required for true communication.

At the beginning of this chapter, I pointed out that there have been confusions of schizophrenics with brain-damaged patients. From language behavior alone, it seems that it should be easy to differentiate the groups, although they may score similarly on subtests of the aphasia batteries (Landre et al., 1992). In brain damage, we would expect to see particular problems with syntax, especially in deriving constituent structures and in producing complex sentences with embeddings, which we would not expect to see in schizophrenia. (Landre's tests did not include this.) In brain damage, we would expect to find problems with a linguistic category of words—function words in Broca's aphasia and substantive content words in Wernicke's aphasia—while in schizophrenia, word-related abnormalities may appear without regard to linguistic or semantic structure. In Wernicke's aphasia, but not in schizophrenia, we should find impairment of access to the associative network, in naming and associations. And there are other possible linguistic and psycholinguistic differentiators, which you might try to find.

In sum, comparison of schizophrenic language processes with aphasic language processes suggests that the disorders should be discriminable and, moreover, that the schizophrenics' difficulties are not primarily linguistic. Perhaps the best way to demonstrate that the breakdowns are different is to examine two quotations, one from a schizophrenic patient (Bleuler, 1911/1950, p. 156) and the other from a Wernicke's aphasic (Gardner, 1975, p. 68). How easy is it to label the schizophrenic and the aphasic "language"? Can you tell which is which?

1. Oh sure, go ahead, any old think you want. If I could I would. Oh, I'm taking the word the wrong way to say, all of the barbers here whenever they stop you it's going

around and around, if you know what I mean, that is tying and tying for repucer, for repuceration, well, we were trying the best that we could while another time it was with the beds over there the same thing.

2. At Apell plain church-state, the people have customs and habits taken partly from glos-faith because the father wanted to enter new f. situation since they believed the father had a Babeli comediation only with music. Therefore they went to the high Osetion and on the cabbage earth and all sorts of malice, and against everything good. On their inverted Osetion Valley will come and within thus is the father righteousness.

---

(Note: #2 is from a schizophrenic patient.)

---

## REFERENCES

Alpert, M., Clark, A., & Pouget, E. R. (1994). The syntactic role of pauses in the speech of schizophrenic patients with alogia. *Journal of Abnormal Psychology, 103,* 750-757.

Alpert, M., Rosen, A., Welkowitz, J., Sobin, C., & Borod, J. C. (1989). Vocal acoustic correlates of flat affect in schizophrenia: Similarity to Parkinson's disease and right hemisphere disease and contrast with depression. *British Journal of Psychiatry, 154,* 51-56.

Anand, A., & Wales, R. J. (1994). Psychotic speech: A neurolinguistic perspective. *Australian and New Zealand Journal of Psychiatry, 28,* 229-238.

Anand, A., Wales, R. J., Jackson, H. J., & Copolov, D. L. (1994). Linguistic impairment in early psychosis. *Journal of Nervous and Mental Disease, 182,* 488-493.

Andreasen, N. C., Hoffman, R. E., & Grove, W. M. (1985). Language abnormalities in schizophrenia. In M. N. Menuck & M. V. Seeman (Eds.), *New perspectives in schizophrenia* (pp. 97-120). New York: Macmillan.

Angyal, A. (1951). Disturbances of thinking in schizophrenia. In J. S. Kasanin (Ed.), *Language and thought in schizophrenia* (pp. 65-90). Los Angeles: University of California Press.

Benjamin, J. D. (1951). A method for distinguishing and evaluating formal thinking in schizophrenia. In J. S. Kasanin (Ed.), *Language and thought in schizophrenia* (pp. 65-90). Los Angeles: University of California Press.

Bleuler, E. (1950). *Dementia praecox or the group of schizophrenias* (J. Zinkin, Trans.). New York: International Universities Press. (Original work published 1911)

Bloom, L., & Lehey, M. (1978). *Language development and language disorders.* New York: John Wiley.

Bonvillian, J. D., & Blackburn, D. W. (1991). Manual communication and autism: Factors relating to sign language acquisition. In P. Siple & S. D. Fischer (Eds.), *Theoretical issues in sign language research: Vol. 2. Psychology* (pp. 255-277). Chicago: University of Chicago Press.

Brown, R. (1958). *Words and things.* New York: Free Press.

Brown, R. (1973). Schizophrenia, language, and reality. *American Psychologist, 28,* 395-403.

Cameron, N. (1951). Experimental analysis of schizophrenic thinking. In J. S. Kasanin (Ed.), *Language and thought in schizophrenia* (pp. 50-64). Los Angeles: University of California Press.

Carpenter, M. D. (1976). Sensitivity to syntactic structure: Good vs bad premorbid schizophrenics. *Journal of Abnormal Psychology, 85,* 41-50.

Chaika, E. (1974). A linguist looks at schizophrenic language. *Brain and Language, 1,* 257-276.

Chaika, E. O. (1990). *Understanding psychotic speech: Beyond Freud and Chomsky.* Springfield, IL: Charles C Thomas.

Chapman, L. J., & Chapman, J. P. (1965). Interpretation of words in schizophrenia. *Journal of Personality and Social Psychology, 1,* 135-146.

Chapman, L. J., Chapman, J. P., & Daut, R. L. (1976). Schizophrenic inability to disattend from strong aspects of meaning. *Journal of Abnormal Psychology, 85,* 35-40.

Chomsky, N. (1957). *Syntactic structures.* The Hague, The Netherlands: Mouton.

Cohen, B. D. (1978). Referent communication disturbances in schizophrenia. In S. Schwartz (Ed.), *Language and cognition in schizophrenia* (pp. 1-34). Hillsdale, NJ: Lawrence Erlbaum.

Colby, K. M. (1968). Computer-aided language development in nonspeaking children. *Archives of General Psychiatry, 19,* 641-651.

Davis, K. M., & Blaney, P. H. (1976). Overinclusion and self-editing in schizophrenia. *Journal of Abnormal Psychology, 85,* 51-60.

Forrester, J. (1980). *Language and the origins of psychoanalysis.* New York: Columbia University Press.

Freud, S. (1960). *The psychopathology of everyday life* (A. Tyson, Trans.; J. Strachey, Ed.). London: Ernest Benn. (Original work published 1901)

Freud, S. (1961). *Introductory lectures on psychoanalysis.* Toronto: Clark, Irwin. (Original work published 1917)

Fromkin, V. A. (1975). A linguist looks at "A linguist looks at 'schizophrenic language.' " *Brain and Language, 2,* 498-503.

Gardner, H. (1975). *The shattered mind.* New York: Knopf.

Garfield, D. A. S. (1989). The order of schizophrenic thought. *Bulletin of the Menninger Clinic, 53,* 442-454.

Goldfarb, W., Goldfarb, N., & Scholl, H. H. (1966). The speech of mothers of schizophrenic children. *American Journal of Psychiatry, 122,* 1220-1227.

Goldstein, K. (1951). Methodological approach to the study of schizophrenic thought disorder. In J. S. Kasanin (Ed.), *Language and thought in schizophrenia* (pp. 17-40). Los Angeles: University of California Press.

Herbert, R. K., & Waltensperger, K. Z. (1982). Linguistics, psychiatry, and psychopathology: The case of schizophrenic language. In L. Obler & L. Menn (Eds.), *Exceptional language and linguistics* (pp. 217-246). New York: Academic Press.

Hewett, F. M. (1965). Teaching speech to an autistic child through operant conditioning. *American Journal of Orthopsychiatry, 35,* 927-936.

Hoffman, R. E. (1992). Language planning and alterations in the experience of will. In M. Spitzer, F. Uehlein, M. A. Schwartz, & C. Mundt (Eds.), *Phenomenology, language & schizophrenia* (pp. 197-210). New York: Springer-Verlag.

Jung, C. G. (1973). *Experimental researches* (L. Stein in collaboration with D. Riviere, Trans.). Princeton, NJ: Princeton University Press. (Original work published 1905)

Koh, S. D. (1978). Remembering of verbal materials by young schizophrenic adults. In S. Schwartz (Ed.), *Language and cognition in schizophrenia* (pp. 55-99). Hillsdale, NJ: Lawrence Erlbaum.

Kwapil, T. R., Hegley, D. C., Chapman, L. J., & Chapman, J. P. (1990). Facilitation of word recognition by semantic priming. *Journal of Abnormal Psychology, 99,* 215-221.

Landre, N. A., Taylor, M. A., & Kearns, K. P. (1992). Language functioning in schizophrenic and aphasic patients. *Neuropsychiatry, Neuropsychology, and Behavioral Neurology, 5,* 7-14.

Larsen, S. F., & Fromholt, P. (1976). Mnemonic organization and free recall in schizophrenia. *Journal of Abnormal Psychology, 85,* 61-65.

Leudar, I., Thomas, P., & Johnston, M. (1992). Self-repair in dialogues of schizophrenics: Effects of hallucinations and negative symptoms. *Brain and Language, 43,* 487-511.

Lovaas, O. I., Berberich, J. P., Perloff, B. F., & Schaeffer, B. (1966). Acquisition of imitative speech in schizophrenic children. *Science, 151,* 705-707.

Maher, B. (1972). The language of schizophrenia: A review and interpretation. *British Journal of Psychiatry, 120,* 3-17.

Moon, A. F., Mefferd, M. B., Jr., Wieland, B. A., Pokorny, A. D., & Falconer, G. A. (1968). Perceptual dysfunctions as a determinant of schizophrenic word associations. *Journal of Nervous and Mental Disease, 146,* 80-84.

Osgood, C. E., Luria, Z., Jeans, R. F., & Smith, S. W. (1976). The three faces of Evelyn: A case report. *Journal of Abnormal Psychology, 85,* 247-286.

Osgood, C. E., Suci, G. J., & Tannenbaum, P. H. (1978). *The measurement of meaning.* Urbana: University of Illinois Press. (Original work published 1957)

Pavy, D. (1968). Verbal behavior in schizophrenia: A review of recent studies. *Psychological Bulletin, 70,* 164-178.

Rausch, M. A., Prescott, J. E., & DeWolfe, A. S. (1980). Schizophrenic and aphasic language: Discriminable or not? *Journal of Clinical and Consulting Psychology, 48,* 63-70.

Rieber, R. W., & Vetter, H. (1994). The problem of language and thought in schizophrenia: A review. *Journal of Psycholinguistic Research, 23,* 149-193.

Rubin, A. I., Doneson, S. L., & Jentons, R. L. (1979). Studies of psychological function in schizophrenia. In L. Bellack (Ed.), *Disorders of the schizophrenic syndrome* (pp. 181-231). New York: Basic Books.

Salzinger, K., Portnoy, S., & Feldman, R. S. (1978). Communicability deficit in schizophrenia resulting from a more general deficit. In S. Schwartz (Ed.), *Language and cognition in schizophrenia* (pp. 35-53). Hillsdale, NJ: Lawrence Erlbaum.

Scherer, K. R. (1979). Nonlinguistic vocal indicators of emotion and psychopathology. In C. E. Izard (Ed.), *Emotions in personality and psychopathology* (pp. 493-530). New York: Plenum.

Schwartz, S. (1978). Language and cognition in schizophrenia: A review and synthesis. In S. Schwartz (Ed.), *Language and cognition in schizophrenia* (pp. 237-274). Hillsdale, NJ: Lawrence Erlbaum.

Seidman, L. J. (1983). Schizophrenia and brain dysfunction: An integration of recent neurolinguistic findings. *Psychological Bulletin, 94,* 195-238.

Shapiro, T., Roberts, A., & Fish, B. (1970). Imitation and echoing in young schizophrenic children. *Journal of the American Academy of Child Psychiatry, 9,* 421-439.

Smith, E. E. (1970). Associative and editing processes in schizophrenic communication. *Journal of Abnormal Psychology, 75,* 182-186.

Spitzer, M. (1992). Word-associations in experimental psychiatry: A historical perspective. In M. Spitzer, F. Uehlein, M. A. Schwartz, & C. Mundt (Eds.), *Phenomenology, language and schizophrenia* (pp. 160-196). New York: Springer-Verlag.

Thacker, A. J. (1994). Formal communication disorder: Sign language in deaf people with schizophrenia. *British Journal of Psychiatry, 165,* 818-823.

Thomas, P., Leudar, I., Newby, D., & Johnston, M. (1993). Syntactic processing and written language output in first onset psychosis. *Journal of Communication Disorders, 26,* 209-230.

Vigotsky, L. S. (1934). Thought in schizophrenia (J. Kasanin, Trans.). *Archives of Neurology and Psychiatry, 31,* 1063-1077.

Whitehorn, J. C., & Zipf, G. K. (1943). Schizophrenic language. *Archives of Neurology and Psychiatry, 49,* 831-851.

Wolff, S., & Chess, S. (1965). An analysis of the language of fourteen schizophrenic children. *Journal of Child Psychology and Psychiatry, 6,* 29-41.

## STUDY QUESTIONS

1. Discuss the use of standard psycholinguistic techniques as personality diagnostics. Consider the relation of language to thought in your discussion with respect to why linguistic indicators may be effective diagnostic tools.

2. Review the analyses of the language abnormalities in schizophrenia. Be critical and consider whether you feel that there is a language deficit indicated by the disorder. Support your position with results from the literature and consider how to incorporate conflicting results with your position.

3. Suppose a person were presented to you whose speech was fluent but seemed nonsensical. To diagnose whether the individual was psychotic or aphasic, which features would you look for in the speech? Which tests would you consider performing? Discuss which results you would expect for each disorder. Try to come up with your own tests, based on your knowledge of normal psycholinguistic methods, in addition to those suggested specifically in this chapter.

4. Discuss how deviancies in social, pragmatic, and communicative aspects of language manifest as a schizophrenic (or autistic) language syndrome. Describe the features of speech (or sign) when it is stripped of the need to communicate or the ability to intuit the viewpoint of the other and the purpose of talking. (How) Is this a patterned difference from other language disorders, such as in the social isolates, language-delayed children, Williams syndrome children, and aphasics?

# Retrospectives on Atypical Language

We began our exploration of language in atypical populations by noting that philosophical interest in human language is age-old. The apparently intimate relationship between language and thought has stimulated speculation on whether language can be disordered independently of thought and, conversely, whether animals or humans lacking language do not think as we do. People also long have wondered whether language is intrinsic to human makeup, if animal communication is qualitatively different from human language, whether animals can be taught to do language, whether isolated children can develop (a particular) language, and if biological dysfunction produces language dysfunction.

The thinking about these issues in this century has been motivated by particular advances in science, which we explored, such as the following:

1. The theory of evolution, which promotes a more equal view of humans and our place in the animal kingdom (Chapter 2)

2. Behaviorism and connectionism, which suggest methods of learning and teaching common to all animals (Chapters 2 and 3, as well as the recurring finding in both normal and brain-damaged populations of the importance of habit strength and frequency in acquisition and resilience of language)

3. Cognitive psychology, the tools of which enable scientific study of mental processes (Chapters 1, 4, 5, 6)

4. New methods and findings of linguistics, which generate and compare descriptions of languages and how they are used (Chapters 1, 4)

5. Increased knowledge of and access to neural mechanisms, with which we can consider issues of brain and language specifically (Chapters 2, 3, 4, 5, and 6)

## SUMMARY OF OUR EXPLORATIONS

Chapter 1 presented the book's themes: defining language and discovering social, perceptual, and cognitive constraints on it, essentially placing language in an evolutionary context. We reviewed how some scholars of language have considered it unique to us, a genetically specified "module," UG, that has no analogue in the currently existing animal kingdom. We also explored data relevant to biological and cognitive constraints, which in fact could indicate analogues.

In Chapter 2, we discussed evolutionary mechanisms that might have contributed to our language, such as sexual selection and genetic specification of a "blueprint" for the vital features of a communication system. We compared our main communication system with other aspects of human communication and with animal signal and communication systems to see that language develops within a defined social community, expressing particular needs and using specific cognitive structures.

In Chapter 3, we looked at language acquisition when biology or environment were disrupted to determine whether human beings learn language using innate language blueprints, of which UG could be one, and how these interact with the language environment to develop language. We found some lines of strong evidence for a genetically controlled blueprint for language that unfolds during a critical period: Genie, a child not exposed to language before puberty, failed to acquire or represent it normally in the brain; there are individuals with familial or clearly genetic disturbances in language learning with no other cognitive dysfunction; conversely, some biological anomalies preserve language skills while severely disrupting other cognitive functions; deaf children born in hearing homes without sign language show an innate urge to communicate through language.

However, we also saw successful late language learning in some deaf or socially deprived individuals, suggesting that the system, if under biological control, is adaptable. Our examination underscored the importance of social as well as biological factors: Children raised in a nurturing environment without language develop one and/or are set to acquire language (even perhaps as adults) when it is presented, but children raised without social contact have difficulty acquiring language when language and socialization are introduced.

Chapter 4 underscored how basic features of language are shaped by cognitive and perceptual-motor constraints, such as a preferred rate of information exchange and the speed with which articulators can move. Sign and speech are deeply similar despite modality differences. And they are processed similarly, both showing left-hemisphere language organization, both symbolic and hierarchic despite the transparent iconic origin of many signs.

The neural underpinnings of language were explored in Chapter 5 as we discussed how brain damage affects language processing and language structures. We found that brain damage can have a selective effect, damaging some language processes but not others. The processing components reflected in brain damage support distinguishing pragmatics and paralanguage (affected with right-hemisphere damage) from language proper (left hemisphere), and suggest separating perception and comprehension (more affected with posterior lesions) from production (anterior). This processing distinction was also suggested in acquisition and in animal language projects (Chapter 2). The pattern in brain damage supported independence of automatic/implicit processing (affected by anterior lesions) and slow, labored processing, including self-monitoring (posterior). These processes give rise to the appearance of semantic preservation with anterior lesions, and syntactic preservation with posterior lesions, but the separation of semantics and syntax per se is not reflected in refined tests.

We saw in Chapter 3 that, for neurological reasons, language and literacy may not be acquired without special intervention, sometimes apparently because of specific language disabilities, and sometimes because of more general cognitive or perceptual disabilities. In primary language, there is so much redundancy through context sensitivity and the interdependence of levels that a specific defect can often be compensated for without loss of function. With print, there is less redundancy and a great dependence on intact language knowledge to model as well as greater language-analytic skills. This makes reading disabilities more common and harder to compensate for than language-learning disabilities.

In Chapter 6, we saw how language processes can be stretched. With personality disorder, we see a break between language and communication, with language intact, but odd, because of its dissociation from its principal social function. This again underscores the importance of social constraints and also supports the processing independence of language and paralanguage, with both needed for normal human communication.

Now that we have looked at the findings and theories about language structure and processing, it is time to return to the initial questions: What is the relation of language and thought? Is language or any aspect of it innate? What is language? Is language special? Returning to these questions will allow us to sum up and see where the research has taken us.

## LANGUAGE AND THOUGHT

### Evidence for Thought Without Language

There are several lines of evidence that point to a form of thought that is not specifically linguistic. For one, in normal adults, there is evidence of imaging and of dual coding into imagery and propositional representations. This suggests that there is a form of thought that is nonverbal. Perhaps more compellingly, right-hemisphere cognitive processes indicate nonlinguistic forms of thought for spatial tasks, object recognition, and so on. There is the dissociation in aphasia between concept organization and both naming and basic syntactic processes, indicating conceptual processes independent of language. Each of these examples employs linguistic adults, who have nonlinguistic modes of thought.

We also find evidence for nonlinguistic thought in prelinguistic adults and children. There seems no doubt that Idelfonso, Victor, language-delayed children, and other functional, but alinguistic people have conceptualized their worlds without, or prior to, acquiring language. (They may even have some protolinguistic conceptualizations, as they watch others interact.) As we reviewed in Chapter 1, careful examination of normal child language acquisition has suggested that "form follows function" (MacWhinney, 1987)—both words and complex syntactic structures (negation, causality, questions) map to existing and emerging conceptual categories. Therefore the conceptual categories exist prior to language; nonlinguistic thought precedes and shapes linguistic thought.

Another line of evidence comes from natural animal behavior and communication. Many animals seem to have deep and complex conceptualizations. However, we find very little evidence that they have language and, except perhaps for the pygmy chimpanzee (Kanzi), no compelling evidence that they can learn it. Thus the complex animal cognitions exemplify thought without language.

## The Influence of Language on Thought

This is not to argue that language or language structure plays no role in shaping conceptual structures. We have seen that the formational characteristics of speech (articulatory features) or sign language (formational dimensions) affect short-term recall and that we all, at times, associate by language sound (clang) rather than conceptual meaning. Semantic meaning derives from other meanings in language and is its own form of thought that is not isomorphic with extralinguistic thought. Indeed, the Williams syndrome children may develop linguistic thought exclusively of extralinguistic anchors. Finally, language experience changes perception of its underlying features. People fluent in speech or sign see them differently from those not fluent.

## Thought for Language

There is, of course, also a part of conceptual structure devoted specifically to language, the part responsible for our tacit knowledge of language structure and our metalinguistic knowledge. In Wernicke's aphasia, this may be preserved while much of the rest of the conceptual structure is destroyed, allowing for apparently good syntax and fluent production but empty propositions. Our at least tacit awareness of linguistic aspects of conceptual structure shapes our behavior in playing language games and creating jokes and poetry. It may even provide structure and explanation for such deviancies in language breakdown as neologisms (which usually preserve the language's phonology) and creation of false personas in split personalities (the split personality uses the normal conceptual space without the normal variability, indicating a tacit awareness of the dimensions of that space).

*Summary*
_____

Thus, with respect to the question of thought's relationship to language, we may consider that in humans normally, thought precedes language with language mapping onto it, but that complex thoughts are possible without language in both humans and animals. Once we have acquired language, linguistic thinking may be a dominant mode of thought, or at least of thought by one cerebral hemisphere, shaping additional knowledge acquisition.

## LANGUAGE AS A BIOLOGICAL HERITAGE

*Evidence From Language Acquisition*
_____

Some aspects of language acquisition appear to be innate. All children raised in normal environments develop language, internalizing formational rules, meaning, and syntax. In contrast, primates reared like human children or given special training do not develop syntax. And children with familial and/or clearly genetic disorders can have disturbed language acquisition but little other cognitive disability (LIs) or, conversely, disturbed cognitive development with little language disability (Laura and the Williams syndrome children). So the normal acquisition pattern also could be under genetic control.

The effects of brain damage at different ages suggest that mapping of language in the brain may be biologically controlled during early childhood. If language learning is interrupted by injury to the language areas of the brain, it resumes following similar steps, but on the undamaged side. If the brain is damaged after language acquisition has been completed, language skills are irrevocably lost, with the right hemisphere apparently no longer able to take over.

Additional evidence for the biological predetermination of language structures is provided by contrasting Genie's language acquisition with that of the younger neglected children. Genie began language training after puberty, had difficulty learning language (but not learning generally), acquired abnormal language skills ultimately, and showed a highly abnormal pattern of cerebral specialization. Genie's learning exemplifies a critical period for left-hemisphere language acquisition ending before puberty—but we must worry about her highly abnormal history and be cautious about generalizing from a single case.

While childhood brain damage and Genie's unusual pattern suggest a critical period for left-hemisphere (perhaps the site of UG?) language learning, there is other acquisition evidence that indicates greater adaptability than the biological-determinism model suggests (Snow, 1987). First, note that estimates of the alleged critical period vary enormously: At birth, there is already cerebral asymmetry (Witelson & Pallie, 1973); at the age of 2, the brain has reached most of its adult size (Lenneberg, 1967); at the age of 5, lateralization is complete (Krashen, 1973); at the age of 7, there is a steep decline in the ability to acquire morphological and syntactic niceties in a new language (Newport, 1994), but this decline continues steeply after puberty (Birdsong, 1992), although in some epileptic children studied recently, removal of the left hemisphere at puberty did not prevent language (Zuger, 1997). In addition, as Snow points out, there is little evidence of actual changes in the brain at any age beyond 2 to support the idea of a change in flexibility in the hemispheres. Finally, people successfully (Nobel prize-winning fluency!) have acquired a second language late and even a first language late (Idelfonso): We should need only one such counterexample to disconfirm a strong biological-determinism position.

## Evidence From Brain Damage and Recordings

Whether age and style of language acquisition is under biological control is questionable, but it seems clear that organization of language in the brain is predetermined. For nearly all right-handed adults, damage to some particular region of the brain has a predictable effect on language. The pattern of language impairment as a result of brain damage indicates that "production" is disturbed by injury to the front of the left hemisphere, and "comprehension" to the rear; that function words have a dual representation in front (automatic, syntactic aspect) and rear (semantic aspect); and that concrete, early-learned words have a dual representation in the left and right hemispheres. Automatic and/or syntactic strategies are disturbed by damage to the front of the left hemisphere, with slow monitoring of conceptual strategies spared. Word naming may be impaired independently of conceptual structure, indicating that the names are mapped to, but dissociated from, conceptual structure.

This pattern occurs again and again: in spoken language as well as in the formationally very different signed language (Chapter 4), and in early- and late-acquired languages of the multilingual. And brain stimulation confirms overlap of brain structures serving spoken and written words and different languages (Ojemann, 1983, 1991). Thus mapping of brain structures to linguistic functions may be predetermined biologically, as the increased size of the language regions even in fetal brains suggests. It perhaps results from languages' evolving to meet the cognitive capabilities of the developing brain (Deacon, 1997).

## Evidence From Language Universals

### Cautions for Interpretation

The last and most controversial line of evidence for biological determinism of language derives from an examination of normal languages in typical populations the world over: the putative discovery of universal features. We considered this in the companion volume, and, as I noted there, it is a tricky line of argument because what might seem to be a universal feature may, in fact, reflect common environmental features (like we all look up to the warm sun, so "warm-light-pleasant-up" may be universally associated because of common experience rather than innate endowment).

Environmental commonality, not universal biological determinism, may account for the similarity of children's language acquisition around the world: All babies are exposed to mothers and milk and are fascinated by objects appearing and disappearing from sight (allgone, bye-bye, peek-a-boo); all parents need to sleep and therefore to get their babies to sleep, lulling them with universal rhythmic movements and soothing sounds in lullabies. Infants worldwide experience similar environments that are different, perhaps critically, from those provided older first-language learners like Genie.

Apparently universal properties may also reflect contamination of one language by another, not biological forces shaping each independently. So, some similarities in structure between ASL and English, such as the move from free word order to SVO order, may have derived from the continual cross-fertilization of the deaf community with the English-speaking community, not from an innate tendency toward SVO.

### Communication and Articulatory Structure Universals

Be that as it may, we might *cautiously* suggest some features that seem universal and therefore perhaps innate. The first is the urge to communicate (which is probably present for all social animals, at least during mating season). We see this most clearly in children (deaf children raised orally or, perhaps, hearing children raised by pidgin speakers) who develop their own symbol system, and we also see it in the fact that all human cultures have developed a language. The second is the use of the vocal-auditory system, if available, for communication. Again, all cultures—except deaf cultures—seem to prefer oral language for communication, although sign systems have been developed secondarily among speaking peoples. Within the oral language systems the world over, we find the same speech features, innately determined by the characteristics of the auditory system and the possibilities for articulation. Analogous perceptual and motor constraints apply in sign systems so that all use, for example, the same dimensions and fine-tuning of articulation on the face. Thus they look superficially alike in all cultures.

### Higher-Level Language Universals

At perhaps more interesting linguistic levels, we find units corresponding to words, phrases, and sentences in all languages, perhaps indicating an innate tendency to categorize and construct propositionlike representations and to construct them hierarchically from smaller constituents. We also see, universally, the *symbolic* use of words rather than a signaling use. No culture uses words rigidly to refer to single concrete objects in a stereotyped fashion. All cultures use figurative language, play language games, and have a mythology, demonstrating symbolic use of words. The tendency for language to be symbolic is most striking in the change by deaf children of nonarbitrary gestures, like indexing or pointing, to symbolic gestures of pronominal reference. This occurs also as hearing children internalize their language system, but is dramatic in sign language where the "word" that is used symbolically and iconically stands for the referent.

Another general feature of language (and perhaps of all human information processing) that may be universal and innate is hierarchical organization. We see this at all levels of English structure and processing. There exists hierarchical organization of motor commands in speech production, hierarchical organization of speech perception reflected in part through the interaction of top-down and bottom-up processing, hierarchical organization of categories in conceptualization, and hierarchical organization of words into phrases, phrases into sentences, sentences into (embedded) clauses and recursively back into sentences, sentences into coherent discourse, and so on. Psychologically we represent, separately and interactively, words in semantic memory, semantic relations within propositions, mental propositions, and connections between propositions through inference, anaphoric, or filler-gap reference and related meanings.

It is perhaps in hierarchical organization that we see the greatest difference between normal human language and what is learned by animals or what remains after breakdown. Chimpanzees certainly have been taught to use words, may use them symbolically, and may string them together. With the possible exception of Kanzi (Chapter 2; Savage-Rumbaugh & Lewin, 1994), they do not create higher-order units using these skills or exhibit hierarchical structuring.

We saw both in aphasia and in some instances of schizophrenic language the nonlanguage-like look resulting from a loss of hierarchical structures. Chains composed of the main words of the thought (Broca's aphasia), overlearned syntactic "fillers" like "It is likely that" (Wernicke's aphasia), or of partially associated but nonintegrated concepts (schizophrenia) were noticeably bizarre and nonlanguage-like. It is only when the pieces are integrated hierarchically that the output looks like language. Given that the hierarchical organization occurs at all levels of language and in all languages, we may want to suggest that it is innate, either for language specifically or for human thinking generally.

### Processing Universals

My last suggestion for innateness in language is human processing capabilities. In considering sign language and spoken language, we noted two striking similarities against a big background of differences. First, the rate of information transmission was similar with respect to both speed of production of propositions and the amount of information sufficient to minimally transmit intelligible reduced signals. Second, recognition and use of the physical and meaning features of the languages were similar. These similarities were striking because different modalities are used to convey the two languages and the tongue is quicker than the hand. Moreover, unlike speech, signs often mimic physical features of their referents, but this does not affect sign processing or acquisition. That none of these factors seems to affect language processing suggests that perhaps innate processes interpret input symbolically, independently of its form. Such innate processes may influence language structure—language evolving to fit our constraints—as in compensating for the slowness of individual sign articulation by simultaneous production of several morphemes, or moving from asymmetric, two-handed productions to ones more efficiently coordinated, or making sign precision conform to visual acuity and the human social need for eye contact.

## Other Universals?

Many investigators have suggested more features of language as innate. For example, it has been suggested that there are innate ideas like time and motion, innate syntactic structures like that of phrases with heads and arguments (to their left or right), innate constraints on government and binding, and innately perceived phonetic feature distinctions. (There are also investigators who think very little is innate, with only the basic abilities to form associations predetermined.)

It is, of course, possible that some or all of these language characteristics are innate and specific to language, but to me the evidence does not compellingly point only in this direction. Consider, for example, observations that *initially* suggested innateness, only to be disconfirmed later, such as that SVO word order is understood earlier than other orders used in the language, or that under strained communication conditions (say, after brain damage, in Broca's aphasia), inflections disappear and word order is used to express semantic relations. But it turns out that order is only preferentially preserved if it is more consistently used than inflection in the language; what is universal is neither attention to order nor parameter-setting but faster learning and better maintenance of frequent, regular, and meaningful structures. So when inflections are neither regular nor phonologically or semantically salient, they are omitted, for attentional, not innate linguistic, reasons. The argument that the inconstancy of language input makes it unlearnable is belied by finding that infants respond to statistical regularity and do not need perfect constancy (Saffran, Aslin, & Newport, 1996).

Therefore the evidence for many "universal" language features can be explained by perceptual, cognitive (attention, memory, and learning), and social constraints: regions of general auditory or visual hypersensitivity that languages have mapped onto, and frequency, regularity (not constancy), and relevance of experience (form follows function). Combining such constraints with common human experience could explain the relative universality of concepts like time and motion.

## Summary

So, as I concluded in *Language and Its Normal Processing* (see pp. 527-528), the innate determinants of language may include only

1. the urge to communicate and establish social bonds,
2. use of the vocal-auditory system if possible for communication,
3. some general idea of what language looks like (words and so on),
4. the tendency to make *symbolic* associations,

5. a general blueprint for neural organization of language,

6. some general psychophysical processing constraints imposed by articulatory abilities (vocal or gestural), perceptual abilities (auditory or visual), and general cognitive abilities (attention, memory, and information processing preferences as in hierarchical organization).

As they evolve, languages move toward optimizing these determinants. Thus they share features we can attribute to the common restrictions imposed by the human mind and body and the common experiences provided by the environment and our nurturing.

## WHAT IS LANGUAGE?

In Chapter 1, I defined language as the way humans communicate. As we compared communication processes in atypical populations, that definition may not seem as trivial as it perhaps did at first. Human beings, through their social needs and cognitive and perceptual structures, have shaped their communication system. Animals, with different social needs and different inherent constraints, communicate differently. To define what it is that makes language language, therefore, we must consider the heritage of its creators and users.

The use of human makeup to define language may seem unfair and unnecessary. I will return to this point at the end of this section and here consider why we should bother to define language at all. There are two reasons people have given for undertaking the process of defining language: (a) to prove that we are specially and better endowed than other organisms and (b) to be able to recognize what is and what is not language—a pattern recognition problem—given a newly encountered communication system.

The first reason, although interesting philosophically, is not my concern: From an evolutionary perspective, all species are specially and uniquely (although not necessarily optimally!) endowed for their biological niche. For me, the second reason is of interest, but its end validly includes specifying the *human* characteristics in language structure and processing—as it is valid to specify "feathers" in defining bird flight apart from, for example, airplane flight.

### Low-Level Design Features

The last section summarized characteristics of language specifically and human information processing generally that might be innate and determine the shape of language. These underlie the design features for language discussed in Chapter 2.

An innate push to use the vocal auditory channel for communication, combined with some innate constraints on information processing, could underlie the following features: rapid fading, broadcast transmission and reception, total feedback, specialization, and, for us, interchangeability. (Transmission and reception are not sex-linked, for example, as they are in many birds.) If our information processing system were incapable of handling rapidly fading messages, as it would be if our short-term memory were more limited, we could not use such a system without increasing redundancy.

Language using the vocal-auditory channel has these low-level design features (which also occur in visual primary language, in sign). Because use of gesture and vocalization are innate, and features of rapid fading and so on are their intrinsic properties, they are characteristic of language.

If we wish to define language as special because of what it communicates, features like rapid fading and so on may be dropped. However, if we consider language a function of its users, the vocal-auditory system (and its characteristics) seems to be the primary mode for language, although we are flexible enough to use other modes. Therefore, although the characteristics of language determined by its usual modality *do not define language as a special symbolic process, they do help define it as a specific communication system.*

## Higher-Level Design Features

An information processing influence on language that we have considered innate is the tendency for symbolic thinking. In language, this could underlie the proposed features of semanticity, arbitrariness, discreteness, and displacement. Once an association between two experiences is recognized (e.g., between a word and its referents, a phonology and a geographic location, a clothing style and a time period, lightning and thunder, relationships and journeys), the association is transcended to allow for additional idea manipulation. This means words are used symbolically rather than referentially or iconically (as may be other characteristics of behavior like clothing or dialect, to stand for a culture). It also means that unobservable associations may be sought, like the nature of lightning and the causes of sound and so on. And it means that metaphors may be applied and reapplied to structure cognitions.

Within language, this innate tendency for symbolic thought means that no matter how concrete the initial association (remember, semanticity entails association), as in iconic signs or onomatopoeia, within a few uses the concreteness is not attended to, and the word (or whatever) is processed as arbitrary and discrete. Once this occurs, it may be used to discuss displaced events and create relations to concepts by analogy.

Another suggestion for an innate force in language, derived from general cognitive constraints, is the tendency for hierarchical organization. Together with symbolic thought, this accounts for many of our design features: productivity, duality of patterning, deception, metalanguage, simultaneity, and recursiveness. If information processing occurs in hierarchically arranged stages, one element may be considered simultaneously on many levels: as a sound, as a morpheme or word, as a contributor to syntactic structure of the sentence. This phenomenon we called duality (actually, multiplicity) of patterning. The most efficient use of the hierar-chical processes would be to consider each element on all these levels at once, so that processing at the highest level is not waiting for output from lower levels. This leads to simultaneity (perhaps best modeled by parallel, distributed representations). Once an element has been identified, it can be used as a symbol itself and be processed through the same hierarchy, leading to productivity, including the use of language deceptively and recursively. And once the elements are recognized simultaneously, at different hierarchical levels, as existing as elements as well as associations to their referents, metalanguage—words like *word, phoneme, language,* and *metalanguage*—may develop so we can discuss the elements of processing as elements of processing.

## Other Design Features

Through much of this book, we have considered whether an innate determinant of language may be exposure to language at a young age, and we have emphasized the importance of language as a social regulator in determining its structures and function. Hockett's last design feature, traditional transmission, depends on the interaction between those knowing language (usually parents) and the learners (usually dependent young people)—that is, on a social setting for language acquisition. Language is necessarily a social phenomenon—that is one function that form must follow. Pragmatic considerations for human language are captured in the features of interchangeability and traditional transmission.

Finally, we might note that the innate human information processor is imperfect; there are lapses of attention and memory, regions of hypersensitivity (and therefore regions of less sensitivity), and so forth. These characteristics produce our last design features: smear and the human thought transmission rate. We need redundancy because of imperfect processing and this is accomplished through smear. We cannot incorporate new thoughts at excessively rapid rates or maintain attention at excessively low rates, and so simultaneity, sequentiality, and smear are balanced in the language to produce an optimal transmission rate.

## Language Defined as Unique to Us

By founding our criteria for language in our biology, we have eliminated the possibility that chimpanzees or any other animal could use or learn language or that computers (as they exist today) could use language as we know it. It is worthwhile considering whether this anthropocentric conclusion is warranted.

Turing (1963/1995) proposed a test to determine whether human intelligence had been truly simulated by machine. If human questioners addressing questions to a machine could not tell from the answers whether the machine was "manned" by a computer or by a human, artificial intelligence would have been achieved.

The Turing test may be considered from two points of view: whether the answers themselves seem human and whether the way that they are generated seems human. With respect to language, it seems possible that at some point either a nonhuman animal or a machine might produce answers that could not be differentiated structurally or symbolically from human answers. However, it is highly unlikely that the *process* of deriving the answer could not distinguish the imposter from the human. Now, we might ask: Is there a way to get at the process rather than the answer? The answer is yes, and this book and its companion were full of such ways: lexical decision times and priming, ratings on the semantic differential, word associations, reaction time for processing grammatically complex sentences, evoked potential changes to semantic anomaly, priming effects of traces on fillers, effects of a bullet wound to a particular spot in the "brain," and so forth. Any and all of these tests could be administered (barring ethical considerations for the last) to draw the conclusion that that machine (or animal) may be clever but is no human.

Some may protest (as Turing did) that this is not a particularly interesting criterion for language simulation or artificial intelligence. After all, the important thing is flying, not doing it with feathers. That is fine, and in that case, probably we do not need most of our design features for language. And probably we would consider that language now, already, is not unique to us. If we define the "task" as communicating, we do that no better than the "lowest" of animals in terms of communicating social needs and surviving. If we define the task as use of symbols and syntax (using the middle-level design features—semanticity, . . . , recursiveness), we can also conclude that language is not unique to us. Computers already use symbols, syntax, hierarchical processing, and recursiveness, in even simple "nonintelligent" programs.

Thus we seem to be in a position either of forfeiting what we perceive as unique about language *as a pattern* or of conceding that the "specialness" derives from particular properties housed within a particular biological medium. The concession suggests that tests for language include processing tests, which no machine or other animal can pass, by definition. As I said, there are two reasons to try to define language: One is to recognize language as a pattern, in which case the Turing test using processing is fair, and the other is to try to argue that we are in some particular way special. For the second purpose, it seems only honest to be clear about being self-serving, and so define language with respect to "special" human qualities.

## CONCLUDING REMARKS

### *Applications*

In closing, we should consider the use to which discoveries about language have been put, that is, mention areas of application of psycholinguistic research.

One important consequence of linguistic and psycholinguistic research has been the recognition that *there are no inferior languages in terms of structure or processing,* and therefore that it is not imperative that all children be made to conform to a specific language or dialect. This has caused a gradual move from considering sign language as a crude gestural system to recognition that it is a complex and beautiful language, notably resulting in the establishment in 1983 of Swedish sign language along with Swedish as the official language of Sweden.

As I discussed in *Language and Its Normal Processing,* comparison of standard English to the African American English Vernacular (Labov, 1972) likewise has shown that AAEV is a *nonstandard dialect, not a substandard language:* It shares many words, structures, and internal processes with standard English but is different in pronunciation, morphology, and, to a lesser extent, syntax. This has permitted understanding of why AAEV speakers may have problems learning to read: (Like deaf children) They are taught spelling-to-sound correspondences for sounds they do not hear; they are taught morphemes that do not correspond to their use of tense and aspect. The solution to this problem is far from settled because there are social stigmas attached to being taught a nonstandard dialect in schools, but, presumably, making teachers aware of the differences and the possibilities of "code-switching" will help.

Aside from modifying attitudes toward language, research in language has been applied to techniques of teaching or reteaching language and testing linguistic competence. As discussed in the companion volume, there have been changes in foreign language instruction from rote memorization of vocabulary items and overt grammatical rules to concentration on language *as used* with emphasis on acquisition of tacit knowledge of structure. Language rehabilitation programs for aphasics not only give practice in the person's original language skills but also to try to recruit what are believed to be spared cognitive functions by teaching language through song or visual patterns (see Gardner, 1975; Helm-Estabrooks, 1983, for example). Language assessment and rehabilitation programs for language-learning disabled and developmental dyslexics or poor readers have isolated, for specific subpopulations, treatable general cognitive/perceptual causes (like temporal processing; Tallal, Galaburda, Llinas, & von Euler, 1993) and, sometimes, specific and treatable linguistic causes, as in failure to make grapheme-to-phoneme correspondences or recognize orthographic units (Bradley & Bryant, 1983).

Increased understanding of language structure and processing has led to better diagnostics of patients, separating aphasics from schizophrenics, real from contrived personalities in multiple personalities, and subpopulations of language-disordered individuals.

As a result of our increased knowledge of language and language processing (combined with technological advances), and despite the great gaps in knowledge, there are now adequate reading machines for the blind (they take text and convert it to speech), computer programs that correct or teach spelling and grammar, and automated knowledge bases that can be accessed for information about virtually anything. Although humans may have to modify their language somewhat to interact with these systems, the systems are increasingly "user-friendly," requiring less adaptation on the part of the human users. A computer that can pass the Turing test (regardless of processing differences) may still seem to be a long way in the future, but machines that require us to think to figure out how to trick them into failing the Turing test have been around for some time.

## Conclusion

We still have a long way to go to understand language and its processing, and many exciting years of research ahead. But we have come a long way since Psammetichus!

## REFERENCES

Birdsong, D. (1992). Ultimate attainment in second language acquisition. *Language, 68,* 706-755.

Bradley, L., & Bryant, P. E. (1983). Categorizing sounds and learning to read: A causal connection. *Nature, 3,* 419-421.

Deacon, T. W. (1997). *The symbolic species: The co-evolution of language and the brain.* New York: Norton.

Gardner, H. (1975). *The shattered mind.* New York: Knopf.

Helm-Estabrooks, N. (1983). Exploiting the right hemisphere for language rehabilitation: Melodic intonation therapy. In E. Perecman (Ed.), *Cognitive processing in the right hemisphere* (pp. 229-240). New York: Academic Press.

Krashen, S. D. (1973). Lateralization, language learning, and the critical period: Some new evidence. *Language Learning, 23,* 63-74.

Labov, W. (1972). *Language in the inner city: Studies in the Black English vernacular.* Philadelphia: University of Pennsylvania Press.

Lenneberg, E. (1967). *Biological foundations of language.* New York: John Wiley.

MacWhinney, B. (1987). The competition model. In B. MacWhinney (Ed.), *Mechanisms of language acquisition* (pp. 249-308). Hillsdale, NJ: Lawrence Erlbaum.

Newport, E. L. (1994). Maturational constraints in second language learning. In P. Bloom (Ed.), *Language acquisition: Core readings* (pp. 543-560). Cambridge: Bradford Books of MIT Press.

Ojemann, G. A. (1983). Brain organization for language from the perspective of electrical stimulation mapping. *Behavioral and Brain Sciences, 6,* 189-230.

Ojemann, G. A. (1991). Cortical organization of language. *Journal of Neuroscience, 11,* 2281-2287.

Saffran, J. R., Aslin, R. N., & Newport, E. L. (1996). Statistical learning by 8-month-old infants. *Science, 274,* 1926-1928.

Savage-Rumbaugh, E. S., & Lewin, R. (1994). *Kanzi: The ape at the brink of the human mind.* New York: John Wiley.

Snow, C. (1987). Relevance of the notion of critical period to language acquisition. In M. H. Bornstein (Ed.), *Sensitive periods in development: Interdisciplinary perspectives* (pp. 183-209). Hillsdale, NJ: Lawrence Erlbaum.

Tallal, P., Galaburda, A. M., Llinas, R. R., & von Euler, C. (Eds.). (1993). *Annals of the New York Academy of Sciences: Vol. 682. Temporal information processing in the nervous system.* New York: New York Academy of Sciences.

Turing, A. M. (1995). Computing machinery and intelligence? In E. A. Feigenbam & J. Feldman (Eds.), *Computers and thought* (pp. 11-35). Menlo Park, CA: AAAI Press/MIT Press. (Original work published 1963)

Witelson, S. F., & Pallie, W. (1973). Left hemisphere specialization for language in the newborn: Neuroanatomical evidence of asymmetry. *Brain, 96,* 641-646.

Zuger, A. (1997, August 19). Removing half of brain improves young epileptics' lives. *New York Times,* p. C4.

# Index

# About the Author

**Vivien C. (Vicky) Tartter** is Professor of Psychology at City College and member of the doctoral faculty of psychology and speech and hearing sciences at the Graduate and University Center of CUNY. She received her doctorate in psychology from Brown University and completed an undergraduate "cognitive sciences" major there, before such a major formally existed. Her research has been funded by the NSF, the National Institute of Deafness and Communication Disorders, the Deafness Research Foundation, and the U.S. Department of Education. In 1987 she was a Fogarty Senior International Fellow. She is a committed teacher at both graduate and undergraduate levels, and strives to involve all students in the excitement of research. From her own educational experience through to her research, she strongly advocates interdisciplinary study. Her research focuses on speech perception in normal and hearing-impaired adults and children but includes excursions into language in aphasia, sign language perception, and literacy acquisition. She is married and has two children who have taught her much about language and literacy acquisition.